More Praise for *One Person, No Vote*

"Throughout *One Person, No Vote*, Anderson's tone, at turns urgent and indignant, seems to arise from the ease with which she can document abundantly—via investigative journalism, popular history and historical scholarship—'the GOP's determined efforts to purge American citizens and cull and homogenize the electorate.'" —*Los Angeles Times*

"Carol Anderson's prose is unflinching, and she wastes no time as she marches the reader from the openly racist, clear-cutting suppression tactics of the early 20th century toward the carefully veneered, ruthlessly efficient disenfranchisement campaign of the present. Whether you only think about voting on a single Tuesday in November or you're passionately engaged in the fight for the ballot, you will set this book down with the knowledge that it's all so much worse than you thought." —NPR.org, Best Books of the Year

"[Anderson's] description of the perpetual war that blacks and now Latinos have fought to get and keep the right to vote is impeccably researched, deftly written and, sadly, prescient . . . *One Person, No Vote* punches above its weight, like a lecture from a professor with superb command of language." —*Star Tribune* (Minneapolis–St. Paul)

"*One Person, No Vote* is a careful documentation of the ways in which Republican voter suppression efforts disproportionately and specifically affect minority voters . . . Anderson's new book, along with her 2017 volume *White Rage*, shows how difficult it is to separate out our current political situation from the legacy of Jim Crow's racial apartheid system. The Republican war on the fairness of American elections is, by its nature, a project that targets one of the core victories of the civil rights movement." —*Vox*

"All of the books on this list have present-day implications, but perhaps none more so than this charged dive into voter suppression from the Chair of African American Studies at Emory University. *One Person, No Vote* looks at this history of this anti-democratic tactic, particularly its racist roots." —EntertainmentWeekly.com

"Voter suppression and disenfranchisement might be the most serious issue in American politics today. In this vastly important read, *White*

Rage author Carol Anderson unpacks how the 2013 Supreme Court decision to roll back the Voting Rights Act of 1965 led to a storm of government-led racial discrimination and voter suppression." —*Bustle*

"Serves as a gimlet-eyed analysis of President Lyndon B. Johnson, Chief Justice John Roberts, and Jim Crow laws." —*O, The Oprah Magazine*

"Voter suppression is one of the most important threats to American democracy. You might already think this before reading Anderson's book, but if not, the copious, well-researched evidence she presents here—that shows how Republican politicians have been systematically and purposefully stripping voting abilities from black and low-income voters—is difficult to refute. Immediately relevant and deeply disturbing." —*Lit Hub*

"Looking at gerrymandering, voter ID laws, the closure of polling places, and a host of other forms of voter suppression; Carol Anderson brilliantly shows how African Americans have systematically lost their voting rights since the Voting Rights Act of 1965. Today, as voter suppression disproportionately affects Black voters and our elections, *One Person, No Vote* is a necessary read that explains how disguised racism continues to impact our political institutions." —*Black Perspectives*, Best Black History Books of the Year

"This is a whiplash-inducing chronicle of how a nation that just a few short years ago elected its first black president now finds itself in the throes of a deceitful and craven effort to rip this most essential of American rights from millions of its citizens." —*Booklist* (starred review)

"A ripped-from-the-headlines book . . . Anderson is a highly praised academic who has mastered the art of gathering information and writing for a general readership, and her latest book could not be more timely." —*Kirkus*

"Insightful . . . [Anderson] scrupulously details the history of racially and politically motivated disenfranchisement in the United States . . . Anyone interested in American democracy or how equality can be not only legislated but realized will find this account illuminating and clarifying." —*Publishers Weekly*

"A clear, concise, and compelling exploration of racialized voter suppression from Jim Crow through today . . . This book is impeccably researched and perfectly argued. It's a must-read for anyone interested in politics, policy, and polling." —*Book Riot*, Best Books of the Year

"In *White Rage*, a *New York Times* best seller that won the National Book Critics Circle Award, Emory professor Anderson chronicled efforts since 1865 to block the advancement of African Americans. Here she concentrates on efforts to curtail the African American vote since the 2013 *Shelby* ruling gutted the Voting Rights Act of 1965. Anderson considers both consequences—e.g., photo ID requirements, poll closures—and means of redress." —*Library Journal*, Barbara's Nonfiction Picks for the Month

"Well-timed . . . In a slim volume, Anderson details the outrages of Republican efforts to target largely minority voters and to limit their influence in elections . . . Blood-boiling stories like these come rapid-fire in Anderson's narrative, which is also peppered with a brief history of voter suppression dating back to Reconstruction." —*Washington Monthly*

"In her impeccably timed 2016 best-seller, *White Rage*, historian and Emory professor Carol Anderson took readers on a jarring and illuminating journey through America's deep history of structural racism. Her new book, *One Person, No Vote*, connects that historical legacy with the resurgence of voter suppression that's capturing headlines in 2018, thanks not only to the ascendance of Trumpism, but the state-level depredations of voting-rights foes like Brian Kemp in Georgia, John Husted in Ohio, and Kris Kobach in Kansas." —*The American Prospect*

"Reading Carol Anderson's *One Person, No Vote: How Voter Suppression Is Destroying Our Democracy* makes it clear that [voter suppression] is alive and well. With exhaustive research and documentation and compelling narrative style, Anderson conveys how the overtly racist poll taxes, literacy tests, targeted violence and intimidation that evolved after Reconstruction to prevent African-Americans and other minorities from voting have been supplanted by ostensibly color-blind efforts to fight voter fraud and game the electoral system." —*Citizen Times* (Asheville, NC)

"Most of us are well aware that there is something fundamentally broken about the way we vote—but not why. In *One Person, No Vote*, Carol Anderson offers up a timely, powerfully written, and comprehensive indictment of the (relatively recent) history of brutal race-based vote suppression, and its many modern iterations—from voter ID requirements and voter purges, to fraudulent election fraud commissions and stolen elections. Along the way Anderson traces the rise and fall of the landmark Voting Rights Act and how the Supreme Court continues to blinker itself to the ways in which American elections are neither free nor fair, and how the dignity of states and white voters continues to be privileged above the franchise itself. A must-read for anyone wondering why voting is the most important issue we continue to misapprehend." —Dahlia Lithwick, chief legal correspondent for *Slate* and host of the *Amicus* podcast

"As Carol Anderson makes clear in *One Person, No Vote*, the right to vote is under even greater assault today. For the sake of those who fought and died for it, it is up to all of us to insist that this most basic American right be protected. Reading this well-crafted book will arm you with the facts." —Senator Dick Durbin, from the foreword

"Carol Anderson is one of our most incisive and cogent thinkers regarding history's fingerprints on current affairs. With *One Person, No Vote* she has produced a crucial examination of a critical issue: voter suppression. At a time when democracy is under siege and the worst elements of the racial past are being resurrected, we can scarcely afford to avert our eyes from our most pressing challenges. Carol Anderson looks at these issues directly, unflinchingly, and offers us an invaluable insight regarding where we are, how we got here, and how we might navigate our way to safer shores." —Jelani Cobb, author of *The Substance of Hope*

One Person, No Vote

BY THE SAME AUTHOR

White Rage: The Unspoken Truth of Our Racial Divide

Bourgeois Radicals: The NAACP and the Struggle for Colonial Liberation, 1941–1960

Eyes off the Prize: The United Nations and the African American Struggle for Human Rights, 1944–1955

ONE PERSON, NO VOTE

*How Voter Suppression Is Destroying
Our Democracy*

Carol Anderson

Foreword by **SENATOR DICK DURBIN**

BLOOMSBURY PUBLISHING

NEW YORK · LONDON · OXFORD · NEW DELHI · SYDNEY

BLOOMSBURY PUBLISHING
Bloomsbury Publishing Inc.
1385 Broadway, New York, NY 10018, USA

BLOOMSBURY, BLOOMSBURY PUBLISHING, and the Diana logo
are trademarks of Bloomsbury Publishing Plc

First published in the United States 2018
This paperback edition published 2019

Bloomsbury Publishing Plc does not have any control over, or responsibility for,
any third-party websites referred to or in this book. All internet addresses given
in this book were correct at the time of going to press. The author and publisher
regret any inconvenience caused if addresses have changed or sites have ceased
to exist, but can accept no responsibility for any such changes.

ISBN: HB: 978-1-63557-137-0; PB: 978-1-63557-1-394; eBook: 978-1-63557-138-7

Library of Congress Cataloging-in-Publication Data is available.

6 8 10 9 7 5

Typeset by Westchester Publishing Services
Printed and bound in the U.S.A. by Berryville Graphics Inc., Berryville, Virginia

To find out more about our authors and books visit www.bloomsbury.com
and sign up for our newsletters.

Bloomsbury books may be purchased for business or promotional use.
For information on bulk purchases please contact Macmillan Corporate and
Premium Sales Department at specialmarkets@macmillan.com.

To all of the voting rights warriors and activists who have fought and continue to fight to protect Democracy

Contents

Foreword
by Senator Dick Durbin

In *White Rage*, Carol Anderson gave us a carefully researched history of American civil rights and race politics from the Civil War to current times. Her work marched us through the painful chapters of Reconstruction, Jim Crow, the Great Migration, and the Civil Rights Movement to the battles we face today.

When I read *White Rage*, I recommended it to my Democratic colleagues in the U.S. Senate. Senator Harry Reid was so impressed that he invited Professor Anderson to address our Senate Democratic Conference. Her passion and scholarship made a real impact.

In her new work, *One Person, No Vote*, Carol Anderson turns her focus to the central issue of racial justice in our time: the right to vote.

Under the specious banner of combating "voter fraud," the Republican Party has launched a nationwide voter suppression effort. Using voter ID laws, reduced voting opportunities, gerrymandering, and even the national census, Republicans clearly believe their future success depends more on constricting rather than convincing the electorate.

When you follow the money behind this national push, the usual suspects surface. The Koch brothers and their allies bankroll operatives like the American Legislative Exchange Council (ALEC). They produce "model legislation" to combat alleged voter fraud by requiring photo identification at the polls. Republican legislators pass and Republican governors sign these laws, which restrict and discourage voting by minorities, the elderly, the young, the poor—anyone who might oppose their partisan agenda.

The rationale for these laws has been repeatedly debunked. For example, a 2014 analysis by Professor Justin Levitt of Loyola Law School, Los Angeles, found only thirty-one incidents of voter fraud out of hundreds of millions of votes cast since 2000.

In 2012, as chairman of the U.S. Senate Judiciary Committee's Subcommittee on the Constitution, Civil Rights, and Human Rights, I chaired national hearings on barriers to the ballot in Ohio and Florida, states that had recently passed restrictive voting laws. We called election officials of both parties, put them under oath, and asked a simple question: What was the incidence of voter fraud or voter irregularity in your state which gave rise to these state laws restricting voters' rights? Their answer was the same in both states: There were few incidents, and virtually none was worthy of prosecution.

This lack of evidence underscores an ugly truth: It's not "voter fraud" that has inspired this new wave of voter suppression laws. Instead, it's the same animus that led to poll taxes, literacy tests, and the infamous Mississippi Plan, which became the template for voter discrimination for decades. That ugly animus was denounced in 2016 by a three-judge federal appeals court that examined a 2013 North Carolina voting law that required strict voter photo identification and limited early voting. The law, the judges wrote, "target[ed] African Americans with almost surgical precision." This was no coincidence, the court found, noting that "before enacting [the] law, the legislature requested data on the use, by race, of a number of voting practices. Upon receipt of the race data, the General Assembly enacted legislation that restricted voting and registration in five different ways, all of which disproportionately affected African Americans."

Unfortunately, this movement is not confined to state legislatures. In his 2005 confirmation hearings to serve as Chief Justice of the United States Supreme Court, John Roberts said that the right to vote "is preservative . . . of all the other rights." His new black robe was barely wrinkled eight years later when, in the *Shelby County v. Holder* case, he cast the deciding vote to overturn a key provision of the Voting Rights Act requiring preclearance of new election laws in states with a history of voter discrimination. The Republican-dominated Supreme Court gave a green light to the "No Vote" Republican strategy—and the Voting Rights Act, which had enjoyed virtually unanimous bipartisan support in Congress as recently as 2006, became a casualty of the GOP voter suppression campaign.

Since then, efforts to restore the Voting Rights Act through measures such as the Voting Rights Amendment Act and the Voting Rights Advancement Act have stalled in Congress. Meanwhile, Republican-led state legislatures continue to enact laws making it harder for a significant number of Americans to exercise their fundamental right to vote.

Evidence suggests that their plan is working. A recent study found that in the 2016 election, Wisconsin's voter ID law deterred nearly 17,000—and perhaps as many as 23,000—eligible voters in two counties from casting ballots. President Trump's margin of victory in Wisconsin was only 22,748 votes.

In her *Shelby County* dissent, Justice Ruth Bader Ginsburg noted that though progress had been made in protecting the vote, Congress reauthorized the Voting Rights Act in 2006 because "the scourge of discrimination was not yet extirpated." She was right.

As Carol Anderson makes clear in *One Person, No Vote*, the right to vote is under even greater assault today. For the sake of those who fought and died for it, it is up to all of us to insist that this most basic American right be protected. Reading this well-crafted book will arm you with the facts.

One

A History of Disfranchisement

It was a mystery worthy of Raymond Chandler. On November 8, 2016, African Americans did not show up. It was like a day of absence. African Americans had virtually boycotted the election because they "simply saw no affirmative reason to vote for Hillary," as one reporter explained, before adding, with a hint of an old refrain, that "some saw her as corrupt."[1] Another journalist concluded that because Clinton lacked the ability, charisma, or magic to keep Barack Obama's coalition together, "African-American, Latino and younger voters failed to show up at the polls."[2] As proof of blacks' coolness toward her, journalists pointed to the much greater turnout for Obama in 2008 and 2012.[3]

It is true that, nationwide, black voter turnout had dropped by 7 percent overall. Moreover, less than half of Hispanic and Asian American voters came to the polls.[4] This was, without question, a sea change. The tide of African American, Hispanic, and Asian voters that had previously carried Barack Obama into the White House and kept him there had now visibly ebbed. Journalist Ari Berman called it the most underreported story of the 2016 campaign.[5] But it's more than that. The disappearing minority voter is the campaign's most misunderstood story.

One Person, No Vote seeks to change that. Minority voters did not just refuse to show up; Republican legislatures and governors systematically blocked African Americans, Hispanics, and Asian Americans from the polls. Pushed by both the impending demographic collapse of the Republican Party, whose overwhelmingly white constituency is becoming an ever smaller share of the electorate, and the GOP's extremist inability to craft policies that speak to an increasingly diverse nation, the Republicans opted to disfranchise rather than reform. The GOP, therefore, enacted a range of undemocratic and desperate measures to block the access of African American, Latino, and other minority voters to the ballot box.[6] Using a series of voter suppression tactics, the GOP harassed, obstructed, frustrated, and purged American citizens from having a say in their own democracy. The devices the Republicans used are variations on a theme going back more than 150 years. They target the socioeconomic characteristics of a people (poverty, lack of mobility, illiteracy, etc.) and then soak the new laws in "racially neutral justifications—such as administrative efficiency" or "fiscal responsibility"—to cover the discriminatory intent. Republican lawmakers then act aggrieved, shocked, and wounded that anyone would question their stated purpose for excluding millions of American citizens from the ballot box.[7]

The millions of votes *and* voters that disappeared behind a firewall of hate and partisan politics was a long time in the making. The decisions to purposely disfranchise African Americans, in particular, can be best understood by going back to the close of the Civil War. As a southerner explained, "Many Texans refused to accept the fact that the Negro was 'free and equal,' and stopped at nothing to prevent him from enjoying civic and political rights."[8] After Reconstruction, the plan was to take years of state-sponsored "trickery and fraud" and transform those schemes into laws that would keep blacks away from the voting booth, disfranchise as many as possible, and, most important, ensure that no African American would ever assume real political power again.[9]

The last point resonated. Reconstruction had brought a number of blacks into government. And despite their helping to craft "the laws relative to finance, the building of penal and charitable institutions, and, greatest of all, the establishment of the public school system," the myth of incompetent, disastrous "black rule" dominated.[10] Or, as one newspaper editor summarized it: "No negro is fit to make laws for white people." Of course, the white lawmakers couldn't be *that* blatant about their plans to disfranchise; there was, after all, that pesky Constitution to contend with, not to mention the Fifteenth Amendment covering the right to vote with its language barring discrimination "on account of race." But, undaunted, they devised ways to meet the letter of the law while doing an absolute slash-and-burn through its spirit.[11]

That became most apparent in 1890 when the Magnolia State passed the Mississippi Plan, a dizzying array of poll taxes, literacy tests, understanding clauses, newfangled voter registration rules, and "good character" clauses—all intentionally racially discriminatory but dressed up in the genteel garb of bringing "integrity" to the voting booth. This feigned legal innocence was legislative evil genius.

Virginia representative Carter Glass, like so many others, swooned at the thought of bringing the Mississippi Plan to his own state, especially after he saw how well it had worked. He rushed to champion a bill in the legislature that would "eliminate the darkey as a political factor . . . in less than five years." Glass, whom President Franklin Roosevelt would one day describe as an "unreconstructed rebel," planned not to "deprive a single white man of the ballot, but [to] inevitably cut from the existing electorate four-fifths of the Negro voters" in Virginia.

One delegate questioned him: "Will it not be done by fraud and discrimination?"

"By fraud, no. By discrimination, yes," Glass retorted. "Discrimination! Why, that is precisely what we propose . . . to discriminate to the very extremity . . . permissible . . . under . . . the Federal Constitution, with a view to the elimination of every negro voter who can be gotten rid of, legally, without materially impairing the numerical strength of the white electorate."[12]

The determination to wipe out the black vote ensnared whites as well, however. Though, for many of those in power, that was just fine. One Mississippi politician remarked that his state had to disfranchise "the ignorant and vicious white," too, so that the electorate was "confined to those, and to those alone, who are qualified by intelligence and character for the proper and patriotic exercise of this great franchise."[13] The resulting "voter mortality rate" was staggering. Throughout the South after the widespread adoption of the Mississippi Plan, voter turnout plummeted to less than half of age-eligible whites, after it had peaked in 1896 at 79.6 percent.[14] In Texas, for example, only 27 percent of age-eligible whites voted in the 1956 election (the national rate was 60 percent).[15] The decline was even more dramatic in the Magnolia State. In the late nineteenth century, Mississippi's voter turnout was close to 70 percent; "by the early twentieth century it scraped near 15 percent."[16]

While there was a steady erosion of white voters, the collapse of black voter turnout was precipitous. In Louisiana, where "more than 130,000 blacks had been registered to vote in 1896, the figure dropped to a bleak 1,342 by 1904."[17] African American registered voters in Alabama plunged from 180,000 to fewer than 3,000 in just three years.[18] As historian C. Vann Woodward concluded, "The restrictions imposed by these devices [in the Mississippi Plan] were enormously effective in decimating the Negro vote."[19] Indeed, by 1940, shortly before the United States entered the war against the Nazis, only 3 percent of age-eligible blacks were registered to vote in the South.[20]

That the states arranged to achieve this remarkable, systematic denial of the vote, while staying within the bounds of the Fifteenth Amendment, is a testament to the warped brilliance of the Mississippi Plan. Senator Theodore Bilbo (D-MS), one of the most virulent racists to grace the halls of Congress, boasted of the chicanery nearly half a century later. "What keeps 'em [blacks] from voting is section 244 of the [Mississippi] Constitution of 1890 . . . It says that a man to register must be able to read and explain the Constitution or explain the Constitution when read to him." Mississippi, the senator bragged, "then wrote a constitution that damn few white men and no niggers at all can explain."[21]

Bilbo was pointing to the power of the literacy test and understanding clause, which were tailor-made for societies that systematically refused to educate millions of their citizens and ensured that the bulk of the population remained functionally illiterate. By 1940, more than half of all African American adults in Mississippi had fewer than five years of formal education; almost 12 percent had no schooling whatsoever. The figures were even more dismal in South Carolina, Louisiana, Georgia, and Alabama.[22] Deliberate underfunding of black schools was critical to the literacy test's disfranchising success. During World War II, for example, Louisiana spent almost four times as much per capita on white elementary schoolchildren as on African American students.[23] Amite County in Mississippi scraped together $3.51 per black child but nearly ten times that amount to educate its white students.[24] In addition, for most of the twentieth century, many Jim Crow school systems did not have high schools for African Americans. That set the stage for states such as Alabama—where more than 54 percent of black adults had fewer than five years of formal education—to require those who came through resource-deprived school systems and who wanted to register to vote to wrangle with the intricacies of constitutional law.[25]

The process was, by design, simultaneously mundane and pernicious. At the registrar's office, while whites might have had a one-sentence section of the Alabama or U.S. Constitution as their litmus test for worthiness to vote, African Americans would get difficult, complex passages in order to prove their literacy, and then they would have to interpret that legal treatise to gauge how well they could actually understand what they had just read. This combination of literacy tests and understanding clauses was designed to thwart blacks' voting rights as they confronted a passage such as this:

SECTION 260: The income arising from the sixteenth section trust fund, the surplus revenue fund, until it is called for by the United States government, and the funds enumerated in sections 257 and 258 of this Constitution, together with a special annual tax of thirty cents on each one hundred dollars of taxable property in this state, which the legislature shall levy, shall be applied to the support and maintenance of the public schools, and it shall be the duty of the legislature to increase the public school fund from time to time as the necessity therefor and the condition of the treasury and the resources of the state may justify; provided, that nothing herein contained shall be so construed as to authorize the legislature to levy in any one year a greater rate of state taxation for all purposes, including schools, than sixty-five cents on each one hundred dollars' worth of taxable property; and provided further, that nothing herein contained shall prevent the legislature from first providing for the payment of the bonded indebtedness of the state and interest thereon out of all the revenue of the state.

And the registrar's decision on whether the would-be voter passed through this maze of legal gobbledygook was final. Non-appealable.[26]

Black coal miner Leon Alexander knew this firsthand. He recalled the moment, shortly after World War II, when he tried to register to vote in Alabama. He stood there at the counter waiting and waiting while the registrar made a big show of deliberately ignoring him. Finally, when whites came into the office, the registrar greeted them, provided the paperwork, and promptly registered them to vote. Alexander nevertheless remained standing there, refusing to leave. Irritated, the registrar finally asked, "What you want, boy?"

"I wants to register to vote," the coal miner replied.

The registrar got the form and took it over to Alexander, knowing perfectly well what the final result would be before the pen had even scratched the paper. The coal miner went through the literacy test writing, and writing, and writing. The moment he was done, without even reviewing the sheet, the registrar took Alexander's registration, "balled it up and threw it in the wastebasket."

"You disqualified," he said. "You didn't answer the question."

In the end, it took the intervention of three white officials in the local United Mine Workers union, who had to get Governor Jim Folsom involved, before Alexander was finally registered to vote. And even then, as the coal miner recalled, it was the registrar who got the last laugh. Alexander may have now been a registered voter, but there was one small problem: "They didn't put me on the voting list!" His name never made it onto the official rolls; therefore, he couldn't vote after all. Looking back, Alexander recalled, "this guy had no intention of registering [me], not only no intention of registering me, he had no intention of registering any black to vote."[27]

Despite the fact that this scene played out over and over in registrars' offices across the South—where a registrar in Mississippi could even ask African Americans, "How many bubbles in a bar of soap?"—the law itself was just race-neutral enough to withstand judicial scrutiny.[28] Not only did literacy tests appear nondiscriminatory; they also carried the aura of plausibility. Voters, everyone could agree, ought to be able to understand their state's laws. Yet when that device was made operational, it had nothing to do with the law, of course, nothing to do with an engaged citizenry, and precisely everything to do with eliminating as many age-eligible African Americans from the voter rolls as possible. Eighty percent was Carter Glass's goal. But the actual numbers were even more brutal. By 1953 in the Deep South, "eleven counties where the black population equaled or exceeded that of whites" had only 1.3 percent of all eligible blacks registered to vote. Two counties had no African American voters at all.[29]

And then there was the poll tax, which all eleven states of the former Confederacy had adopted. Initially, after the Civil War, the poll tax "was intended not so much to disenfranchise the Negro as to place him again under the white man's domination, since failure to pay the tax was made prima facie evidence of vagrancy," which was the catchall term to criminalize, jail, and auction off African Americans. The "Negro who desired to stay off the chain gang was . . . forced to place himself under the protection of a white man who would pay the tax for him."[30] It was only years later, during the rise of Jim Crow, that the deliberate intent to choke off the black vote came into play when the states required all age-eligible males to pay an annual fee in order to vote.[31] Its proponents wielded the seemingly rational arguments that it costs money to hold elections and that extra funds were necessary to meet the needs of democracy. Moreover, they said the poll tax simply provided additional revenue for public schools. As a revenue producer, it was "a flop," however; Arkansas, for example, raised "only 5 percent of [its] total school budget by the poll tax, a tax that [kept] a good 80 percent of [the state's] adult citizens from voting."[32] But to many of the poll tax's proponents, the high "voter mortality rate" proved how important it was for vetting and weeding out those unworthy of democracy.

"Any person unwilling to pay a small fee in order to enjoy such a precious privilege did not deserve the franchise," its advocates proclaimed. Behind the veil of fiscal and patriotic duty, however, was the full understanding that without the poll tax, "Negroes would again be an important factor in southern politics." One man in Arkansas put it succinctly enough: "Do you want to see niggers in the state capital with their feet on the desk?"[33]

The power of the poll tax derived from several key components. First were the arcane rules about when and where to even pay the tax. The "procedures," C. Vann Woodward observed, were "artfully devised to discourage payment."[34] And, as it was law enforcement that collected the poll tax, the intimidation factor was very real in many locales. Sheriffs, notorious in the black community for their racism and brutality, were now the gatekeepers to the franchise.[35] In Tallahatchie County, Mississippi, for example, "where most whites but few Negroes had registered to vote," the sheriff admitted "that he instructed his deputies to require all persons paying poll taxes for the first time to apply to him personally."[36] There was another built-in obstacle, as well. In most states, the tax was due months before the election. One man noted that "paying a poll tax in February to vote in November is to most folks in Texas like buying a ticket to a show nine months ahead of time, and before you know who's playing or really what the thing is all about. It is easy to forget to do, too."[37]

Second, the tax was cumulative, a feature that alone would prove virtually insurmountable. For every year the resident was eligible to vote, a payment was due. For example, if after twenty years of not voting or having been unable to vote, an African American in Alabama in 1944 was finally able to pay, he or she would need not $1.50 to do so but rather $30, which is the equivalent of $722 in 2016.[38] By design, then, those back taxes "effectively depressed the black turnout."[39]

The economics of disfranchisement were brutally simple. In the mid-1940s, the National Committee to Abolish the Poll Tax estimated that 10 million Americans were denied the right to vote because they simply could not pay.[40] Many poor blacks were sharecroppers, living on credit until the harvest came in. Without cash throughout most of the year, they had no ability to pay the poll tax.[41] In Mississippi, the average farm family's income was "less than $100 a year." The state was, therefore, requiring that the impoverished give up 2 percent of their annual income "to cast a ballot." In households with three adults, this demand on limited resources could require them "giv[ing] up 6 percent of their income for the franchise."[42]

Southern lawmakers knew exactly what they were doing here. In 1950, African Americans' median income was but 54 percent that of whites', and the poll tax, absorbing a disproportionate share of blacks' "disposable" income, was often a burden too heavy to bear.[43] As late as November 9, 1963, Texas saw the enormous value of the poll tax and voted to maintain this tool of disfranchisement because "removing the poll tax requirement . . . would 'allow' minorities to 'flood the polls.' "[44]

In short, while the poll tax may have read as race-neutral—seemingly applicable to all—its reality was anything but, as the disparities in wealth, education, and relations with law enforcement had everything to do with the disparities in access between blacks and whites. Moreover, the registrars' discretion, as with the literacy test, inevitably undermined any sense of fairness or nondiscrimination, as they "thwarted black aspirants by not showing up at the office or by simply refusing to register blacks to vote when they did."[45]

There was another built-in inequity in the system. Mississippi, for instance, required receipts for two years of poll taxes in order to vote. The tilt in the playing field was apparent when arch-segregationist Theodore Bilbo's political operation worked with election officials to handle the difficulty of keeping track of multiyear receipts. His all-white constituency's "receipts are not only bought for them but are kept on file, issued on election day, re-collected and saved for the next year." The political machines in Texas did something similar. They would "buy up as many poll tax receipts as they [could], . . . keep them on file and pass them out . . . on election day—with instructions, of course, and an extra dollar or so for sweetenin'."[46] It was a total debasement and corruption of democracy, and it worked. During World War II, the overall voter turnout in the seven poll tax states was just 3 percent for the midterm election. The 1944 presidential election was only marginally better. The poll tax states could barely generate an 18 percent turnout rate, as compared with the nearly 69 percent national average.[47]

Another powerful tool to stop African Americans from having any political voice was the white primary. Key to the white primary's effectiveness was the fact that from Reconstruction until 1968 the South was a one-party system—only Democrats needed apply, so despised was the party of Lincoln. Several of the states, therefore, began to discern that one way to skirt around the Fifteenth Amendment was to tinker with the primary election, during which the Democratic candidate was chosen. This seemed foolproof for two reasons. First, because the South was a one-party region, whoever won in the spring would certainly be the victor in November. As long as the all-important and decisive primary was a whites-only affair, the results would be foreordained. And second, in 1921 the U.S. Supreme Court had ruled in *Newberry v. United States* that the federal government, and, thus, the U.S. Constitution itself, had no authority over the conduct of primary elections in the states.[48] With no federal interference and a hermetically sealed party system, the white primary became a masterful way to "emasculate politically the entire body of Negro voters," especially those who had successfully defied the other methods of disfranchisement, such as poll taxes and literacy tests.[49] In fact, one Georgia legislator strenuously "opposed another [proposed] disfranchisement device" because he believed it was unnecessary: "We already had the Negro eliminated from politics by the white primary," he proudly asserted.[50] And then a paper-thin aura of legality was achieved because blacks were welcome to vote in the irrelevant and perfunctory general election.

Except black people fought back. Over the span of twenty years they launched four separate lawsuits that went all the way to the U.S. Supreme Court. Texas was the site of this battle, because while all eleven states of the Old Confederacy had the white primary, the Lone Star State did it in "a more brutally direct fashion."[51] Its 1923 statute expressly forbid anyone but whites from voting in the Democratic primary. That was too explicit even for a U.S. Supreme Court that had previously decided that the poll tax and the literacy test were constitutional.[52] After reviewing Texas's white primary law, and seeing such an explicit violation of the equal protection clause, the court was unanimous and unequivocal: "It seems to us hard to imagine a more direct and obvious infringement of the Fourteenth Amendment."[53]

Texas was, however, undaunted. Satisfied that the court hadn't questioned whether the white primary actually violated the Fifteenth Amendment right to vote, the legislature simply redrafted the statute to turn the Democratic Party into a private organization—one to which the state just happened to delegate the authority to hold a primary. The point of this ruse was perfectly clear. In the *Cruikshank* decision, almost fifty years earlier in 1875, the U.S. Supreme Court had established that private actors were "immune from the strictures of the Fourteenth and Fifteenth Amendments."[54]

Again, blacks challenged Texas's law, and again they prevailed—though this time by only a 5–4 decision. The statute, justices ruled, was unconstitutional because the so-called private Democratic Party received its authority directly from the state. Therefore, it was not a "private" actor at all but an agent of the State of Texas. Lawmakers in Austin soldiered on, unfazed, cleverly picking up on the part of the court's ruling that laid out that African Americans "could be excluded from primaries" by putting the authority for that exclusion in the state Democratic convention.[55] Less than a month after the Supreme Court provided the roadmap to disfranchisement, then, the Democratic Party called a statewide convention and passed a resolution "restricting membership in the Party plus participation in party primaries to white citizens of Texas."[56]

Once again, the state had effectively eliminated African Americans and Mexican Americans (this was, after all, Texas) from having any real voice in determining their representatives in government or the policies that would affect their lives. And so in 1935, blacks sued Texas for a third time. Only this time, the Supreme Court, in Thurgood Marshall's words, "blinded themselves as judges to what they knew as men" and unanimously held that the Democratic primary was now a private matter. An organization had the right to choose the qualifications for membership and that, according to the Supreme Court, is exactly what the Democratic Party did. Therefore, the State of Texas had not violated African Americans' rights.[57]

Ridding this nation of the white primary now looked impossible but a subsequent U.S. Supreme Court decision in 1940 finally "pierced the façade . . . which had shielded primaries from the reach of Federal laws regulating the conduct of elections."[58] This landmark case, *United States v. Classic* (1941), erased much of the ambiguity about how far the Fourteenth and Fifteenth Amendments could reach into the election process. "If a state law made the primary an integral part of the election machinery and if the primary did effectively control the choice of the elected official then Congress had the right and the duty to regulate and control such primaries."[59] That clarity created a legal basis for the fourth white primary case, *Smith v. Allwright* (1944).[60] A black Texan wrote, "One thing is certain, as a result of the *Classic* case . . . the tables are turned . . . now the Negroes are on top."[61] In an 8–1 decision, the Supreme Court affirmed that sentiment when it ruled that the white primary, although supposedly a private affair, was central to the election process and, therefore, fell under the domain of federal law and the U.S. Constitution. Marshall was overjoyed that the justices had finally "looked behind the law and ferreted out the trickery."[62]

But the shenanigans continued. South Carolina decided to maintain the white primary while at the same time purging its books of all election laws. The rationale was simple: With nothing written down, there was nothing that the courts could find in violation of the Fourteenth or Fifteenth Amendments.[63] Not to be outdone, Texas offered up yet another scheme, this one with a pre-primary in the guise of the all-white, private Jaybird Democratic Association, that would then feed into the Democratic primary without any official machinery involved—no election laws, public funding, or certification by the party. The state reasoned that because this was supposedly before any real election activities took place and there appeared to be a firewall between this private club and government officialdom, Texas could avoid running afoul of the U.S. Constitution. In 1953, in *Terry v. Adams*, the Supreme Court disagreed, saying that the scheme in whatever guise was unconstitutional, and, with that, finally and completely driving a stake through the heart of the white primary.[64]

What the states could not accomplish by law, they were more than willing to achieve by violence. The wholesale slaughter of African Americans in Colfax, Louisiana (1873), Wilmington, North Carolina (1898), and Ocoee, Florida (1920), resulted in the loss of hundreds of lives simply because whites were enraged that black people had voted.[65] As states encouraged or winked at the murders, as killers stepped over the bodies and gobbled up the stolen land and property, black political power evaporated in a hail of gunfire and flames.

In 1946, former Georgia governor Eugene Talmadge was determined to keep it that way especially because World War II had lit a political fire in Black America.[66] He knew that the number of African Americans registered to vote had skyrocketed from 20,000 statewide in 1944 to 135,000 just two years later. During his run to regain the governor's office, he therefore vowed to reinstate the white primary, welcomed the endorsement of the Ku Klux Klan, and "campaigned largely on the issue of 'keep the niggers where they belong!'" His followers launched a major purge of the voting rolls, especially in the rural counties, followed by "cross burnings, night riders, and violence." Talmadge didn't flinch in the face of all this bloodshed and terror. Instead, he encouraged "the good white people [to] explain it to the negroes around the state just right." If African Americans were appropriately persuaded, Talmadge concluded, "I don't think they will want to vote." One white man responded enthusiastically, "[Lynching has] got to be done to keep Mister Nigger in his place . . . Gene told us what was happening, and what he was going to do about it."[67]

What Talmadge had done was to give his blessing to waves of anti-black violence.[68] A World War II veteran, Maceo Snipes, was one of the first to get caught in the tide of state-sponsored lynching. This was no surprise. Black veterans were particular targets throughout the South because their sense of rights and racial justice had grown especially acute during the battles to defeat the Nazis.[69] Snipes knew that he had already put his life on the line for democracy. He was willing to do it again. But what World War II didn't kill, Georgia most certainly did. The 1946 primary was the first since the U.S. Supreme Court's *Smith v. Allwright* decision, and Snipes, as an American citizen, believed that he actually had the right to participate in his state's election. He was mistaken. Whites had already posted a sign on the black church in Taylor County, Georgia: "The first Negro to vote will never vote again."[70] Snipes was not deterred. In July 1946, he cast his ballot in Taylor County's primary. In fact, he was the only black person to do so; and with that act of democratic bravery, Maceo Snipes signed his death warrant.

A few days later four white men showed up at Snipes's house and demanded that he step outside. As he stood on the porch, they pointed their guns at him and began firing. Snipes staggered and fell to the ground. They just walked away. His mother ran out of the house and got him to the hospital, but in Jim Crow America, black patients did not have the right to health care. He lay in a room the size of a closet unattended for six hours bleeding, just bleeding. This strong man, this veteran, lingered for two more days, but the damage was too extensive, the medical treatment too slow, and Georgia's hate too deep. In the wake of his murder, there was barely an investigation, and given that his death was "a direct result of the violence preached by Governor-elect Talmadge," Snipes's killers walked.[71]

In Mississippi, Senator Theodore Bilbo was also determined that his state's black population would have no rights that the white man was bound to respect. During the 1946 primary, he riled up his "red-blooded Anglo-Saxon" followers with orders that "the best way to keep the nigger from voting . . . [was to] do it the night before the election." Then, as if additional clarification were required, he sneered, "If any nigger tries to organize to vote, use the tar and feathers and don't forget the matches." In some cases, blacks were simply turned away; but in others, officials taunted African Americans demanding that they "paint . . . their faces white" if they wanted to vote in the white primary. Others were just beaten. Etoy Fletcher, a veteran, was actually "flogged." V. R. Collier, the president of the NAACP branch in Gulfport, was "physically assaulted." When he turned to the Federal Bureau of Investigation for help, the agent told him that the bureau didn't protect; it investigated. When he called the U.S. attorney in Jackson, Collier was directed to seek help from the FBI. The realization was wrenching: "We Negroes are without any protection at all," he said.[72]

Intimidation and violence simply prevented access to the polls for African Americans. Over and over those who tried to register to vote would be photographed by the police and harassed and threatened by gun-toting, pickup-driving toughs. Blacks who dared register had a virtual target on their backs. They would soon receive a visit from the sheriff, endure arrest on some trumped-up charge, and face jail time or an exorbitant fine.[73] In Rankin County, Mississippi, the sheriff stopped a black man from registering to vote at the courthouse by beating him. "I hit him and kept on hitting him," the sheriff bragged, "and if he hadn't run I would have kept on hitting him." The beating was not just about stopping this one man; "it was meant to send a message" that this "was the fate for others seeking this precious right."[74]

The tools of Jim Crow disfranchisement worked all too well. In 1867, the percentage of African American adults registered to vote in Mississippi was 66.9 percent; by 1955, it was 4.3 percent.[75] Between 1954 and 1962, only eight blacks in all of Claiborne County had managed to come through Mississippi's gauntlet.[76] Those vote-chilling numbers scarred the southern electoral landscape. Five counties in Alabama had zero to less than 2 percent of African Americans registered.[77] In Georgia, "less than 10% of the age-eligible African Americans were registered in 1962" in thirty counties with significant black populations. In fact, four entire counties had fewer than ten nonwhites registered.[78]

Denying the vote to millions of American citizens was so deeply rooted in the fabric of the nation, twisted into the mechanics of government, and embedded in the political strategy and thinking of powerful government officials that this clear affront to democracy was not going to change on its own. Fortunately, local resistance and global condemnation combined to take America to the brink of democracy.

Starting in 1947, the United States found itself in a pitched battle for global leadership against the Soviet Union. Two hegemons, two warring ideologies, two economies were amassed and ready to destroy the other. The reality of nuclear weapons, however, made any head-on confrontation an existential impossibility. Therefore, they fought a series of proxy wars in Asia, Africa, and Latin America "with the ferocity that only civil wars can bring forth." As each superpower chose sides and armed and financed the combatants, "the Cold War took demonic possession of a local transition."[79]

The Cold War also weaponized culture and propaganda.[80] The Soviet Union prided itself on meeting the basic material needs—housing, employment, health care—of its people. There was, of course, a steep price to be paid in terms of individual freedom and liberty. The Soviet weakness, therefore, played directly into the Americans' strength: democracy. But, given Jim Crow, those vaunted democratic ideals turned out to be the U.S.'s Achilles heel as well—a fundamental hypocrisy the Soviets set out to exploit at every turn.[81]

Each lynching, each bombing of a black home or business, each miscarriage of justice became grist for the Kremlin's mill. One article in the party-controlled Soviet press laid out the "numerous examples of racial terrorism in the U.S.A., such as the lynching of the Negro [Emmitt] Till, the brutal persecution of the Negro girl Autherine Lucy, the arrests of Negro leaders in Montgomery and the explosions of bombs near the homes of Negroes in northern and southern states."[82]

While each of those troubled the American narrative of democracy, Little Rock sent shockwaves and ripped it apart. White resistance to the *Brown v. Board* (1954) decision to integrate schools was fiery, furious, and fevered as it erupted, most visibly in Little Rock, Arkansas, in 1957, when nine black honor students sought to desegregate Central High. The crisis "brought Jim Crow violence to vivid life in world media" and led Secretary of State John Foster Dulles to exclaim that "this situation was ruining our foreign policy."[83] The Soviets wanted to be sure of it as they published their exposé: "National guard soldiers and policemen armed to the teeth bar Negro children from entering the schools, threaten them with bayonets and tear-gas bombs and encourage hooligans to engage in violence with impunity."[84]

The racial violence also caught the attention of nations the United States wanted firmly allied with the West, and no amount of State Department assertions about Soviet propaganda could allay the damage. The U.S. ambassador to the United Nations Henry Cabot Lodge asserted, "I can see clearly the harm that [Little Rock is] doing . . . More than two-thirds of the world is non-white and the reactions of [their] representatives is easy to see."[85] The *Times of India* ran with a front-page story, "Armed Men Cordon Off White School: Racial Desegregation in Arkansas Prevented." Similar articles dominated the news in Egypt, Tanganyika, and other places. The *Irish Times* laid out the costs: The crisis in Little Rock had "given Communist propagandists the text for innumerable sermons to coloured peoples everywhere."[86]

What ruined the U.S.'s credibility, the Soviets gleefully claimed, was that people who "dream of nooses and dynamite . . . who throw rocks at defenseless Negro children—these gentlemen have the audacity to talk about 'democracy' and speak as supporters of 'freedom.' "[87] Don't be fooled, the Kremlin warned—the U.S. goal was to export Jim Crow, not democracy. "American racism and its

savage practice of cruel persecution and abuse of minorities is . . .
the true nature of the American 'democracy' which the United States
is trying to foist on other countries and peoples."[88]

African Americans were well aware of the global Cold War context
of their own struggle for freedom and never forgot it.[89] But it was a
series of local insurgencies in the black community erupting across
the South that gave that uprising the aura of a "movement."[90]
Recognizing the importance of the media in documenting and broad-
casting that confrontation, leadership in Montgomery, Atlanta,
Birmingham, and other cities adopted a nonviolent strategy to
confront the evil that African Americans faced when trying to vote,
go to good schools, shop, dine, and just live.

Although it came to the realization slowly, the U.S. government
was now confronted with a nation-defining decision. America was
paralyzed, on one hand, by the power of the Southern Democrats in
Congress, whose inordinate political strength and control of key
committees was based on their ability to win reelection after reelection because of massive disfranchisement and racial terror; and on
the other, by the missionary-like belief that America was the champion of democracy and freedom in the battle against the Soviet Union,
whose death grip on human rights had no limits. The dilemma
was clear. Domestic politics and the disproportionate power of the
Southern Democrats demanded that the federal government fully
capitulate to Jim Crow, while foreign policy, and the need to woo the
emerging Third World nations and defeat the Soviets, required that
racial discrimination end once and for all.[91]

President Dwight Eisenhower's "solution" to this Gordian knot,
however, only pulled the rope tighter. In 1957, Attorney General
Herbert Brownell, with a full assist from the wily junior senator from
Texas, Lyndon Johnson, crafted and pushed through Congress the
first civil rights bill in nearly ninety years. This was America taking
care of the "unfinished business of democracy." Except it wasn't.

The Civil Rights Act (1957), while seemingly a landmark piece of
legislation, was actually a paper tiger that had no ability to protect

the right to vote. The act did create the Civil Rights Commission, upgrade the Department of Justice's section on civil rights to a division, and authorize the U.S. attorney general to sue those violating the voting rights of American citizens.[92] But it was—by design and implementation—no match for the entrenched resistance to black citizenship.

The core of the act gave the U.S. Department of Justice the authority to sue jurisdictions that blocked citizens from voting "on account of race." But, the lawsuit mechanism, while an improvement, had any number of insurmountable problems. First and foremost, litigation would be a reaction to voting rights violations, rather than any sort of meaningful prevention. The "crime" had to occur, in other words, before the Department of Justice stepped in. Which meant that skewed election results, where a candidate assumed office because citizens had been systematically disfranchised, could affect years of policy and lawmaking while the long, drawn-out court process slowly unfolded.[93] After investigation, these suits would take, on average, an additional 17.8 months between the trial and the judges' ruling, and then another year for the appeal. And if the registrar who was the named defendant in the lawsuit were to leave office at any point during this process (which was a common ploy), then the case became moot and was thrown out.[94] Meanwhile, the black populations could and would continue to be terrorized and harassed for daring to vote, with little to no protection.

The litigation route was hampered, too, by that fact that the Civil Rights Act "did not provide access to [voter] registration records prior to filing suit. Nor did it prohibit the destruction of these records."[95] Without that vital evidence, cases would simply stall or, worse, collapse. Moreover, "southern federal judges were sometimes unreceptive" to the suits, and all-white juries rarely returned a guilty verdict when blacks were the victims.[96]

And then there was the reluctance in the Department of Justice to pursue these cases with any true vigor. From the FBI to the U.S.

attorney general, resentment, caution, and hesitancy were the watch-words.[97] As a result, there were no systemic changes "even when there were victories," and the Civil Rights Act of 1957 proved, just as many African Americans had feared, to be but a very "modest piece of legislation . . . [with] few teeth and little impact."[98]

The unrelenting pressure of the Civil Rights Movement, however, meant that America's tepid response to the denial of the basic right to vote would not go unchallenged. In Alabama's Marion, Lowndes, and Dallas counties, years of nonviolent, direct-action protest led to a cinematic explosion in March 1965 on the Edmund Pettus Bridge in Selma. As peaceful marchers ran into the hailstorm of Alabama state troopers and Dallas County sheriff Jim Clark and his deputies, news cameras captured the horror of tear gas, barbed-wire bullwhips, and police on horseback trampling over the fallen. A nation sat in stunned silence, almost traumatized by the spectacle. And then the ensuing bludgeoning death in Selma of a white minister because he had the audacity to believe that black citizens had the right to vote became the tipping point, and now, shaken out of its compla-cency, a civil rights assembly mobilized.[99]

Congress, itself, and the White House, too, had seen enough. President Lyndon Johnson demanded that the attorney general craft a law with teeth. The "goddamdest, toughest voting rights act that [attorney general] Nicholas Katzenbach and his aides could devise targeted southern jurisdictions that had a tradition of discrimination against African Americans."[100] During the hearings to finally make the Fifteenth Amendment viable, Congress noted the ineffectiveness of the Civil Rights Act of 1957, especially in the face of entrenched resistance. The House Committee on the Judiciary stated:

> The litigation in Dallas County took more than 4 years to open the door
> to the exercise of constitutional rights conferred almost a century ago.

The problem on a national scale is that the difficulties experienced in suits in Dallas County have been encountered over and over again under existing voting laws. Four years is too long. The burden is too heavy—the wrong to our citizens is too serious—the damage to our national conscience is too great not to adopt more effective measures than exist today.[101]

The Voting Rights Act (VRA) passed with overwhelming majorities in the House of Representatives (328–74) and the Senate (79–18). Johnson signed the bill into law on August 6, 1965.[101] Clarence Mitchell, the chief Washington lobbyist for the NAACP, said, "After five years of shameful events that increased tensions at home and caused embarrassment abroad, Congress finally gave a remedy it could have given in 1960."[103]

The VRA was nevertheless a seismic shift in thought, action, and execution for the U.S. government when compared with the Civil Rights Act of 1957 and its equally enfeebled companion legislation of 1960. Rather than passively waiting for locales to violate the rights of American citizens and then sitting still until those who had been routinely brutalized by this system made a formal complaint, the VRA put the responsibility for adhering to the Constitution onto state and local governments.

In other words, the days of discriminatory laws and so-called race-neutral machinations were over; the years of relying on long, drawn-out, costly, and often ineffective litigation to address disfranchisement changed in 1965. The Voting Rights Act "thrust the federal government into the role of supervising voting in large parts of the country to protect African Americans' right to vote, a duty it had not assumed since Reconstruction."[104] The VRA identified jurisdictions that had a long, documented history of racial discrimination in voting, and required that the Department of Justice or the federal court in Washington, D.C., approve any change to the voting laws or requirements that those districts wanted to make *before* it was enacted.[105] The preventative thrust of the VRA was landmark.[106] Alabama civil rights attorney Hank Sanders recognized the revolutionary, transformative impact that the preclearance provision could have. Section 5 of the VRA, he explained, "can complete something this country started 200 years ago. That something is not complete, it is called Democracy."[107]

As might have been expected, that potential for an actual thriving, viable democracy was the threat that set the stage for a backlash that would gain momentum and velocity in the ensuing decades, all the way to 2013, when the act would be largely gutted.

In 1966, just a year after the Voting Rights Act was first passed, South Carolina challenged its constitutionality, arguing that the act infringed upon the state's sovereignty and ability to carry out its own elections. South Carolina resented mightily the insertion of federal electors at registrars' offices and polling places to ensure that the state no longer used literacy tests, which the VRA had banned. In *South Carolina v. Katzenbach* (1966), the justices, in an 8–1 decision, reaffirmed both the constitutionality and the need for the legislation. "The Voting Rights Act was designed by Congress to banish the blight of racial discrimination in voting, which has infected the electoral process in parts of our country for nearly a century. Congress felt itself confronted by an insidious and pervasive evil which had been perpetuated in certain parts of our country through unremitting and ingenious defiance of the Constitution."[108]

When South Carolina's frontal challenge to the law did not work, Mississippi and Virginia took up the battle and tried to undermine it by arguing that the scope of the activities subject to the VRA was actually quite limited. Yes, they asserted, disfranchisement via literacy tests, understanding clauses, and the poll tax was now illegal. Understood. But Virginia and Mississippi, they argued, merely sought to make minor changes to aid the efficiency of elections. Certainly, those mere tweaks did not require prior approval—what the Act calls "preclearance," from the federal government.

Operating under this assumption, Virginia changed the way it handled voters who were illiterate. Prior to the VRA, there were helpers at the polls to aid those who could not read. After the Voting Rights Act, though, the state changed the rules so that voters would have to physically write in the candidates whose names were not printed on the ballot. In the 1966 state election, those who were illiterate tried to use labels and stickers to indicate their preference only to have those votes be discarded and uncounted according to the new rule requiring the names be handwritten. This latest iteration was as "race-neutral" as the literacy test. After the *Brown* decision, Virginia led the effort to make the Supreme Court decision to end segregation in the schools unenforceable and untenable. So determined were state lawmakers to resist *Brown* that they shut down school districts throughout Virginia, funneled tax dollars into all-white private academies so that white children could continue their education, and provided no educational opportunities whatsoever for black students. This went on for years. In short, Virginia ensured that there would be schooling for whites but not blacks; and after that, the state changed its laws so that those who were illiterate would not be able to vote.[109]

Mississippi's alterations in voting were equally subtle in their discrimination. After the advent of *Brown* and the VRA, positions such as school superintendent suddenly became appointed rather than elected offices. And whereas county supervisors had once been voted on within their respective, defined districts, now they would be installed via at-large elections. While seemingly innocuous, at-large voting is particularly insidious in areas where African Americans are a sizable part but not a majority of the population. It works like this: In the original confined districts, African Americans' numbers were large enough to carry enormous electoral weight. Yet literacy tests, poll taxes, and Election Day terror had nullified that power and reduced black voter registration to the single digits. Therefore, there was no possibility of an African American candidate, or even a candidate openly attuned to the black community's concerns, winning an election. So long as disfranchisement shut down the black vote, white Mississippi felt safe. After the Voting Rights Act, however, those districts could easily produce African American elected officials. Mississippi opted, therefore, to diffuse or dilute the black vote among a sea of whites by erasing the district boundaries and requiring candidates to run and succeed in a much wider geographical (and demographic) area. These supposedly race-neutral changes, one Mississippi legislator candidly admitted, would "preserve our way of doing business."[110]

Chief Justice Earl Warren certainly thought so and, in one of his court's last decisions, he pushed back hard. It was clear that Mississippi and Virginia believed that as long as they weren't restricting access to the polls via a literacy test or poll tax, every other change they made was beyond the scope of the VRA. The U.S. Supreme Court strongly disagreed. Voting is not just the act itself, Warren chided, but includes "all action necessary to make a vote effective." Then, to ensure that the range of activities subject to the VRA was clear, he insisted that the Voting Rights Act "was aimed at the subtle, as well as the obvious, state regulations which have the effect of denying citizens their right to vote because of race."[111]

That hardly settled the issue of course. States and reluctant presidential administrations, Richard Nixon's and Ronald Reagan's in particular, were less than enthusiastic about securing the right to vote for those previously denied access to the polls. Entirely willing to dilute and weaken the VRA, these GOP presidents were supported in their efforts by states chafing against the restraints imposed by enforced federal law.[112]

In those challenges were the seeds of 2013, when the U.S. Supreme Court, in *Shelby County v. Holder*, looked at the VRA, "the most effective legislation ever passed by Congress," and proceeded to eviscerate that law.[113] Many of the arguments that Chief Justice John Roberts made at that time had already, over the course of several decades, been carefully crafted, reframed, and stacked to wall off the ballot box from millions of American citizens.

These arguments began shortly after the law's passage. Justice Hugo Black's lone dissent in the 1966 *South Carolina v. Katzenbach* case went directly after one of the core components of the VRA: preclearance. Justice Black argued that Congress had overstepped its authority "by providing that some of the States cannot pass state laws or adopt state constitutional amendments without first being compelled to beg federal authorities to approve their policies." That preclearance proviso, he argued, "so distorts our constitutional structure of government as to render any distinction drawn in the Constitution between state and federal power almost meaningless."[114] Of course, Congress had tried in 1867, 1870, 1957, and again in 1960 to put authority for voting, even in federal elections, in the hands of the states. And repeatedly, Mississippi, South Carolina, Georgia, and the usual suspects willfully, deliberately, and painstakingly barred eligible American citizens from the polls. What remedy, then, was available to the federal government for those who mocked the Fifteenth Amendment, skewed and skewered elections, and placed in power those who held the Constitution in contempt? The Supreme Court admitted that the Civil Rights Act of 1957 and 1960 simply did not work:

> Litigation has been exceedingly slow, in part because of the ample opportunities for delay . . . Even when favorable decisions have finally been obtained, some of the States . . . merely switched to discriminatory devices not covered by the federal decrees, or . . . enacted difficult new tests designed to prolong the existing disparity between white and Negro registration. Alternatively, certain local officials have defied and evaded court orders or have simply closed their registration offices to freeze the voting rolls.[115]

Yet Justice Black's sense of an intrusive, unconstitutional federal leviathan lingered and, over time, gained enormous political strength.[116]

Ironically, the second element used to wall off the Voting Rights Act was its own success. The impact of the VRA on African Americans was immediate:

> In Mississippi, black registration went from less than 10% in 1964 to almost 60% in 1968; in Alabama, the figure rose from 24% to 57%. In the region as a whole, roughly a million new voters were registered within a few years after the bill became law, bringing African American registration to a record 62%.[117]

In addition, there was a "dramatic" increase in the number and percentage of blacks registered to vote in South Carolina.[118] In 1967, Mississippi elected its first African American to office since Reconstruction.[119] Those successes, after decades of crushing, brutalizing disfranchisement, led "spokesmen for the white South" during the 1970 VRA reauthorization hearings to "claim . . . that the law had served its purpose and should be allowed to expire."[120] What was left unsaid, of course, was that the reason the Voting Rights Act worked was the advent of vigorous federal intervention, not because the racism that required the law in the first place had stopped.[121]

One of the key vestiges of that racism transformed the demographic and geographic composition of the two major parties. The Solid Democratic South dissolved as, ironically enough, Texan Lyndon Johnson lobbied for and signed acts that legally acknowledged the citizenship rights of African Americans. He lamented that his advocacy for the Civil Rights Act of 1964 and the Voting Rights Act of 1965, while the right thing to do, meant that "the Democrats have lost the South for a generation."[122] It would actually turn out to be much, much longer. The GOP quickly adopted the Southern Strategy to woo the white South into the Republican Party.

The key was to pitch the GOP's message and policies as designed to short-circuit the civil rights gains of African Americans and, equally important, to cast conservative whites as victims besieged by liberalism, minorities, and the Democrats' big, intrusive government.[123]

The third element that undergirded John Roberts's destruction of the Voting Rights Act, then, was the notion that that remarkable piece of legislation had singled out the South. Picked on it even, with a law that was "punitive." The VRA, in this scenario, was a sentence without a crime. In 1970, Senator Strom Thurmond of South Carolina, one of the most powerful members of Congress and a former presidential candidate for the Dixiecrat Party, insisted that "this act is nothing more than a device created to inflict political punishment upon one section of the country."[124] That haze of victimhood and innocence diffused the hard edges of decades of Election Day terror, literacy tests, poll taxes, and white primaries. And the resultant fog blurred the reality of the systematic disfranchisement of African Americans in which, as late as World War II, fewer than 1 percent of age-eligible blacks were registered to vote in South Carolina. It also occluded the active leadership role the state took from 1944 to 1952 in circumventing the *Smith v. Allwright* decision and providing a "model for other Southern States seeking to keep their party affairs free from Negro participation."[125] And although the VRA had had an impact, by 1970, only "28 percent of blacks were registered in Thurmond's home of Edgefield County, compared with 96 percent of whites."[126] Yet five years later, the senator still complained about the very existence of the law. The "so-called voting rights act," he railed, "should be allowed to expire unceremoniously." He then added that the VRA was "unconstitutional" because its supporters "were guilty of discrimination" against the South. The sense that Dixie had changed, had stopped encouraging sheriffs to beat down African Americans who wanted to register to vote, meant that there was no need for this "unfortunate" law.[127]

The Old South was still there, of course—just in a new dress. In 1971, Mississippi wanted to redesign its primaries and redraw district boundaries, and argued that its new and improved election plans required only that residents in "a third of Mississippi's counties— constituting 40 percent of the state's black voters"—re-register.[128] The state had pulled this stunt before. Prior to the *Brown* decision, the NAACP had mounted a serious voter-registration campaign in the state and, despite the odds, achieved measurable results. After *Brown*, however, Mississippi passed a law in 1955 requiring every registered voter to go through the gauntlet the state had created, which included heightened literacy and understanding tests, as well as registrars who understood their orders as if Theodore Bilbo was there barking out instructions on how to stop blacks from voting. Not surprisingly, the number of African American voters plummeted by two-thirds.[129]

Sixteen years later, Mississippi tried, once again, to send black citizens through an impenetrable reregistration process. This time, however, after intense wrangling, the Department of Justice and the Voting Rights Act stopped the Magnolia State.[130] Not that this dissuaded others from testing how far the VRA could be stretched to stay just on this side of the Fifteenth Amendment, maintain the facade of race-neutral innocence, and still achieve the goal of disfranchisement, which is exactly what Alabama accomplished in 1981 with the acquiescence of Reagan's Department of Justice. The state passed a "reidentification" bill that purged the voting rolls in three counties with sizable black populations and required previously registered voters to go to the courthouse to identify themselves. African American registration dropped by 43 percent.[131]

The fourth element, then, was an especially pernicious lie that hovered like a storm cloud over the VRA and became darker and more threatening as black political power grew. Key segments in the criminal justice and political system, especially as the nation made a right turn during the Reagan years, insisted that the real violators were not the states at all but actually African Americans who committed outright voter fraud.[132] Hank Sanders had witnessed this vicious scenario play out. Whenever blacks won political office or started to assert their voting rights, he remarked, the prosecutor's office would launch an extensive investigation. This move had but one purpose: intimidation. "Every time people start investigating you," he explained, "you start drawing back and decide no matter how right you are to leave that alone," because if you don't, the criminal justice system will rip you apart for simply exercising your voting rights.[133]

In 1979 two black women, Julia Wilder and Maggie Bozeman, felt the full wrath of Alabama's legal system. Wilder, the sixty-nine-year-old president of Pickens County Voters League and an officer of the Southern Christian Leadership Conference (SCLC), had been hard at work to make the Voting Rights Act a living, viable document in rural Alabama. By the late 1970s, no African American had ever been elected to office in Pickens County, which was 42 percent black. Joining Wilder in this work was fifty-one-year-old Maggie Bozeman, president of the local NAACP branch. They had collected absentee ballots from more than three dozen elderly and disabled African Americans, had those forms certified as valid by the local funeral director, who was a notary, and sent those ballots in to the Board of Elections.

That's when the trouble began. Later that year, Sophie Spann, an African American woman, went down to the local grocery store to cast her vote in the election and was turned away because, the election official said, she had already voted absentee.

That set off an investigation by the Pickens County district attorney followed by a tumultuous, haphazard trial that was so riddled with holes and contradictions that the appeals court labeled the key witnesses' testimony "confusing," "conflicting," and an indecipherable "hodgepodge." Of the thirteen "victims," the only one who remained steadfast in insisting that her vote was stolen was Sophie Spann, who just happened to have "reared the sheriff's deputy and son-in-law" and who was brought lunch by the sheriff personally before she took the stand. Based on Spann's testimony alone, both women were found guilty by an all-white jury, whose verdict was upheld by the appeals court. Bozeman received a four-year prison sentence, and Wilder got hit with the maximum, five years, which for a sixty-nine-year-old could easily be a life sentence. These were "the stiffest [sentences] ever given in an Alabama voting fraud case."[134] The SCLC president, the Reverend Joseph Lowery, wailed that Bozeman and Wilder were "politically lynched."[135]

But as far as the white power structure in Pickens County was concerned, these women had gotten just what they deserved. Bozeman and Wilder, community leaders who insisted that African Americans had rights, including the right to vote, had "guts" and "nerve." And that, remarked the newspaper editor, "brought out the worst in white people." "If they could get out and march at their ages," sneered one deputy, "they could have done just fine in jail." Robert Kirksey, a county commissioner, complained, "They constantly harassed public officials . . . they were always creating disturbances" by showing up at every county commission and school board meeting and having the audacity to ask questions of elected officials.

The two activists had pushed for and won better wages for sanitation workers and to have the roads paved "on the black side of town." But they weren't done. Wilder's commitment to black voting rights was unshakable. If it meant giving someone her last fifty cents "to get to the polls," she was going to do it. If it meant teaching a civics lesson to those who had been beaten down for so long that they didn't think their vote mattered, she had no problem with that either. Wilder would answer the defeated refrain of "It don't make much difference how I vote, the white folks will do what they want anyway," with a self-empowering rejoinder: "Because we let them." Community self-respect, she taught, was inextricably tied to the vote. And that sense of political awareness and backbone led Bozeman to declare and warn, "If you teach black people to stand up for their rights in Pickens

County, white folks will starve you out, or suffer you so until you move out of town." She knew it and African Americans knew it, too.

One black resident simply said of Maggie, "She made white folks mad." For many in the black community, therefore, the district attorney going after Bozeman and Wilder was nothing but retribution "for trying to make democracy work."[136] The sheriff disagreed vigorously. There was no need for what "those women" did. African Americans had it good in Pickens County. "We have a policy of not beating 'em," he bragged, "We treat 'em right. We don't run over 'em just because they are black." But the message was also clear: If they're black and, as one African American woman pointed out, "promote better living for colored" people, the full force of the state's legal machinery would hound, harass, and imprison them for helping the disfranchised vote.[137]

In 1985, U.S. attorney Jefferson Beauregard Sessions III slapped three civil rights workers, including a former aide to Martin Luther King, with a twenty-nine-count indictment for forging or changing and then mailing bogus absentee ballots. Albert Turner Sr. was the primary target. He had come to the voting rights battle in the early 1960s when, even as a college-educated man, he failed Alabama's literacy test.[138] Infuriated, and "determined to be free," Turner began the long, hard work of grassroots organizing.[139] He was knee-deep in the battles in Selma. He led the mule train that carried Martin Luther King's body to its final resting place. He formed the Perry County Civic League to register more African Americans to vote and change what democracy looked like in Alabama.

Working with his wife, Evelyn, and a colleague, Spencer Hogue, Turner noticed that despite the VRA, and despite the large number of African Americans in the state's Black Belt counties, whites consistently won every election. As he dug deeper, he learned that the difference was the sheer volume of absentee ballots coming in from whites who were landowners in Perry, Lowndes, and other counties but lived in Birmingham, Chicago, and beyond. They, in fact, were strongly and actively encouraged by election officials in the Black Belt, including Perry County, to use absentee ballots to keep the political power in white hands. White candidates, as historian Allen Tullos observed, "found electoral deliverance inside dependable absentee voting boxes."[140]

Turner believed he had now cracked the code. Years of registering blacks to vote, especially in a county that was 60 percent African American, and years of encouraging black candidates to run for office, yet still to have all the elected officials be white, came down to, he grasped, absentee ballots. This was a device that blacks didn't use extensively, certainly not like other voters did. Yet Perry County was prime for it. One-third of African American adults who lived there actually worked in another county. In addition, 15 percent of black residents were over sixty-five years old. In short, 48 percent of the black vote was already in jeopardy because of employment obligations and a lack of mobility. Then, to make the likelihood of their voting even more difficult, the polls were open for only four hours in the afternoon on Election Day.[141] If blacks could not vote because of their work schedule, distance to the polls, or limited mobility during that narrow four-hour window, then, Turner concluded, the absentee-ballot procedure would solve the problem. He went to the Alabama attorney general's office for training sessions and then began to apply that knowledge in Perry and surrounding counties. Not surprisingly, Election Day 1982 brought a very different result. African Americans won their first positions on the school boards and county commissions.[142]

Those victories "put the old-guard white elite on the defensive."[143] Or, more accurately, on the offensive. The Perry County district attorney was convinced there was fraud and, more important, that Turner and his group committed it. The D.A. quickly informed the U.S. attorney, Jeff Sessions. When the next primary rolled around in 1984, Sessions called in the FBI to tail the Turners and Spencer Hogue. As the civil rights workers mailed hundreds of absentee ballots that they had collected (mostly from the elderly), the agents, who had been hiding in the bushes, rushed to the mailbox, seized the ballots, and, after picking through them, believed they had identified seventy-five that had been tampered with. Sessions, then, identified the victims of the alleged voter fraud, moved them south to Mobile, and interviewed them there.[144]

One way to see this effort is through the gauze of colorblind justice, which would depict Sessions as an efficient U.S. attorney: Seeing a potential problem, he moved to secure the rights of voters by secreting them 160 miles away from the power base of the man who may have violated their rights. Sessions also painstakingly gathered the evidence he needed to make sure that identity and ballot fraud had not sullied Alabama's elections.

But that's not at all what happened, despite his subsequent denials.[145]

Instead, Sessions was "someone who thinks that the VRA ought not to have ever been in existence" because, for him, it was an "intrusive piece of legislation."[146] Thus, in a move that flipped the Voting Rights Act on its head, his investigation targeted only counties where African Americans had won office. He deliberately ignored districts that maintained white political control via absentee ballots and summarily dismissed evidence of irregularities in those votes as not being "credible."[147] He then rounded up twenty elderly blacks and had Alabama state troopers drive them away from their community, into a predominately white area to be fingerprinted, photographed, and grilled before a grand jury. Every step of this process was designed to intimidate, especially those who were more than aware of what sheriffs, police, and Alabama state troopers, with the acquiescence of the FBI, had done to black people who had dared to vote. Reverend O. C. Dobynes recalled that long, "degrading" bus ride to Mobile and all that followed: "To me, it was just simply saying, 'We are going to scare you into saying what we want you to say.'" It worked. Fannie Mae Williams told the grand jury that this was her "first and last" time voting using an absentee ballot. Two others were even more emphatic: "They were done with voting." Period.[148] And as Ari Berman reports, "Ninety-two-year-old Willie Bright was so frightened of 'the law' that he wouldn't even admit he'd voted."[149]

Even when the judge threw out most of the charges and the jury came back with a "not guilty" verdict on the few remaining counts, the damage had been done. Both the trial of the Marion Three and that of Bozeman and Wilder signaled how to use "the criminal processes . . . to slow down the development of progressive black leadership." And it laid out how to marshal the forces of legal intimidation to trigger communal memories of brutality, Jim Crow, and disfranchisement.[150] Even years after her ordeal with Jeff Sessions, Evelyn Turner declared, "I'll never forget, as long as I stay black."[151]

The fifth element that laid the groundwork for gutting the Voting Rights Act was the ease with which the U.S. Supreme Court overturned a federal election, ignoring blatant violations of the Fifteenth Amendment and swaddling it all in the language of the Fourteenth Amendment's equal protection clause. It demonstrated how far the court's slim majority would go to create a political outcome, despite all the evidence.

This happened in 2000, of course, when the presidency hung by a chad. Republican George W. Bush and Democrat Al Gore, with forty-nine states having tallied their ballots, were suddenly in a virtual tie, such that whoever won Florida's twenty-five Electoral College votes would become president of the United States.

Florida, however, was a festering election cesspool—as racially backward as it was bureaucratically inept. Secretary of State Katherine Harris had used faulty data to purge approximately twenty thousand names, mostly of blacks and Hispanics, from the voter rolls.[152] In polling stations in Jacksonville's black neighborhoods, police officers stationed themselves conspicuously around the buildings and at entry points as if this were Mississippi in the 1950s all over again. In other cases, voters who knew they were registered learned on Election Day that their names were nowhere to be found on the registrar's list. Poll workers could not get in touch with election officials to do any kind of verification because the phone lines were jammed. There was a more effective method via laptop computers; however, those were placed in predominately white, Republican precincts. There was also a limited number of working voting machines in polling stations that had sizable minority populations. In some areas, none of the machines tallied even one vote for a presidential candidate. Not one. And then there were the hanging chads. Some of the voting machines punched a hole next to a candidate's name, others made a dent, while others left the little circular piece of paper dangling.[153]

Florida in 2000 was, without question, a perfect storm of incompetence and Election Day treachery. Unfortunately, there was a presidency hanging in the balance and the final tally, even *with* the massive disfranchisement effort to keep blacks and Hispanics from voting, was still too close to call. The voting machines, unable to get an accurate count, not least because of the ballots with imperfect chad punches, were blamed. Gore therefore requested a hand recount. And that's when the momentum swung, as Bush's margin of victory began to shrink rapidly, from 1,784 votes to 327, then to 154.[154]

It was at this nail-biting moment that the U.S. Supreme Court stepped in, overruling Florida's highest court, and ordered that the recount stop. Five conservative justices, who often denounced what they called an activist judiciary, and federal overreach in general, now ruled that Florida did not have the right to count the ballots in the election held in its own state.[155] In fact, *no* entity could tally those votes. The recount violated the Fourteenth Amendment's equal protection clause, the justices contended, because the process was for those counties with numerous electoral failures and, therefore, some people, somehow, somewhere (that would be in those counties where the polling machines actually worked) weren't going to have their votes counted again.

The inanity of the argument was "so brazen a departure for the conservatives and so ferocious an assault on . . . conventional . . . doctrinal understandings" about federalism and originalist constitutional philosophy that it defied logic. That is, until it became clear that this was about one thing and one thing alone: putting Republican George W. Bush in the White House.[156] Prominent lawyer Vincent Bugliosi called it a "judicial coup d'etat."[157]

That 2000 presidential election set the stage for the sixth component that Roberts would use to undermine the Voting Rights Act. Over time, more and more members of the U.S. Supreme Court had begun to openly question the constitutionality of preclearance.

The election, and particularly how it was won, had driven home how racially polarized and divided the electorate was.[158] George W. Bush, however, didn't believe the situation was hopeless. While only 9 percent of African Americans voted for him, 35 percent of Hispanics had cast their ballot for Bush.[159] His strategist, therefore, argued that the Republicans could broaden their appeal to minorities and thus avert the demographic apocalypse that awaited a party that was nearly 90 percent white. In addition to immigration reform, one of his key strategies was to have full White House and bipartisan support for the 2006 reauthorization of the Voting Rights Act.[160]

Aided by a phalanx of civil rights organizations, Congress amassed and reviewed reams of research and data on discrimination in voting, and with a 390–33 vote in the House of Representatives and 98–0 vote in the Senate, reauthorized the Voting Rights Act for another twenty-five years.[161] Many of the VRA's original or subsequent features still remained, including "target[ing] the same states and counties for special coverage, while preserving both Section 5 preclearance requirement and the language assistance provisions," which had arisen during the 1982 reauthorization hearings to acknowledge the documented attempts to disfranchise Latinos.[162]

Barely a week after the bill passed, however, a small, recently formed municipality in Texas sued, alleging that because it did not have some sordid history of racial discrimination, it should not have to abide by the preclearance statute just because it was located in the Lone Star State. In short, city officials argued, Texas had a history of discrimination. Not the Northwest Austin Municipal Utility District Number One (NAMUDNO). The lawsuit argued more than that though. NAMUDNO depicted the Voting Rights Act as a dinosaur that should be as extinct by now as the forces that had once created it. The suit charged that "racial discrimination was no longer the problem it had been in 1965 and that Section 5 imposed unfair and unnecessary burdens on the jurisdictions that it covered."[163]

The court wasn't quite ready to go that far. At least not yet. While allowing the Voting Rights Act to stay in place for now, key members of the court, especially Chief Justice John Roberts, signaled discontent with what they saw as a stagnant VRA, which failed to take into account that Jim Crow was dead and America had moved on. This was not 1899, after all, or even 1969.

Long an opponent of the Voting Rights Act, Roberts had clerked under Justice William Rehnquist, whose initial foray into voting rights prior to his ascent to the Supreme Court included a project to purge as many minorities as possible from voting rolls in Phoenix.[164] Rehnquist's appointment to the bench only strengthened that resolve. In one case, the U.S. Supreme Court had overturned a multiyear scheme in Rome, Georgia, that, without gaining preclearance approval, repeatedly annexed white areas to the city to reduce the electoral potential of black voters. Rehnquist was unfazed by the city's (illegal) actions and instead depicted the VRA as simply African Americans' way to get revenge on the heirs of slaveholders. "The enforcement provisions of the Civil War Amendments [Fourteenth and Fifteenth]," he wrote in his dissent, "were not premised on the notion that Congress could empower a later generation of blacks to 'get even' for wrongs inflicted on their forebears."[165]

This was the man who served as an ideological light for John Roberts. "Rehnquist reinforced John's preexisting philosophies," observed a colleague clerking for another justice. "John was not a believer in the courts giving rights to minorities and the down-trodden. That was the basic Rehnquist philosophy." The framing of the Rehnquist-Roberts philosophy is key. Note that the word used is "giving" instead of simply recognizing that minorities have rights. Thus Roberts's subsequent stint in Reagan's Civil Rights Division of the Department of Justice honed his antipathy to the VRA. "John seemed like he always had it in for the Voting Rights Act," remembered J. Gerald Hebert, one of the chief litigators for the DOJ on voting. "I remember him being a zealot when it came to having fundamental suspicions about the Voting Rights Act's utility."[166]

Adding to Roberts's disdain was the way Congress, during its 1982 reauthorization of the Voting Rights Act, wiped away an earlier court ruling that required the Department of Justice to prove that there was a deliberate intent to discriminate in order for there to be a VRA violation. That decision said that prima facie evidence of discrimi-nation was not enough, even when staring right at a city like Mobile, Alabama, which was 35 percent black and had never—even after the VRA—elected any African American as a city commissioner. Instead, the court ruled that the DOJ would have to prove that offi-cials in Mobile deliberately crafted the voting requirements to dilute the electoral strength of its black population. Intent, of course, was nearly an impossible threshold of proof, requiring racially explicit memos or taped conversations, especially in an era that was so consciously colorblind but race-aware.[167]

The 1982 reauthorization of the VRA removed Roberts's beloved "intent to discriminate" standard, which led him to predict, insist even, that the Voting Rights Act would require election results ruled by quotas and affirmative action.[168] But as Berman noted, "In the seven southern states originally covered by the VRA . . . blacks made up 25 percent of the population but held only 5 percent of elected seats." Roberts's fears were just that, fears. "In a lot of cases . . . there were no blacks elected," said civil rights lawyer Armand Derfner. "We were trying to get from none to some."[169] Roberts didn't see the virtual shutout in many municipalities and counties; instead he focused on districts such as Atlanta and Houston, which had elected African Americans and Latinos, and, therefore, to him it was unfair that Georgia and Texas remained under the preclearance provisions.[170]

Thus, when *NAMUDNO v. Holder* was decided in 2009, years of doubt about the Voting Rights Act, years of questioning whether racism existed anymore, came to a boil. "Since 1982," Roberts wrote in his decision, "only 17 jurisdictions—out of the more than 12,000 covered political subdivisions—have successfully bailed out of the Act." That only seventeen had been able to prove they no longer discriminated against their minority populations' voting rights and thus no longer needed federal oversight seemed absurd to Roberts. He, of course, did not reckon with the fact that places in Georgia and Alabama such as Pickens County, Perry County, Rome, and others had repeatedly tried to disfranchise American citizens despite the Fifteenth Amendment, and that is the reason only seventeen jurisdictions had been released from scrutiny in more than four decades. Instead, came the court's warning shot: seventeen was not enough. "It is unlikely that Congress intended the provision to have such limited effect."[171]

Thus, when the commissioners in Shelby County, Alabama, challenged the Voting Rights Act by outright defying it, the U.S. Supreme Court was already primed and just waiting for a test case. Calera City, Alabama, had a city council that included one African American councilman. His district was 65 percent black, in a city that was over 30 percent African American. Then the commissioners in Shelby County began annexing land surrounding Calera City, and with each annexation they began to redraw the electoral districts, so much so that the black councilman's district population shrank from 65 percent African American to 29 percent. Running now in a predominately white district, where more than three-fourths of the electorate voted against Barack Obama, the lone black councilman lost the next election.[172]

This was not the first time that the Supreme Court had dealt with the redrawing of a city's boundaries designed to dilute the voting strength of a town's black population. In the late 1950s, African Americans in Tuskegee, Alabama, had begun, against all odds, to amass some semblance of voting strength. The state legislature quickly countered by annexing plot after plot of land surrounding Tuskegee until the town's perfectly symmetrical square boundaries had been horribly disfigured into a twenty-eight-sided blob. But this is exactly what it took to remove all but four or five of the four hundred voting-age eligible African Americans from the city and ensure that no white voter was excluded. Alabama argued that it had the authority to change its city boundaries whenever and however it chose and it didn't need a reason. Justice William O. Douglas explained how mistaken Alabama truly was. He systematically laid out how the state, despite multiple queries, could come up with no viable reason for its actions. There was only one way to explain why four hundred black voters became a mere four or five, to explain why a perfectly logical city boundary devolved into one with twenty-eight sides, to explain why, even with all those changes, Tuskegee did not lose one white voter. Alabama had set out to strip African Americans of their right to vote. And that, Douglas insisted, violated the Fifteenth Amendment.[173]

Fifty-three years later, Chief Justice John Roberts looked directly at a similar situation where county commissioners in Alabama had annexed plot after plot, redrew boundaries, diluted the voting strength of black voters, and, this time, did so in violation of the Voting Rights Act. Unlike before, however, the Supreme Court, in a 5–4, decision, ignored all the evidence and drew instead upon the arguments hurled against the VRA since 1966. Refrains about states' rights, black electoral success, regional discrimination, the end of racism, and the seeming calcification of the VRA became the key elements in the decision penned by Chief Justice Roberts in *Shelby County v. Holder.*

The court decided that the VRA was unfair because it singled out and punished the South (which obviously meant whites in the South), unfair because the 2006 reauthorization included the same states and counties as in the original bill, unfair because blacks had won multiple elections and were voting in record numbers, and thus unfair because the racism of the past, which had led to the creation of the VRA, obviously no longer determined access to the polls. The *Shelby County v. Holder* decision thus gutted Section 4 of the Voting Rights Act, which determined which locales came under federal oversight. With that, GOP-led states, as if this were Alabama in the early 1980s, asserted that it was actually voter fraud, not voter suppression, that required the full machinery of government to eradicate.[174]

Therefore, 2016 was the first federal election in fifty years held without the protection of the Voting Rights Act. As a result, the rash of voter ID laws, purged voting rolls, redrawn district boundaries, and closed and moved polling places were the quiet and barely detected fire that burned through the 2016 presidential election, evaporating millions of votes and searing those who hadn't even been under the original VRA.[175] In Wisconsin, for example, black voting rates plummeted from a high of 78 percent in 2012 to less than 50 percent in 2016. In Milwaukee County, which is overwhelmingly African American, fifty thousand fewer votes were cast in a state that Donald Trump won by only twenty-seven thousand ballots.[176] Meanwhile, Republican officials in North Carolina congratulated themselves that "African American Early Voting is down 8.5% from this time [four years earlier] in 2012."[177]

Not only had the tide of expanding the franchise and the robustness of American democracy apparently turned, but its ebb continued. During the 2017 special congressional election in an Atlanta suburb, for example, the *Christian Science Monitor* asked, "What's behind fewer African-American voters at the polls?" Polling expert Nate Silver was puzzled; the *14 percent* drop-off in the number of blacks voting had been even greater than expected.[178]

It's puzzling only if you don't understand how the various methods of voter suppression actually work.

Two

Voter ID

He was a proud Korean War veteran. He was also black and in Texas. And by 2013, that put his voting rights in the state's crosshairs even though he was "Army strong." When he proudly presented his Veterans Administration card to the registrar, it was repelled by the force of the state's new voting requirement for government-issued *photo* ID. The eighty-six-year-old, whom even the North Koreans couldn't break, conceded defeat: "I wasn't a citizen no more. I wasn't."[1] Others also realized that they, too, had just crossed into the twilight zone of American-lite: a citizen without full citizenship rights. A disabled man exclaimed, "I have not been able to vote in any election since Texas passed its voter ID law in 2013. My constitutional rights have been stripped from me."[2] Another man, a retiree, had been repeatedly blocked from the ballot box because his mother changed his name when he was a teenager and now that fifty-year-old paperwork was lost in a "bureaucratic nightmare." After spending hundreds of dollars trying to find the wayward document and then struggling to get certified by the name he's used for more than half a century, he knew, beyond all doubt, that he was targeted. "The intent of this law is to suppress the vote. I feel like I'm not wanted in this state."[3]

But it wasn't just Texas that had thrown up new barriers. Almost thirteen hundred miles away, a Navy veteran who had returned home in 2015 after serving in Iraq and Afghanistan went to the polls and received the same rude awakening. His valid Illinois driver's license was irrelevant in his new home state, Wisconsin. The veteran's fifty-hour work week was hard enough, especially because it precluded getting to the local Department of Motor Vehicles and securing a new license. Governor Scott Walker made sure of that. The Republican had curtailed the operating hours or removed many of the DMVs in the Democratic stronghold of Milwaukee, where 70 percent of the state's black population lived, and in the Navy veteran's university town of Madison. "Coming home" from a war zone, he said, "and being denied the right to vote because I didn't have a specific driver's license" was "very frustrating."[4]

Americans in Iowa, Indiana, and Pennsylvania could relate.[5] In the twenty-first century, the geography of voter suppression had clearly changed. It was no longer only a phenomenon of the Jim Crow South. Voter suppression had now gone nationwide as it became a Republican-fueled chimera that by 2017 had gripped thirty-three states and cast a pall over more than half the American voting-age population.[6]

The latest iteration of this disfranchising beast had been born in Florida. Its genesis was the 2000 presidential election. Hanging chads, broken machines, police hovering around the polls, and purged voter rolls had "put great stress on the public's faith in electoral integrity."[7] African Americans certainly didn't trust the state's election officials. Blacks "found themselves in the position of having to complain to the people they were complaining about—filling out a police report about alleged police intimidation or filing a formal complaint about poll workers with canvassing boards." Seeing the futility, most African Americans bypassed Florida's severely compromised machinery and went directly to a trusted ally, the NAACP, with their concerns and affidavits.[8] With the electoral chaos in Florida and the inability to get an accurate tally, it soon began to dawn on many that democracy in the United States was not the well-oiled machine it purported to be. Instead, it became all too apparent that "racial discrimination may have persisted despite the VRA" and that even "the nation's ability to correctly count votes was in question."[9]

As law professor Richard Hasen noted, "Belief in the integrity of elections is essential to any democracy," but in Florida in 2000, that belief was shaken to its core.[10]

Congress immediately moved to reestablish and regain trust in the system. It was not going to be easy. The debacle in Florida "shook Americans from all walks of life and of all political persuasions. Many were left wondering about the viability of America's democratic system."[11] It was "a wake-up call."[12] To regain the nation's trust, a bipartisan commission, led by former presidents Jimmy Carter and Gerald Ford, set out to identify the deficiencies in the election process and make solid recommendations to address the weaknesses. But the carefully laid-out process and, more important, the overall goal had already been hijacked in Missouri.

Just as in Florida, Election Day 2000 in St. Louis was a "chaotic mess."[13] The St. Louis City Board of Elections had not only illegally purged nearly fifty thousand names from the voter rolls in key Democratic precincts but had also failed, as the law required, to notify the people the board had just disfranchised. Not surprisingly, then, when those voters showed up to cast their ballots, they were "told they were no longer registered." Besieged precinct workers couldn't get through on the jammed phone lines to check or double-check much of anything and opted at that point to send frustrated would-be voters downtown to the Board of Elections office to resolve the issue. This was a train to nowhere. Poor record-keeping and ill-prepared and ill-informed officials meant that hours and hours dissolved away as the clock on Election Day wound down.[14] "By early evening, the lobby [at the Board] was shoulder to shoulder with people who wanted to vote."[15] But by then it was near closing time at the polls.

Democrats filed for an injunction to keep the doors open at the precincts for a few more hours to accommodate voters who had been caught in the Board of Election's illegal purge and runaround. The local judge agreed and ordered the polls to stay open for three additional hours. Moments later, however, the Republicans pleaded with a higher court to close the polls at the agreed-upon time. Senator Christopher "Kit" Bond (R-MO) said that the initial ruling "to keep the polls open until 10 P.M. 'represents the biggest fraud on the voters in this state and nation that we have ever seen.'"[16] Other Republicans on the team, including Mark "Thor" Hearne representing the Bush-Cheney campaign, made the case that this was just a Democratic maneuver that would result "in voter fraud and the casting of hundreds of illegal votes." The higher court concurred, and within only forty-five minutes of the initial decision, the doors slammed shut on hundreds of people waiting in line to cast their ballots.[17] But it would get worse.

Missouri Republicans twisted this clear case of election board wrongdoing into a torrent of accusations against the overwhelmingly black residents in St. Louis and the Democrats.[18] Missouri secretary of state Matt Blunt called the effort to keep the polls open a "conspiracy to create bedlam so that election fraud could be perpetrated." Senator Bond was even more specific. He alleged that the attempt to keep the polls open was a "brazen, shocking, astonishing, and stunning" effort to commit "voter fraud . . . with dead people registering and voting from the grave, fake names and phony addresses proliferating across the nation's voter rolls, dogs registering, and people signing up to vote from vacant lots." This was, he continued, "a major criminal enterprise designed to defraud voters."[19] It was not. It was, instead, an illegal purge of 49,589 eligible voters by the Board of Elections. It was also sloppy recordkeeping and bureaucratic malfeasance.[20] But, for the GOP, that was not the point. Rather, the Republicans used this bungled election to walk away with several key lessons.[21]

The first was that demographics were not destiny.[22] The voting-age population was becoming increasingly African American, Latino, and Asian. In 1992, for example, nonwhite voters made up 13 percent of the electorate; by 2012 they made up 28 percent.[23] Because of

GOP policies, that growing share of the electorate tilted heavily toward the Democrats. A late 1980s poll by the Joint Center for Political and Economic Studies, for example, "found that only 17 percent of blacks and about half of black Republicans believed that the GOP cared about African Americans' problems."[24] In the 2000 presidential election, therefore, 90 percent of black, 62 percent of Hispanic, and 55 percent of Asian voters cast their ballots for Al Gore.[25] The big takeaway for the GOP from Florida and St. Louis therefore was the imperative of blocking members of those groups from the polls by virtually any means necessary. Paul Weyrich, a conservative activist and founder of the American Legislative Exchange Council (ALEC), which eventually crafted voter suppression legislation that spread like a cancer throughout the United States, was brutally clear: "I don't want everybody to vote." The Republican Party's "leverage in the elections quite candidly goes up as the voting populace goes down."[26] That is to say, the GOP learned that voter suppression applied ruthlessly and relentlessly could deliver victory.

The second lesson was the importance of controlling the electoral machinery that decided the rules for voting, the conditions upon which those votes would be cast, and whose vote counted and whose did not. Florida secretary of state Katherine Harris proved this point beyond all doubt. A delegate at the Republican National Convention and one of George W. Bush's "campaign co-chairs for Florida right up until Election Day," she used her authority and power to undermine the recount.[27] Harris was not alone. She had the full support of the presidential candidate's brother, Florida governor Jeb Bush, who surreptitiously sent in his "coolly efficient" fixer, Mac Stipanovich, to keep the secretary of state focused on the job at hand. Knowing that his presence would be "provocative," Stipanovich came in and out of back doors to avoid the media while he advised Harris on how to subvert the process. The key was to override the state's law that identified "intent of the voter" as the "gold standard" for a manual recount in Florida. For example, was the hanging chad or indentation clear on the ballot but unreadable by the machine; had the voter written in the preferred candidate's name instead of marking the oval, etc.? When some of the counties began their manual tabulation of a representative sample of the ballots, they used the "gold standard" to guide their process. Suddenly, Gore was gaining ground fast, which meant this could trigger a full-blown recount. Harris and Stipanovich immediately sent in an undercover ally, attorney Kerey Carpenter, to advise the Palm Beach County Canvassing Board. Carpenter's supposedly unbiased legal advice tilted the scales dramatically. She raised the standard for "intent" so maddeningly high that "Gore's vote gain dropped to half a dozen." Then she persuaded the chairman of the election board to get Harris's opinion on whether a full recount was even necessary. Of course, the preordained answer was no. The voting machines had to be completely broken, not simply malfunctioning, the secretary of state ruled. Then Harris tried to short-circuit the process further by moving up the deadline date for when the manual count had to be completed, which was actually well before two of the major counties, including Miami-Dade, "had even decided whether to recount, and before Broward had finished." Harris simply "sowed confusion." In one egregious case, she altered the rules to determine which absentee ballots were valid and which were not, and the most salient feature in that advice was the political tilt of the county: Republican-leaning counties received a much more expansive set of parameters and were advised that they could count overseas ballots that were completed—and not necessarily postmarked—on Election Day. Democratic counties, however, had been handed the opposite advice, which diminished greatly the number of eligible ballots. As a result, George W. Bush, although losing the nationwide popular vote, carried Florida by 537 votes, won the Electoral College, and, with a very key assist by the U.S. Supreme Court, became the forty-third president of the United States.[28] This was a powerful demonstration, like none other, how those that controlled the key levers of the electoral and political machinery could give purges, bureaucratic runarounds, and other types of chicanery the aura of legality.

The final, and perhaps most important, lesson, was to lie. Lie often, loudly, boldly, unashamedly, and consistently. Lie until it drowned out the truth. Lie until no amount of evidence could prove otherwise. Lie until there was no other reigning narrative. Just lie. Senator Bond learned the lesson well. He claimed that scores of Democrats were using the names of dead people and dogs to vote repeatedly. He insisted that others were basically stuffing the ballot box by creating fictitious addresses where there were only vacant lots.[29] Just as the best lies hold a kernel of truth, Bond chose well. Some prankster had, indeed, registered a thirteen-year-old springer spaniel, Ritzy Mekler, to vote.[30] Yet there is no record anywhere of Fido, Rover, Lassie, or even the infamous Ritzy casting a ballot. Similarly, the specter of a swarm of fraudulent voters using the addresses of vacant lots to tilt the election to the Democrats, while salacious and tantalizing, collapsed under scrutiny. When the *St. Louis Post-Dispatch* investigated, it found that 82 percent of the suspicious addresses were "wrongly classified by the city assessor's office as vacant" because they "in fact contained legitimate residences."[31] This bureaucratic snafu even "snared" St. Louis's top budget official, Frank Jackson, whose ten-year-old condominium had never, even after a decade, made it off the city's vacant lot register. That lapse in administrative efficiency landed him and his neighbors on Secretary of State Matt Blunt's "suspect voter" list.[32] Most of the remaining suspicious voters had been flagged because a large number of adults had registered the same address as their respective home. When reporters visited those sites, however, it turned out that, indeed, while these might not be group homes, apartments, or nursing homes, "more than eight people properly lived at the address noted." The vast majority of the other "suspect voters" were mislabeled as fraudulent because of typographical errors or because they had actually moved within the city and did not have to reregister.[33] And, just as with Ritzy the dog, Bond did eventually find a dead person on the voter registration rolls, a former city alderman, but, again, there was no evidence that the deceased or anyone with his name voted in the 2000 election. In fact, by the time every one of Bond's three hundred plus claims was investigated, it was clear that out of 2.3 million voters in Missouri, the four people who committed some type of malfeasance at the polls hardly constituted the "brazen, shocking, astonishing, and stunning voter fraud" that he claimed. And it was also obvious that "none of these problems could have been resolved by requiring photo ID at the polls."[34] Yet, from the tattered cloths of bureaucratic snafus, administrative incompetency, and typographical errors, the lie of rampant voter fraud hung there, dangling, as the senator kept fashioning democracy's noose.

In 2001, Bond became the senator tasked with guiding a bill through Congress to re-instill the American public's confidence in the electoral system. The nation's concern about the racism and inadequacies that were on full display on November 7, 2000, was real. Bond, however, was determined to also prioritize the fiction of rampant voter fraud. The result was the 2002 Help America Vote Act (HAVA). It was filled, because of the good work of the Carter-Ford Commission, with all kinds of legitimate treats like an Election Assistance Commission to help states modernize and standardize voting systems. The law also provided a clear mandate to update voting machines and a mechanism to register complaints. HAVA, however, also included a poison pill.[35] Kit Bond insisted on it. As a quid pro quo for allowing the replacement of the infamous hanging chad machines, he demanded language requiring that people have identification in order to vote.[36] Initially, it seemed harmless enough. Even the human rights president, Jimmy Carter, agreed, noting that "in the old days and in small towns where everyone knows each other, voters did not need to identify themselves. But in the United States, where 40 million people move each year, and in urban areas where some people do not even know the people living in their own apartment building let alone their precinct, some form of identification is needed."[37] The requirement for ID was supposed to be limited, however, to voters who had originally registered by mail. It was also supposed to allow a range of documents by which a citizen could verify his or her identity, including employee IDs, student IDs, and paychecks, as well as driver's licenses. What it actually did, though, was give federal credence, in law, to the lie of rampant voter fraud. Thus, a dangerous false equivalency emerged. There was the hard-core reality of voter suppression in Florida and St. Louis (purged rolls, faulty machines, and more) that had disfranchised tens of thousands of American citizens. And then there was Kit Bond's fantasy of stuffed ballot boxes. With HAVA, the lie had become the truth.

What made the law even more problematic was that the Carter-Ford Commission had estimated that "as many as 19 million potential voters nationwide did not possess either a driver's license or a state issued photo ID" and those "most likely to be adversely affected . . . were disproportionately young, elderly, poor, and African American."[38] That was key. All that had to happen was for the GOP to reinforce the lie of voter fraud, create the public perception of democracy imperiled, increase the groundswell to "protect the integrity of the ballot box," require exactly the type of identification that blacks, the poor, the young, and the elderly did not have, and, equally important, mask these acts of aggressive voter suppression behind the nobility of being "civic-minded."[39]

From 2005 to 2013, the Republicans did just that. In congressional hearings on strengthening election integrity, Thor Hearne, who had made such an effective advocate in the courts for shutting down the polls in Missouri and who now represented the American Center for Voting Rights (ACVR), became a frequent expert witness on rampant voter fraud. The ACVR, however, was about as real as the claim itself, a modern-day Potemkin village. It had a bright, shiny webpage featuring a photo of an array of racially diverse Americans, links to "policy papers" and "data," and a very impressive bio of its director, Thor Hearne. ACVR had the " 'think tank' academic cachet" that made it seem substantial enough to be the major source of information to Congress about massive voting irregularities throughout the United States. It all seemed so real. Except it was "the only prominent nongovernmental organization claiming that voter fraud is a major problem, a problem warranting strict rules such as voter-ID laws."[40] What it was, in the end, was pure Hollywood stagecraft:

> ACVR was founded just days before its representatives testified before a congressional committee hearing on election-administration issues chaired by then-Rep. (and now federal inmate) Bob Ney. The group was headed by Hearne, national election counsel to Bush-Cheney '04, and staffed with other Republican operatives, including Jim Dyke, a former RNC communications director. Consisting of little more than a post-office box and some staffers who wrote reports and gave helpful quotes about the pervasive problems of voter fraud to the press, the group identified Democratic cities as hot spots for voter fraud, then pushed the line that "election integrity" required making it harder for people to vote.[41]

Hearne gave it his all. In hearing after hearing, press conference after press conference, op-ed after op-ed, he was there filling the ether with tales of people impersonating someone else to destroy the integrity of America's elections. In 2004, Fox News reported on a study completed by ACVR that actually cited as its marching orders the 1941 *Classic* decision that opened the door for ending the white primary. In this upside-down world, though, the language used to end disfranchisement now became the tool to reemploy it with ruthless efficiency. ACVR identified five "hot spots" of systemic voter fraud, each with a black or at least nonwhite population that made up 32 to 95 percent of the city's residents. As if it were an FBI Most Wanted list, ACVR trotted out a rogues' gallery of voter fraud:

1. Philadelphia, PA
2. Milwaukee, WI
3. Seattle, WA
4. St. Louis/East St. Louis, MO/IL
5. Cleveland, OH

The report served up old canards and false anecdotes dressed as fact, providing new, tantalizing, and wholly erroneous reports of the NAACP paying for votes with crack cocaine, and, therefore, providing excellent, digestible fodder for Fox News and other broadcasts.[42] The disinformation program was malevolently brilliant and effective. In 2005, "Hearne was pushing allegations about voter fraud in St. Louis from 2000 that had been thoroughly debunked in 2002. It didn't matter. Republican voters came to believe there was a vote fraud epidemic."[43]

But almost as soon as that narrative was out there, gaining traction, providing sound bites for politicians and creating the basis to shape voter ID legislation, ACVR and its P.O. box and website, with its Getty stock photos of diverse America, disappeared. As did any mention on Hearne's résumé of his role in this scam.[44]

President George W. Bush had also turned the supposed need to protect the integrity of the ballot box from rampant voter fraud into "public policy." In 2002, his attorney general, John Ashcroft, a former senator from Missouri, made this a top priority for the Department of Justice and federal prosecutors.[45] They scoured major cities with large minority populations looking for cases to substantiate Kit Bond's, Matt Blunt's, and Thor Hearne's tales of electoral chicanery. They found a few felons who didn't know they couldn't vote yet. They uncovered a handful of permanent residents who misunderstood the laws about voting. That was it.[46] Nevertheless, inordinate pressure from Republican U.S. senators and Department of Justice officials continued. Some federal prosecutors dug in and refused to bring charges and give credence to the GOP's voter fraud claims right before the 2006 midterm election because there was little to no evidence of wrongdoing. David Iglesias, the U.S. attorney in New Mexico, for example, saw no reason to file charges against a thirteen-year-old because the "boy had been registered [to vote] without his or his parents' knowledge."[47] For that and similar acts of integrity, Iglesias and seven other federal prosecutors were fired.[48] As far as turning up proof of a wide-ranging conspiracy to subvert elections, however, Richard G. Frohling, the assistant U.S. attorney in Milwaukee, conceded, "There was nothing that we uncovered that suggested some sort of concerted effort to tilt the election."[49] But all this activity, all this searching, gave the illusion of widespread voter fraud that needed to be ferreted out and stopped. And that was the point.

Indiana stepped into the breach. Secretary of State Todd Rokita, a Republican, recalled, "Back in 2001 and 2002, election integrity was a huge issue . . . The problem was that people were losing confidence in the system . . . there was a fear of votes being stolen. Even," he added, "if the fear didn't pan out to be true, . . . the fear was still there."[50] In other words, based on a perception that had been carefully crafted, cultivated, and stoked by the GOP, state governments believed they had a mandate, a calling even, to wrestle this virtually nonexistent voter impersonation fraud to the ground. Rokita and Indiana's Republican legislators, therefore, set out to add a powerful barrier to the polls while, he said, "making sure we were balanced and honest in our approach to prove it was not politically motivated," although every Democrat voted against the bill, Senate Enrolled Act (SEA) 483, and every Republican supported it.[51] The 2006 law required government-issued photo ID to vote; defined what types of identification were acceptable; offered to provide, at state expense, an identification card to those who could not afford it; and secured an off-ramp of a provisional ballot for those who did not have the ID at the time of the election but, in order to have their vote count, could supply the identification or an affidavit to the appropriate authorities within a limited number of days.[52]

The ACLU and NAACP, as well as the state's Democratic Party, immediately challenged SEA 483. Given that there was "no evidence . . . that Indiana's voter ID law is justified by any actual voting fraud problem," the real motivation, they discerned, was partisan and geared to disfranchise as many minority voters as possible.[53] The Seventh Circuit, however, had heard the constant drumbeat since the 2000 election and believed that stopping and preventing voter fraud was worth the cost and "declined to judge the law by the strict standard set for poll taxes in *Harper v. Virginia Bd. of Elections*, finding the burden on voters offset by the benefit of reducing the risk of fraud."[54]

The organizations, therefore, appealed the decision to the U.S. Supreme Court. The ACLU and NAACP went right after the core of the issue—there was no voter fraud. Therefore, there was no state interest at stake—certainly nothing that could warrant this assault on the Fifteenth Amendment. It "bear[s] repeating," they asserted, that Indiana had "not identified even a single instance of voter impersonation fraud occurring at the polls in the history of Indiana" and no one in the state has "ever been charged" with that crime. Ever. Moreover, when the bill was being drafted, "no evidence of in-person impersonation fraud was presented to the legislature," making SEA 483, at best, a solution in search of a problem. And, to punctuate that point, the ACLU and NAACP attorneys emphasized that even in this hearing before the U.S. Supreme Court, "no such evidence was presented in this litigation." There were, of course, the same old tried and true anecdotes about the dead voting in St. Louis, etc., but all those stories had been debunked. So, they asked, what "state interest" could possibly justify the burdens placed on citizens' right to vote?[55]

Indiana, of course, had pointed to free identification cards and provisional ballots as the salves to ensure that there were "protections [against disenfranchisement]."[56] The state also assured the court that only 1 percent of Indiana's voting-age eligible population lacked the necessary identification. And, most important, it claimed that the law had not dampened voter turnout at all. In fact, the state pointed to a study showing that in 2006 the voter turnout actually increased.[57]

The NAACP and ACLU countered that the state's numbers, study, and analysis were inaccurate and full-blown misrepresentations. For example, the fact that supposedly 1 percent did not have an ID was "hardly negligible" because that was 43,000 citizens. But, it was much worse than that, they argued. A recent survey of Indiana voters "found that approximately 16% of all voting eligible residents did not have either a current license or state identification card and 13% of current registered voters did not have licenses or identification cards." In fact, a subsequent study found that in Indiana, "white citizens were 11.5 percentage points more likely than black citizens to have the accepted credentials to vote." The situation was exacerbated by the state's "Byzantine requirements imposed on persons attempting to obtain identification from the BMV [Bureau of Motor Vehicles] . . . In a given week 60% of applicants for licenses or state identification cards are turned away because they fail to have the appropriate documents mandated by the BMV." In other words, the state's offer of "free ID" was a brilliant smokescreen that masked that the actual documents required to obtain an Indiana driver's license or state identification were not so easy to get and often came with costs borne solely by the would-be voter. The NAACP and ACLU noted, for example, that a birth certificate was necessary to get a driver's license, but in an obvious "Catch-22 of classic proportions" in Marion County, where more than two hundred thousand of the state's black population lived, the health department required a driver's license as proof of identification to get a copy of a birth certificate. The tangle of rules, regulations, and the state voter ID law had consequences—real-life consequences. The attorneys told the story of Therese Clemente, who "made multiple fruitless trips to her local BMV in an effort to present the proper combination of documents in order to be able to vote." And in Muncie, Indiana, a tight mayoral race, with only nine votes separating the candidates, hung in the balance of fourteen provisional ballots and "five contested absentee ballots." But because, under the rules for provisional ballots, they had only ten days to get the necessary documentation to prove their identity, "their votes went uncounted in the final total" which the victor won by eleven votes.[58] Elections, representatives, and the policies that emanate from them were now, once again, being determined by disfranchisement.

The Supreme Court didn't see it that way. The majority of justices had imbibed the tonic of voter fraud and saw before them the hallucination of ne'er-do-wells in the cities stealing elections and undermining democracy. The court recognized, Justice John Paul Stevens wrote, that the "only kind of voter fraud that SEA 483 addresses is in-person voter impersonation at polling places." And, he was forced to admit, that the "record contains no evidence of any such fraud actually occurring in Indiana at any time in its history." That easily should have been the end of it. But it wasn't. Instead, he continued, "flagrant examples of such fraud in other parts of the country . . . have been documented throughout this Nation's history by respected historians and journalists." He then pulled out the story of New York City's William "Boss" Tweed from an 1868 election. That was followed by a swan dive into the fictional swamp of St. Louis's canine and dead voters.[59]

Not only did the court swallow whole the myth of rampant voter fraud, but equally important, the justices could not fathom that something as simple as needing an ID constituted any type of overwhelming burden—especially because Indiana offered to provide the driver's license or state ID for free. The court's reasoning was simple: Just because SEA 483 would require that "the Democratic Party and the other organizational plaintiffs . . . [would have to] work harder to get every last one of their supporters to the polls" did not make the voter ID law unconstitutional. Worse yet, Stevens chided, neither the NAACP, the ACLU, nor the Democratic Party could provide hard numbers about the "magnitude of the burden . . . or the portion of the burden imposed" on those who ostensibly would be disfranchised by SEA 483. "Much of the argument about numbers of such voters," Stevens scoffed, "comes from extrarecord, postjudgement studies, the accuracy of which has not been tested in the trial court." The court, therefore, ruled that the state's needs were compelling and there was no concomitant evidence that SEA 483 placed any substantive burden on voters to block their access to the polls. Indiana's voter ID law was, under this reasoning, constitutional.[60]

This was judicial legerdemain and sophistry at its worst. On one hand, Indiana did not need to provide any proof whatsoever that voter fraud—much less, rampant voter fraud—existed. Or, for that matter, that anyone in the history of the state had ever been charged or convicted of the crime. Instead, each of the examples of voter fraud the justices held up would not and could not have been stopped by voter ID requirements, especially absentee ballots, which—because they're overwhelmingly used by whites—Indiana had exempted from the law. Yet, on the basis of nothing—fables and urban legends—the majority of the justices took the state's claims of democracy in peril seriously. On the other hand, the plaintiffs' studies and statistics were not enough. The stories not enough. The data not enough. As hard as the NAACP and ACLU attorneys tried, there seemed to be no amount of evidence and no documentation that the justices could accept as persuasive. The plaintiff's lawyers laid out information about the limited number of BMVs, the scarcity of public transportation to get to those scattered facilities, and the difficulty and costs of obtaining a birth certificate. They worked to explain how this innocuous sounding law was a targeted hit, especially for those who did not have the financial resources to amass the documentation to get the necessary ID. The NAACP and ACLU, therefore, noted the strong correlation between race and poverty in Indiana and that SEA 483 would strip those populations of their basic right to vote.[61] As far as the court was concerned, however, what the NAACP and the ACLU identified as a "constitutional danger sign" was no more than smoke and mirrors while the mythical beast of voter fraud was real.[62]

In 2005, Georgia, even though it was under the Voting Rights Act's preclearance mandate, also crafted a voter ID law. The Peach State's version eliminated twelve types of acceptable identification to vote, including utility bills, bank statements, and private employer IDs, and put in their place a narrowed list of six types of government-issued photo IDs. Thus, only a few short years after the passage of HAVA, a preclearance state took a virtual machete to the federal law's much more expansive list of IDs and created a stump of severely curtailed acceptable forms of identification to vote. Because that stump had a clear racial bias, black and Hispanic lawmakers' concerns were ignored as white Republicans steamrolled this legislation, H.B. 244, through the statehouse. African Americans had, to no avail, raised the need for voter education on the new requirements, voiced concern about the maldistribution of the driver's license bureaus throughout the state, and explained the difficulty for those not born in hospitals to get a birth certificate that would allow them to get a license. Indeed, despite Georgia's Section 5 status, the state was beyond cavalier in considering the racial implications of the change in voter ID requirements. The chief policy adviser to the Georgia House of Representatives admitted that the legislature "did not conduct any statistical analysis of the effect of the photo ID requirement on minority voters." In fact, when asked about the need for this law, Representative Sue Burmeister from Augusta explained that it was to prevent fraud and if that meant "there are fewer black voters because of the voter ID law it will be because there is less opportunity for fraud." She then clarified: "When black voters in her black precincts are not paid to vote, they do not go to the polls."[63]

Even a statement that blatant, however, couldn't damage H.B. 244's momentum. The state's GOP had not only been fed voter-fraud talking points by a well-resourced, well-coordinated group of right-wing activists, such as John Fund, whose book *Stealing Elections* was one of the bibles for demanding photo IDs to vote; but Georgia also had allies ensconced in the U.S. Department of Justice.[64] The Bush administration was still going full throttle on its "voter fraud" witch hunt, and the disregard the department's political appointees had for career civil servants decidedly tilted the balance of power.

The staff attorneys in the DOJ's Civil Rights Division had actually rejected H.B. 244 because of its disparate impact on black voters. Their investigation found that only one-third of the state's counties actually had a Department of Drivers Services (DDS) and that there was not a single driver's license bureau in the entire city of Atlanta. Moreover, of the fifty-six DDS locations throughout the state, only five were "accessible via public transportation." In short, H.B. 244 required a personal vehicle and a license to be able to get to the DDS. As the attorneys dug deeper into the data, they uncovered that 17.7 percent of black households did not have access to a vehicle, while only 4.4 percent of white households had no motorized form of personal transportation. And even more troubling, in the two counties that Atlanta spread across, almost three-fourths of those without a vehicle in Fulton County were African American, and in DeKalb, 63.5 percent. When the attorneys then overlaid the map of where the DDS offices were located with the information on the lack of personal vehicles, it soon became clear that racial disparity and disparate impact were embedded in H.B. 244. Indeed, "census data show that five times more black households in counties without DDS offices lack access to a motor vehicle compared to white households." Similar analysis on poverty rates, access to birth certificates, and unemployment rates (given that government work IDs were acceptable) resulted in the same pattern of racial inequality that would easily impact the ability to vote. Theodore Shaw, the director of the NAACP Legal Defense and Educational Fund (LDF), told the attorneys that H.B. 244 was actually a new version of "reregistration" à la Mississippi 1955 and "reidentification" Alabama-style "that the Department has objected to in the past." On August 25, 2005, the staff attorneys agreed and recommended that H.B. 244 be rejected "on the ground that the state has failed to meet its burden of proof to demonstrate that it does not have the effect of retrogressing minority voting strength."[65] The very next day, however, political appointee John Tanner, the chief of the Voting Section of the Civil Rights Division, overruled the staff attorneys and allowed Georgia to implement what would become one of the "strictest" voter ID laws in the United States.[66]

The election of Barack Obama to the presidency increased the GOP pressure at the state level for this very effective tool of disfranchisement. Obama had managed to bring fifteen million new voters to the polls in 2008. They were overwhelmingly African American, Hispanic, Asian American, and poor. Moreover, 69 percent of these new participants in democracy voted for him and, as a result, put a black man in the White House.[67] All that hope for change, though, dissipated in the midst of a recession that had begun under George W. Bush and which had already destroyed twenty-two trillion dollars of wealth, fueled and entrenched double-digit unemployment for African Americans, and led to economic stimulus packages that were targeted at those whose greed and recklessness had put the global economy in a tailspin. There was also an obstructionist and extremist Republican-led Congress whose sole mission was to "make Obama a one-term president."[68] As a result, in the 2010 midterm elections the GOP swept several long-term Democrats out of Congress, picking up six seats in the Senate and sixty-three in the House of Representatives, and adding six governors to the roster. Moreover, as the *Washington Post* reported, "before the midterm elections, Democrats controlled 27 state legislatures outright. Republicans were in charge in 14 states, and eight states were split . . . Today, Republicans control 26 state legislatures, Democrats 17." It was, without question, a political bloodbath.[69]

In 2011 and 2012, therefore, the floodgates for voter ID laws opened and "180 bills to restrict who could vote and how" simultaneously appeared in forty-one states. This proposed legislation, which "seemed aimed at low-income voters, particularly minority voters, and at young people and the less mobile elderly" was something that "hadn't been seen . . . since the end of Reconstruction, when every southern state placed severe limits on the franchise."[70] Paul Weyrich's ALEC was behind this well-coordinated effort. In 2009, the group, which was founded in the 1970s and views itself as advancing "free market and limited government principles" by linking state legislators with corporate lobbyists, began to draft model voter ID legislation. With the GOP control of more than half the nation's state governments, these bills arose like dragon's teeth out of the soil of racism and disfranchisement; out of a Republican vision of democracy that views most citizens as unwashed, "uninformed," and, therefore, unworthy.[71] Iowa congressman Steve King lamented the passing of "a time in American history when you had to be a male property owner in order to vote." Florida congressional candidate Ted Yoho echoed that sentiment when he also proffered, "You used to have to be a property owner to vote." Of course, after the Great Recession, with African American homeownership lower than it had been during the 1930s and the lowest of all ethnic and racial groups in the United States, the implications of the GOP longings were obvious. Right-wing pundit Ann Coulter, however, was even more forthright. "I just think it should be a little more difficult to vote. There's nothing," she wrongly insisted, "unconstitutional about literacy tests."[72] The point was to eliminate the voters who were resistant to right-wing policies and, thereby, have a much smoother road to re-create the civil rights order of the early 1950s and the economic environment of unregulated capitalism of the 1920s.[73]

Two key U.S. Supreme Court decisions greased the path. One, *Shelby County v. Holder*, made the Voting Rights Act as ineffective as the 1957 Civil Rights Act. Prior to this ruling, as Justice Ruth Bader Ginsburg's dissent noted, "between 1982 and 2006, DOJ objections blocked over 700 voting changes based on a determination that the changes were discriminatory." The Department of Justice's findings were reinforced during congressional hearings on the 2006 reauthorization of the VRA when it became apparent that those proposed changes that the DOJ had denied were actually the preclearance states' "calculated decisions to keep minority voters from fully participating in the political process."[74] And now that protection was gone.

The other key Supreme Court decision was *Citizens United v. Federal Election Commission* (2010), which ruled that the laws borne out of the Watergate scandal that limited corporate donations to political campaigns actually violated businesses' right to free speech.[75] Like a twin-pincer motion in a two-front war on American democracy and its people, the flood of hundreds of millions of virtually untraceable dollars, so-called dark money, poured into the coffers of the GOP while the counterbalance of a majority of citizens who wanted a nation more vibrant, more inclusive, and less discriminatory came under vigorous assault by the rash of ALEC-drafted voter suppression bills.

Now that the Republicans controlled most of the states' electoral machinery, as well as Congress and the U.S. Supreme Court, they continued to saturate the air with the lie of massive voter fraud until "nearly half of Americans believe voter fraud happens at least somewhat often, and 70 percent think it happens at least occasionally."[76] While many Americans came to accept the lie as truth, there was no evidence that it was the scourge of democracy that Republicans had portrayed. The real threat, in fact, was the damage this lie did to governance and to the sanctity of the right to vote. Todd Allbaugh, an aide to a Republican state senator in Wisconsin, recoiled when he saw how "GOP Senators were giddy" about the way a proposed voter ID bill "literally singled out the prospects of suppressing minority and college voters. Think about that for a minute," he wrote. "Elected officials planning and happy to deny a fellow American's constitutional right to vote in order to increase their own chances to hang onto power."[77] This was no fluke. In a series of emails where Republicans were concerned that their candidate for the Wisconsin Supreme Court just might lose, GOP operatives, as *Esquire* reported, began plotting:

> Steve Baas, a lobbyist for the Metropolitan Milwaukee Association of Commerce and former Republican legislative staffer, floated an idea on the email thread: "Do we need to start messaging 'widespread reports of election fraud' so we are positively set up for the recount regardless of the final number? I obviously think we should." Scott Jensen—the former GOP Assembly Speaker turned lobbyist for American Federation for Children, a private school voucher advocacy group—quickly responded: "Yes. Anything fishy should be highlighted. Stories should be solicited by talk radio hosts." In another email, Jensen writes that [Judge] Prosser "needs to be on talk radio in the morning saying he is confident he won and talk radio needs to scream the Dems are trying to steal the race."[78]

The bogeyman of voter fraud has also proven useful in North Carolina where Republican governor Pat McCrory insisted that the only way to keep the monster at bay was the draconian ID law that state instituted. But a systematic analysis by the North Carolina State Board of Elections of nearly 4.8 million votes in the 2016 election found only one vote that could have possibly been stopped by voter ID.[79] The story was the same across the United States. Law professor Justin Levitt conducted an extensive study and uncovered that from 2000 to 2014, there were thirty-one voter impersonation cases out of one billion votes nationwide.[80] But the lie of voter fraud remains a salient part of the American political landscape; indeed, it continues to be a powerful and effective "political weapon" wielded against minorities, youths, and the poor.[81]

The effectiveness of voter ID laws is based on three key features. First, from the very beginning the dog whistle target has been "urban" areas.[82] Kit Bond railed against the electoral corruption in St. Louis. ACVR identified a rogues' gallery of cities where millions of African Americans lived, including some where they were the majority population. Representative Burmeister singled out blacks in Augusta who were supposedly willing to sell their votes and democracy for a few pieces of silver. Psychologically, the word association of "crime," "urban," and "African Americans" made the connection of "stealing" an election via fraud cognitively palpable to the broader population, which had linked crime and blackness together for more than a century.[83]

Conversely, and this is the second key factor, respectable members of society leveled the charges—U.S. senators, attorneys with law degrees from the Ivy League, governors, and others—fervently and doggedly warning the nation about voter fraud, voter fraud, voter fraud. The credibility of those accusations was amplified by newscasts that, initially, did not question the assertions of voter fraud but simply reported them.[84]

And, finally, the third factor is that the response, given the depth of the threat, seemed measured, reasonable, and commonsensical. This is why the Supreme Court in the *Crawford v. Marion County Election Board* case was mystified about why having to show an ID would be a problem. This is what allowed Kansas secretary of state Kris Kobach to quip, "I don't think it's a burden to reach into one's wallet or one's purse and pull out a photo ID."[85] Virginia state senator Mark Obenshain was equally dismissive. "There's only one class of people who are going to be discouraged from voting," he said, "and that's fraudulent voters."[86]

Those factors of assumed criminality, presumed respectability, and commonsense reasonableness provided ample cover for state after state after state to systematically target and disfranchise millions of American citizens.

In 2011, Alabama passed a photo ID law but never sought preclearance from the Department of Justice. In crafting this legislation, the state tossed out HAVA's range of valid identification such as a utility bill or social security card and homed in on only certain types of government-issued photo ID, which, disproportionately, African Americans and the poor did not have. Without preclearance, though, the law lay dormant for years. After the 2013 *Shelby County v. Holder* decision, however, Alabama attorney general Luther Strange announced that in 2014 "the photo voter ID law . . . can go ahead without any additional hoop jumping by the state."[87]

Citizens, however, were now going to have to run an obstacle course to acquire the appropriate identification to vote. Alabama, for example, refused to accept public housing ID, although this clearly is government-issued and, as the LDF explained, "for many people of color [it] is their only form of ID."[88] This refusal is despite—or, rather, because of—the racialized poverty that has made Alabama one of the poorest states in the nation. Nearly 34 percent of Hispanics and 31 percent of blacks live below the poverty line, compared with 14 percent of whites in the state. Moreover, in nine of the Black Belt counties, those in poverty exceeded the state average and echoed the impoverished conditions found during the Great Depression: Barbour (32 percent), Macon (32.2 percent), Sumter (33.2 percent), Wilcox (33.2 percent), Dallas (34.6 percent), Lowndes (35.2 percent), Greene (37.7 percent), Bullock (39.6 percent), and Perry (40 percent).[89]

In the midst of this grinding poverty and the rejection of public housing IDs to vote, Governor Robert Bentley, upon the suggestion of his mistress and aide, Rebekah Mason, then "closed 31 driver's license offices in mostly black counties." He used the excuse that fiscal exigencies required paring down the number of DMVs. But the "closures were estimated to save around $200,000, an extremely small savings in a General Fund that typically has annual shortfalls ranging from $100 million to $200 million."[90]

While the financial savings were meager, the impact on access to the ballot box was profound. A study by the NAACP Legal Defense

Fund found that "more than 100,000 registered voters in Alabama can't vote because they don't have the photo identification required by the state." Further analysis showed that most of the disfranchised were poor, making less than ten thousand dollars a year, and were black or Latino.[91] With no viable public transportation, no access to vehicles, and the closest DMV sometimes nearly fifty miles away and open for only a few days a month, many Black Belt county residents were simply and completely disfranchised. U.S. attorney general Eric Holder slammed voter ID as nothing but "a poll tax." Legal scholars called it "a financial barrier to the ballot box."[92] The Alabama secretary of state's office, though, brushed aside the criticisms although its staff calculated that five times as many as the LDF estimate, nearly five hundred thousand Alabamians, "would be blocked from voting under the new photo ID law."[93]

As if reading from the ALEC playbook, North Carolina instituted "America's worst voter suppression law."[94] Driving that decision was the grim reality for the Republicans that in the twenty-first century, African American voter registration had increased by 51.1 percent in the state *and* blacks also had a higher voter turnout "rate than white registered voters in both the 2008 and 2012 presidential elections."[95] Republican legislators, therefore, gathered the data on the types of identification blacks had and didn't have, then tailored the list of vote-worthy IDs to favor whites. Their actions were so brazen that the federal court ruled that the law was targeted at African Americans "with almost surgical precision." The Fourth Circuit also blasted North Carolina's voter identification legislation as designed to "impose cures for problems that did not exist." Indeed, Judge Diana Gribbon Motz wrote that all North Carolina's claims about the dangers of voter fraud "cannot and do not conceal the state's true motivation." The law not only has a discriminatory impact; it has "a discriminatory intent."[96]

Just as North Carolina was concerned about how to stanch the growing voter turnout rate of African Americans, Texas lawmakers also set out to neutralize the sizable demographic shift in their state. With more than 80 percent of Texas urbanized, and Dallas now a Democratic stronghold, Houston overwhelmingly minority, and San Antonio as well, it was clear that the burgeoning Latino and African American population had the ability to turn a red state not just purple, but blue.[97]

Texas's answer was S.B. 14, passed a mere two hours after the *Shelby County v. Holder* decision came down. The law skewed acceptable government-issued photo IDs to those "which white people are more likely to carry," such as gun licenses. It made driver's licenses the virtual holy grail of IDs because nearly one-third of the state's counties, including some of those that are heavily minority, do not have DMVs. Republican legislators recognized that it would require some citizens to travel up to 250 miles round-trip to obtain a license, but the lawmakers decided to remove language from S.B. 14 that would have reimbursed those who had to make that poll tax–like trip. In fact, one of the state's lawyers "brushed aside geographical obstacles as the 'reality to life of choosing to live in that part of Texas.'"[98]

The NAACP and the LDF, meanwhile, dealt with the fact that six hundred thousand black, Latino, and poor voters who were currently registered did not have the prerequisite ID. And, even more frightening for the future of democracy in Texas, an additional one million, who had not yet registered, also lacked any of the identification on the state's "exceptionally narrow" list. State officials, such as Governor Greg Abbott, were determined to keep it that way and refused to provide any tangible funding or resources to ameliorate the situation.[99]

Yet despite repeated court rulings about the discriminatory impact, and most recently, the discriminatory intent of the legislation, Texas, which has already spent more than $3.5 million and tweaked a bad bill to make it worse by adding felony penalties, is determined to make voter suppression the law of its land. Thus, whether it was S.B. 14 or the reincarnated S.B. 5, Sherrilyn Ifill, LDF president and director-counsel, intoned, "Make no mistake: this bill is old poison in a new bottle."[100]

The goal of all the GOP voter ID laws is to reduce significantly the demographic and political impact of a growing share of the American electorate. To diminish the ability of blacks, Latinos, and Asians, as well as the poor and students to choose government representatives and the types of policies they support. Unfortunately, it's working. A recent study shows that "the turnout gaps between white and ethnic minority voters are far higher in states where people must show ID during or after voting." There is a 4.9 percent gap between Latino and white voters in states that do not require an ID, but this "leaps to a 13.2 percent" difference in states like Texas, North Carolina, Georgia, and Wisconsin. For African Americans, the gap "rises from 2.9 percent to 5.4 percent; among Asians, the gap increases from 6.5 percent to 11.5 percent."[101] In Wisconsin, 8.3 percent of white voters who were surveyed said they were "deterred" from voting in the 2016 election because of voter ID laws; that number more than tripled for African Americans (27.5 percent).[102] A Government Accounting Office report "suggests that . . . turnout dropped among both young people and African Americans in Kansas and Tennessee after new voter ID requirements took effect."[103] Another study posits, however, that it's not the advent of voter ID laws but the confusion over what the correct identification is that actually drives down voter turnout, especially among blacks and Latinos.[104] This also explains why states such as Texas, Georgia, and Indiana have resisted mightily expending virtually any resources on voter education about the new standards. Wisconsin, in fact, used a federal court's ruling that upended the state's ID law to sow even greater confusion about what the revised guidelines, post–court decision, actually were. The flat-out refusal to train the staff at the Department of Motor Vehicles on the new court-ordered requirements left Wisconsinites "at the mercy" of DMV employees who had no idea about the necessary documents and IDs required to vote. The state's willful defiance also led to a harsh rebuke from the judge who had already called Wisconsin's efforts at credentialing voters a "wretched failure" because of the disparate impact on African Americans and Hispanics.[105] The results of the confusion and defiance of a federal court order were amazingly predictable, with a precipitous decline in voter turnout in 2016, especially in the overwhelmingly black, Democratic stronghold of Milwaukee.

A Republican seizure of power based not on the strength of the party's ideas but on massive disfranchisement denies citizens not only their rights, but also the "talisman" of humanity that voting represents.[106] The lie of voter fraud breaks a World War II veteran down into a simple, horrifying statement: "I wasn't a citizen no more." It forces a man, a retired engineer who was instrumental in building this nation, into facing a bitter truth: "I am not wanted in this state." It eviscerates the key sense of self-worth in a disabled man who has to pen the painful words "My constitutional rights have been stripped from me." It maligns thousands of African Americans who resiliently weathered the Missouri cold and hours of bureaucratic runarounds as nothing but criminals and frauds. It leaves a woman suffering from lung cancer absolutely "distraught" and convinced that "they prevented us from voting," because none of her IDs could penetrate Wisconsin's law. It shatters the dying wish of a woman who, in her last moments on earth, wanted to cast a vote for possibly the first woman president of the United States. But an expired driver's license meant none of that was to be.[107]

Three

Voter Roll Purge

The story read like something straight out of Stalinist Russia. But this casualty list was in the United States in the twenty-first century. Virginia: 41,637 purged.[1] Florida: 182,000 purged.[2] Indiana: 481,235 purged.[3] Georgia: 591,549 purged.[4] Ohio: two million purged.[5] With the flick of a bureaucratic wrist, millions of Americans—veterans, congressional representatives, judges, county officials, and most decidedly minorities—were erased.[6] To be clear, they still had their lives, but in the course of simply trying to cast a ballot, they soon learned that as far as the government was concerned, they did not exist. They were electorally dead. Their very right to vote had disappeared into the black hole of voter roll purges, Interstate Crosscheck, and felony disfranchisement. Some of the walking dead were viscerally "angry."[7] Others fumed, "This is screwed up!"[8] Most felt "like an outcast," "empty and unimportant," and one man was actually reduced to "crying right there in the county elections office."[9] These were the latest casualties in the war on democracy.

They had been eliminated by a GOP deftly wielding a law that had actually been designed to broaden access to the polls. The modern-day version of voter purging began in the aftermath of a dismal election. The 1988 presidential contest between Democrat Michael Dukakis and Republican George H. W. Bush not only brought out the racial dog whistle skills of GOP strategist Lee Atwater, who crafted the infamous Willie Horton ad, but it also resulted in one of the lowest voter-turnout rates since 1924. Barely 50 percent of age-eligible adults cast a ballot. Columbia University professor Richard Cloward identified the culprit. "When there's no organizing structures to help people get registered, the voter registration barriers just sort of gradually erode the electorate."[10] In some counties in Mississippi, for example, the only place to register to vote was in the clerk's office during traditional business hours. In other locales, such as Indianapolis, voter registration drives were hampered by a "rule" that doled out a maximum of twenty-five forms to each volunteer. Limited access to registration had a visible and disparate impact on the electorate. According to a report by Demos, a progressive think tank, while top income brackets achieved more than 80 percent voter registration rates, "from 1972 to 1992, voter registration among the lowest income quintile saw a nearly 18 percentage point drop—from 61.2 percent in 1972 to 43.5 percent in 1992."[11]

Congress, therefore, passed the National Voter Registration Act (NVRA), also known as the Motor Voter law, in 1993.[12] The statute's opening preamble is clear. The right to vote "is a fundamental right." And, it is "the duty of the Federal, State, and local government to promote the exercise of that right." This obligation requires paying particular attention to "discriminatory and unfair registration laws and procedures" that "disproportionately harm voter participation by various groups, including racial minorities."[13] As a result, the NVRA expanded the venues for and standardized the process of registration. Now citizens could register at the Department of Motor Vehicles and public assistance and disability offices, as well as through the mail with a brand-new standardized federal form.[14]

As important as this was—indeed, the number of registered voters increased by more than 3.3 million in just a few years—the lag time between the initial "concern" in 1988 and the passage of the law in 1993 was significant.[15] During the negotiations, Republicans at first stalled, and then demanded a quid pro quo for increasing access to the ballot box. They insisted that the law had to require routine maintenance, scrubbing even, of the voter rolls. This would ensure that people who had moved out of the district or state and those who had died were no longer listed as eligible voters. It all sounded so reasonable and so mundane. Except it wasn't. That innocuous language— just like Kit Bond's demand to insert a requirement for voter IDs into the Help America Vote Act—became yet another weapon in the Republicans' arsenal to disfranchise as many citizens as possible.

What the law requires and how it has been implemented are two different things. The NVRA mandates that election officials update the voter rolls regularly. There are, however, strict guidelines about who is removed, how that is accomplished, and why.[16] And on each of these parameters, the GOP has violated not only the spirit of the law but the letter as well. The NVRA outlines that officials can remove someone from the roll of eligible voters if he or she requests it; has had a name change and didn't notify authorities within ninety days; dies; is convicted of a felony that under state law renders them ineligible to vote; "has moved outside the county of registration or has registered to vote in another jurisdiction"; *and* after that does not respond to a follow-up inquiry, usually a mailing, from election officials concerning a change in status. Then, and only then, is the process of purging supposed to begin.[17]

In other words, the trip wire is a two-step process triggered first by a change in status of the voter (name change, felony conviction, move) and then by an inquiry from a state election official about his or her continued eligibility to vote in that jurisdiction. Unfortunately, far too many secretaries of state have bypassed this carefully laid-out two-step process, ignored a change in status, and, instead, used one specific criterion (non-voting) that is expressly forbidden in the NVRA to wipe out otherwise eligible voters. The point of this illegal tactic is to cull the electorate of millions of citizens, most of whom are young, poor, and/or minorities, who statistically do not vote for Republicans and whose voting activities are often sporadic. Despite the targeting of key demographic groups, this wide-scale purging remains virtually undercover. It is effective, "powerful," and "dangerous precisely because it is easy to justify to the public in the name of 'keeping our voter rolls up to date.' "[18]

Ohio has been in the forefront with this lethal maneuver. In fact, no state has been more aggressive or more consistent in attacking the heart of the NVRA. From 2011 to 2016, Secretary of State Jon Husted has wiped two million people from the state's list of registered voters. Most important, 1.2 million of those have been eliminated solely because they voted infrequently.[19] Yet the NVRA is crystal clear: people cannot be struck from the registration rolls simply because they did not vote in a few federal elections.[20]

Nonetheless, that is exactly what happened to software engineer and Navy veteran Larry Harmon. In 2008, he eagerly voted in a historic presidential election. Four years later, however, Harmon sat out because he was somewhat disenchanted with President Barack Obama and partially swayed by Republican challenger Mitt Romney's platform. Unable to choose, he deliberately chose not to vote. When the 2014 midterm elections came around, Harmon was not impressed with any of the candidates for Congress and, therefore, just stayed home. But in 2015, with a local initiative concerning legalized marijuana on the ballot, he wanted his voice to be heard and went to the polling place. There he received a rude awakening. To the State of Ohio, this veteran, this taxpayer, this citizen did not exist. At least not at the ballot box. When he stepped up to the table to show his ID, poll workers told him that he "could not vote." He wasn't registered. At first, Harmon "felt embarrassed and stupid," then it began to sink in and he became "madder" and madder. How could he simply be erased like that? "I'm a veteran, my father's a veteran, my grandfather's a veteran," he said, stewing; we fought "for the country . . . now they aren't giving me my right to vote, the most fundamental right I have? I just can't believe it." As he dug deeper, as he learned that the sheer constitutionally protected act of not voting had just cost him his right to vote, he became more infuriated. It turns out that in 1994, Ohio had "updated its elections law to add what is known as a 'supplemental process'" to the NVRA. That means that "voters may be purged from the rolls after six years just because they didn't vote—even if they are otherwise eligible." Ohio, in other words, had flipped federal law on its head. "I've been paying my taxes, paying my property taxes, registering my car," he said. "All the data was there for (election officials) to know" that he still lived in the same house, on the same block, in the same jurisdiction. He had not moved. Nor had he changed his name. He was Larry Harmon in 2008. He remained Larry Harmon in 2015. And he clearly had not died. In short, not one of the federal law's requirements for the secretary of state to remove him from the rolls had occurred. He simply had not voted in two federal elections.[21] But, in Ohio, despite the NVRA, apparently that was all it took.

Jon Husted argued that his office met its statutory obligations and mailed postcards to Harmon and millions like him alerting them that if they did not respond within thirty days, the process of removal would begin. "If this is really [an] important thing to you in your life, voting," the secretary of state chided, "you probably would have done so within a six-year period."[22] That argument, however, misses the basic point: failure to vote is not a legal, viable reason to purge someone from the voter rolls.

Besides its sheer illegality, Ohio's method had another fatal flaw: mailing postcards crammed with fine print is fraught with discriminatory impact. The Census Bureau, for example, uncovered that when it sends out mail, "white voters are 21 percent more likely than blacks or Hispanics to respond to their official requests; homeowners are 32 percent more likely to respond than renters; and the young are 74 percent less likely than the old to respond."[23] Thus, the differential response rates for Husted's mailings translate into disproportionate purges in key neighborhoods of Cleveland, Columbus, and Cincinnati—areas that are overwhelmingly minority and composed of renters and young adults. In Cleveland, for example, whites make up only 34.5 percent of the residents while 50.1 percent of the city's residents are black and 10.5 percent are Hispanic.[24] Moreover, nearly 60 percent of homes in the city are rented, not owned.[25] It is also a town where 69 percent of the voters went for Obama in 2012. By 2016, however, the percentage of Democratic voters had dropped to 66 percent, while the Republican share stayed virtually the same.[26] That little bit of magic might be explained by the fact that "voters in neighborhoods that backed Obama by more than 60 percent in 2012" had more than twice as many registered voters purged "for inactivity" than "neighborhoods where Obama got less than 40 percent of the vote."[27] Indeed, more than one-fourth of the two hundred thousand Ohioans Husted purged from the voter rolls in 2015 were in Cuyahoga County alone, where Cleveland is located.[28]

Moreover, despite Husted's insistence on personal responsibility, the question of showing up regularly to vote is not solely an individual choice. For years, Ohio has taken an active role in culling the electorate and dissuading citizens from voting (or even having those votes count). Secretary of State Husted and his Republican predecessor Kenneth Blackwell have, for example, limited the number of polling stations for early voting in urban areas, thus creating untenable four-to-five-hour wait times in cities. These election officials have also tossed tens of thousands of absentee ballots, supposedly because they were cast on incorrect paper stock or had a spelling error.[29] And, in a deposition, Husted's top aide admitted that these so-called enforcement activities were actually targeted at the cities, while "white rural areas went nearly untouched."[30] In essence, the state has set up the equivalence of the old literacy tests, in which those Jim Crow states ensured that many of their citizens could not get a decent education and then turned around and required literacy to vote. Similarly, Ohio has set up a system whereby it blocks American citizens from voting and then purges them from the rolls . . . for not voting.

Ohio is not alone. Georgia and its secretary of state, Brian Kemp, have also mastered the art of the purge. Georgia has been so good at it, in fact, that even as its population climbed, its number of registered voters since 2012 has actually dropped.[31] Kemp, it turns out, is a voter-suppression warrior who wears his triumphs in fighting nonexistent voter-impersonation fraud as a fundraising badge of honor while, all along, his "actions have undermined voting systems, election security and democracy in general."[32] He has displayed a tendency to consistently err on the side of disfranchisement: such as "when his office lost voter registrations for 40,000 Georgians, the vast majority of whom *happened* to be people of color"; and when his office leaked the social security numbers and driver's license data of voters not once but twice; and when he refused to upgrade the voting machines throughout the state that had received an F rating because they were easily hackable and "haven't been updated since 2005 and run on Windows 2000."[33] Kemp had also "crusaded against" and "investigated" voter registration drives by Asian Americans and predominately black groups. He actually launched a criminal inquiry into the registration of 85,000 new voters, "many of them minorities," but "found problems with only 25 of the registrants, and" not surprisingly, after all the time, money, and publicity, "no charges were filed." Yet the intimidation was real—too real and too familiar.[34] While Jim Crow Georgia had implemented a potent disfranchisement cocktail of literacy tests, poll taxes, and terrorism to keep the voting booth as white as possible, now, in the twenty-first century, James Crow Georgia has concocted its own witch's brew of feigned innocence, the elimination of a million citizens for the sheer act of not voting, and a highly unreliable and therefore effective program called Exact Match.

Georgia's perfidy has not gone unnoticed and has resulted in an onslaught of lawsuits from the NAACP, the ACLU, and the League of Women Voters. Kemp's response, however, has been Orwellian. Confronted with 732,800 voters who, between October 2012 and November 2014, had their "registration status canceled 'due to failure to vote'" and then the 591,548 who were wiped off the rolls just two years later, Candice Broce, a spokeswoman for Kemp's office, took umbrage at the charge and explained that the "secretary of state's office does not 'purge' any voters." That's just not a word that his office was willing to use. Instead, his staff explained, in language that the public would find reassuring, the elimination of more than one million citizens from the rolls was nothing more than "voter list maintenance . . . to safeguard . . . the integrity of the ballot box . . . and prevent fraud and ensure that all votes are cast by eligible Georgia voters."[35] Kemp's specter of waves of people impersonating the dead to cast ballots in Georgia has been disproved repeatedly. Political scientists M. V. Hood III from the University of Georgia and William Gillespie from Kennesaw State University concluded that "after examining approximately 2.1 million votes cast during the 2006 general election in Georgia, we find no evidence that election fraud was committed under the auspices of deceased registrants."[36] A decade later, as the *Washington Post* reported, despite all the baying at the moon, there were no cases prosecuted in Georgia for voter impersonation fraud.[37] Kemp, however, did not hesitate to raise the bogeyman of voter fraud to mask the state's voter suppression efforts.

The subterfuge continued as the secretary of state explained the rationale for wiping more than one million citizens from the rolls. Kemp argued that he was merely following state law and that the catalyst for removal was simply that the voter had had no contact with election officials over a span of seven years, not, as his critics charged, because of non-voting. The hocus-pocus in that statement is obvious. If a citizen doesn't move and doesn't change his or her name, there is absolutely no reason to contact the secretary of state's office. None. It is not about changes of addresses or even name changes; it's realizing that minorities, the poor, and the young are less likely to vote than affluent whites are.[38] Just as the Mississippi Plan in the 1890s used the poll tax to identify the characteristics of those the state did not want to vote, Georgia's twist of the law does something similar.

Even when they do vote, the poor, minorities, and the young are also more likely to move, to be more transient than the typical Republican voter. "I've had enough of that," declared one woman who received Kemp's pre-purge notice. No one is arguing that voter rolls shouldn't be updated, she declared, but she moved to a home in the same county, in the same voting jurisdiction. Kemp's notice, therefore, felt like harassment. It felt like the first step to kicking her off the rolls.[39] Yet the NVRA is as clear on this point as it is about non-voting. If a "registrant who has moved from an address in the area covered by a polling place to an address in the same area," he or she "shall be permitted to vote at that polling place upon oral or written affirmation by the registrant of the change of address before an election official at that polling place." That is to say, under these circumstances, there should never be a purge notice or its attendant threat. Instead, the citizen simply informs the election official of the new address when he or she goes to vote.[40] That's the law. Except in Georgia.

Francys Johnson, the former president of the Georgia NAACP, who was known for bringing "street heat and legal teeth" into the voting rights battles in the state, branded Kemp's maneuvers as designed for no other purpose than "to close opportunities for Georgians to be able to exercise the right to vote."[41] The monstrous little program named Exact Match did just that.

In March 2007, using the specter of voter fraud and the cover of the NVRA's requirement for voter roll maintenance, Georgia insisted that the names in its voter registration database match those in the Department of Motor Vehicles in every way. Jon Greenbaum, an attorney with the Lawyers' Committee for Civil Rights, knew instinctively that the state was "going out of its way to look to purge voters."[42] Though it didn't necessarily appear so initially, at least two problems with the Exact Match plan indicated that this was the goal. First, at the time, Georgia was under the preclearance provision of the VRA and hadn't bothered to ask the Department of

Justice for approval. Yet because the counsel to the head of the Civil Rights Division, Hans von Spakovsky, was a George W. Bush appointee who, over the strenuous objections of the career attorneys at the DOJ, had already approved Georgia's voter ID law, the state rightfully assumed that it had little to fear. Second, the databases of the DMV and secretary of state's offices were fraught with errors—a missing "e" in the name Carole, a hyphen where one was not supposed to be, an errant "y" instead of an "i" in Nicki, or any of the other numerous typographical errors that can happen when two large bureaucracies are processing millions of applications. All this had a horrific effect on voter registration, especially for minorities. African Americans, who were one-third of the applicants, accounted for 64 percent of the tens of thousands of voter registrations that Georgia's secretary of state canceled or "placed in 'pending status'" for data mismatches between 2013 and 2016. Meanwhile, "Asian-Americans and Latinos were more than six times as likely as white voters to have their applications halted."[43]

The devastation of Georgia's Exact Match was amplified in nearly thirty states by the Interstate Crosscheck program. It gave the illusion of being clean, clinical, efficient, and fair. Its implementation and use were anything but. Crosscheck began in 2005 as a small, regional three-state endeavor, similar to Georgia's. In many ways, the premise was the same: the alignment of databases would be able to flag fraudulent voters and purge them from the rolls. For a few years, the program limped along, virtually unnoticed. Then, a new secretary of state took over in Kansas, and he hitched his star and his agenda, which had been nurtured in the worlds of virulent anti-immigrant, anti–civil rights conservative circles for decades, to making Crosscheck more robust, more pronounced, and, frankly, more electorally lethal.

That man was Kris Kobach. He was a Harvard graduate and Yale law alum, son of a Midwestern Buick dealership owner, who began his career in George W. Bush's Department of Justice and exuded the certainty, absorbed from his mentor Samuel Huntington, that America was under attack from brown immigrants and black voters. There was, as a result, a zealotry to all of Kobach's work. He "has been a key architect behind many of the nation's anti-voter and anti-immigration policies." At the DOJ in 2001, he developed a database screening program to identify Muslims as terrorist threats. Though thousands were deported, no terrorists were ever found. But Kobach saw the program as a "great success." After he left the DOJ, he eventually moved on to Arizona to help bolster the infamous "Driving While Brown" anti-immigrant law that made Maricopa County's Sheriff Joe Arpaio so notorious. Riding on the wave of his reputation in staunch conservative circles, he ran for office in Kansas and in 2010 successfully won his campaign to be secretary of state. As Ari Berman reported, Kobach told the *Kansas City Star* that the "position of secretary of state was not an especially glamorous one, but it offered an enormous amount of power by virtue of its authority to enforce state voting laws, particularly as American elections were being decided by increasingly narrow margins."[44]

Once he was at the helm, Kobach's first electoral battle cry was a menacing thrust at the "massive" and "pervasive" voter fraud that had purportedly engulfed Kansas. As "Exhibit A," he pointed to a case where a man named Albert Brewer, who had been dead for years, showed up and voted in the last primary election. Kobach held up this instance as one of thousands lurking in the voter rolls, skewing elections, canceling out the legitimate votes from hardworking, honest Americans. It was vintage Kobach, and vintage GOP. It was also not true. Yes, there was an Albert Brewer who had died. And there was one who voted. But they were not one and the same. The Albert Brewer who voted, Albert Brewer Jr., was the son of the man who had died. Kobach hadn't even bothered to check before he started slinging accusations.[45]

That kind of deliberate sloppiness would, however, be his trademark; it's the way he garners the support necessary to wipe thousands off the rolls in Kansas and millions throughout the United States. In the 2016 election, Kobach's office, for instance, rejected more ballots than even Florida did, despite Florida's population being seven times larger. That sledgehammer approach makes clear that Kobach's goal is not to get it right. The goal is to tilt the electorate to the right. Jason Kander, Missouri's former secretary of state, said that "Kobach uses every trick that he can to make it as hard as possible for eligible voters to cast a ballot—whether it's unconstitutional legislation, targeting immigrants or forcing more eligible voters to use provisional ballots."[46]

Kobach, thus, helped draft a Kansas law based on the lies of voter fraud and immigrant takeover of the ballot box. Under the absolutely misnamed Secure and Fair Elections (SAFE) Act, the state required voters to "1) present photo IDs prior to casting a ballot, 2) present a full driver's license number and have their signatures verified in order to absentee vote and 3) provide proof of citizenship to register to vote."[47] The last element, which could be satisfied with a birth certificate or a U.S. passport, was supposed to address Kobach's claim (based on a roundly refuted and widely discredited study) that eighteen thousand noncitizens "may have registered to vote in Kansas."[48] Although, as one politician noted, immigrants don't "com[e] here to vote . . . They come here to work," Kobach insisted that they were stealing elections or, equally frightening, were more than capable of doing so.[49] "We had margins of less than 10 for water commissioner, school board and mayors," Kobach claimed. And, with eighteen thousand noncitizens supposedly poised to usurp the rights of Americans, immigrants could take over key positions in government. It was a Samuel Huntington *Clash of Civilizations* nightmare.[50] So Kobach sounded the alarm. Through his Captain Queeg–like hunt for culprits, he turned Kansas upside down, wrangling prosecutorial power from the legislature, but found only a Peruvian immigrant who was actually in the process of naturalizing and erroneously thought he could cast a ballot. One lone immigrant cannot and simply does not convey "massive" and "pervasive." So, the secretary of state billed it as "the tip of the iceberg."[51]

Kobach, therefore, suspended the right to vote of 35,314 Kansans because they could not produce "proof of U.S. citizenship." More than 12,000 of those he simply purged outright because the disparate access to citizenship documents played right into Kobach's belief about who is American and who is not, and thus who has the right to vote. He "associated minority voters with 'ethnic cleansing' . . . [in] a conspiracy to 'replace American voters with illegal aliens.'" The U.S. Commission on Civil Rights rightfully concluded that the SAFE Act "may disparately impact voters on the basis of age, sex, disability, race, income level and affiliation." And, the commission continued, what it costs, especially for the poor, to obtain a passport or a birth certificate is a "barrier" that amounts to "an unconstitutional poll tax." A contemptuous Kobach sneered that the commission's report "is not worth the paper that it was written on."[52] Yet a study by the Brennan Center for Justice found that "7 percent of Americans, mostly minorities, do not have these [citizenship] documents readily available." Moreover, as scholar Chelsie Bright explained, "it is unclear that proof of citizenship requirements actually add any real value to the integrity of the election process. Federal law already requires that individuals registering to vote affirm in writing that they are a U.S. citizen. Lying carries serious criminal penalties. Further, research consistently finds that voting by noncitizens is extremely rare."[53]

The ACLU sued. Kobach's purge was not driven by any exigent need or crisis. There was no threat to the integrity of the ballot box. What there was, however, was Kobach's need to remove the poor and minorities from the voting rolls. In October 2016, the Tenth Circuit of the U.S. Court of Appeals agreed. Kobach's "theory of Kansas' widespread problem of noncitizens voting" was "pure speculation" with "precious little . . . evidence."[54] Yet Kobach was undeterred;

he went on to set up a two-tiered federal/state registration form and continued to harangue registrants for proof of U.S. citizenship to vote in the *state*'s elections. One of those registrants was ninety-one-year-old World War II veteran Marvin Brown, who had been around long enough to remember the poll tax. When Kobach deigned to question whether "Brown was truly a citizen," the veteran found an ally in the ACLU and went back to court. There, U.S. District judge Julie Robinson chided that Kobach once again had "scant evidence of noncitizen voter fraud."[55] Unfazed by what would be yet another one of his losses to the American Civil Liberties Union, Kobach continued to work toward disfranchising as many "threats" to American democracy as he could find. In fact, he had already "block[ed] 18,000 motor voter applicants from registering to vote in Kansas."[56]

His most devastating weapon to date, however, has been Interstate Crosscheck, which he has nurtured and promoted as an important device to eliminate voter fraud from the American political landscape. The program is supposed to root out those who are registered to vote in two different states as part of "a national move to bring more integrity to the voter rolls" and provide a solution to "registration systems [that] cannot keep up with a society of voters who move from state to state." It works through an alliance of twenty-seven states, which sends voter information to Arkansas to upload. Kobach's Kansas then pulls and runs the data for every member of the consortium, searching for comparisons "of registered voters to weed out duplicates."[57] Interstate Crosscheck, which by 2012 had more than forty-five million voter records, matches first, middle, and last names, date of birth, last four digits of the social security number, and suffix, if applicable, to identify those who may be going from state to state to vote, tainting election after election.[58]

At least that's the narrative Kobach told when he stumbled upon Lincoln L. Wilson, a sixty-six-year-old Republican who owned homes in both Kansas and Colorado. Wilson felt he was well within his rights to vote in local elections in both states. "I'd vote for president in one state, and local issues in both places," Wilson explained, especially when he saw his property tax bill skyrocket and resolved that there would be no taxation without representation. What looked logical to Wilson, however, and, frankly, not that much of a big deal to the local prosecutor, was a red flag to Kobach, who pursued charges against the elderly man with a vengeance. Kobach simply needed to make an example of him. Eighteen months and nearly $50,000 in legal fees, a $6,000 fine, $158 in court costs, and a guilty plea to three misdemeanors later, Kobach had his victory. Wilson simmered, saying, "Kris Kobach came after me for an honest mistake . . . Damn right, I'm upset . . . I'm a convicted man now."[59]

Wilson, however, was in many ways a fluke. Crosscheck is such a fundamentally flawed database that its "success" rate is actually an epic fail for democracy. Since the database's launch, 7.2 million voters have been flagged as suspect. Based on the individual lists the states received back from Kobach, massive purges have wiped more than one million American citizens from the electoral map. In Virginia, for example, 342,556 names were immediately identified as suspect because they appeared to be registered in another state. Those who were already on an "inactive voters" list were summarily removed, "meaning a stunning 41,637 names were 'canceled' from voter rolls, most of them just before Election Day" in November 2014. Texas set out to purge 80,000 voters, even though the Crosscheck match was "weak." Only a court order, prompted by a lawsuit from a man the system had marked as "dead," stopped the process. In Ohio, Crosscheck "flagged close to half a million voters." North Carolina's secretary of state alerted the Republican-dominated legislature that at least 35,750 dual voters were stalking the rolls. In Georgia and Washington, Crosscheck seemed to identify a total of more than one million unscrupulous voters.[60] In the 2016 election, it was even worse, especially given the slim popular vote margins that ultimately determined who won the Electoral College.[61] Arizona purged almost

271,000 voters. Michigan removed nearly 450,000 voters, and North Carolina managed to eliminate close to 600,000 from the system.[62] The staggering numbers fueled the narrative of massive, rampant voter fraud; of voter rolls so unkempt that the dead had ample opportunity to rise from the grave and tilt an election. That, of course, meant Kobach's pet program had successfully spun its web of lies, at least, in the view from thirty thousand feet.

But up close, neither the lists nor the database could withstand scrutiny. The problem is twofold. First, despite the hype and the marketing, the program does not actually match on every parameter. Not all states require the same information that Crosscheck uses to purge the rolls. Social security numbers, for example, are rarely used. Ohio doesn't bother with a person's middle name either. Suffixes rarely make it in, as well. As a result, it believes that James Willie Brown is the same voter as James Arthur Brown, as James Clifford Brown, as James Lynn Brown. The possibility for error is exponential. In Georgia alone there are nearly four hundred James Browns. And in North Carolina, the supposedly more than thirty-five thousand illegal voters simply evaporated when the state hired an ex-FBI agent to ferret them out and bring them to justice. He found "exactly zero double voters from the Crosscheck list." In fact, researchers at Stanford, Harvard, Yale, and the University of Pennsylvania discovered that Crosscheck has an error rate of more than 99 percent.[63] The lack of consistency, rigor, and accuracy led a "shocked" Mark Swedlund, a database expert whose clients include several Fortune 500 companies, to dismiss Crosscheck's "childish methodology." It's too error-prone. "God forbid," he noted, if "your name is Garcia, of which there are 858,000 in the U.S. and your name is Joseph or Jose. You're probably suspected of voting in 27 states."[64]

Crosscheck's overreliance on a handful of selective data points, therefore, feeds into the second major problem: it is a program "infected with racial and ethnic bias."[65] Minorities in America tend to have common or shared last names. If your last name is Washington, for example, there is an 89 percent chance that you're African American; Hernandez, a 94 percent chance that you're Hispanic; Kim, a 95 percent chance that you're Asian.[66] Similarly, Garcia, Lee, and Jackson all signal a strong probability of being a minority in the United States because "minorities are overrepresented in 85 of 100 of the most common last names."[67] As a result, when Crosscheck zeros in on name matches, whites are underrepresented by 8 percent on the purge lists, while African Americans are overrepresented by 45 percent; Asian Americans by 31 percent, and Hispanics by 24 percent.[68] With Crosscheck perseverating on similar last names, it has blasted a hole through minority voting rights. Indeed, as *The Root* reported: "Roughly 14 percent of all black voters were purged from databases under the guise of preventing 'double-voting' and 'fraud'."[69]

The depth of disfranchisement, of wringing the right to vote out of American citizens, led award-winning columnist Charles P. Pierce to conclude that "Kobach is Jim Crow walking."[70] Investigative journalist Greg Palast, after surveying the racial casualties in Ohio, knew that it wasn't just Kansas's secretary of state but an entire GOP apparatus that decided the "only way" to win an election was "by stealing American citizens' votes." "It's a brand-new Jim Crow. Today, on Election Day, they're not going to use white sheets to keep away black voters. Today they're using spreadsheets."[71]

Kobach's track record, therefore, set off alarm bells when he stepped out of a meeting with President-elect Donald Trump carrying some papers that were partially visible with talking points about how to restrict access to the polls under the new regime.[72] Papers, by the way, that he consistently lied about and refused to produce until a court order and a thousand-dollar fine forced him to reveal that he proposed altering the NVRA to require proof of citizenship.[73] The fears were heightened further by Trump's fantastical claim that he would have won the popular vote if it hadn't been for three million to five million illegal voters.[74] Concern mounted as the president, who was determined to prove his lie was the truth, signed an executive order creating the Presidential Advisory Commission on Election Integrity and appointed as its chair Vice President Mike Pence, who as governor of Indiana had the state police raid and destabilize an organization registering African Americans to vote, and Kris Kobach as its vice chair.[75] A *New York Times* editorial summed it up: the "Commission on Election Integrity . . . is a sham and a scam . . . born out of a marriage of convenience between conservative anti-voter-fraud crusaders, who refuse to accept actual data, and a president who refuses to accept that he lost the popular vote fair and square."[76] The lie of voter fraud now had the presidential stamp of approval. It also had additional federal funding, a presidential commission, and several key members who were part of a rogues' gallery of voter suppressors.[77]

In addition to Kobach, Kenneth Blackwell, and Hans von Spakovsky, whose appointment was like "a big middle finger" from Trump to minorities, there was J. Christian Adams.[78] Similar to Kobach, Adams was also in Bush's Department of Justice. There he flipped the Voting Rights Act on its head and went after African Americans for supposedly violating whites' right to vote.[79] He also made it clear that he deplored the NVRA because, in his view, "voter registration takes forethought and initiative, something lacking in large segments of the Democrat base."[80] Under the cover of his organizations, the American Civil Rights Union (ACRU) and the Public Interest Legal Foundation (PILF), he bullied and targeted minority and poor districts, and threatened lawsuit after lawsuit unless they purged their voter rolls, forcing many to capitulate because they simply didn't have the resources to fight him in court.[81] He argued, in his own Huntington-like version of *The Clash of Civilizations*, that the "Obama Administration was attempting to 'import populations with cultural and legal traditions foreign to American traditions,' and that 'noncitizen voting helps the left win elections'—statements," as the NAACP Legal Defense Fund chair Sherrilyn Ifill notes, "with no factual basis whatsoever."[82]

Fully packed with voter suppression crusaders, Trump, over the objections of von Spakovsky, then added a few Democrats for "window dressing." But it soon became clear that their role was to be even less than that. They were invisible. The Democrats on the commission, such as Maine secretary of state Matt Dunlap, were shocked to learn that the Pence Commission actually had a staff. That little piece of information only came to light through news reports, however, because Ronald Williams II, who had previously worked for Adams at the DOJ and was now identified by the media as working for the commission, was arrested on child pornography charges.[83] The Democrats were also blindsided by the commission's request for data that was sent to all fifty secretaries of state. In addition to voters' names, dates of birth, and the last four digits of their social security numbers, the Pence Commission wanted party affiliation and voting patterns for every voter on the rolls, as well as information on any felony convictions. This would have been Crosscheck on anabolic steroids, a Bane doing massive damage to the body politic by heightening and spreading the flaws in Kobach's pet database across the nation.[84] The juiced-up pounding on Asian Americans, African Americans, and those with Hispanic surnames would have demolished their voting rights and, as much as possible, made the electorate white again. This would have been virtually assured, given the ideological, anti-black, anti-minority, anti-immigrant bent of the power center on the Pence Commission. That nationwide data in their hands spelled disfranchisement from sea to shining sea.

The backlash to the request for voter information was therefore intense. There were major concerns about privacy, about the security of the database, about the intentions of the commission for amassing this data. The immediate response was a 2,150 percent increase in citizens in Denver canceling their voter registration, and there were similar cancelations in Arizona, Florida, and North

Carolina.[85] The other public response to Kobach and the commissioners was as pointed: "You are all about voter suppression to rig elections . . . you are evil, pray there is no hell."[86] Another concerned citizen was equally succinct: "This commission is a sham and Kris Kobach has been put on it expressly to disenfranchise minority voters."[87] A New Yorker got to the point, as well: "You have no right to my voting record or anyone else's; and to use it to eventually suppress voting is unconscionable in American Democracy." And, then, as if echoing a recent horror movie, he wrote, "We saw what you did in Kansas . . ."[88]

Even Republicans seemed to agree. Forty-four states, including Kobach's Kansas, balked at the Pence Commission's data request.[89] Mississippi planted its feet squarely on the ground of states' rights and told the commission "it could go jump in the Gulf."[90] Democrats were equally opposed. "This is a coordinated attempt to create a national voter registration file that would reside in the White House . . . We might as well let [Russian President Vladimir] Putin just get a zip drive of every registered voter's information in the nation," Kentucky's Alison Grimes remarked, alluding to the ongoing federal investigation of whether the Kremlin sought to tip the scales in the 2016 race to Trump.[91]

The concerns about the Pence Commission's integrity continued to mount during its first meeting in New Hampshire. Even the site was problematic. Jeffrey Toobin in the *New Yorker* observed that the "choice of this location is characteristic of the incompetence and malevolence that is at the heart of the vote-suppression agenda."[92] Trump had lied about thousands of Massachusetts residents coming over in buses and voting in New Hampshire, costing him and the Republican senate candidate the state in the last election. Kobach buttressed the lie and then spun a fairy tale in *Breitbart* as if voter fraud were real.[93] It was harrowing, he wrote. A "pivotal, close election was likely changed through voter fraud on November 8, 2016." He claimed he had "proof" that "5,313 people who voted in New

Hampshire in 2016 do not actually reside in the state."[94] Yet, just like the 18,000 phantom noncitizens on the rolls in Kansas, just like the "massive" and "pervasive" evidence of widespread voter fraud that has yet to appear, just like the dead-then-not-so-dead Albert Brewer, who rose from the grave and voted in the primary election, Kobach's charges were once again, as the *New York Times* noted, "baseless allegations." Those 5,300-plus voters were overwhelmingly college students, whose nine-month tenure at the state's higher education institutions made them in 2016 legally eligible to vote in New Hampshire.[95]

In addition to being built on lie after lie, the Pence Commission's shaky beginning also included getting hit with eight separate lawsuits for violating a range of federal laws about the setup and operation of government commissions.[96] "That kind of recklessness," columnist Mark Joseph Stern concluded, "can only heighten the widespread suspicion that the commission is interested in something other than 'election integrity.' "[97] The suspicion was exacerbated by the selection of witnesses called to testify during its first meeting. For a commission that, according to the vice president, "had no preconceived notions," its initial fact-finding venture featured a cavalcade of "prominent" white conservative men pounding on the "overblown charges of voter fraud."[98] The most controversial and telling witness, however, was a gun researcher, John Lott Jr., who advocated running voters through the same background-check system—mental health, dishonorable military discharges, substance abuse issues, and criminal history—as someone purchasing a gun. Lott's suggestion had a powerful agenda behind it. As Pema Levy and Ari Berman pointed out, such a system would easily "deter people from voting who are distrustful of law enforcement and want to stay away from a criminal background check."[99] One journalist noted, in fact, that Kobach, von Spakovsky, and Lott "are playing a very serious game, burrowing into the fine print and corners of the voting process to find and exploit ways to rig the rules."[100] Exploiting the toxic relationship between law enforcement and African Americans is one way, as when Mississippi and then Florida posted sheriffs at polling places to reduce the turnout rate. Indeed, a Gallup study found that "there's a more-than-20-point gap between the portion of blacks and whites who mostly trust the police."[101]

General distrust is one thing, but the reality of mass incarceration is another, because the impact on voting rights is profound. In 2016, one in thirteen African Americans had lost their right to vote because of a felony conviction, compared with one in fifty-six of every non-black voter.[102] The major villain in this set piece is the War on Drugs, which was a targeted hit on black people.[103] African Americans statistically do drugs no more than any other racial or ethnic group but are imprisoned for drug charges at almost six times the rate of whites. Hyper-policing in black communities has meant that while "African Americans represent 12.5% of illicit drug users," they are "29% of those arrested for drug offenses and 33% of those incarcerated in state facilities for drug offenses."[104]

In America, mass incarceration equals mass felony disfranchisement. With the launch of the War on Drugs, millions of African Americans were swept into the criminal justice system, many never to exercise their voting rights again. Indeed, the felony disfranchisement rate in the United States has grown by 500 percent since 1980.[105] Each state, to be sure, has its own rules. In Vermont and Maine, there is no felony disfranchisement, even when the person is incarcerated. But that has little impact on the vote totals for African Americans, who are only 1.3 and 1.5 percent, respectively, of those states' populations.[106] The other forty-eight states have some form of disfranchisement. Generally, the incarcerated cannot vote, but once they have served their time, which sometimes includes parole or probation, there is a process—often arcane and opaque—that allows for the restoration of voting rights. Overall, 6.1 million Americans have lost their voting rights. Currently, because of the Byzantine rules, "approximately 2.6 million individuals who have completed their sentences remain disenfranchised due to restrictive state laws."[107]

The majority are in Florida. The Sunshine State is actually an electorally dark place for 1.7 million citizens because "Florida is the national champion of voter disenfranchisement."[108] The state leads the way in racializing felony disfranchisement as well. "Nearly one-third of those who have lost the right to vote for life in Florida are black, although African Americans make up just 16 percent of the state's population." In fact, "Florida's law disenfranchises 21 percent of its total African American voting-age population."[109]

The push to eliminate blacks' access to the ballot box dates back to the end of the Civil War. As white Southern leaders strained to maintain their power and curtail the potential strength of the newly freed, Florida wrote felony disfranchisement into its new constitution. Then the state, like others in the old Confederacy, deployed the burgeoning criminal justice system to craft laws designed for or enforced only against African Americans. The criminalization of blackness led to labor camps, with the added bonus of the curtailment of blacks' constitutional rights, including voting.[110]

Florida is one of only four states, including Kentucky, Iowa, and Virginia, that "permanently" disfranchises felons.[111] The term "permanent" means that there is no automatic restoration of voting rights. Instead, there is a process to plead for dispensation, which usually requires petitioning all the way up to the governor after a specified waiting period. Republican governor Rick Scott has made that task doubly difficult. The Florida Office of Executive Clemency, which he leads, meets only four times a year and has more than ten thousand applications waiting to be heard. An ex-offender cannot even apply to have his or her voting rights restored until five to seven years after all the sentencing requirements have been met. The process is therefore daunting enough as it is, but Scott has slowed it down considerably.[112] His predecessor, a moderate Republican turned Democrat, "restored rights to 155,315 ex-offenders" over a four-year span. Since 2011, however, Scott has approved only 2,340 cases.[113] As a result, the state is able to gain the extra representatives in Congress that its population—including the prison population—warrants, while, similar to the Constitution's Three-Fifths Compromise, politically silencing millions of citizens who give the state its additional clout and power in Washington, D.C.

The Department of Justice has exacerbated the threat. In June 2017, its Civil Rights Division sent a letter to forty-four states demanding details on "how they keep their voter rolls up-to-date." There was nothing in the letter at all inquiring about what the states were doing, via the NVRA, to expand access to the ballot box. Rather, using language that echoed that of Kris Kobach, Jon Husted, Brian Kemp, J. Christian Adams, and every other vote suppressor in power, Attorney General Jeff Sessions focused on "voter roll maintenance," which has been the key to purging millions of American citizens from the voter rolls.[114] The seeming legality of hiding behind the language of the "integrity of the ballot box" and merely following the mandate of the NVRA for "voter roll maintenance," all the while gutting the Fifteenth Amendment, is why purging voter rolls is really "undercover racism."[115]

The United States is now at the tipping point where the concerted efforts at the state and federal level to purge American citizens and cull and homogenize the electorate is a clear and present danger to democracy.[116]

Four

Rigging the Rules

The numbers didn't add up. They couldn't. The system, by design, was "rigged," "ratfucked," and "sabotaged."[1] Republican political strategist Karl Rove warned, however, that what everyone had witnessed was really only a "half-assed" effort. The "right-wing" was ready to get "serious."[2] The Democrats had done it for years, and now it was the GOP's turn. But it was going to be of a degree that no one had ever seen before. The point was to make the outcome of elections a foregone conclusion; to have the winner decided before the first vote was ever cast. The question, therefore, was never how do we open up this democracy and make it as vibrant, responsive, and inclusive as we can, but rather, how do we maximize the frustration of millions of citizens to minimize their participation in the electoral process? How do we let candidates identify and choose their voters instead of the other way around? And how do we make all this look legitimate?

The subtle but destructive tinkering with the very sinews of the nation's elections has shredded the constitutional logic of "one person, one vote."[3] Whether it was reconfiguring congressional district boundaries, removing polling stations from minority neighborhoods, reducing the dates for early voting, or ratcheting up the standards for those conducting voter registration drives, all those little, virtually unnoticeable-until-it's-too-late bureaucratic tricks had major consequences. They inflated congressional representation to create an impregnable majority that was also impervious to the will of the voters. They led to thousands of people waiting in line for hours to cast a ballot. They shut down the operations of storied organizations that had worked for decades to register citizens to vote. And as a result, they created "a sense that something has gone amiss with American democracy, that there is this effort to rig the rules of the game."[4]

In 2016, the Economist Intelligence Unit, which had evaluated 167 nations on sixty different indicators, reported that the United States had slipped into the category of a "flawed democracy," where, frankly, it had been "teetering for years."[5] Similarly, the Electoral Integrity Project, using a number of benchmarks and measurements, was stunned to find that when it applied those same calculations in the United States as it had in Egypt, Yemen, and Sudan, North Carolina was "no longer considered to be a fully functioning democracy." Indeed, if it were an independent nation, the state would rank somewhere between Iran and Venezuela. The basic problem in North Carolina was that, despite the overt performance of ballots, precincts, and vote tallies, legislators and congressional representatives were actually *selected* for office rather than elected.[6]

The deft art of gerrymandering, "the nastiest form of politics that there is," is key to understanding the decline of democracy in America.[7]

It wasn't supposed to be that way. The Founding Fathers, disgusted with the "rotten borough" system that had crept into British politics, making safe electoral havens for corrupt, unresponsive politicians, were determined to create something better.[8] The U.S. Constitution, therefore, requires that legislative boundaries be drawn every decade after the Census to align and realign congressional representatives with population shifts and changes. From the very beginning, however, chicanery was afoot. Revolutionary hero Patrick Henry recognized that whoever drew those legislative district lines could reward friends with political power and simultaneously banish enemies into the electoral wilderness. He therefore went after his nemesis James Madison to keep him out of Congress. Henry convinced the Virginia legislature to manipulate the boundaries of his enemy's district so that the election eventually pitted Madison against the revered James Monroe for the coveted seat. In 1810, when Massachusetts governor Elbridge Gerry drew a district in the shape of a salamander to corral his rivals and neutralize their influence, the term "gerrymander" became a descriptive and ongoing part of the American political lexicon and life. By the late nineteenth century, gerrymandering was so pervasive and disruptive that President Benjamin Harrison called it nothing but "political robbery."[9]

Two distinct types of gerrymandering emerged on the American landscape. One was racial; the other, partisan. Both were lethal. Racial gerrymandering, especially after the passage of the Voting Rights Act, would lead the courts on a circuitous path of trying to discern how to ensure that minorities had the chance to elect representatives whose interest aligned with theirs while guarding against the "packing" of African Americans or Latinos in one or two isolated districts, which meant those congressional representatives were mere tokens who would have absolutely no influence in the larger halls of power.[10] That is to say, racial gerrymandering is designed to create an all-white power structure virtually impervious to the rights, claims, and public policy needs of minorities.

Partisan gerrymandering, on the other hand, supposedly eschews race altogether for party affiliation and seeks to ensconce in power, regardless of the vote count, a particular party's candidates while eliminating the competition (and constituents) from having any real say in the development and implementation of laws and public policy. As a result, partisan gerrymandering has "designed wombs for [its] team and tombs for the other guys" by controlling the executive, legislative, and judicial branches of government.[11]

Thus, regardless of whether it's all white or all one party, the ultimate goal of gerrymandering makes clear that this is no way to run a democracy.

Beginning in the 1960s, the Civil Rights Movement's call for moral clarity and legal equality finally began to disrupt business as usual. The NAACP, the Student Nonviolent Coordinating Committee, the SCLC, and the Congress on Racial Equality were demanding desegregation of the schools, the end of disfranchisement, an equal justice system, and the full array of African Americans' citizenship rights. Their activism in the courts and the streets had put the all-white, one-party Democratic South under enormous pressure. Arch-segregationists, however, were not going to give up without a fight, which meant, in part, culling those white politicians who were a bit too liberal so that the government could speak with one unified, resounding voice as it crushed the quest for racial equality.

Mississippi exemplified this ideologically inflexible move to the right endemic in one-party systems. In the South, that meant, in the words of Alabama's George Wallace, that no politician who wanted to win an election was going to get "out-niggered."[12] Voters had already jettisoned Mississippi governor J. P. Coleman because, although he was an avowed segregationist, he had the audacity to believe that the lynchers who dragged a black man out of a jail, beat and chained him, then threw him into the river, should actually be prosecuted. "Coleman's insistence on the rule of law, opposition to the Citizens Councils, and call for reason" was heresy bordering on blasphemy. He was pilloried by two-time gubernatorial loser Ross Barnett, whose "sole campaign theme" was white supremacy. Barnett "denounced Democratic opponents in the state house as moderates . . . for inviting Federal agents to investigate the lynching of a black man." He promised, instead, to protect Mississippi's sovereignty and unleash the full force and fury of the state on civil rights agitators.[13] In 1960, Barnett was not going to be a three-time loser. Instead, he became governor.

Just as with the jettisoning of Coleman, Mississippi congressman Frank Smith would also have to go. When he was initially elected in 1951 to District Three, he had flown under the racial radar because his credentials for maintaining the status quo appeared unassailable. His father had been killed by a black man and he was from the Delta, one of the most entrenched, racially stratified, violent, and treacherous places in Mississippi. Smith, therefore, appeared to be "one of them." But he wasn't. He was truly heretical—a Deep South white politician who believed in and supported the cause of the Civil Rights Movement. There was simply no space in Mississippi's Democratic Party for someone like him: a politician "deemed too moderate by whites." The results of the 1960 Census and the mandatory reapportionment, where Mississippi lost one of its congressional seats, provided the mechanism to "rid" the state "of this meddlesome priest." As political scientist K. C. Morrison described it, "The legislators devised a reapportionment plan that obliterated the district by consolidating it with the Second District," which placed Smith in head-to-head competition with "another incumbent, Jamie Whitten." Equally important, the "new district had been gerrymandered in such a way that Whitten," who blasted Smith for supporting desegregation, "was guaranteed a victory."[14]

In the same year that Congressman Smith was gerrymandered out of a job, the U.S. Supreme Court issued a landmark ruling in *Baker v. Carr* that finally began to place restrictions on how state legislatures drew the boundaries for districts. Tennessee had been using a 1901 statute to determine the electoral districts for state and congressional representatives. The law locked in place the political domination of the countryside and ignored that there had been major shifts in population to urban areas like Memphis and Nashville. While the cities were exploding, rural Tennessee was atrophying, but its clout in the legislature was as powerful as ever. By 1960, in fact, "roughly two-thirds of Tennessee's representatives were being elected by one-third of the state's population."[15]

Memphis resident Charles Baker therefore led a group that sued the state, arguing that the 1901 statute was unconstitutional because even at the time of its passage, it "made no apportionment of

Representatives and Senators in accordance with the constitutional formula . . . but instead arbitrarily and capriciously apportioned representatives in the Senate and House without reference . . . to any logical or reasonable formula whatever." And, Baker continued, the court should recognize that legislative redress was impossible. The legislature was created and sustained by this unconstitutional law and, thus, those representatives, who owed their very positions to maintaining the status quo, had no viable reason to legislate themselves out of a job. The court, Baker's suit continued, was the only viable mechanism to correct this wrong, because Tennessee's adherence to a calcified statute had caused a "debasement of their votes" that denied those who lived in the cities the equal protection of the laws guaranteed to them by the Fourteenth Amendment.[16]

The state's counterargument was simple. This was a "political," not a constitutional, matter, and the court simply did not want to breach that threshold and wade knee-deep into a political quagmire. Given years of precedent, that viewpoint seemed to hold. At least initially. The district court concurred with Tennessee even though the judges recognized that "the evil" of stripping citizens in major population centers of the real weight of their vote "is a serious one which should be corrected without further delay." Still, that court held, there was no standard and no rationale for judicial intervention. The U.S. Supreme Court disagreed and ruled that this was a "justiciable" matter, and the courts did have authority to weigh in on this issue. The constitutional rights of American citizens had been impinged upon by state action. In using the 1901 statute to draw congressional districts, Tennessee had diluted the votes of some citizens while privileging others. That dilution violated the Fourteenth Amendment's equal protection clause. In its decision, in pointing to the disparity in the weight of votes, the court, thus, defined "one person, one vote" as the standard benchmark for democracy. This was reaffirmed in two major subsequent decisions in the 1960s.[17]

That seemingly rock-solid constitutional standard, however, was under assault almost immediately. States looked for ways to circumvent the law using the dominance of party affiliation in determining districts in part because partisan gerrymandering seemed to bedevil the court. Indeed, the befuddlement that haunted the court's *Davis v. Bandemer* (1986) decision, which made partisan gerrymandering justiciable but not yet legally measurable, was akin to Justice Potter Stewart's 1964 assertion on hard-core pornography: "I know it when I see it."[18] The uncertainty of exactly what it was and what it wasn't, the difficulty in determining when it existed and when it didn't, only egged on the states as they violated "one person, one vote" as shrewdly, as cleverly, and as ruthlessly as they could.[19]

Maryland Democrats had crafted districts that looked "as if they were drawn by a child experimenting with an Etch-A-Sketch." Georgia Democrats had managed to eliminate Republican strongholds even as the state gained congressional seats. Pennsylvania Republicans, egged on by those in the GOP's national leadership, vowed to make what happened in Georgia "look like a picnic." In Texas, the 1990 Census allowed Democratic representative Martin Frost to spearhead a redistricting process that virtually gerrymandered the Republicans out of power. "For the next decade, Democrats received a substantially larger share of the seats than their share of the popular vote." By 2000, although the Republicans won 50.8 percent of the congressional vote, they only secured thirteen of thirty seats.[20] In 2002, Texas Republicans staged a virtual coup, a "knee-capping" even, by using state troopers, the Department of Justice, and the Federal Aviation Administration to track down and corral enough Democrats, who had fled into New Mexico and Oklahoma, to avoid a special session in the legislature. With a handful of Democratic legislators dragged back to Austin to ensure a quorum, the Republicans redrew the congressional districts to assure GOP dominance well into the future.[21]

What happened in Pennsylvania, however, would finally give the U.S. Supreme Court a chance to rectify the problem. The 2000

Census required the state's congressional delegation to be reduced by two seats. The Republicans, who controlled both houses of the legislature and the governor's office, received marching orders from "prominent national figures in the Republican Party"—House Majority Leader Tom DeLay and Speaker of the House Dennis Hastert—"to adopt a partisan redistricting plan as a punitive measure against Democrats for having enacted pro-Democrat redistricting plans elsewhere."[22] The resulting gerrymandered map was even more effective than what Mississippi had done to Frank Smith in 1962. Before the redistricting, Pennsylvania's congressional delegation was composed of eleven Republicans and ten Democrats. The Census-driven reduction of two seats did not lead to an eleven-to-eight ratio, however, but one that would yield thirteen or fourteen Republicans out of a total of nineteen seats.[23] This gerrymandered map, this reconfiguration of power that gave inordinate power to mid-Pennsylvania and diluted the political voice of those in Philadelphia and Pittsburgh, landed the state before the U.S. Supreme Court in 2003 as Democrats sued.

At that point, the ACLU and the Brennan Center for Justice filed an amicus curia brief that issued a warning as loud and clear—and, unfortunately, as ignored—as Cassandra's right before Agamemnon stepped into the house and met his death. They laid out that partisan gerrymandering was a scourge on democracy—that it silenced the will of the people and exchanged it for computer-assisted, carefully drafted maps that entrenched power in the hands of the few. They hammered on the long history of partisan gerrymandering and how it eroded citizens' confidence in the government, in the meaningfulness of voting, and in democracy. They warned that to continue down this road would entrench a one-party system in power whose only threat would be challengers from the extremist wing. They predicted that the rotten-borough districts would make these so-called representatives absolutely unrepresentative because they would be impervious to the will of voters. We are creating, they insisted, a system in which "elections do not matter." As long as the system puts in power those who received the least number of votes, American democracy is imperiled.[24]

Four of the justices were not persuaded. Led by Justice Antonin Scalia, they asserted in *Vieth v. Jubelirer* (2004) that partisan gerrymandering was beyond the scope of any judicial scrutiny. It was a political issue and not one where the court could insert itself.[25] There was no standard to determine the difference between plain old gerrymandering and partisan gerrymandering, they ruled. And eighteen years of cases after *Bandemer* hadn't brought the Supreme Court any closer to a workable standard. While Scalia and three others threw up their hands in seeming despair about trying to adjudicate something as legally vague as "fairness," one justice, Anthony Kennedy, held out a flicker of hope that although there was no standard in 2004 that could determine partisan gerrymandering, that may not always be the case. Still, his doubt led to a plurality decision that gave a green light to partisan gerrymandering and left the states without even the threat of judicial review.[26]

That decision combined with the increasing diversity of the cities, the mounting whiteness of the suburbs and rural areas, the rightward shift in the Republican Party, the role of dark money and the *Citizens United* decision in elections, and the rise of powerful computer mapping software and analytics created a perfect gerrymandering storm that has not only affected state legislatures but also determined the ideological configuration and policy stances of the U.S. Congress, and, thus, the nation.[27] *Vieth*, therefore, "is not simply a technical decision about whether it is possible to detect political gerrymander . . . Rather, it strikes at the heart of the right to equal representation that the Supreme Court championed in the 1960s."[28] The Supreme Court's abdication—just as in *Citizens United* and *Shelby County v. Holder*—unleashed anti-democracy forces across the American political landscape. The ultimate tipping point was after the 2010 midterm elections, when the GOP swept legislative and gubernatorial elections and used that victory to "declare war on democracy."[29]

Control of the legislature and the governor's office in twenty-six states, especially after the completion of the 2010 Census, gave the GOP the authority to draw congressional district boundaries at will. Control of the statehouse also provided the opportunity to craft a series of voter suppression laws and jigger the mechanisms determining how, where, when, and for whom citizens in their state could vote.

The key step was to unleash "brute force, computer-driven gerrymandering" to render democracy obsolete.[30] Some Republicans, like those in North Carolina, brought in their top mapmaker, Tom Hofeller, who provided "the most cravenly political results . . . with calculating prudence." His "exceptionally smart" maps transformed a once 7–6 Democratic congressional majority into a "10–3 GOP stronghold." Similarly, Michigan, Pennsylvania, Texas (which didn't consult with Hofeller), Wisconsin, and other states began to have districts that looked like contorted yoga positions or Rorschach tests: the North Carolina Gimpy Leg, the Texas Glock, the Georgia Flat-Cat Road Kill that became the Squirrel Not Yet Hit by a Car, and the Texas 27th Bottle Opener. Hofeller, using the most powerful mapping software linked to demographic data and trends, was able to wring every last available GOP district out of a state and do so in a way that provided safe districts where there could never be a viable challenge from a Democratic candidate. Indeed, after the high-powered gerrymandering, "more Americans lived in areas with uncontested elections than . . . before." And when there is a competition, it usually isn't much. Only 4.9 percent live in districts where the margin of difference between the winner and loser was 5 percent or less.[31]

Meanwhile, the GOP "pack[ed] the rival party's voters tightly into far fewer districts," creating a power "asymmetry."[32] Because of the population disparity between the numerous Republican districts, which represent suburbs and rural areas, and the handful of Democratic districts that are drawn around urban areas, "there is a 20% Republican advantage when both parties have equal votes, and the Democrats would in some cases need to win almost 60% of the vote to have a fifty-fifty chance of having a majority of the state's delegation to the House of Representatives."[33] This deliberate feature in the electoral system has resulted in the muting or erasure of the political concerns of those who live and vote in the most populous areas. Senators John McCain and Sheldon Whitehouse recognized this harsh reality for what it is: "wasted votes and silenced voices."[34]

For example, in 2017, it was obvious that from the Affordable Care Act, to the Deferred Action for Childhood Arrivals (DACA), to the Children's Health Insurance Program (CHIP), the majority of the American people have been on one side of the issue and Republicans in Congress on the other; and the Republicans have won.[35] One of the most striking examples of this jarring phenomenon was the passage of the 2017 tax bill (H.R. 1). In many ways, its features are absolutely injurious to middle- and working-class Americans.[36] Hence, a majority of the people were strongly opposed to the bill. A Gallup poll found that while 70 percent of those identifying as Republicans supported the measure, a mere 7 percent of Democrats and 25 percent of Independents supported the bill. Most important, only 29 percent overall approved of H.R. 1.[37] The media continued to publish one stark poll after the next, astonished that the GOP leadership, as well as the rank and file, could and would ignore the clamor and outrage coming from the public.[38] But with wealthy donors threatening to cut off campaign contributions unless the tax bill passed and transferred the lion's share of the $1.5 trillion in resources to them, the GOP pressed forward.[39]

This was relatively easy to do because many Republicans were convinced that their carefully drawn districts provided ample protection from ballot box anger and retribution. Their districts had already proved to be "impregnable garrisons from which they [could] maintain political power while avoiding demographic realities."[40] As the Brennan Center for Justice noted, "Citizens can't just vote the gerrymandering party out of office, because the maps are too heavily skewed. In fact, that's the whole point of extreme partisan gerrymanders; to insulate the legislative majority from the will of the voters."[41] In the 2016 election, for example, Democrats running for seats in the House of Representatives received 1.4 million more votes than their opponents, but Republicans secured thirty-three more seats.[42] And those meticulously crafted districts provided another important benefit as well: they inflated the number of Republican districts and provided an additional sixteen to twenty-six representatives in Congress, which was more than enough to pass the extremely unpopular tax bill.[43]

Despite the judicial distinction between the partisan gerrymandering that Scalia asserted was beyond the pale of the Supreme Court's authority and racial gerrymandering that requires the highest level of judicial review, known as strict scrutiny, partisan gerrymandering is also about race. As U.S. district judges Xavier Rodriguez and Orlando Garcia observed, this seemingly colorblind method of drawing districts is, instead, all about a "party's willingness to use race for partisan advantage."[44] The demographic composition of the parties almost dictates it. The Pew Research Center notes that in 2016, while 86 percent of Republican voters were white, those who were African American had stayed at 2 percent since 1992. Meanwhile, Democratic voters were much more diverse: 57 percent were white, 21 percent were black, 12 percent were Hispanic, 3 percent were Asian, and 5 percent described themselves as mixed race or their race as "other."[45] The racial demographics of the parties, therefore, carry over into the ways that the district lines are constructed. In Georgia, when two Republican incumbents barely won reelection in 2016 because their platforms did not resonate with the growing African American population in the Atlanta suburbs, the GOP-controlled legislature simply redrew their districts, moving the black neighborhoods over to a Democrat and extracting her white constituents to Republican districts.[46]

In fact, just as Mississippi in the 1960s exemplified the contortions a state was willing to undertake to politically silence its sizable minority population, Texas is the poster child for trying to accomplish something similar in the twenty-first century. The 2010 Census indicated that Texas's population had grown significantly. As a result of 4.3 million new residents, four additional seats were added to the state's congressional delegation. That growth, however, was the direct result of the Hispanic and African American population increasing by 42 and 22 percent, respectively. "In other words, without the minority growth, Texas—now officially a majority-minority state—would not have received a single new district." The GOP-dominated legislature, nevertheless, then set out to produce "lavishly brazen maps" where "white Republicans were awarded three of the four new seats that resulted from Democratic-leaning minority population growth."[47] The racial gerrymandering in Texas is so institutionalized that, frankly, it has the aura of the apartheid era's "white minority rule." In the Lone Star State, whites are 45 percent of the state's population but control 70 percent of the congressional districts. This disparity is even more obvious in the Dallas–Fort Worth area, where whites are only 20 percent of the population but have 80 percent of the congressional seats.[48] As an editorial in the *Dallas Morning News* explained, "Current voting maps erode minority voters' right to choose who they want to represent them—and threaten our democracy more broadly."[49] The state has, therefore, faced a number of lawsuits and has had to go back and redraw, redraw, and redraw, again.[50]

Yet it is Wisconsin, one of the most segregated states in the nation, that has become the major legal battlefield over the issue of partisan gerrymandering.[51] An epic struggle is playing out in the U.S. Supreme Court in the *Gill v. Whitford* case, on which, as former attorney general Eric Holder noted, the justices "will have a chance to rein in an aggressive new breed of data-driven gerrymandering that divides communities and diminishes the voice of many Americans."[52]

After gaining control of the Wisconsin legislature in the 2010 election, the GOP set out to "create a map for state assembly elections that would guarantee them large legislative majorities even with a minority of the statewide vote." A handful of Republican legislators and aides virtually sequestered themselves in a hotel room working diligently over the course of four months to "engineer maps with the aid of sophisticated" social science statistical techniques. During this process, the mapmakers excluded all Democrats from participation and "even rank-and-file Republicans were largely left in the dark, shown only information relating to their specific districts and only after signing nondisclosure agreements."[53] As the mapmakers drafted one map after the next, each tweak only tightened the noose on Democratic voters. There would be no scenario, regardless of the votes, in which the Republicans would not come out dominating the state legislature.[54] The lines they had drawn to carve up Wisconsin had created a "perpetual-motion entrenchment machine" in which "Democrats could not regain control even if they won all swing districts."[55]

When put to the test, the redistricting exceeded the Wisconsin GOP's expectations. In the 2012 election, although Obama carried the state by seven points and Democrats received more than 50 percent of the vote, they garnered only 39 percent of the seats in the general assembly.[56] And each subsequent election yielded an increasing number of Republican seats that was decidedly disproportionate to the votes GOP candidates received.[57]

The *Vieth* decision seemed to indicate that there was nothing—no force, no authority—that could stop this. But a retired law professor, Bill Whitford, had been meeting with a group in a Madison tea shop regularly, talking politics and believing that extreme partisan gerrymandering was dangerous to democracy. Once they learned that various teams of social scientists had been working on ways to actually measure extreme partisan gerrymandering, the small opening that Justice Kennedy had left in *Vieth* provided the window that

Whitford, a dozen Democratic voters, and their team of lawyers needed. They filed suit.[58]

Wisconsin's defense was simple. The state claimed that it did nothing wrong. It was just politics, and *Vieth* made clear that there was no role for the court in politics. Moreover, if Democrats had fewer districts, it was only because their voters tend to be concentrated in the cities. The districts were drawn based on political geography, the state contended, nothing more. Whitford's lawyers, however, countered that American citizens' right to equal protection under the law had taken a beating because of the extreme partisan gerrymandering that the state executed. The trail of inequality was easily discernible, from the sixty out of ninety-nine seats the GOP won in 2012 to the sixty-three out of ninety-nine in 2014, with nothing approaching that kind of dominance at the ballot box. Democratic voters had been meticulously, ruthlessly, and unconstitutionally undercut and silenced.[59] And while the Supreme Court had earlier ruled that no one could expect proportional representation (e.g., that 48 percent of the population should receive 48 percent of the representatives), what was happening in Wisconsin was not about proportional representation; it was about representation, period.[60] Then, Whitford's team addressed Kennedy's concern and provided not only a way to measure partisan gerrymandering to determine whether it was extreme but also laid out the standards that, taken in conjunction with the measurement, could identify the most egregious cases and separate them from traditional redistricting, so that the courts would not be inundated with frivolous lawsuits.

First, of course, came the problem of how to even measure. What separates a Wisconsin from, say, an Illinois? Or, for that matter, Michigan and Pennsylvania from California or New York? Law professor Nicholas Stephanopoulos and political scientist Eric McGhee had developed a mathematical formula to assess districting maps.[61] They had looked at geography to see whether the concentration of likely Democratic voters in the cities accounted for the vast seat differential, as Wisconsin had contended. But as they ran their equations and various models, it was apparent that the seats flipped too rapidly from Democratic to Republican for geography to be the driving force. The key, instead, were the maps crafted in that locked room and the "efficiency gap" they created. Wasted votes are the sine qua non in this equation—whether they are in districts that are so uncompetitive that the winners garnered 94 percent of the vote, as has happened in several Wisconsin elections, or in other districts where voting for a candidate who has absolutely no chance of winning is a vote that has gone for absolute naught. A "gerry-mander," the research team explained, "is simply a district plan that results in one party wasting many more votes than its adversary." Losers are to be expected, of course. It is the structure determining the full extent of that loss that is under scrutiny. Stephanopoulos and McGhee have determined that "an efficiency gap larger than 7% may show that one party holds an unconstitutional 'systemic advantage' over the other."[62] For example, between the 1970s and 1990s, Republicans averaged a 1.5 percent efficiency gap in their favor. Yet, "in the three elections since 2010, that figure rose to 12.3%."[63] In other words, when a plurality of the votes garners only 39 percent of the seats in the state assembly, those wasted votes are like the canary in the mine signaling that something toxic may be happening down in the shaft.

The efficiency gap is, however, only one component.[64] Other tests must be used in conjunction with it to verify those findings. First, is there a *durable partisan effect*, such as Wisconsin undergoing three elections in which the Republicans' vote gains were not overwhelming but their share of the number of seats in the General Assembly continued to grow. The next part of the standard is *intent* to seek a partisan edge. When Wisconsin's GOP took a small cabal to an off-site room, worked away at the maps for four months, excluded every Democrat from the process, and required nondisclosure agreements from their Republican colleagues before they could be shown their own districts, intent had been more than established. To be clear, unitary party control of the government apparatus—both houses of the legislature and the governor's office—is usually an essential condition of intent. Finally, if the *districts do not meet previous constitutional standards*, such as being compact, contiguous, and within established political subdivisions, but instead begin to take on the shape of a bug splattered against a windshield or are joined together only during low tide, something could be awry.[65] None of these alone will suffice, but combined they spell out democracy's SOS.

The district court weighed the evidence, assessed the arguments, evaluated the efficiency gap's reliability and validity, and parsed through the other standards and how they strengthened the judiciary's ability to determine whether partisan gerrymandering was in operation. Then the court, in a 2–1 decision, found that Wisconsin had violated American citizens' Fourteenth Amendment rights. With that, partisan gerrymandering was back in the judicial crosshairs. Kennedy's opening in *Vieth* appeared to be just what democracy needed.

Wisconsin, of course, appealed, and the arguments before the U.S. Supreme Court set off judicial fireworks. The ideological fissures within the court were on full display. Neil Gorsuch, who owed his very seat to the rules Senate Majority Leader Mitch McConnell (R-KY) bent, rigged, and contorted, showed his contempt for the efficiency gap's methodology. He mocked the "standard" as being no more than a "touch" of this and a "touch" of that, "a pinch of this, a pinch of that," as if it were his "steak rub" and "not a real set of criteria." He questioned whether the court had any business meddling in a state's political affairs. There seemed, to him, no constitutional reason for this case to exist.[66]

As Gorsuch harangued Whitford's attorney on this point, Justice Ruth Bader Ginsburg had had just about enough and asked a basic question that any first-year law student would know the answer to: What is the basis for "one person, one vote"? As Whitford's lawyer, Paul M. Smith, recited the Supreme Court's decisions in *Baker v. Carr, Reynolds v. Sims*, et al., Ginsburg's pointed query sent a powerful signal. Later she cut to the core of the issue: "The precious right to vote" was "what's really behind all of this . . . if you can stack a legislature in this way, what incentive is there for a voter to exercise his vote? . . . What becomes of the precious right to vote?"[67]

That did not appear to be the issue for Chief Justice John Roberts, of *Citizens United* and *Shelby County v. Holder* fame. He derided the "efficiency gap" as "gobbledygook" and "a bunch of baloney." Roberts insisted that what Whitford and the Democrats wanted was "proportional representation, which has never been accepted as a political principle in the history of this country." Smith countered quickly and brilliantly that this was about symmetry. If in one election, party A received 54 percent of the vote and received 58 percent of the seats, then the same should hold true when party B wins 54 percent of the vote. "That's symmetry." But, Smith continued, what Wisconsin's GOP did was to spend "those four months in that locked room doing two things, trying to maximize the amount of bias and eliminating . . . competitive districts." Where there had once been twenty of those types of districts, the Republicans had reduced that number down to ten and "tinkered with it and tinkered with it to make sure that even of that 10, they thought they could get at least seven. They ended up getting eight and then eventually all 10."[68]

Justice Stephen Breyer proffered an approach to see if there was some "way of reducing" "all of that social science stuff and the computer stuff . . . to something manageable." Something that the courts could use. In four steps he laid it out. First, "was there one-party control of the redistricting"? Second, "is there partisan asymmetry? In other words, does the map treat the political parties differently? . . . Good evidence of that," Breyer added, "is a party that got 48 percent of the vote got a majority of the legislature." Third, "is there going to be persistent asymmetry over a range of votes?" Wisconsin's 2012, 2014, and 2016 elections "shows you that," he said. And fourth, was there any "justification," any "motive," for crafting a districting map that is one of "the worst in the country?" As Breyer admired his handiwork, he concluded, "Now, I suspect that that's manageable."[69]

Kennedy began to ask deep questions about the efficiency gap and how it could reliably identify extreme partisan gerrymandering. Wisconsin's attorney tried to counter that some formula based on hypothetical social science models would only drag election decisions out of the political realm where they rightfully belonged and place that decision-making in the hands of the federal courts.[70]

At that point, Justice Elena Kagan cut him off. There was nothing "hypothetical, airy-fairy, we guess, and then we guess again" happening in this case, she said. "This is pretty scientific by this point."[71]

Justice Sonia Sotomayor then picked up from there. When the GOP used social science methods to devise maps, the group in the locked hotel room ran enough models to know that the first one would not yield the results they wanted. "Your map drawer . . . started out with the Court plan, they created three or four different maps, they weren't partisan enough. They created three or four more maps, they weren't partisan enough. And they finally got to the final map, after maybe 10 different tries of making it more partisan, and they achieved a map that was the most partisan . . . And it worked. It worked better than they even expected." "So," she asked, "if it's the most extreme map they could make, why isn't that enough to prove partisan asymmetry and unconstitutional gerrymandering?"[72]

As Wisconsin's attorney tried to answer but fumbled badly, Sotomayor circled around again. They "kept going back to fix the map to make it more gerrymandered," she noted. "That's undisputed. People involved in the process had traditional maps that complied with traditional criteria and then went back and threw out those maps and created more—some that were more partisan . . . So why didn't they take one of the earlier maps?"[73]

The answer, the confession, in fact, explained everything. "Because there was no constitutional requirement that they do so."[74]

Through all the oral arguments, it became clear. The conservatives on the bench had dug in behind Scalia's claim in *Vieth* that partisan gerrymandering was not justiciable. And that it would sully the court to insert itself in the political process. Meanwhile, the liberals on the bench were greatly concerned about how absolute power had corrupted the democratic process absolutely. With the GOP takeover, Ginsburg had cut to the core of the issue: What happened to "the precious right to vote"? Sotomayor was just as concerned: "It's okay to stack the decks so . . . even though it [one party] gets a minority of votes . . . [it] can get the majority of seats?" She was, therefore, compelled to ask, "Could you tell me what the value is to democracy from political gerrymandering? How—how does that help our system of government?"[75]

In fact, gerrymandering's pernicious, corrosive effects on democracy and our system of government are well understood and documented. Karl Rove brazenly explained, "Control redistricting . . . and you could control Congress."[76] Indeed, a Brennan Center report noted that gerrymandering in a handful of swing states—Michigan, North Carolina, Pennsylvania, Florida, Ohio, Virginia, and Texas—could "completely warp the composition of Congress." The redistricting maps "are the product of a flawed, undemocratic process which usurps the basic power of voters to choose their representation."[77]

Gerrymandering has a horrific effect on voter behavior. Those in competitive districts are more likely to vote; those in safe, uncompetitive districts stay home more often on Election Day. Just as Ginsburg surmised, there appears to be no "incentive to vote." Moreover, that "redistricting dampens turnout in the subsequent election cycle, especially among black registrants." The import for what this means to Democratic candidates is profound. "The drop in overall turnout among [African Americans] attributed to redistricting can produce sizable electoral effects."[78] As expected, black voter turnout declined in every gerrymandered swing state during the 2016 election.[79]

The damage to democracy is exacerbated by another feature of partisan gerrymandering: there are deliberately fewer competitive districts. Not surprisingly, then, in the 2016 election, 97 percent of incumbents in the U.S. House of Representatives won reelection.[80] In California, before the state adopted the process for a nonpartisan commission to draw district lines, former governor Arnold Schwarzenegger noted that " 'the former Soviet Politburo had more turnover' than pre-reform California, which between 2002 and 2010 held 265 congressional races, of which just one saw a seat change its party control."[81]

The lack of accountability to the public, therefore, creates another vicious dynamic. On one hand, there's the calcification inherent in one-party rule. On the other, there's the internal party catalyst that pushes the agenda further and further to the extreme in order for challengers to differentiate themselves from what is now orthodoxy. Alabama governor George Wallace had called it being "out-niggered." It creates a hardening in legislative positions that requires those in power to refuse to compromise or seek solutions across the political aisle for fear of running into a modern-day Ross Barnett, where even the most commonsensical stance (e.g., that lynchers should be brought to justice) becomes inflammatory and politically untenable.

Virginian and former House majority leader Eric Cantor, who made his mark as a "very conservative" Tea Party darling who challenged President Obama at every turn, learned this lesson the hard way. In 2014, he was "out-niggered" on the issue of immigration. His hard-core stances turned out to be not hard-core enough in a gerrymandered district where there was no leavening, no diversity, only "new and very conservative voters who had been moved in to strengthen him in the general election." Instead, he was "felled in a primary for being insufficiently faithful to the ideas of the right."[82]

Unfortunately, the assault on democracy is not only about the way congressional and legislative district lines are drawn. The undermining of democracy is also achieved in the way long, seemingly interminable lines at the voting booth have been artificially created. We've seen the results: A five-hour wait in Maricopa County, Arizona.[83] A line with four thousand people stretching for one quarter mile in Cincinnati.[84] Lines in Miami-Dade County, Florida, bending beyond the photographer's lens and melding into the horizon.[85]

Those lines, and so many others just like them, take their toll. Studies are clear that long lines "discourage voting, lower confidence" that a ballot will actually be counted, "and impose economic costs on voters."[86] Moreover, just as voting is "habit-forming," not voting is as well. Once discouraged, it becomes a difficult pattern to break.[87]

As endemic as long lines have become, however, they are not a fixture in most communities. The conditions that bring about five-hour wait times, or thousands standing in line, or only forty people able to get through and cast their ballots after three hours, are concentrated overwhelmingly in minority precincts.[88] In short, this is a burden that is disproportionately borne in order to exercise that fundamental right to vote. In 2012, on average, blacks had to wait in line twice as long as whites. In the "10 Florida precincts with the longest delays . . . almost 70 percent of voters were Latino or black." Nationwide, in the 2012 election, whites who lived in white neighborhoods had the shortest wait times of all citizens—just seven minutes.[89]

Behind the lines, beneath the sometimes hours of waiting, is a deliberate and cruel hoax played on millions of citizens. Minority neighborhoods, despite their population density, have been allocated significantly fewer resources by election officials.[90] There are fewer poll workers. Fewer operable machines. And fewer opportunities to vote, as Republican legislatures, such as those in Ohio, Indiana, Florida, and North Carolina, have slashed the days and times available for early voting.[91] Early voting had, in previous elections, been one of the key ways to take the economic burden off a generally working-class population that had been forced to choose between voting on Tuesday and missing hours at the job, or going to work and not participating in electing the officials and policies that affect one's life. Latinos, for example, are the least likely racial or ethnic group to vote in person on Election Day.[92] In 2008, before Florida reduced early voting, African Americans were 13 percent of the electorate but more than 35 percent of those who voted before Election Day.[93] The conscious decision of election officials to shortchange Latino and black neighborhoods' access to the polls, to place older, barely working, and, in the case of Detroit in 2016, nonworking machines at their precincts wreaks havoc on democracy.[94]

In Ohio, for example, the secretary of state allocates only one polling station per county for early voting. On the surface, that gives the aura of fairness and equity. But all counties are not equal. Pickaway County has fewer than sixty thousand residents total.[95] Hamilton County, where Cincinnati is located, however, has a population of more than eight hundred thousand.[96] Yet despite this seismic disparity, each had only one early voting polling place available. There were, obviously, no lines in Pickaway County, home to Circleville. Hamilton County, however, in trying to squeeze a population of that magnitude through only one facility, had a line that stretched a quarter mile.

This electoral resource distribution policy uses geography as a proxy for race and puts a distinct burden on voters who live in major urban areas in the state—Cleveland, Columbus, Cincinnati, Dayton, etc.—and, therefore, disadvantages blacks. Whereas Pickaway County, for example, has only 1,881 African Americans, Franklin County, where Columbus is located, has more than 274,000 African

American residents.[97] The allocation of one early voting spot, especially for a population whose median income is a little more than thirty-one thousand dollars (a full twenty thousand dollars below the state median), is designed to corrosively and subtly lower black voter turnout.[98] When pressed to account for a policy that could have this kind of deleterious impact, the chairman of the Franklin County Republican Party explained, "I guess I really actually feel we shouldn't contort the voting process to accommodate the urban— read African American—voter turnout machine."[99]

Other ploys to strip election resources from minority communities abound. By the time the 2016 election was held, for example, there were 868 fewer polling places available in previous VRA preclearance counties.[100] Scholars have found that "moving a polling place can affect"—and not for the better—"the decision to vote."[101] North Carolina, in a "subtler maneuver" than the gerrymandering and voter ID laws that landed the state in court, "moved the location of almost one-third of the state's early voting sites," which then "significantly increased the distance African Americans have to travel to vote early, while leaving white voters largely unaffected." This was deliberate. An earlier study indicated that for every one-tenth of a mile increase to a polling place, voting by registered black voters declines by 0.5 percent. The ratio in that study suggests that "North Carolina's changes might have kept nearly 19,000 black voters from the polls."[102] In Macon, Georgia, election officials voted to move the new polling station for the African American precinct to the sheriff's office. In Sparta, Georgia, a poll consolidation left the one assigned to the majority black neighborhood seventeen miles away. Only heightened vigilance and major protests in both cases stopped those moves.[103] In Florida and Texas, the legislatures changed the laws to make voter registration drives or assistance "a risky business" by requiring months of courses or sworn oaths under the penalty of felony criminal prosecution, short and unreasonable turnaround times to submit registration cards to election authorities, and unnatural county barriers on registration activities that ignored the growth of multicounty metropolises. The result in Florida was that the League of Women Voters, which had led voter registration drives for seven decades, ceased operations, pulled out of the state, and sued. In Texas, voter registration is so onerous, criminalized even, that there are more unregistered voters there than the total population of twenty states.[104] Texas and Georgia have also interpreted laws about "assisting" at the polls to ensnare a young man helping his Bengali-speaking mother translate a ballot, and an African American second-generation civil rights warrior in southern Georgia, who, when asked, simply showed a young woman how to use the voting machine. Both the son and the black doyenne then faced felony charges, which, by design, sent a strong warning signal to both their communities.[105]

In short, rigging the rules to suppress or dilute the vote of millions of citizens to affect the outcome of an election has come almost naturally to many of these politicians and public officials. Tweaking a line here or creating a longer line there has displayed the high-tech wizardry of "blunt-force computer-driven" gerrymandering and the low-tech, traditional means of starving minority communities of resources necessary to participate fully in American democracy.

Yet, none of this has gone unchallenged. The numerous lawsuits, the protests, the op-eds, the investigative journalists digging into the arcane minutiae of electoral law and legislative intent, all indicate that the light cannot be snuffed out. As one woman who took on Georgia's attempt to move the polling place for the black community to the sheriff's office noted, "When voter suppression still exists and when we have to stand up for what we believe in and what is right, we will do it."[106]

Five

The Resistance

While Nina Simone sang "Mississippi Goddam," Alabama showed how it's really done.[1] The images are seared in our national memory. A firebombed Greyhound bus, listing to one side near Anniston, its tires shredded, doors jammed shut, and Molotov cocktails sending terror, screams, and thick black smoke pouring out its windows. Freedom Riders gingerly picking broken teeth out of their blood-soaked mouths. Firehoses in Birmingham slamming black bodies against brick walls and hurling nonviolent protesters, often children, down the street. Snarling, fangs-bared German shepherds, straining to rip open the flesh of unarmed black people with the full encouragement of law enforcement. Pint-size stretchers emerging from the bombed-out hell of a church with tiny white sheets draped over the lifeless bodies of four little girls. State police and horseback-mounted sheriff's deputies trampling, teargassing, and whipping men, women, and children on Selma's Edmund Pettus Bridge.

The consequences of that brutality, of that way of governing, have permeated the state long beyond the Civil Rights Movement and well into the twenty-first century.[2] Although its form of oppression is now much subtler, it is equally devastating. Alabama ranks dead last in the nation in public health.[3] The United Nations Special Rapporteur on Extreme Poverty found extensive pools of human fecal matter in the woods behind homes because there is no waste-disposal infrastructure for large swaths of the state's Black Belt counties and, equally important, the government refuses to build any. State officials, however, are fully aware of the need. According to the Alabama Department of Public Health, "The number of households in Lowndes County with inadequate or no septic systems range from 40 to 90 per cent; . . . 50 per cent of the conventional, onsite septic systems are currently failing or are expected to fail in the future." As a result, fecal-contaminated water has made *E. coli* and hookworm, indicative of extreme systemic poverty, prevalent throughout the Black Belt counties.[4] Not surprisingly, the state is next to last in infant health. In fact, the "death rate for African American infants is more than two times higher than the rate for white infants, a stubborn trend that has persisted for the last several years."[5] Alabama is also ranked forty-seventh in education, forty-fifth in low poverty rate, forty-sixth in low unemployment rate, and forty-second in quality of government.[6]

This is the toxic bouillabaisse that gave rise to Judge Roy Moore as the Republican candidate for the U.S. Senate in a 2017 special election. His Bible-thumping diatribes embodied the sense of righteous, God-ordained racism that had already doomed the state to the bottom tier. His résumé was a testament to homegrown rebel canon masquerading as homespun patriotic symbolism. Moore had been a reckless MP in Vietnam whose violations of the rules and insistence on "strutting around" so that his rank and honor were recognized consistently put American soldiers in danger. Similarly, he was a mediocre law student whose pugnaciousness could not mask that he was absolutely "immune to logic and reason."[7] When he was a thirtysomething assistant district attorney, young women, many in their teens and one as young as fourteen years old, accused him of stalking and, in the case of the minor, committing sexual assault.[8] He was a "dangerous" chief justice who had to be removed twice from the Alabama Supreme Court because he openly and proudly flouted and defied the U.S. Constitution.[9] He publicly questioned whether women were qualified to hold elected office.[10] He was a gay-bashing, Islam-hating, "conservative extremist" who thought the last time America was truly great was during slavery.[11] Yet, after the 2017 Republican primary, this was the man poised to be the next U.S. senator from Alabama.

Despite his obvious shortcomings (although the sexual assault allegations came later in the campaign), the idea of Senator Roy Moore wasn't so farfetched. Not only had Republicans won every U.S. Senate election in Alabama over the past twenty-five years, but since the advent of *Shelby County v. Holder*, the state had amassed a powerful array of voter suppression techniques and laws targeted at the one constituency that could possibly give Doug Jones, Moore's Democratic opponent, something beyond a "snowball's chance in hell" and a "sliver of hope" of winning.[12]

Once Alabama was freed from the oversight of the VRA and preclearance, every twist and turn of the assault on voting rights was mobilized to go after black and poor folk, which the state had in abundance. A recent study showed that *all* Alabama's Black Belt counties have "a poverty rate higher than 25 percent." Moreover, *only* the Black Belt counties have that distinction. And, at the sites of historic voting rights battles—Dallas County, Lowndes County, and Perry County—the poverty rate ranged from 34.6 percent to 40 percent.[13] The state, therefore, looked at its citizens and didn't see, as Kristina Scott, executive director of the nonprofit organization Alabama Possible, stated, that "poverty is . . . a complex series of barriers that hardworking people have to overcome every day."[14] Instead, Alabama created an additional series of hurdles to get to the ballot box that increased the intensity of that struggle.

Each redrawn boundary, each closed polling place, each understaffed, barely equipped polling station, each long line, and each ID requirement all negatively affected voter turnout. The first test was the 2014 midterm election. As NAACP Legal Defense Fund president Sherrilyn Ifill noted, "Alabama voter turnout reached a shameful nadir, plummeting to the lowest it had been in decades."[15] In counties with sizable minority populations, in fact, Alabama achieved what no other state had: a full 5 percent decline in voter turnout—the most precipitous drop in the nation.[16]

The road to this "shameful nadir" began even before *Shelby County v. Holder.* In 2011, the Alabama legislature rushed through a strict voter ID law that eliminated utility bills, bank statements, and other documents as viable proof of residency and instead required government-issued photo IDs to cast a ballot. The law was so intentionally racist, though, that the state didn't even bother to send it up to the DOJ for preclearance. It's easy to see why. Republican lawmakers had actually recorded themselves discussing how to "depress the turnout of black voters—whom they called 'aborigines' and 'illiterates' who would ride 'H.U.D.-financed buses' to the polls."[17] That bill, not surprisingly, lay dormant for years. But a day after the Supreme Court came down with its decision gutting the Voting Rights Act, Alabama implemented this law—one that never could have passed the VRA's litmus test.[18]

As with the 1890 Mississippi Plan, though, this voter ID law had an overtly discriminatory intent, while its implementation was full of subterfuge. For example, with the city of Birmingham alone struggling under the weight of a 30.9 percent poverty rate, with the state capitol, Montgomery, hovering just above a 24 percent poverty rate, and with 32 percent of Latinos and 30.3 percent of African Americans in the state living below the poverty line (compared with 13.7 percent of whites), not surprisingly tens of thousands of Alabamians received federal assistance for housing, including public housing.[19] In fact, African Americans made up 71 percent of "the State's federal public housing residents."[20] And yet the key government-issued photo identification for those who lived in public housing was not on the "approved" list for voter IDs.[21]

That seemed like an easy fix. But as Deuel Ross, an attorney with the NAACP LDF, explained, it wasn't so easy: "Alabama has rejected even modest suggestions to lessen the photo ID law's impact . . . Last year, for example, Alabama officials ruled that people could not vote

using the photo IDs issued to them by public housing authorities."
In response, Secretary of State John Merrill did not address that issue
head-on but used the cloak of protecting the ballot box from fraud
to justify a law with both discriminatory intent and impact. This was
his attempt to plant the state's flag in something less toxic than overt
racism. "The photo ID requirement was designed to preserve the
credibility and the integrity of the electoral process," he said. "I voted
for and was a co-sponsor of House Bill 19 that became Act Number
2011-673 in 2011, and I will defend the rights and freedoms of all
our eligible citizens to register to vote, obtain a qualified photo voter
ID, and participate in the electoral process!"[22]

Those qualified voter IDs could be obtained at the Department
of Motor Vehicles, but then Governor Robert Bentley closed the DMV
locations in the six counties where African Americans made up more
than 70 percent of the population, and he shuttered the DMVs in
another eleven counties where blacks made up more than half of the
residents.[23] The impact was devastating. A Brennan Center report,
in fact, showed that "almost a third of Alabama's voting-age population lived more than 10 miles away from the nearest license-issuing
office that was open more than two days per week."[24]

The state tried to pretend that its alternate-ID mobile unit would
supplant the brick-and-mortar sites, but, by design, it didn't even
come close. Alabama issued only 5,070 voter cards out of the quarter
of a million its own calculations estimated were actually needed, and
the link on the secretary of state's website "directing voters to places
where they could get a free ID led to a blank page." Kathleen Unger,
the president and CEO of VoteRiders, which assists citizens in getting
the ID they need to vote, saw this as a typical move. "The lack of
clear information, frankly, . . . the lack of correct information or
internally consistent information online . . . It's a big problem . . .
Sadly," Unger concluded, "I am not surprised."[25]

Despite the closing of the DMVs in the Black Belt counties, the
demonstrated inadequacy of the mobile units, and the lack of

information on the secretary of state's website, Alabama, nonetheless, claimed that its online registration would solve the problem. However, 56 percent of those living in Alabama's rural counties, including the Black Belt, do not have access to the internet. Neither do 20 percent of those in urban areas.[26]

Another possibility was to physically travel to another county to get a driver's license, but "13.8 percent of Black households in Alabama as compared to 4 percent of white households . . . have no access to a vehicle." For those without a car, public transportation was the only viable means to get the card required to vote. But Alabama "invests no state money in public transportation" and, therefore, is ranked forty-eighth in the nation in "intercity transit access" for 844,000 rural residents.[27]

There was still, supposedly, one more option: the local courthouse. Secretary of State Merrill, in fact, praised this opportunity where "anybody can go any day of the week . . . and apply for a voter ID."[28] Like everything else the state touted as an option, though, there were major structural flaws with this choice as well. First, as Merrill had to admit, one could apply "*as long as the courthouse is open*," but what he didn't say was that since "2013, many Alabama court-houses have been operating on reduced hours, due to budget cuts."[29] The second unspoken and significant flaw was to treat the local courthouse—a central component of a notorious criminal justice system—as a viable, race-neutral space to obtain a voter ID card. This despite the fact that the name Scottsboro haunts the halls of justice, where "Yellow Mama," the electric chair, sent flames shooting out of the head of one of the condemned and took nineteen minutes to burn to death another inmate, where more than half of those on death row in the state are African American, and where the prison population is 54 percent black although African Americans are only 26 percent of the population.[30]

John Merrill and other Republican lawmakers claimed that they simply did not see the problem. The issue of access to the ballot box had nothing to do with Alabama rejecting government-issued public housing ID, closing the DMVs in the Black Belt counties, curtailing the hours at the courthouses, placing broken links and misleading and inconsistent information on the state's website, offering the mirage of online registration for people without even the basic fiber optics (much less computers) in their rural areas, suggesting that Alabamians could ride nonexistent public transportation to other counties, or touting a mobile voter-ID-card unit that provided only 2 percent of the cards needed. The problem, John Merrill said, was the people. "If you're too sorry or lazy to get up off of your rear and to go register to vote, or to register electronically, and then to go vote, then you don't deserve that privilege," he said, as he twisted not only state-constructed barriers into personal failings but also the Fifteenth Amendment into a "privilege" and not a right. "As long as I'm secretary of state of Alabama," he boasted, "you're going to have to show some initiative to become a registered voter in this state."[31]

Alabama was, in other words, going to continue to treat the right to vote for African Americans as an obstacle course, creating more hurdles and trenches to jump over and walls to climb. Thus, although the state's population grew by "nearly 2 percent from 2010 to 2016," Alabama closed down "almost 7 percent" of its precincts. Because of *Shelby County v. Holder*, by 2016, there were 868 fewer precincts in Section 5 jurisdictions. Sixty-six of those were in Alabama alone.[32]

As if that weren't enough, by August 2017 Merrill purged the voter rolls, "putting 340,162 people . . . on inactive voter status." He explained that he was merely "following federal and state law" and had used the established postcard method, where his office mailed a notice that required a response within a limited, defined time or the recipient would be removed as a registered voter and placed in electoral limbo—the inactive roll.[33] That a state representative landed on the "inactive" roll although she "never got [a postcard] and neither did [her] wife" or that subsequent complaints identified, among others, a woman who had voted in the same precinct since 2005 only to be turned away at the polling station, suggested, as the Southern Poverty Law Center asserted, that "the process used by the secretary of state is deeply flawed." Merrill actually conceded that "many voters might be discouraged from voting, because they don't have time to pursue the matter."[34] And then, he left the issue right there—with discouraged voters and a deeply flawed process.

That sense of confusion, obfuscation, and discouragement eddied right over to the issue of felony disfranchisement. In 1901, Alabama stripped voting rights from those convicted of crimes of "moral turpitude." For more than one hundred years, though, the state refused to lay out what crimes actually fell under that broad, amorphous definition. In fact, some registrars interpreted it to mean misdemeanors, such as vagrancy, and other charges that law enforcement liked to reserve for black people. By the twenty-first century, 15 percent of African American adults in the state were, therefore, disfranchised by this 1901 Jim Crow statute specifically designed to limit black voters and, as the U.S. Supreme Court had observed, " 'to establish white supremacy in this State.' "[35] Finally, after much pressure and further litigation from the ACLU, the NAACP, the League of Women Voters, the NAACP LDF, and other civil rights organizations, in 2017, under H.B. 282, Alabama crafted a definitive list of crimes—murder, rape, treason, etc.—which fell under the banner of "moral turpitude." That meant, of course, that there were more than "250,000 otherwise qualified citizens—nearly 8 percent of the population"—who had previously lost their voting rights but were unaware those rights were now restored.[36] Merrill, nonetheless, did not see the need to take any initiative "to inform those who previously were unable to vote that they can now register."[37]

Finally, in addition to all the other methods of voter suppression, the state had gerrymandered districts that were so obviously racially biased that the federal courts eventually slapped them down. Alabama drew its legislative boundaries to "pack" as many minority voters in as few districts as possible, thus giving disproportionate weight to white voters and, as the research is clear, seeking to demoralize blacks and Latinos so that they wouldn't even bother to vote.[38]

The *Atlantic* journalist Vann R. Newkirk II summed up how intentionally daunting the barricades to voting in 2017 were. "Voting has always been burdensome for black people in Alabama," he noted. There were the standard obstacles of ID, limited polling places, purged voter rolls, and more, which had all been deployed, and meanwhile, the tried-and-true voter modernization techniques were simply not available. Newkirk explained, "Early voting, which has been a key factor for other states in increasing black turnout, is not permitted in Alabama. The state also doesn't have no-fault absentee voting, preregistration for teens, or same-day registration. In all, it's harder to vote in Alabama than just about anywhere else."[39]

Frankly, it looked hopeless. Roy Moore was on the cusp of shaping the laws for the United States of America in the twenty-first century, with a vision that was clearly nineteenth-century antebellum. He had repeatedly said that "getting rid of constitutional amendments after the Tenth Amendment," which included the ones ending slavery (Thirteenth), defining citizenship and due process (Fourteenth), guaranteeing the right to vote without racial discrimination (Fifteenth), providing for women's right to vote (Nineteenth), and ending the poll tax (Twenty-Fourth), "would 'eliminate many problems' in the way the US government is structured."[40] With that vision of what would make America great, he now had the financial backing of the Republican Party and the endorsement of President Donald Trump. The *Guardian* summed it up: It just "seemed the pit was bottomless."[41]

Worse yet, nothing seemed to be powerful enough to stop this juggernaut.

The wing-and-a-prayer consensus was that it would require finding enough disgusted whites combined with a black voter turnout rate that surpassed even that for Obama to stop an avowed bigot and alleged serial pedophile from being elected as a U.S. senator.[42] One of Moore's legal colleagues added another hard-core reality fact about Red State Alabama. "Southern Baptists control the damn state," he said. "And they'll vote for Roy. It'll be a landslide."[43] Alabamian Devon Crawford, a divinity student at the University of Chicago who came home to vote against the judge, knew exactly what that meant: "Mr. Moore's version of Christianity was 'really just a masquerade for white supremacy.'"[44]

Yet there has always been more than one kind of Christianity roiling and churning in Alabama.[45] As Martin Luther King Jr. called upon it in 1963 from a Birmingham jail, so, too, did the Greater Birmingham Ministries and Brown Chapel AME Church in 2017. And it can never be forgotten that the state that produced the Eugene "Bull" Connors, the Sheriff Jim Clarks, and the Judge Roy Moores also created the civil rights warriors who took down and defeated Bull and Jim, and now had Roy in their crosshairs.

It wasn't just the churches, either. There were the historically black colleges and universities (HBCUs), as well, that became key organizing sites for the millennials. There was also the NAACP, which was so powerful that the state had once tried and almost succeeded in driving it out of business.[46] Now, the NAACP, with branches spread throughout Alabama, mounted a fierce, "muscular" ground game that drew praise on social media for being "perhaps one of the most relevant progressive political organizations in the South."[47] Other groups, such as the storied ACLU and NAACP LDF, and the lesser-known The Ordinary People Society (TOPS) and BlackPAC, each played key, important roles in taking on voter suppression and fighting for democracy. They did it through grassroots mobilization, legal challenges in the courts, organizing communities, and providing citizenship education and restoration to those who had wrongly lost their rights via "moral turpitude." There was neighbor-to-neighbor, neighbor-for-neighbor advocacy. There was a shrewd understanding of where key resources were needed and then a system put in place to meet that need.

What emerged on the electoral battlefield in 2017, in fact, was a modern-day version of resistance that drew upon the historical strengths and tactics of mobilizing against a state determined to quash the right to vote. LaTosha Brown, co-founder of the Black Voters Matter Fund, therefore, scoffed at media representations of a demoralized, low-energy, apathetic black community.[48] "They never could see black people in Alabama, in a highly conservative racially polarized state . . . They never could see our power, even when we did."[49] But, just as before, as in Selma, the resistance used the strengths and talents of progressive civil society, those organizations that arise to protect democracy. The resistance relied on traditional as well as new media to message key constituencies about the consequences of this election. The resistance recognized deep political fissures, especially within the ruling party, and had the savvy to communicate the impact of standing on the wrong side of history. The resistance also tapped into necessary outside funding but knew that the effectiveness of those resources depended on *local* ownership of the process.

We had seen this previously. In 1963, John Lewis, then the chairman of the Student Nonviolent Coordinating Committee, returned from the March on Washington and asserted that the key battle they were getting ready to wage in Selma was about "one man, one vote." As civil rights activist Andrew Young stated, however, "We knew enough about the political situation to know you couldn't prepackage a movement." The local "people had a dynamic, and you had to get in and work with those people," Young said. They, and only they, knew the lay of the land. They knew who the movers, the shakers, and the fakers were. They knew the strengths and the weaknesses of the place, the people, and the values that had put them in that moment. For the activists in the 1960s, they knew who brought Alabama to its knees, who made the nation listen, and who was responsible for the Voting Rights Act. Young's answer was simple: "The local black leadership in Selma was really responsible for the Selma movement."[50]

In 2017, that same local savvy, determination, and expertise kicked in again, and, to be clear, the efforts started well before the election. While the media depicted a "last-minute push," this was, in fact, the long game.[51] "Unlike traditional get-out-the-vote campaigns implemented by Democrats in key African American communities close to elections, many of the moving pieces in the Alabama election were funded by entities other than the party or the candidate's campaign, and had been proceeding in stealth for months," Newkirk wrote. Local activists "had been working to bolster black turnout long before the Senate race gained national attention" because they understood better than anyone else what a tangled, knotted cord the state had woven around voting rights.[52]

It was clear almost immediately how Alabama had withheld, obfuscated, elided, and contradicted so much basic information about eligibility, polling places, and ID availability that confusion could easily create frustration and lead to anemic voter turnout rates.[53] In fact, fewer than 18 percent of eligible citizens voted in the August 2017 primary.[54] John Merrill, therefore, predicted that the subsequent race between Roy Moore and Doug Jones would require only enough resources for an arthritic 25 percent voter turnout rate.[55]

Democracy dies in that kind of darkness.

The Alabama NAACP, working with local churches, the National Pan-Hellenic Council (Black Greek fraternities and sororities), the ACLU, and Planned Parenthood, therefore, held a series of rallies throughout the state to shine a klieg light on all that was at stake. They emphasized that, despite the barriers Alabama threw up to block the people's access to the ballot box, it was essential to "Vote Out Loud!"[56] There would be horrific "consequences if the Black voters in Alabama stayed silent."[57] Hezekiah Jackson, president of the Metro Birmingham NAACP, exclaimed, "We're at a crossroad in the city, in the state, in the country." At stake, continued another speaker, were "healthcare, education and gay rights." Another explained, "For us . . . what's on the ballot is women's rights, human rights, the 1965 Voting Rights [Act]."[58] Benard Simelton, president of the Alabama State Conference of the NAACP, emphasized that "there's things that [you'll] have to lose if you don't get out and vote. Social Security—it's not a guarantee . . . And health care—it's not a guarantee . . . education—you know, Alabama is—like so many other Southern states, the education system is in shambles." Those issues, Simelton understood, "resonated particularly with African-American voters."[59] But it was even more than that. There was a foreboding "concern that the country, in the Trump era, was going back to a place best left in the past."[60] Simelton explained: "Look where the Trump administration is headed. It's taking us backwards, and we cannot allow that to set the tone for where African-Americans will be five, 10 years from now. We need to stop it right now."[61]

That was the charge. It stops here. It stops now. And it starts with us. Alabama's civil rights activists were clear: "We have to do this for ourselves . . . No one is going to do this for us."[62]

The state, for example, had had no problem sending out mailers telling citizens "they were ineligible to vote because of a past conviction, when they were in fact eligible." Yet, despite the May 2017 law that finally defined "moral turpitude," John Merrill refused to "spend state resources" to correct the error or clarify the new law. Meanwhile, there was a dangerous double-dare in this manufactured ambiguity: the "Alabama voter registration form requires applicants to swear under penalty of perjury that they are a qualified voter, but it does not include a list of crimes that are disqualifying." Merrill, however, said the notion that people would be "scared away from filling out voter applications" because they might get charged with a felony because their conviction was for a crime that actually constituted "moral turpitude" was nothing but a "well-laid excuse by liberal minions from around the world."[63]

The threat of criminal prosecution, however, was not a piece of fiction. Alabama had strung criminal penalties and booby traps all around voting. At nearly the very moment Merrill was mocking the baited trap of "moral turpitude" and perjury, he was wielding a brand-new law that allowed him to go after "674 Alabama citizens who voted both in the 2017 Democratic primary and Republican runoff elections."[64] Jail, frankly, was how Alabama threatened the poor and minorities for daring to vote—it was how in the 1980s the state imprisoned Julia Wilder and Maggie Bozeman; it was how Jeff Sessions went after the Marion Three. This was no idle threat.

Therefore, Legal Services Alabama (LSA) and the local ACLU stepped in to do the hard work of citizenship education regarding "moral turpitude" and voting rights. First, the groups started running a series of ads on both radio and social media "to get the word out to as many convicted felons as possible" that the new law was going to provide a chance "to regain the right to vote."[65] The key, however, was not just awareness about H.B. 282 but immediate follow-up with workshops and clinics on how to restore one's voting rights.

LSA and the ACLU then launched "restoration clinics" in the historic Brown Chapel AME Church in Selma, which in the 1960s was a key site for voting rights organizing and had become a make-shift hospital for those beaten mercilessly on the Edmund Pettus Bridge during Bloody Sunday. In July 2017, the ACLU and the LSA held their first restoration clinic at Brown Chapel, where volunteers and legal professionals went painstakingly through the conviction records, discerning whether the felonies fell under the disfranchising categories or not. If the latter, then the next step was a workshop on how to register to vote—what materials and documents were needed, such as birth certificates, and how to attain them. There was also an understanding that traditional forms of identification—a passport, a driver's license—are a class-based phenomenon and that alternate IDs, such as official mugshots, could be used to vote.[66]

These restoration clinics took place in churches in Birmingham, Dothan, and Mobile, as well as traveled in high-visibility caravans that went throughout the state, particularly to economically impoverished areas. As one of the directors noted shortly before the program had launched, "Effective legal aid for the poor requires taking your work to the neighborhoods where the disadvantaged people live. That is why we are drawing on the clergy community and why we will literally be going on the road in Birmingham, Mobile and the Black Belt."[67] They provided "the resources and the legal assistance [people] need to check their voter registration status and eligibility for restoration, to fill out their applications, and to increase their chances at successfully restoring their right to vote."[68] These clinics and caravans simply cut through the miasma of mis- and disinformation that swallowed the voting rights of poor and black folk in Alabama. The clinics provided a pathway to resurrection from the "civil death" that Alabama had imposed on those with a felony conviction.[69]

Grassroots Alabama wasn't done yet, though. There was still more to be accomplished on the felony disfranchisement front. However, the right-wing organ *Breitbart*, in a toxic mélange of anti-Semitic, anti-black dog whistles, didn't see the indigenous battle for voting rights. Instead, its headline warned that its bête noire, billionaire George Soros, had an "Army in Alabama to Register Convicted Felons to Vote Against Roy Moore." There was something close to apoplexy that civil rights activists were "taking advantage" of a new law that clarified "moral turpitude" and that Soros was behind it all, providing funding for the ACLU, the NAACP, and, perhaps worst of all, an organization based in Dothan called The Ordinary People Society, led by Pastor Kenneth Glasgow, who had once been incarcerated and was now on a mission to "fill the void left by Alabama's legal refusal to actively notify potentially tens of thousands of former felons that they regained their voting rights."[70]

Glasgow was, in fact, on a mission. After he had emerged from prison for a drug conviction, he "spent three years fighting through the pardon process to have his voting rights restored." It was only years later that he learned "the state had made a mistake. He should never have been disenfranchised in the first place because his drug charge was not a 'moral turpitude' offense." He knew he wasn't alone. The state had done this to others, far too many others. Glasgow, therefore, worked with the ACLU to get H.B. 282 passed and was now on the second phase of that restoration project.[71] There were so "many felons [who] simply believed they could never regain the franchise." But, with the new law, Glasgow said, "I've got people all over the state registering people [to vote] . . . in Tuscaloosa, Birmingham, Montgomery, Enterprise, Dothan, Abbeville, Geneva, Gordon, Bessemer, we have a lot." One of the most important sites of this work was in the local jails and prisons. State law actually allowed absentee ballots for those incarcerated—as long as they had not been convicted of a crime of "moral turpitude." Glasgow and TOPS members, therefore, fanned out and began voting rights and citizenship education sessions in thirty-two carceral facilities. One man, Spencer Trawick, "lost the franchise in 2015 when he was convicted of third-degree burglary, a felony." As he sat in Dothan jail, Glasgow informed him that this crime did not fall under the definition of "moral turpitude." Trawick was stunned as he went "ahead that same day and filled out the required [voter] registration forms." The incarcerated man explained, "A lot of people get felonies and they just feel like their whole world's shattered because there's a lot of things that you can't do, but now that they passed that law a lot of people are going to run towards it." In fact, Glasgow estimated that since he began this effort in June 2017, that "thousands of felons across Alabama have registered to vote."[72]

Despite that success, it wasn't enough. The state had worked to cut off the ballot box from more than just convicted felons. Alabama had also put African Americans' voting rights, in general, on its hit list. The NAACP, therefore, organized a campaign to dodge, deflect, and blunt every one of the shots that the state took at citizens' voting rights. Just as during the Civil Rights Movement, it didn't seem to be a fair fight. The state had weapons of mass civic destruction. The resistance appeared to be unarmed. But it actually had a determination that would stun Alabama. There was no other viable choice; the toll that voter suppression had already taken on the nation was all too clear. It had placed in the White House, even according to former CIA director John Brennan, a president who is "unstable, inept, inexperienced, and also unethical."[73] Voter suppression had also resulted in that same unethical man controlling the public policies that affected millions of lives, although "57 percent of adults— including 8 in 10 blacks, three-quarters of Hispanics and almost half of all whites—say [he] is a racist."[74] And it looked as if Alabama was trying to replicate that debacle with Roy Moore.

Civil society knew that 2016 was a wake-up call. And those who were part of it answered the alarm. The *Atlantic*'s Newkirk noted that "GOP dominance, voter suppression, and the stubborn support for Moore among white voters in the state helped revive the kind of black political entities originally built in the state to grapple with Jim Crow."[75] Those organizations drew upon that history and the lessons learned from 2016. They needed to be more deliberate, more purposeful, more focused, and more vigorous. To take Roy Moore down would, in short, require fewer TV ads and more person-to-person interactions.[76] One activist recalled, "I remember right before the polls closed, I sat down and I felt good because the one thing that I did know was that we left it all out there."[77] Simelton understood: "We have never had this kind of effort before."[78]

In addition to numerous rallies to spread the word about the special election for the Senate seat and its consequences, the next wave was to make direct one-on-one contact with the state's citizens.[79] As one college student who attended the rallies remarked, "I don't want Alabama to go backwards."[80] The Alabama NAACP identified registered voters who had not cast a ballot in 2016 or who had been sporadic voters, and using that list, its local branches began calling, and calling, and calling. In addition, the NAACP "created phone banks" so that volunteers in a number of other organizations, including Indivisible, a "progressive grassroots network of local groups to resist the Trump Agenda," could "contact African American voters in urban Alabama as well as the rural 'Black Belt.' "[81] Based on research out of Stanford, the activists knew that the message wasn't to ask whether someone was going to vote; the point was to define the person as a voter because a "voter is who you are" whereas "voting can be a task competing with lots of other ones." The volunteers were, therefore, instructed to use "HIGH VOTER TURNOUT LANGUAGE AND ASK HIGH VOTER TURNOUT QUESTIONS LIKE: 'I know you're a reliable/consistent voter' and 'We rely on reliable voters like you' and 'What time of day are you going to vote?' "[82]

And while the NAACP, Indivisible, the Collective PAC, and BlackPAC—which "uses the power of year-round political engagement and elections" to enact long-term transformation of the economic, political, and justice systems—made 1.32 million phone calls, mailed more than 220,000 postcards, produced video ads that "garnered 1.4 million Facebook ad impressions, targeting 650,000 African American voters in every county in Alabama," and sent one million texts, all that work was merely tilling the ground. As one activist noted, "in the south, culture will eat strategy for breakfast." The phone calls, technology, social media, and mailing bombardment would not have made a dent if the organizers hadn't "swarmed communities" and knocked on as many doors as possible. "We had a lot of Alabamians talking to Alabamians," remarked one member of Indivisible's Huntsville branch.[83] Randall Woodfin, the thirty-six-year-old mayor of Birmingham, who had previously won his own upset election victory, laid out the magic formula: "Doors. Doors. Doors. Turn ya folk out," he entreated.[84] "It is relationship capital on both the black and the white side" to relay a compelling, virtually irresistible message: "So much of the future is in our hands . . . We cannot afford to" just sit and "watch an administration turn the clock back on future generations."[85] Moore was not only "reflective of the Alabama of the past," but he also, as one NAACP official noted, "offered the black voter nothing but a return to the way things used to be."[86]

Therefore, another grassroots organization that was focused on the millennials, Woke Vote, "centered its efforts on potential sites of latent black political power, including the HBCUs and black churches."[87] Woke Vote had "dozens of students working on 12 Alabama campuses" and had secured "11,000 signatures on a petition promising to cast a ballot."[88] Then the Sunday before the election, the organization deployed 270 canvassers, who "knocked on more than 14,000 doors . . . committing 6,000 voters on that day alone."[89] Meanwhile Righteous Vote, whose emphasis was on "turning out black churches, had 120 captains representing 146 churches across Alabama." That effort "reached an estimated 300,000 people."[90] The Mobile NAACP, also recognizing the centrality of religion to African Americans—indeed, 83 percent of blacks absolutely believe in God, with another 11 percent fairly certain of God's existence—also targeted the all-important churches.[91] That branch of the NAACP "crunched the numbers" and showed local ministers that "whatever they had done in recent years to turn out voters wasn't working. The pastors then pushed for and got resources to do congregation-wide robo calls and voter reg[istration] tables at church events."[92]

Regardless of how impressive and blanketing that outreach was, however, it would have been an exercise in futility without the next component: ensuring that the people had access to the crucial information they needed to cast their ballots. Alabama's voter ID law posed a formidable barrier, and while the NAACP LDF, NAACP, and Greater Birmingham Ministries sued first to soften, and then overturn the law, VoteRiders focused its efforts on helping Alabamians get the documents they needed to gain access to that all-precious ID to vote.[93] Working with grassroots organizations well before the election, VoteRiders launched voter ID clinics to "help citizens obtain their birth certificate, change-of-name and other documents required to secure a state-mandated ID for voting purposes."[94] As law professor Rick Hasen tweeted, it's "not glamorous but it is the painstaking work of @VoteRiders which makes the difference in whether thousands of people get to vote or are disenfranchised."[95]

Similarly, because quelling the doubts raised by the state's dis- and misinformation campaigns was so important, the NAACP set up call centers to deal with the rampant confusion caused by the closure of sixty-six polling places as voters searched for where they were supposed to cast their ballots. It also handled questions about what types of identification are acceptable and how to attain them, as well as queries, given Merrill's purge of more than three hundred thousand citizens from the voter rolls, about how to determine whether one was still registered to vote.[96] In addition, at school alumni and reunion parties, NAACP branches also "handed out several thousand flyers with election dates, registration deadlines, absentee deadlines, [and] voter ID requirements." They followed up by distributing this same packet of vital information in their door-to-door canvassing.[97]

And, still, the battle was far from won. Poll closures and the resulting increasing distances voters had to travel, coupled with the disparities in access to public and private transportation and exacerbated by staggering poverty rates, suggested that all the information in the world would have gone for naught if Alabamians could not physically get to the voting booth. This was a major stumbling block. Or, as Indivisible succinctly summarized the problem: "Transportation to the polls is a HUGE issue in Alabama."[98] Media attention, therefore, zeroed in on Perman Hardy, who, working independently of any of the organizations, did what she has done for the past twenty-five years. She got in her minivan and, over the course of the day, took to the polls fifty registered voters in Lowndes County, who had no other way to get to the one voting machine at Old Bethel Baptist Church in Collirene. She convinced those who didn't think they were dressed well enough to step into a church and vote, she picked up sisters from their mobile home, and she shepherded a man from his job picking pecans to the polls and back to work in the orchard.[99]

That kind of effort, multiplied across the state, amplified by numerous vehicles, was exactly what Alabama needed. And that's exactly what it got. Reminiscent of the highly effective private car service established in the wake of the 1956 Montgomery Bus Boycott, the NAACP and other organizations, such as Black Belt Citizens and Indivisible chapters in several counties, were determined to "help our neighbors get to the polls and make their choice on this Special Election Day, December 12th."[100] The organizations put in place a system of drivers, buses, and rideshares to ferry place-bound voters to and from the polls. In fact, originally fifteen and then at least twenty NAACP branches throughout Alabama worked to ensure that those voters who needed a ride got one.[101]

None of this—the phone banks, the organizers going door-to-door, the vast information systems on the radio and social media and call centers, and getting voters to the polls—was cheap. It cost money. Senate Majority PAC, which was founded to counter the dark money pouring into the GOP, therefore, pumped over $6 million into Alabama. That funding helped finance the incredible ground game mounted by local organizations, including BlackPAC, which received $600,000.[102] The executive director of BlackPAC, Adrianne Shropshire, acknowledged the importance of the funding. Instead of having to rely on volunteers to knock "on over half a million doors," she said, BlackPAC could pay organizers, "a tactic that helped offset the strain and demands of canvassing rural and hard-to-reach communities in the state."[103] The Black Voters Matter Fund, meanwhile, "crowdfunded $200,000 a week before the election . . . that paid for 460 canvassers to work with 30 organizations across 19 Alabama counties in the Black Belt and beyond."[104] In doing so, it provided "dozens of grants to smaller get-out-the-vote organizations, organized transportation to the polls, and printed thousands of pieces of voter literature."[105] This funding cyclone was augmented with resources from the NAACP, the Democratic National Committee, and Priorities USA, which focuses on traditional voter-mobilization techniques. Priorities USA, in fact, spent $1.5 million in Alabama, $1 million of that "specifically . . . on mobilizing black voters."[106] Yet, as is clear, knocking on doors is only half the battle. Getting voters to the polls is the holy grail. Senate Majority PAC, therefore, spent $2 million alone on voter turnout.[107]

All this effort, without question, was aided by the GOP selecting one of the worst possible candidates imaginable. Roy Moore's well-documented litany of racist, sexist, homophobic, and anti–religious freedom stances should have made him immediately unacceptable. But it did not. It was only on November 9, when the *Washington Post* published its horrifying, well-researched, and verified story of Moore's serial attempts to date and sometimes sexually assault teenage girls while he was an assistant district attorney that his ascent to Congress seemed imperiled.[108] Then, another well-documented account in the *New Yorker* of his tendency to cruise the local mall looking for girls was published a few days later. It became clear that Moore's predilections were a well-known secret. Journalist Charles Bethea "spoke with more than a dozen people—including a major political figure in the state—who told [him] that they had heard, over the years, that Moore had been banned from the mall because he repeatedly badgered teen-age girls."[109] Revulsion began to course through some Republicans, who drew the line right there. Their resolve, however, held as long as the polls or advertisers did. Once white evangelical Alabama came roaring back showing Moore had a chance to win, which then dangled the slim Republican majority in the U.S. Senate before the stalwarts, many in the GOP "slinked back" to the alleged serial pedophile.[110]

Yet there were some who remained repulsed.[111] Most important, the senior senator from Alabama, Richard Shelby, refused to sit quietly in disgust. A few days before the election, on CNN's Sunday show *State of the Union*, he matter-of-factly remarked that when he cast his absentee ballot, "I didn't vote for Roy Moore . . . I wouldn't vote for Roy Moore. I think the Republican Party can do better."[112] And even though the RealClearPolitics poll actually showed the disgraced judge with nearly a 4 percent lead over Jones, Shelby insisted, nonetheless, that not only could the GOP do better; the "state of Alabama deserves better."[113] The sexual assault charges were credible. The string of women who continued to come forth was compelling. And Moore could not keep any of his stories straight about what had happened and what hadn't happened except to say, "I don't remember ever dating any girl without the permission of her mother."[114]

For Shelby, however, Democratic candidate Doug Jones was not an option. Indeed, the Alabama GOP has a rule that any Republican who endorses a Democrat would lose ballot access for six years.[115] Jones, therefore, was most definitely not an option. But who was? Shelby told viewers that he opted to use his absentee ballot to write in "a distinguished Republican name" and he "encouraged fellow Alabama voters to do as he did."[116] His message was clear. Save the GOP and save Alabama by not voting for Moore. Rather, write in the name of someone worthy and deserving to represent the state.

That may have been Shelby's admonition, but shortly before the election, CBS reported some sobering news: polling showing that "Moore leads 49 percent to 43 percent among the likely voters who are most apt to vote on Dec. 12." Even more telling, the "poll also finds more than 80 percent of Republicans plan to vote for their party's candidate" and "a higher number of Moore's backers call themselves definite voters than do Jones' backers."[117]

Doug Jones had not been idle, however. First, he had to rebuild a disintegrated Democratic Party apparatus that had collapsed under the weight of the GOP's crushing victory in 2010. As the *New York Times* reported, Jones confronted a "Democratic operation [in

Alabama] with the lights out. With a fairly anemic state party, there [was] little existing infrastructure for routine campaign activities like phone banks or canvassing drives."[118] He put all of that in place. Then he went into black churches on "multiple Sundays," as well as attended barbecues and fish frys. He spoke "about health care and jobs and infrastructure." He also reminded African American voters that he was the prosecutor who had successfully gone after the Klansmen who had planted the bomb in the 16th Street Baptist Church that killed four little girls. He clearly realized that he could "not just take" the African American vote "for granted." Nor did he shy away from advertising on billboards in black communities so that African American voters knew his name, his credentials, and that he was not Roy Moore.[119]

Yet when the much-anticipated Election Day rolled around on December 12, 2017, the hazards of being black and voting began to pop up almost immediately. Todd Cox, director of policy for the Legal Defense Fund, told TV host Roland Martin:

> We saw numerous examples of voter problems that confronted African Americans and their opportunity to participate in the electoral process. Voters standing in long lines only to be told they're on inactive lists and not being given the opportunity to vote on a regular ballot. Voters who, when they got there, were given false or incorrect information regarding the photo ID policies of Alabama. Voters who, unfortunately, in certain areas, stood in long lines because facilities lacked the proper or the right number of voter machines or check-in locations.[120]

Kristen Clarke, executive director of the Lawyers' Committee for Civil Rights Under Law, in an interview on WHNT, explained that her organization had already "received about 300 calls from concerned voters before 4 P.M. A number of the calls were from voters—who had apparently not voted in a while—who been moved to 'inactive status'" because of Secretary of State Merrill's aggressive purge. Not only is federal law unequivocal that registered voters cannot be removed simply because they have not voted; Alabama law is equally clear. Clarke noted that "if the voter can prove their identification or their address, they should be allowed to vote without issue." And not, as Simelton later observed, be "directed to use provisional ballots," which, studies show, are frequently used in districts with sizable minority populations and, worse yet, more than 30 percent of votes from provisional ballots are not counted fully or rejected outright.[121]

Sherrilyn Ifill was also alerted to the problem of an "inactive list" that seemed designed to "discourage . . . voters from casting a ballot." She remarked as well on a "shortage of ballots or wrong voting machines at certain African American precincts . . . Long lines in Selma and Mobile due to too-few voting machines or check-in tables."[122] Attorney and president and founder of the Transformative Justice Coalition Barbara Arnwine identified additional failings. Citizens "went into Montgomery to vote," she said, "and found out that the disability ramps had been removed."[123] Given that 17.5 percent of adults in Montgomery County have disabilities, this was not inconsequential.[124] Arnwine continued: "What we also saw was ex-felons who had had their rights restored attempting to vote and being denied that right because they would not accept their 'mugshot pictures' which had been agreed to be accepted as legitimate photo ID."[125]

For many of these shenanigans and system failures, the organizations were ready. The Lawyers' Committee and the National Bar Association, which is the African American analog to the American Bar Association, had their attorneys on the ground to assist with information about citizens' voting rights. Given the tendency to understaff and underresource polling stations in minority neighborhoods, it was imperative that people knew that "if you're in line at the time the polls close, stay in line because you have a right to vote."[126] Similarly, BlackPAC "mobilized a group of lawyers who bounced around precincts and local courts on election day."[127]

Meanwhile, Pastor Glasgow explained election law to poll workers who tried to reject mugshots as an acceptable form of ID, and his intervention ensured that those whose Fifteenth Amendment rights he had helped restore were able to cast their ballots.[128]

Roy Moore, nonetheless, had a lock on the Republican strongholds in most of the northern sectors of the state. As the vote tallies began to roll in, his lead continued to grow. It looked almost insurmountable. But there was a crack in his seemingly invincible electoral armor. His lead was not as large or as commanding as it should have been or would have been if he were a regular Republican candidate. The taint of pedophilia had clearly depressed the white voter turnout in Alabama. And it soon became apparent that Senator Shelby's call to moral arms was having an effect. There was a surge of write-in votes coming out of traditionally Republican counties as well. Indeed, nearly half the 22,819 write-ins came from counties that Moore carried. Moreover, college-educated whites, who had backed Trump in 2016, were peeling off, too. For example, in Madison County, home to Huntsville, where both a major university and a NASA facility are located, the Republican presidential candidate had secured 54.85 percent of the vote. Yet in the 2017 special election, Moore eked out just a little over 46 percent. This was greater than an 8 percent drop and was an omen about what was to come. Meanwhile, Indivisible had focused its efforts on six counties. "Three of them—Madison, Lee, and Mobile—flipped from having a majority of their voters select Trump last November to a majority choosing Jones. In the other three counties . . . Houston, Dale, and Henry—the G.O.P.'s winning margins shrank by more than twenty points." But, even with all that, there was still a glimmer of hope on the Republican side. Although the votes from the more diverse areas of the state had not yet been tallied, Moore still had a sizable lead. And if voter suppression worked as it was supposed to, and those in the Black Belt counties and the cities stayed home, victory was assured and, equally important, as in

2016, it would inevitably be chalked up to African Americans being disengaged and apathetic.[129]

As the votes continued to be counted, the election seemed to mirror the classic Muhammad Ali rope-a-dope, with black voters apparently overwhelmed, outmatched, and headed for sure defeat at the hands of a much more powerful opponent.[130] But then, a blazing uppercut caught Roy Moore squarely on the jaw and sent his hopes snapping back as "black people in Alabama punched above their weight" and delivered an unexpected and well-delivered stunning blow.[131] And, so fittingly, the first indication that Moore was in serious trouble came from a legendary place. "Selma, Lord, Selma," exclaimed Bernice King, daughter of Martin Luther King Jr. "It's no coincidence," she tweeted, "that Selma, where blood was shed in the struggle for voting rights for Black people, pushed #DougJones ahead for good."[132] As the election results kept rolling in, the black voter turnout surprised almost everyone. The "stealth" of the get-out-the-vote campaign, which made it seem so "last-minute," the apparently feigned nonchalance when media and pollsters hovered asking questions, and the "significant barriers" to the voting booth that Alabama crafted, brought about a kind of confidence (or resignation) that blacks would just not vote.[133] Indeed, if the overall voter turnout rate had been the paltry 25 percent that Merrill had predicted, perhaps Moore, for whom Merrill cast his ballot, would have won.[134] But "more than 40% of voters showed up, with surges well beyond 50% in counties favorable to Jones." The people in the Black Belt counties, who were weighed down by everything that Alabama could throw at them, were equally impressive. "Jones won an average of 73.4% of the vote in [those] counties with turnouts that averaged 45.4%, about five percentage points higher than the state average."[135] The Black Belt simply came through. And while Selma had Moore reeling, Birmingham truly delivered the knockout blow. There Jones picked up 83,213 more votes than Moore, Republican turnout was significantly less than in 2016, and there were 3,710 write-ins.[136]

There simply weren't enough white evangelical votes left in Alabama to revive his chances.[137] There would be no recovery. There would be no getting up from the count. And, as a result, there would be no "Senator" in front of Roy Moore's name. He lost by 20,715 votes.[138]

As the results became evident, the disgraced judge immediately raised the specter of voter fraud and pointed to overwhelmingly black Birmingham—the same way Kit Bond had pointed to St. Louis and Trump to Philadelphia—as the culprit. Moore insisted that the black voter turnout rate was simply too high and the Republican vote was mysteriously too low. For him, that could mean only one thing: voter fraud.[139] The charge, of course, was as hollow as the man and, frankly, all those before him who gave voice to that pernicious lie.

Because in Alabama, as in the United States, African Americans know, "Somebody paid a big price so [they] could come and vote . . . There were people who has [*sic*] the hoses turned on them. There were people who had the dogs turn [*sic*] on them."[140] And, unfortunately, in the twenty-first century, there were people who had to overcome every barrier that Alabama put in their way. And they did. But let's be clear, they shouldn't have had to. Voting is neither an obstacle course nor a privilege. It's a right.

Conclusion

At the Crossroads of Half Slave, Half Free

Something had gone horribly wrong. Most Americans knew it.[1] When special counsel Robert Mueller indicted thirteen Russians for subverting the 2016 election, those suspicions were confirmed.[2] The Kremlin's agents, by "weaponizing" Twitter and Facebook and exploiting the racial fissures in America, had gone for the nation's Achilles.[3]

Taking "extraordinary steps to make it appear that they were ordinary American political activists," they opened up a series of social media accounts, and then, after "earning" their stripes as social justice warriors, began a campaign urging African Americans to boycott the election and just stay home.[4] Using the Instagram account Woke Blacks, the Russians posted a message suggesting that African Americans' disdain for Trump was simply manufactured by sinister influences trying to "forc[e] Blacks to vote Killary," the pejorative social media name for Democratic presidential candidate Hillary Clinton, who was cast as "the lesser of two devils." Faced with the distasteful choice between Trump, whom blacks were supposedly manipulated into loathing, and Clinton, who was Satan in a pantsuit, the disguised Russians used their robust social media presence to trumpet that "we'd surely be better off without voting AT ALL."[5]

On Facebook, the Russians posted under the name Blacktivist, which they had used to elbow their way into a series of rallies in Buffalo, New York, that were demanding answers about the mysterious jailhouse death of a young African American woman, India

Cummings. After muscling their way into the protests, the Russians began inflating their stature and profile using an internet bot farm that gave Blacktivist an even larger following than Black Lives Matter had. With their bona fides secured, the undercover Russians then began posting about the upcoming 2016 election. "They would say things like: 'What have the Democrats done for you the last four years, the last 60 years'" and then, when the unspoken reply was "nothing," the Russians in their best cyber-militancy mode would answer: "'Show them your power by not showing up to vote.'" The message spread like a virulent toxin.[6] One election expert observed that "Russians understood how important minority voters were to Hillary Clinton's chances in this election. They were able to read the situation and say, 'If we demobilize this community, it could have enough of an impact.'"[7]

The Kremlin's agents didn't stop there, however. While working to get African Americans to willingly "sit out" the election, the Russians were also focusing on increasing the pressure for stricter voter suppression techniques by "reporting" on rampant voter fraud in heavily contested minority districts.[8] In North Carolina, where Republicans had issued strict voter ID laws and shown no mercy in targeting African Americans "with almost surgical precision," the Russians, using the Twitter handle @TEN_GOP, reported that an investigation was under way to uncover who had committed the latest round of voter fraud in the state, virtually waving a red cape in front of the charging Republican bull. Closer to Election Day, @TEN_GOP issued another tweet using the hashtag #VoterFraud and questioning the validity of tens of thousands of mail-in ballots for Hillary Clinton in Broward County, Florida, where more than half the population was Latino or black.[9]

As insidious as all this was, the Russians, frankly, were merely piggybacking on the years of work done by the GOP to stigmatize, disfranchise, and suppress the votes of African Americans and other minorities. The Republicans, as we've seen, have consistently claimed there is rampant voter fraud, especially in cities and states that have sizable minority communities. Thus, the suspicion thrown by the GOP on St. Louis and Miami-Dade County in the 2000 election is just as dastardly as the Russians conjuring up #VoterFraud in North Carolina and Broward County in 2016. Reverend William Barber best summarized the harsh parallel: "Voter suppression hacked our democracy long before any Russian agents meddled in America's elections."[10]

Obama's election had been a catalyst for the most recent version of massive disfranchisement.[11] And the resulting efforts to strip millions of citizens of their voting rights indicated how easily the electoral system could be manipulated. It was like a neon sign pointing "Enter Here."[12] After Obama surprisingly carried Indiana in 2008, the GOP-dominated state legislature and the governor identified the primary source of that supposed catastrophe: Marion County, home to Indianapolis and the lion's share of African Americans in the state. The Republicans, therefore, passed a law—while Vice President Mike Pence was the governor—designed to prevent blacks from having that kind of influence at the ballot box ever again. The legislative device was simple: Counties with at least 325,000 residents could not have more than one early voting site unless there was unanimous agreement from the bipartisan county election board. Buried in that sanitized language was pure, uncut racial animus. Only three of the ninety-two counties in the state have populations that exceed that threshold—Marion (Indianapolis), Allen (Fort Wayne), and Lake (Gary), and, not surprisingly, 62 percent of the state's African American population live in either Marion or Lake Counties.[13] Meanwhile, smaller (and whiter) counties are not held to that same restriction. Therefore, suburban Hamilton County has had its number of early voting sites expanded to three and, as a result, has witnessed a 63 percent increase in early voting. The *Indianapolis Star*, which uncovered the GOP's "methodical" and "relentless" attack on Democrats' voting rights, found that "three other Republican-friendly counties also added early voting sites and have seen a similar increase in early voting." Yet, because of the Republicans' built-in veto on the Marion County election board, the state's largest city, with nearly one million people, lost two of its early voting stations and has been reduced to a single site for each subsequent election since 2008. As a consequence, and as could be expected, early voting in Marion County plummeted by 26 percent.[14]

Republicans in Georgia have brought their own distinct twist to voter suppression. Secretary of State Brian Kemp has developed a pattern of going after and intimidating organizations that register minorities to vote. In 2012, when the Asian American Legal Advocacy Center (AALAC) realized that a number of its clients, who were newly naturalized citizens, were not on the voter rolls although they had been registered, its staff asked the secretary of state's office why. After waiting and waiting and still receiving no response, AALAC issued an open letter expressing concern that the early voting period would close before they had an answer. Two days later, in a show of raw intimidation, Kemp launched an investigation questioning the methods the organization had used to register new voters. One of the group's attorneys was "aghast . . .'I'm not going to lie: I was shocked, I was scared.'" AALAC remained under this ominous cloud for more than two years before Kemp's office finally concluded there was no wrongdoing.[15]

Kemp then went after the New Georgia Project when in 2014 the organization decided to whittle away at the bloc of 700,000 unregistered African American voters in the state and, in its initial run, registered nearly 130,000 mostly minority voters. Kemp didn't applaud and see democracy in action. Instead, he exclaimed in a TV interview, "We're just not going to put up with fraud." Later, when talking with a group of fellow Republicans behind closed doors, he didn't claim "fraud." It was something much baser. "Democrats are working hard . . . registering all these minority voters that are out there and others that are sitting on the sidelines," he warned. "If they can do that, they can win these elections in November." Not surprisingly, within two months of that discussion, he "announced his criminal investigation into the New Georgia Project." And, just as before, Kemp's hunt for fraud dragged on and on with aspersions and allegations filling the airwaves and print media while no evidence of a crime could be found.[16]

Indiana and Georgia, unfortunately, are not outliers. Voter suppression has become far too commonplace. In 2017, "99 bills to limit access to the ballot have been introduced in 31 states . . . and more states have enacted new voting restrictions in 2017 than in 2016 and 2015 combined."[17] This means that more policymakers and politicians, as in Wisconsin, will be "giddy" about denying the constitutional right to vote to their citizens.[18] More, as in North Carolina, will "celebrate" the precipitous drop in early voting by African Americans.[19] More, as in New Hampshire, will lie about voter fraud in order to install a "poll tax" on college students and keep them from the ballot box.[20]

Yet, while there are far too many states that are eager to reduce "one person, one vote" to a meaningless phrase, others, such as Oregon, are determined to "make voting convenient" and "registration simple" because these "policies are good for civic engagement and voter participation."[21] In 2015, Oregon pioneered automatic voter registration (AVR). Citizens who "apply for or renew their driver's license" at the DMV are automatically registered to vote unless they opt out. Under AVR, Oregon added 68,583 new voters in just six months. By the end of July 2016, the state's "torrid pace" had swelled the rolls by 222,197 new voters. And equally impressive, its voter turnout rate in the 2016 election increased from 64 to 68 percent, "more than any other state"—but also the income, age, and racial diversity of the electorate was enhanced by AVR, as was the participation of first-time and sporadic voters.[22]

California took one look at its neighbor to the north and is "hard on Oregon's heels."[23] Secretary of State Alex Padilla, dissatisfied with his own state's abysmal 42 percent voter turnout rate, had been scouring the nation looking for best practices.[24] "We want to serve as a contrast to what we see happening in other states, where they are making it more difficult to register or actually cast a ballot," he said. California, thus, adopted and then adapted Oregon's AVR program to include preregistration of sixteen- and seventeen-year-olds who are then automatically registered to vote when they turn eighteen.[25] Padilla also installed observers, including himself, in Colorado during the November 2014 election. There they saw the effectiveness of same-day registration, which could "boost turnout 7 to 14 percentage points" and "create . . . a fail-safe for people who missed the 15-day deadline and still want to vote."[26]

These state initiatives to *remove* the barriers to the ballot box, including the use of mail-in ballots, which has had tremendous success in Colorado, are beginning to ricochet around the nation. To date, ten states have implemented AVR and "15 states have introduced automatic voter registration proposals in 2018." Illinois and Rhode Island, in fact, have expanded the program to include other agencies beyond the DMV, such as those "serving people with disabilities" and social service agencies, that also have the capacity to electronically send verified files to election officials.[27] That expansion beyond the DMV helps address the racial and economic disparities between those who drive and those who would have no reason whatsoever to have contact with the DMV. Most telling, given the political polarization of the moment, the bill in Illinois was bipartisan, as Republicans and Democrats "cooperat[ed] to make voter registration work better." AVR provided electronically vetted records that will keep voter rolls up-to-date and "is expected to register more than a million voters" in the state.[28]

Democrats in Congress have also pushed for legislation to enact a federal AVR program, because the United States consistently ranks toward the bottom of developed democracies in terms of voter turnout. In July 2016, Senators Patrick Leahy (D-VT), Dick Durbin

(D-IL), and Amy Klobuchar (D-MN) cosponsored legislation that would take AVR nationwide. Leahy remarked, "There is no reason why every eligible citizen cannot have the option of automatic registration when they visit the DMV, sign up for healthcare or sign up for classes in college."[29] No reason at all, except not one Republican in Congress has stepped up to support the bill.

Yet, a key factor affecting the U.S.'s low ranking among developed democracies is the sheer magnitude of age-eligible adults who are not registered. Currently, seventy-seven million Americans aren't on the voter rolls. To put this in perspective, there are so many unregistered voters in the United States that they exceed the total combined population of the largest one hundred cities in America—from New York City to Birmingham—by nearly sixteen million people.[30]

Moreover, the demographics of the unregistered have greatly affected elections and policies. Texas, for example, has two Republican U.S. senators, John Cornyn and Ted Cruz, who have voted overwhelmingly (97 percent and 92.5 percent, respectively) to support Trump's agenda regarding immigration, taxes, banking regulations that strip the requirement to report on discrimination in lending, and other policies.[31] Yet, the senators' voting profile is antithetical to the composition of Texas, where "Latinos make up about 39% of the state's population." Unfortunately, almost half of those who are eligible to vote are not registered, compared with "only 27% of white eligible voters." Similarly, across the United States, "more than 42% of Latinos are not registered to vote." Nor are 43% of Asians. And "nearly 31% of blacks are unregistered." On the other hand, only 26 percent of eligible white voters are not registered.[32] In short, an increasingly diverse America is poised to have an increasingly racially homogenous electorate, and voter suppression exacerbates the consequences. In 2016 and 2017, whites were the only racial group where the majority cast a ballot for Donald Trump and Roy Moore, two wholly unqualified candidates who paraded their white supremacist views in a suit and tie.[33]

Meanwhile, states *and* cities where the GOP does not have full control have continued to move forward.[34] Delaware eliminated the requirement for absentee ballots to be notarized, thereby "expanding voting access for younger Delawareans attending school out of state."[35] New Mexico's state senate passed legislation to demolish the barrier that required citizens who wanted to cast a ballot to be registered to vote at least twenty-eight days before an election. The new bill knocks more than three weeks off that requirement and allows voting-eligible residents to register three days prior to an election. One of the sponsoring senators explained the rationale for the legislation, which has yet to become law: "When more citizens participate in our democracy, our democracy is stronger."[36] Connecticut passed legislation providing for same-day registration and online voter registration. Miles Rapoport, its former secretary of state, observed, "While other states are busy restricting the vote with new voter ID requirements and barriers to community voter registration drives, Connecticut . . . [is] opening up new avenues to voter participation." Again, the rationale was simple. "Democracy is at its best with active, engaged citizens," he said.[37] Similarly, although Minnesota has the highest voter turnout rate in the nation, the Democrats in the state senate were still not satisfied. Voting along straight party lines, they passed a bill to extend early voting to "15 days before an election, expand mail-in balloting to small communities and permit convicted felons to vote immediately after they are released from prison." Republicans balked at the provisions, but it appears that their major resistance was "political . . . In 2012, Barack Obama carried 17 of the 20 states that had the highest voter turnout."[38]

In 2016, just to the east of Minnesota, Wisconsin's voter turnout dropped by more than sixty thousand. Two-thirds of that decline, by design, happened in Milwaukee. The Republican state leadership made it clear that it was willing to strangle into submission Democratic strongholds like the city that houses 70 percent of the state's African

American population. But now, the mayor and aldermen are fighting back. They have authorized funding to expand the number of early voting sites for Wisconsin's largest city from three in 2016 to eight in 2018. Progressive civil society, such as One Wisconsin Institute, which has sued the state to end voter suppression, was fully behind the expansion. Executive director Scot Ross observed: "We know that when voters are given the opportunity to vote, that voters vote."[39] Similar efforts at expanding access to the franchise are occurring in Madison, Wisconsin; East Lansing, Michigan; New York City; St. Louis, Missouri; and Macon County, Illinois.[40]

Yet, for all these efforts, the work seems to be an "uphill climb."[41] The lie of voter fraud has embedded itself into the American imagination and has proved resistant to facts, studies, court cases, and reports proving otherwise.[42] As the tentacles of the lie continue to sink deeper and deeper into our democracy, they threaten to choke the very life out of the body politic and, in the end, severely weaken the United States.[43] Trevor Tejeda-Gervais, the Midwest organizing director for the nonpartisan group Common Cause, explained the nation's current, dire predicament: "We are only as strong as the most suppressive state."[44]

In short, we're in trouble. Years of gerrymandering, requiring IDs that only certain people have, illegally purging citizens from the voter rolls, and starving minority precincts of resources to create untenable conditions at the polls have exposed our electoral jugular and made the United States vulnerable to Russian attacks on our democracy. Those assaults played out as seamlessly as if they had been made in the USA and not hatched in the bowels of the Kremlin. But it's not just the Russian attack, as horrific as that is. Voter suppression has made the U.S. House of Representatives wholly unrepresentative.[45] It has placed in the presidency a man who is anything but presidential.[46] It has already reshaped the U.S. Supreme Court with the installation of Neil Gorsuch and Brett Kavanaugh, and as a slew of Trump's unqualified nominees to the federal bench get greenlighted by a compromised Senate, it threatens to undermine the judiciary for decades to come.[47]

Thus, when thirty-one states are vying to develop new and more ruthless ways to disfranchise their population, and when the others are searching desperately for ways to bring millions of citizens into the electorate, we have created a nation where democracy is simultaneously atrophying and growing—depending solely on where one lives. History makes clear, however, that this is simply not sustainable. It wasn't sustainable in the antebellum era.[48] It wasn't sustainable when the poll tax and literacy test gave disproportionate power in Congress to Southern Democrats.[49] And it's certainly not sustainable now.[50] Or, as Abraham Lincoln soberly observed, "I believe this government cannot endure, permanently half *slave* and half *free*."[51]

Afterword

"We Are Going to Warrior Up"

She actually said the quiet part out loud. At a campaign stop in Starkville, Mississippi, Republican Senator Cindy Hyde-Smith remarked: "There's a lot of liberal folks . . . we don't want to vote. Maybe we want to make it just a little more difficult. And I think that's a great idea."[1] Later that month, on yet another campaign stop, Hyde-Smith exclaimed that she would be "on the front row" if "invited . . . to a public hanging."[2]

This wasn't from 1890, when Mississippi politicians were putting the finishing touches on massive disfranchisement and the brutal architecture of Jim Crow. This wasn't even from 1964, when the FBI recovered several water-logged corpses while dragging the river looking for the bodies of civil rights workers James Chaney, Andrew Goodman, and Mickey Schwerner.[3] Instead, these were the sound-bites that epitomized the 2018 midterm elections in far too many states, not just Mississippi.

While the tactics were not as visibly violent as during Jim Crow, they were designed to be equally lethal to democracy and the nation's citizens. After two years of the Trump regime's cruelty, corruption, and racism, voters were convinced that the stakes in this election were "sky-high" because this was a "war for the soul of America." In fact, "93 percent of voters in battleground districts said their vote mattered just as much as in a presidential election; and enthusiasm about voting was at its highest level in any midterm in more than two decades."[4] Republicans knew that that enthusiasm had to be squelched; particularly because it was coming from populations that didn't traditionally vote for the GOP and because the party's policies and stances were highly unpopular with the majority of Americans.[5] Therefore, Republican strongholds in Georgia, Florida, North Carolina, Kansas, Wisconsin, Michigan, North Dakota, and Texas unleashed purges, poll closures, uncounted ballots, election fraud, voting machines rationed as if there was a famine, and outright threats of state-sanctioned power in order to shut down millions of Americans demanding democracy.

But the people kept fighting back. They had to. Republican-led attempts to dismantle the right to vote were, as one activist insisted, "a silent war."[6]

In North Dakota, the political power of Native Americans had shocked the state's GOP. First, indigenous voters were instrumental in electing Democrat Heidi Heitkamp to the U.S. Senate in 2012; then, they stood their ground for months at Standing Rock, upsetting all of the plans to quietly put an oil pipeline near the lands and water sources of indigenous peoples. When the Republican legislature got its chance, it struck back.[7] First, in 2013, after Heitkamp's victory, it passed a law that specified only three types of identification would be acceptable to vote—a North Dakota driver's license, a North Dakota identification card, or a tribal ID. Then, in each subsequent bill, the Republicans doubled down and slammed shut the alternate identification escape hatches for those who didn't have IDs; and finally, in 2016, they directly targeted Native Americans. Using the smokescreen of preventing voter fraud, the legislature now required IDs to have street addresses.

While it might sound logical and innocuous, there were three problems with this. Lawmakers couldn't point to any instances of voter fraud to warrant this legislation which, nonetheless, as a preemptive strike, was going to be devastating. There were 580,000 voting-age-eligible residents in North Dakota and 70,000 didn't have any of the state-approved IDs to vote.[8] In fact, Native Americans were twice as likely as other residents in North Dakota to not have the IDs.[9] And, reservations, where 60 percent of indigenous people in North Dakota lived, did not have street addresses for their homes. Until this new law, they weren't necessary. As indigenous journalist Jenni Monet remarked, "people don't need addresses to find neighbors on reservations." Mail was simply handled via P.O. Boxes.[10]

Seven Native American voters immediately sued Secretary of State Al Jaeger. Soon thereafter, the Native American Rights Fund joined the fight and won an injunction stopping North Dakota from implementing a law that made access to the ballot box dependent on something that Republican lawmakers knew the vast majority of indigenous people in the state did not have. But North Dakota kept pushing, pushing, pushing, and finally, in late September 2018, the Eighth Circuit ruled that the needs of the state to protect against voter fraud were compelling and that the midterms, which were just six weeks away, were still far enough out to not "adversely affect" anyone who needed to get a physical address.[11] In October 2018, the Supreme Court allowed the Eighth Circuit's decision to stand.[12]

Native Americans were now "scrambling."[13] How were they going to get street addresses for thousands of indigenous people right before the election? Secretary of State Jaeger offered a solution. He suggested that 911 operators could provide an address once the resident called in and described where he or she lived. Not only was this untried and untested, especially at this scale, it was also untrue. Those 911-generated addresses didn't always correspond to the rubric that county auditors used, thus leading to a legally perilous mismatch. One auditor spelled out the ramifications of the discrepancy for Native Americans: "If the address is incorrect it goes to the Attorney General's office where it will be prosecuted for fraud."[14] In short, a law ostensibly designed to stop voter fraud would, in fact, serve as the legal flytrap that actually created voter fraud. This is what Native Americans were up against. And they knew it. But they didn't flinch.

"We are going to warrior up," said O.J. Semans, co-executive director of Four Directions, a voter rights organization focused on Native Americans. He and his wife, Ruth, drove a thousand miles a week setting up phone banks, creating maps, and working with tribal leaders to get street addresses for all of the voters on the reservations. "You can only push somebody so far," he warned, "before they start pushing back."[15] Indeed, as journalist Jay Michaelson reported, "outrage over the law . . . led to a huge backlash and grassroots efforts to help people vote despite the law."[16] Lakota, Sioux, Chippewa, and Spirit Lake Tribe voters were determined that states like North Dakota "are aware we're here."[17] Phyllis Young, an organizer on the Standing Rock Sioux Reservation, was even more pointed: "The GOP's overt voter suppression 'is only making us more aware of our rights, more energized, and more likely to vote this November.'" The silent war was on.[18]

Meanwhile in Georgia, quietly and without fanfare or press attention, a stealth campaign was underway. A consultant recommended by the secretary of state's office had gone to ten county boards of elections and convinced them to shutter numerous polling stations in predominately black neighborhoods.[19] But then in August, the consultant went after the eleventh county. Citing violations of the Americans with Disabilities Act (ADA), he once again recommended closing the traditional and familiar sites where citizens had cast their ballots for years and had done so as late as the May 22 primary elections and July 24 Republican runoff. Suddenly, seemingly out of nowhere, a small announcement in the legal section of the local newspaper laid out that seven of the nine polling places in Randolph County were slated to be closed as soon as the Board of Elections met in late August.[20]

This had all of the earmarks of a targeted hit. Not only was Randolph County 61.4 percent black, but at least one of the polling places on the chopping block served 98 percent to 99 percent of African American voters in that precinct.[21] Eliminating most of the polling sites in the county would require voters who had no transportation to walk up to three hours, and others to drive twenty miles to cast a ballot.[22]

The consultant, Mike Malone, however, seemed perplexed that shutting down 78 percent of a county's polls was an issue at all. He told the Randolph County Board of Elections, "I don't see how you can say if you consolidate, you're disenfranchising voters."[23] Republican state representative Gerald Greene agreed. He was clear that he didn't like the timing of the closures, especially because the election was just a few months away, but he resented mightily the implications that race had anything to do with Malone's recommendations. Sounding like Selma's mayor in 1965, Greene asserted: "I don't like the outside agitation that brands us as racist . . . or as a place that suppresses the vote."[24]

Yet, just as in 1965, racism and voter suppression were front and center on the agenda. Sean Young of Georgia's ACLU remarked that the attempt to shut down the vast majority of the polling stations in Randolph County would leave "a reasonable observer to wonder whether the real motive behind these closures is indeed to make it harder for African Americans to cast a ballot."[25] The suspicions were well-founded.

The election consultant was directly tied to Secretary of State Brian Kemp, who had a hard-earned reputation for criminalizing organizations that registered minorities to vote, purging more than one million from the rolls, and suspending the registration of tens of thousands of African American voters in 2018.[26] He was the "voter-suppression king, who now wanted to be governor."[27] And Mike Malone had donated to his gubernatorial campaign.[28] Moreover, Kemp, disregarding ethics and even the pleas of President Jimmy Carter, refused to step down as secretary of state when he became the Republican nominee for governor.[29] Instead, like a director of the lottery who certifies the machinery, then draws the winning billion-dollar ticket, Kemp insisted on overseeing the high-profile, contentious election in which he was running in a statistical dead heat against Stacey Abrams, who was poised to be the first African American woman elected governor in the United States.[30]

Randolph County, therefore, looked increasingly like the latest in a string of sniper attacks that had already taken out numerous polling places in black communities, only this time the perpetrator got caught. Malone "explained that Kemp . . . had asked him to go around the state and 'recommend polling place closures' to various counties."[31] Apparently, the more than two hundred polling places that closed in Georgia after the *Shelby County v. Holder* decision weren't enough. Already, as journalist Bob Moser noted, those closures "correlate in near-perfect synchronicity with concentrations of high poverty across the state—the places where fewer people have cars to drive to the polls, where public transportation is often non-existent, and where African Americans vote Democratic."[32] A study by the *Atlanta Journal-Constitution* showed that after *Shelby*, "53 of Georgia's 159 counties have fewer polling sites now than in 2012." In addition, "thirty-nine of those 53 counties have higher poverty rates than the rest of the state and 30 of them have large African-American populations."[33] One activist explained, "Closing polling places in Black areas is a transparently racist tactic in line with literacy tests, poll taxes, and intimidation and harassment by law enforcement agents during the Jim Crow era."[34]

Malone's recommendations were suspicious not only because of his ties to Kemp but also because of the rush to adhere, just months before the election, to the Americans with Disabilities Act. As CBS News reported, "Officials have known about the ADA compliance problems in the county for at least six years." The county, in fact, "used a grant to fix violations at the courthouse" but left the other voting sites untouched and in violation of the code.[35] And, although

Malone was hired in January, ADA noncompliance was the situation throughout the 2018 Republican primary and the Republican runoff. During that time, he did not recommend any closures or identify alternative polling places that met ADA guidelines, nor did he recommend bringing the existing facilities up to code. The sense of urgency to comply with ADA regulations seemed to arise only when Brian Kemp faced a strong Democratic challenger for governor in the general election. Then and only then did Malone's recommendation to shut down seven of nine polling places come snaking through an innocuous legal notice in the local newspaper.[36]

Bobby Jenkins, the county's Democratic Party chairman, said that this notice was the first he knew of the proposal that would leave only two polling stations for nearly six thousand adults and that he had no idea "when they started" planning this. What he did know, however, was that this was not the first time the rights of black voters had come under attack in Randolph County and, just as before, he vowed, "We're going to fight to get this plan stopped."[37]

And fight they did. Kristen Clarke, the president and executive director of the Lawyers' Committee for Civil Rights, sent a take-no-prisoners letter to the Randolph County Board of Elections and Registration. It was, she explained, "letting them know that we intend to sue if they don't reverse course. We're giving them a chance to see the writing on the wall. If they choose to ignore that, we look forward to seeing them in court."[38] In addition, the ACLU and the NAACP Legal Defense and Educational Fund had also mobilized. By the time the battle was over, Mike Malone had been fired, the Randolph County Board of Elections had come under the intense spotlight of the national media, and an enraged citizenry packed the August meeting where the fate of Malone's recommendations would be decided. It wouldn't take longer than sixty seconds. The board rejected the consultant's recommendation then promptly adjourned.[39]

The intense media and public attention to poll closings in Georgia was, up to this point, an anomaly. It's easy to understand why. Generally, the process is so mundane, quiet, and bureaucratic that it goes unnoticed.[40] Nationwide, since the Supreme Court's gutting of the Voting Rights Act, "more than 1,000 polling sites have been closed in nine Republican-run states alone."[41] This slow burn through democracy happened without any significant outcry. But 2018 was different. It was a referendum on Trump; a referendum on accountability; and a referendum on whether this was a people's democracy or one driven by the money that silenced politicians in the face of numerous mass shootings, climate change, and the student loan debt crisis.[42]

It's no surprise, then, that attention soon turned to Dodge City, Kansas. The county clerk there, Debbie Cox, decided in October, with the election just a month away, to move the one and only polling place for thirteen thousand voters to a site beyond the city limits, a mile from public transportation, and not readily accessible by walking.[43] Her office then sent newly registered voters the wrong address to cast their ballot.[44]

None of this suggested happenstance. Dodge City was 60 percent Hispanic. The city had only that one voting site, while the surrounding county, which was majority white, had three locations that remained untouched. And, as in Georgia, Kansas's secretary of state, Kris Kobach, notorious for voter suppression and rabid nativism, was also running for governor and refused to step down from overseeing his own election.[45]

American citizens from across the nation vowed to fight this. They poured resources—buses, cars, funding—into Dodge City to ensure that the people would restore the voting rights that Kansas was trying to take away.[46]

Meanwhile, the ACLU and the League of United Latin American Citizens (LULAC) sued to force Cox to open a second voting site that was accessible at least by public transportation. "We understand," said Micah Kubic, executive director of the ACLU in Kansas, "that there are people who believe voting is a privilege, but we don't. It is a right that must be fiercely protected."[47] When the ACLU also demanded that the organization's voter help hotline be made available to citizens in Dodge City, Cox apparently scoffed, writing "LOL" when she forwarded the letter to Secretary of State Kobach.[48] While Senate Minority Leader Anthony Hensley blasted her response as "despicable," Cox claimed that "she didn't mean anything when she wrote 'LOL'" and that moving the polling place to an inaccessible site out of the city "wasn't done with any racial intention at all." While proclaiming her racial innocence, she hired Bradley Schlozman, who, when he was an attorney in George W. Bush's Department of Justice, worked to "gerrymander all of those crazy libs right out of the [DOJ's civil rights] section" and now, in private practice, had a reputation for "defending states and towns accused of trying to restrict voting."[49]

This had all of the earmarks of high noon. But then the bullet ricocheted. Madai Rivera, LULAC's Kansas state director, testified about the "challenges faced by Dodge City Latino voters" who were the backbone of the meatpacking industry and, thus, the rejuvenation of the town's economy. Many, she explained, "work hourly jobs and can't afford to leave a shift, find a ride across town and wait in a long line." Schlozman, however, mocked the toll on Latinos' voting rights. "The burden has been extremely exaggerated," he countered. He didn't see that a polling station outside of the city limits and away from public transportation would impose any real difficulties on working-class people who had to punch a time clock or lose pay. Rather, Schlozman intoned, what Rivera and the ACLU "have attempted" to do is "elevate typical life vagaries and inconveniences to constitutional magnitude. Neither case law nor common sense support their claims." He was, of course, minimizing the disproportionate impact that moving the polling place had on a population that was 61 percent Hispanic. This move was especially egregious because their voter turnout rate was already significantly lower than that of whites in Dodge City and the surrounding Ford County. Cox insisted that she was racially colorblind because she "didn't recognize either a Latino or white part of town." On the other hand, the defense continued, the ACLU and LULAC were being unreasonable. It was too close to the election to make any further changes such as opening up another polling place. Chaos and confusion would mar the election, one of Kobach's lieutenants testified, and there would be no way to prevent voter fraud because the registration books couldn't be parsed out finely enough at this late date to ensure that the rolls matched the voters in that precinct. The judge, in the end, concurred.[50]

In other words, even though it was Cox who had actually created the "confusion" by moving Dodge City's only polling place a month before the election for a construction project that had yet to occur and sending voters the wrong address to cast their ballots, she would not be sanctioned nor would voters find judicial relief.[51] Instead, the timing of her actions did what carefully planned voter suppression tactics are designed to do. They backed the judiciary into the same corner that Texas's voter ID law had done years earlier and that North Carolina's racially gerrymandered districts did in 2018.[52] Despite all of the telltale signs of a discriminatory policy, judges feared that any remedy with only a few days before the general election would lead to electoral chaos. Therefore, the flawed actions of the state had to stand even if they influenced—or, more likely, tainted—the midterms.

In Waller County, Texas, the rationale was equally logical and pernicious. Election officials cited "limited resources" as the reason there could be no early voting at a historically black university, Prairie View A&M, which had 8,400 students and the largest concentration of African Americans in the county.[53]

The university was already the home of a landmark Supreme Court decision that gave heft to the Twenty-Sixth Amendment, which lowered the voting age to eighteen. In the early 1970s, Waller County officials tried to negate that amendment as surreptitiously as Mississippi had done with the Fifteenth during the advent of Jim Crow. Waller County tax collector and voter registrar LeRoy Symm and his deputies would register people they knew or those listed on the tax rolls. Others, however, had to complete a questionnaire to determine legal residency and the right to vote in the county. Two key criteria were status as a college student and whether the would-be voter had paid property taxes in Waller County. That seemingly mundane, bureaucratic criterion—property tax payment—was as targeted as North Dakota's requirement for a street address. College students weren't buying homes or land in the area and everyone knew that. It was, therefore, a criterion with no real viable purpose other than to eliminate the HBCU students from Waller County's electorate. The students fought back and won in *Symm v. United States* (1979).[54]

Still, even after the Supreme Court ruling, Waller County election officials quietly worked around the decision and refused to place voting machines on campus until three decades later. That is to say, until 2013, students, who were more than half of the county's population, often had to walk along a mile of busy roadway to get to the nearest polling place.[55] As Vann Newkirk II notes, since the 1970s, Waller County has "been a mess of lawsuits, and of both subtle and more brazen plans to dilute the voting strength of Prairie View's mostly black student body" including "curtailing early voting" on campus in 2003 when a student ran for commissioner.[56]

The county's entrenched resistance to black students' voting rights, therefore, made the latest maneuver in 2018 simply another link in the long chain of disfranchisement.[57] Students comprised "a significant voting population in Waller County," and this was no ordinary election. Texas was the battleground for a tight, high-profile senate race between "the most hated man in the U.S. Senate," Republican Ted Cruz, and a $70.2 million grassroots-funded Democrat, Representative Beto O'Rourke.[58]

Waller County officials again went after the ever-popular early voting. At first, they provided no hours and no voting machines whatsoever on Prairie View's campus. None. Meanwhile, the city of Waller, "which has a majority white population and half of the eligible voting-age population of Prairie View," had access to multiple polling machines and eleven full days of early voting.[59] Waller County officials "vehemently denied" that racism had anything to do with it; this was, they claimed, just a function of resources. Theirs were limited and so they deployed the voting machines in the most efficacious way. It just so happened to not be at Prairie View A&M.[60]

Neither the students nor the NAACP LDF bought it. The claim simply made no sense. The county had chosen to place all of the early voting sites in the areas with the fewest voters and, at the same time, provided no hours and no machines in the area that had the largest number of voters. Prairie View students, who have a long civil rights protest tradition, were not going to abide by this clear violation of their right to vote. They had fought Waller County before and won and they were ready to do it again. Kalynn Lakes, president of the NAACP student chapter at Prairie View, said, "Whether I'm a student living here for four or five years or a permanent resident, it doesn't mean my voice doesn't count."[61]

Student protests mounted, national media swarmed in, and LDF sounded the alarm of yet another lawsuit. The county reluctantly responded, but only with as great a half-measure as could be imagined: There would be no early voting at all during the first week. And during the last week, the county would establish three days of early voting for Prairie View A&M but "two of those days will be held at an off-campus location . . . not easily accessible to students that lack transportation." And, "neither site would offer weekend hours."[62] LDF's lawsuit, therefore, cut to the chase: "There is no legitimate, non-discriminatory reason" for black voters to have three days and white voters eleven to cast their ballots.[63] Moreover, LDF was ready to make this a battle for the long haul. Leah Aden,

LDF's deputy director of litigation, laid out that this lawsuit was not just about November 2018. It was to put an end to the need to have lawsuit after lawsuit after lawsuit for every election just to compel officials to uphold the basic constitutional rights of Waller County's citizens. The judge saw things differently. In his estimation, this wasn't about race. He ruled that Democratic chairwoman Rosa Harris asked that there be no first week of voting because she didn't want it to interfere with homecoming. And, even more importantly, the county had done everything it could with its limited resources. Prairie View A&M received three days of voting. That was sufficient. The LDF's response was vintage LDF. This isn't over.[64]

The 2018 midterms not only exposed the quiet burn through voting rights that shuttering, moving, and restricting access to polling stations kindled, but also turned the spotlight on yet another stealth mode of destroying American citizens' ability to cast ballots: voter roll purges. As the Brennan Center reported, in the two years before the 2016 presidential election, sixteen million voters were wiped off the rolls. This wasn't routine or normal. The eliminations, it turns out, were at a substantially higher rate than they were before the Supreme Court's *Shelby County v. Holder* decision. In fact, the "increase in purged voters was most significant in parts of the country with a history of racial discrimination" and that were previously under the preclearance provisions of the Voting Rights Act. Georgia, for example, under Brian Kemp, "purged twice as many voters—1.5 million—between the 2012 and 2016 elections as it did between 2008 and 2012."[65]

Kemp, however, was only just beginning to cull the electorate, to wipe out the voting rights of those who overwhelmingly opposed him. This opposition was deep and strong. In an *Atlanta Journal-Constitution* poll, 90 percent of African Americans in Georgia disapproved of Kemp.[66] He was, therefore, and rightly, afraid of the power of minority voters. He was determined to silence them.[67] During 2017, he erased 668,000 voters from the rolls, most of whom were removed because they had ostensibly left the state. But a further analysis demonstrated that 340,134 of them were "wrongly purged." They still lived in Georgia and had never moved.[68] Investigative journalist Greg Palast remarked, as he surveyed the electoral damage, "If it were random it would be unfair and undemocratic. It's worse. It's racial."[69] Yet, that bludgeoning of citizens' voting rights continued. For Kemp, his political career depended upon it.[70] From 2016 to 2018, he eliminated more than 10 percent of Georgia's voters from the rolls.[71] Three months before the midterm election, his office purged an additional eighty-five thousand.[72]

Stacey Hopkins, a black woman and activist in Atlanta, was one of them. She was indignant as she held the secretary of state's notice of disfranchisement in her hand. "This was the line that got me," she sneered: " 'You have not voted or updated your registration in at least three years.' " How could that be, she asked. "I. Just. Voted!" Hopkins exclaimed. In fact, not only had she voted in the 2018 primary elections, she had also been a registered voter since 1992. But, she railed, "Secretary of State Kemp and Fulton County tried to come for my vote and three of my children." And she was not going to have any of it. "There is blood on this ground," she preached. And, in the fight for the right to vote, "We are the defenders!" The ACLU certainly thought so and dragged Kemp's office to court on her behalf and won. Hopkins was proud that her clarion call and the ACLU's actions "were able to save one hundred fifty-nine thousand voters who were just like me. Yes," she emphasized, "one hundred fifty-nine thousand."[73]

Kemp had used a standard conservative "enemies list" to justify his office's scorched-earth policy through the voter rolls. He claimed he was about defending the integrity of the vote against the "radical leftists," "outside agitators," and "criminal illegals" who were pouring into the state to take democracy away from its rightful owners. At a campaign rally where Donald Trump continued to stoke the baseless fears about "illegals" overrunning the state, Kemp had already tilled the ground with the lie that his opponent, Stacey Abrams, was encouraging "illegals"—documented and undocumented—to build the blue wave and vote for her. He told the throngs that they had the power to stop it: "We can build a wall—a big, red, beautiful wall—around the state of Georgia to knock that blue wave down."[74]

The threat to Kemp's political aspirations, however, was not coming from outside the state. It was homegrown and fed up with voter suppression, his office's cybersecurity incompetence, and his own personal ethics violations.[75] It wasn't about building a wall—although that rhetorical flourish tied in well with Trump's fearmongering xenophobia—it was about purging Georgia's voters at a rate twice as high as that before the *Shelby* decision and continuing to winnow the voter rolls well into 2018 (while running for governor).

Kemp's strategy also required blocking American citizens from becoming registered voters in the first place. Oddly enough, on the surface Georgia almost looked electorally progressive. Kemp's office boasted that "it has never been easier to vote in our state."[76] There are, in fact, electoral innovations in Georgia that states like Mississippi, Alabama, and New York don't have.[77] In addition to no-excuse absentee voting, online voter registration, and early voting, the state also has automatic voter registration. Automatic voter registration has the potential to expand and diversify the electorate as it did in Oregon. But the cutting edge of voting policy is consistently dulled by the archaic knife of racism and disfranchisement, as Kemp so clumsily demonstrated in October 2018 with Georgia's Exact Match program.

An investigation by the Associated Press uncovered that, on the last day to register and be eligible to cast a ballot in the November midterms, Kemp's office had captured fifty-three thousand voter registration cards and put them in "pending" status because of some discrepancy, somewhere, between the registration form and the Department of Driver Services or Social Security databases. It could be an errant or missing accent—Renée rather than Renee—a hyphen in one place but not the other—Marquez-Garcia rather than Marquez Garcia—or even a typo. The courts had already ruled that Exact Match was racially discriminatory because of its built-in methodology that privileged anglicized names. The "new and improved" version—which Kemp lobbied for, and was passed by the GOP-dominated, gerrymandered state legislature—had the same problem, however. Of the fifty-three thousand registrations pulled by Kemp's office, African Americans' registrations comprised 70 percent of those held in electoral purgatory.[78] The heavy imbalance was centered around ten counties that housed the state's major cities of Atlanta, Macon, Albany, Augusta, Savannah, and Columbus. In Fulton County, for example, 75.7 percent of the pending Exact Match voter registrations were from African Americans; in DeKalb, it was 71.1 percent; for Dougherty County, 80.7 percent.[79] Kemp insisted that voters could still go to the polls, they just needed to present the appropriate documentation to clear up whatever the inconsistencies were between the registration card and the state's or the Social Security Administration's database. Yet, it was not clear what triggered the suspension in the first place. So, would a marriage license clarify the problem? Divorce decree? Birth certificate? Tax return? Utility bill? Social Security card? The very essence of ambiguity heightens the confusion about what it would take to be registered and confusion depresses voter turnout. Or, as Stacey Abrams explained, "53,000 have been told, 'You may be able to vote, you may not, it's up to you to prove it.'"[80]

Just a week after news hit about fifty-three thousand voter registration cards in limbo, officials in Jefferson County went after a busload of African American voters. It started with an event at the Jefferson County Leisure Center, where a group of black senior citizens listened intently to LaTosha Brown and Cliff Albright of Black

Voters Matter. The nonpartisan organization and its directors had been traveling throughout the South advocating the power and necessity of the vote. The senior citizens, many of whom had living memories of Jim Crow, were eager to wield that power, especially in this key election. One seventy-year-old woman recalled, "When I was coming up, I didn't know what voting was," and, now, in the twenty-first century, "There's been some issues . . . But," she laughed, "I ain't finna get in no trouble."[81]

But trouble was coming, nonetheless. It was the first day of early voting in Georgia. The senior citizens were pumped up and determined to go vote.[82] They asked if Brown and Albright could take them on the Black Voters Matter bus to the polling place. It was "a moment of epic black joy" as the seniors were "singing songs" and "chanting."[83] It was also a moment of panic, fear, and Old South paternalism on the part of the county commissioners. As the bus was loaded up with more than forty voters and getting ready to pull out of the lot, the center director, who apparently received a phone call from the county clerk, ordered the senior citizens to disembark.[84]

Stunned, one woman asked, "Why we can't vote?"[85]

While the county commissioners fumbled for an answer, Cliff Albright had one:

There's not a candidate on this bus, there's not a party symbol on this bus, but I'm going to tell you what is on this bus—a whole bunch of black fists in the air with the word "power" underneath it. That's what scared them and made them say "Those folks have to come off that bus."[86]

As the incident exploded over traditional and social media, the commissioners insisted that race had nothing to do with it. Rather, they claimed, the center was nonpartisan and "this was a prohibited political activity."[87] Yet, that rationale crumbled beneath the Jefferson

County Leisure Center Facebook post that same day announcing an upcoming talk by a Republican running for reelection.[88]

The commissioners also stressed that they didn't know who this "third party"—Black Voters Matter—was, despite the organization already having been vetted and approved by the center. Nonetheless, they remained "uncomfortable" with this group taking senior citizens off the center's grounds. Atlanta-based music producer Isaac Hayes III scoffed at that: "These are grown adults that went to go vote." But, the county commissioners "made them get off the bus like they were being kidnapped . . . That's a textbook example of voter suppression itself."[89]

County Administrator Adam Brett insisted, however, that this move was simply about the county's obligation to ensure the safety of those at the center and to limit the government's liability if something awful happened. "These senior citizens," he explained, "are under the complete care and supervision of Jefferson County while they are at the Senior Center."[90] To be clear, though, this was not a long-term care facility or a psych ward. This was a community center where people voluntarily came and went as they pleased. As LaTosha Brown said with unyielding clarity, "These are grown people. We're not talking about children . . . They're not a resident of the center, nobody has control or authority over them."[91]

In this county that was 53 percent black, energized African American voters, especially voters engaging in civic life as a group, sent a tremor through the political biosphere. Albright set out the scenario: "Somebody called the County Commission to complain because they saw all these black folks get on this big black bus—it's the blackest bus in America—somebody drove past, saw that, got nervous, got mad, called the County Commission's office, which then called the center. And the bottom line was, all the folks who had just got on the bus . . . had to come off the bus."[92] It was a shockwave felt all the way in the offices of the NAACP LDF, which demanded an investigation into this "unacceptable act of voter intimidation."[93]

While Jefferson County officials blocked a busload of African Americans from voting, Trump's Departments of Justice and Homeland Security set out to cow entire groups of North Carolinians into electoral silence. The state has a burgeoning population of Asians and Hispanics. Some are citizens, some are not. "Since 2000, the state's Asian population has more than doubled, increasing from 114,000 to 268,000, a growth rate of 136% . . . the Hispanic population was nearly 912,000, an increase of more than half a million or 141% over fifteen years."[94] The changing demographics, especially as more gain their American citizenship and register to vote, have the potential to upend electoral politics in North Carolina, a key swing state in presidential elections.

Anti-immigrant policies and repeated lies about millions of voting noncitizens, of course, have been a cornerstone of Trump's regime.[95] During the 2018 election, he fanned the flames with Mad Max imagery about "hordes of immigrants in caravans from Central America threatening to launch an ongoing spree of murder, sex trafficking, and drug running throughout the United States."[96] He weaponized the Department of Homeland Security's Immigration and Customs Enforcement (ICE) in ways virtually unimaginable. ICE ripped asylum-seeking families apart, separating children from their parents and deliberately not documenting familial relationships as the agency deported the adults and locked the children in cages.[97] ICE also terrorized communities by showing up at courthouses and workplaces and seizing people who had been brought to the United States as children decades earlier, deporting them to lands unfamiliar and far, far away.[98] ICE simply brought terror. Terror as policy.[99] And now it was coming to North Carolina.

On the Friday before Labor Day weekend at five o'clock, ICE and the Department of Justice combined to hit a series of North Carolina's County Boards of Elections with a massive and "haphazard" subpoena demanding that forty-four counties provide within twenty-one days fifteen million records on voters.[100] ICE and the justice department wanted "poll books, voting records, voting authorization documents, and executed ballots for the last five years." A revised subpoena expanded the request to all hundred counties for dates going back to January 1, 2010.[101] The document requests were so "sprawling" that it was clear that the feds were on a "fishing expedition."[102] ICE and the Justice Department also demanded "registration application forms, postcard applications, federal write-in absentee ballots, early voting application forms, provisional voting forms, absentee ballot request forms, any record of voter cancellations and any form in which someone admits or denies being a non-citizen."[103] ICE and Justice weren't done. They then subpoenaed the state's Division of Motor Vehicles, which is a key site for voter registration. The federal agencies "demanded eight years of information," including "applications completed in a language other than English."[104]

At first the county boards couldn't believe it; they thought the subpoenas were "fake" and perhaps "a Russian plot to get the ballots." The information requested looked like a dark web phishing expedition: "dates of birth, Social Security numbers and even the actual voted ballots of millions of people."[105] But it soon occurred to many that these subpoenas mirrored the aggressive data requests by Trump's Electoral Integrity Commission, which had earlier tried but failed spectacularly to prove rampant voter fraud committed especially by minorities and immigrants.[106] This time emerging from the darkness was ICE, reinforced by a Department of Justice led by Jeff Sessions with his well-documented contempt for immigrants. The agency hunted for applications not written in English, driver's license applications from non-citizens, and voter cancellations tied to citizenship.[107] As expected, the initial demand for a "tsunami" of documents targeted the areas of North Carolina "with high concentrations of minority voters."[108]

The implications were a democracy's nightmare. Gunther Peck, an associate professor of public policy at Duke University, explained, "There is a genuine fear that by linking voting to ICE, legal citizens might be anxious about voting because ICE has detained and rounded up people that are [U.S.] citizens."[109] Repeatedly.[110] This was voter suppression through intimidation. The NAACP and the ACLU explained that concept to Attorney General Jeff Sessions: "The extremely broad and unprecedented subpoenas extend far beyond the scope of any legitimate law enforcement objective." These subpoenas were, instead, designed to "threaten voters' constitutional right to cast a ballot free from fear and intimidation as well as their expectation that their personally identifiable information . . . and voting preferences will remain private."[111]

The question was whether the bipartisan North Carolina Board of Elections would cave to the enormous pressure from two behemoth federal bureaucracies. Would the board abandon its citizens? The answer was resounding. Although the board comprised four Democrats, four Republicans, and one independent, its members unanimously agreed. The board "stands ready to assist any federal, state, or local investigation into illegal activity." They refused, however, to be part of any scheme "if the purpose of the investigation is to advance a false narrative of voter fraud, if it's to propagandize a voter ID amendment [that was on the state's midterm ballot], if it's to suppress African-American votes, [or] if it's to intimidate Hispanic voters."[112] The board members, therefore, questioned ICE about the "political motivation behind this unprecedented request." They brought up how "President Trump has continually repeated false claims regarding widespread voter fraud in the 2016 election." And, they made the connection between those lies and the subpoenas that now hung over North Carolina like Damocles's sword. "This new North Carolina document request by ICE appears to pick up where the [Pence-Kobach] Commission left off and seeks to use allegations of widespread voter fraud to justify voter suppression and intimidation practices." North Carolina's Board of Elections, with the support of the state's attorney general, decided to fight.[113] The feds backed down. But they didn't back off. There was some faint recognition that an impending midterm election and a slow-moving hurricane that had caused $24 billion in damage had disrupted greatly the state's ability to respond.[114] ICE and the DOJ, however, were planning to come back in 2019.

While North Carolina was dealing with enormous pressure from a federal government intent on intimidation and proving voter fraud, it was also wrestling with the consequences of the Department of Justice's refusal to go after a clear case of *election* fraud and the resulting subsequent attempt to steal a congressional seat.

In North Carolina's Ninth District, Republican Mark Harris hired Leslie McCrae Dowless Jr., a man known as a "guru of elections."[115] Dowless's candidates were virtually invincible. Harris had already confronted this hard, cold reality in 2016, when he lost in the primaries to one of Dowless's men. At the time, however, Harris suspected there was something just not quite right with the final vote count. His opponent had won 221 of Bladen County's 226 mail-in absentee ballots. Harris only received four absentee votes.[116] It appeared that in the counties where Dowless was active the votes came rolling in like a powerful thunderstorm, although the tallies raised Category 4 alarms.[117] But Harris wanted to win, and if what it took was to get Leslie McCrae Dowless on his 2018 campaign payroll, then so be it.[118]

Dowless had previously brushed up against the North Carolina Board of Elections. In 2016, when Republican Governor Pat McCrory and his team of lawyers went hunting for voter fraud to explain his loss to Democrat Roy Cooper, they stumbled across some voting anomalies in Bladen County. They gathered "evidence" and then accused "an African American community group [the Bladen County Improvement Association (BCIA)] for an alleged absentee ballot scheme that in reality was led by Republican operative Leslie McCrae Dowless Jr."[119]

As the Republicans made their case before the board, they got names wrong, had incorrect data, made "sloppy errors," and presented Dowless, who was a candidate for Soil and Water Conservation District supervisor, as a victim of voter fraud, while he was, in fact, a perpetrator of election fraud. He actually sat there listening to testimony presented by the Republican-backed attorneys about how crooked and scandalous the BCIA's actions were, when the evidence and affidavits were actually detailing bit by bit what Dowless's operation had done to steal an election.[120]

The board knew it. It had launched its own investigation and found how Dowless's employees would "'push' absentee voters to choose Donald Trump, McCrory, and other Republican candidates, and that Dowless would pay them for delivering completed absentee ballots, a practice prohibited by North Carolina law except in special cases."[121]

Not only did the North Carolina Board of Elections find against the Republicans' complaint, but also in January 2017 the board's executive director, Kim Strach, urged the U.S. Department of Justice to "file criminal charges against" Leslie McCrae Dowless and his operatives "for illegally gathering absentee ballots in Bladen County." If this enterprise went unpunished, Strach warned, similar "violations would likely recur in future elections."[122] The board was so desperate they not only went to the U.S. attorney's office but also to the local district attorney, and the FBI. Nothing. No movement whatsoever. The board's concerns and pleas simply went unanswered. One of the women whose vote had been jeopardized by Dowless's operation was livid. "Whoever . . . is supposed to be following up on crooked elections, is not doing their job," she railed.[123]

Despite the obvious cloud over Dowless, Harris hired him anyway.[124] And during the 2018 midterms, the campaign operative delivered. He had eighty employees fanned out over Bladen and Robeson Counties, urging people to vote absentee, then following up, collecting the ballots, and sending them in. With a twist. His workers would routinely gather blank or incomplete ballots, fill them in voting a straight Republican ticket, then witness the form as if the actual voter had made all the selections for candidates. Dowless trained his team to use "the same color ink as the voter who filled out other parts of the ballot," put the completed forms in mailboxes close to the homes of the voters, and place the stamps in a certain way so as not to raise the suspicions of the county election boards. Meanwhile, other ballots were dumped at his office for special handling. In fact, there were "stacks of them on his desk." In return his ballot workers received cash for the number of absentee ballots they distributed and collected.[125] It was a smooth, effective operation that helped Mark Harris win the Ninth Congressional District by 905 votes. It was also illegal.

The red flags were many. Numerous absentee ballots had been witnessed by "the same handful of people." In fact, "three witnesses signed more than 40 ballots each, another signed 30, and three other people signed more than 10 apiece." Dowless's operation alone had turned in 592 of the "684 absentee ballots ultimately cast in [Bladen] county." There were other anomalies as well. Harris won 61 percent of the absentee vote in the county. But only "19 percent of Bladen County's accepted mail-in absentee ballots were cast by registered Republicans." Which means "that along with the almost 20% of loyal registered Republicans who voted that method, Harris would have also received almost all the registered unaffiliated voters and/or some Democratic registered voters to make it to 62% [*sic*] of the vote."[126] Bladen County, as well as Robeson County, where Dowless also operated, had another statistical phenomenon—votes that just disappeared. The initial analysis showed that in Robeson County alone "nearly two-thirds of the absentee ballots, or 1,180 ballots, weren't returned." The statewide average was around 25 percent.[127] In fact, "Robeson had more unreturned ballots than Mecklenburg County (home to Charlotte) despite Mecklenburg casting three times as many total votes as Robeson."[128] Worse yet was the racial dynamic of those missing ballots. The Raleigh *News & Observer* noted:

> More than 40 percent of the ballots requested by African Americans and more than 60 percent of those requested by American Indians did not make it back to election officials. For white voters, that figure was just 17 percent.[129]

A Harvard University professor looked at this data and declared that "the rates of unreturned absentee ballots in two Ninth District counties were 'extreme statistical outliers.'"[130] The Wake County District Attorney also had questions including "the possibility that absentee ballots were gathered in areas considered to be supportive of [Harris's opponent Dan] McCready but never turned in."[131]

As an editorial in the *Washington Post* noted, the Republicans "have spent the past decade crying wolf over voter fraud as a pretext for imposing needlessly complicated ID requirements."[132] Yet they refused to acknowledge what happened right in front of them: election fraud, when "a candidate's campaign sets out to manipulate vote tallies to steal an election."[133] The North Carolina Republican Party simply dismissed the magnitude of what Dowless did on Harris's behalf and offered, instead, that the "reality is that there aren't enough ballots in question to change the outcome of this election." That statement required the GOP to ignore the 1,675 unreturned absentee ballots, the hundreds completed by Dowless's operatives and not the voters, and North Carolina law stating that if "irregularities or improprieties . . . taint the results of the entire election and cast doubt on its fairness" the state elections board can order a new election. Instead, the party brushed that aside and "urged the elections board to certify the results," so that Harris with his 905-vote "victory" could take his seat in the U.S. Congress.[134] Harris, of course, agreed. "There is absolutely no public evidence," he had tweeted, "that there are enough ballots in question to affect the outcome of this race." Nate Silver, an expert on election polling and statistics, retorted: "This is simply not true; there ARE enough ballots in question in NC-9 to potentially affect the outcome."[135] The North Carolina GOP didn't care and threatened to sue if Harris wasn't seated.[136]

The North Carolina Board of Elections didn't back down. Instead, it investigated just as it had in 2016 and, once again, Dowless was in the middle of electoral corruption. During the board's hearings in February 2019, his employees testified about how they collected the absentee ballots and what they did with them afterwards. It was damning. Dowless clearly ran an illegal ballot snatch-and-grab operation. But Mark Harris tried to shield himself from the taint behind a wall of innocence—he had no idea there were any red flags about the campaign operative. He didn't know what was going on. He thought his campaign manager was on top of Dowless, ensuring that everything was legitimate. He just didn't know. Harris's wall held, for a moment. Then the Republican's son, an assistant U.S. attorney, took the stand and knocked it down with a sledgehammer of documents that detailed his numerous warnings to his father about Dowless's "shady" reputation and ethical lapses. In other words, Mark Harris knew exactly with whom he was dealing and had hired. And, as the son sat on the stand and testified, the father, a Baptist minister, sat there across from him in tears, exposed as a liar and an election thief.[137] There was going to be a new election in North Carolina's Ninth District, but Mark Harris would not be a candidate and Leslie McCrae Dowless Jr. would be under indictment.[138]

The case of the disappeared votes also haunted Georgia's midterm election. The major issue was how reliable, secure from hacking, and readily available were the voting machines. On all three standards, Brian Kemp abdicated responsibility, blamed others, and oversaw a system where the counties that would lean heaviest toward his opponent did not have the equipment they needed to handle the massive turnout of voters.

In November 2018, Georgia's voting machines were, by technological standards, archaeological relics. They ran on Windows 2000, which Microsoft hadn't supported since the summer of 2010, and left no auditable paper trail.[139] As a result, "there is no way to verify whether the counts are accurate or whether the vote has been hacked."[140]

Even though the Department of Homeland Security warned Kemp that hacking was a possibility, he ignored the DHS and its secretary Jeh Johnson for years.[141] That is, until 2016, when, at a DefCon hacker convention in Las Vegas, an organization took control over the way Georgia's voting machines register and store votes, although it had little expertise in voting matters.[142] At that point, Secretary of State Kemp finally accepted federal dollars, which he had previously refused, to update some of the machines. But his efforts were too little, too late. Two key elections had already occurred.

Groups sued the state, alleging that the 2016 presidential election and a 2017 special election had been hacked. Shortly after Kemp received notification of the lawsuit, officials at Kennesaw State University, which provides logistical support for the state's election machinery, "destroyed the server that housed statewide election data."[143] That series of events, including an April visit to the small campus by Ambassador Sergey Kislyak of Russia, raised warning flags for many observers.[144] But not to Kemp, who said that there was nothing untoward in any of it; the erasure was "in accordance with standard IT procedures."[145]

The lawsuits concerning potential hacking of the 2016 and 2017 elections, however, provided a convenient cover for Kemp to sequester seven hundred voting machines in Fulton County and ensure they would not be available for the 2018 midterms.[146] They remained embargoed even after the plaintiffs in *Curling v. Kemp* informed him that if the machines were needed for the election, it was "possible to have a workable arrangement . . . for sampling or imaging of the data." Kemp just needed to let the plaintiffs know.[147] He never did. An additional three hundred machines didn't make it to November 6, 2018, because they had been used for early voting.[148] In total, Cobb County lost access to 550 voting machines; Fulton, 700; and DeKalb, 585. As journalist Charles P. Pierce noted, Kemp "locked up the voting machines from important Democratic counties so that the voters could watch their fingernails grow while waiting in line." Not surprisingly, "all three counties impacted by the shortage favored Democrat Stacey Abrams over Republican Brian Kemp."[149]

As Georgia prepared for the midterm elections, then, all was not well. There was a secretary of state running for governor, one who held onto his current job while striving for a higher elected office, creating an ethical conflict of interest that he flat-out refused to resolve. There was a high-profile, statistical dead-heat governor's race that promised to drive record voter turnout in the midst of widespread efforts at voter suppression. There were voting machines that were easily hackable with no auditable paper trail. Then, there was Kemp's office, which was tasked with ensuring election integrity but was lax on cybersecurity and so dismissive of expert testimony that U.S. District Judge Amy Totenberg admonished Kemp that "the Defendants and State election officials had buried their heads in the sand" and left the state's election machinery vulnerable.[150] There was also a refusal by Kemp's office to use any of the ten million dollars from the federal government to buy new machines to replace those embargoed.[151] And, an unwillingness to contact the court to release into use some of the seven hundred machines sequestered in Fulton County because of lawsuits. Altogether, a perfect electoral storm blew through Georgia.

It was as chaotic, mismanaged, and frustrating as expected. Predictably, because of Kemp's machinations, precincts "with particularly long lines [were] in African American neighborhoods."[152] In Gwinnett County, a rapidly diversifying area in metro Atlanta whose demography changed from 67 percent white in 2000 to less than 40 percent white in 2017, "machines in at least four voting locations . . . went down."[153] People lost a full day at work (and pay). The lines "were at a standstill." The problems with the voting machines "started around 7 am and were not resolved until around 11:30 am." Then, and only then, did the lines finally begin to move. It took 4½ hours.[154] One voter noted, "It's like waiting on line at Six Flags," a nearby amusement park, but at least those lines, while long, did move. Not so in Gwinnett, the state's second-largest county. "We've got people who are voting with the paper ballots, and we've got people who are standing to wait for the machines to be fixed, and we've got people who said they are planning to come back," a county spokesman explained to the *New York Times*.[155] One voter told reporters, "I wanted to come in, do my voting and get out and that didn't happen today." Another simply said, "It was very frustrating."[156] Someone forgot the power cords to the machines and couldn't find them. Batteries were running down at another voting site. The computer system that logs voters in stopped working. And this was just in Gwinnett. Fulton, DeKalb, and Cobb were plagued with their own and similar problems, such as names of voters suddenly disappearing from the rolls, the rationing of provisional ballots because someone else might need them more, and one predominantly black precinct receiving only one-third the required number of voting machines because of a calculation error.[157] A woman who waited hours to vote wryly noted, "In a way, we were expecting something to go wrong."[158]

Something else, however, had gone horribly awry. More than one hundred thousand votes disappeared. Voters were at the machines but their selections may have never been tallied. The phenomenon showed up in the race for lieutenant governor of Georgia. Usually there's a 0.8 percent drop-off in the number of votes as the ticket goes down ballot from governor to lieutenant governor; e.g., from 100 percent to 99.2 percent. Then there's another decline for the next officeholder, and so on, and so on. But in Georgia a strange anomaly occurred: The insurance commissioner race, which was way down ballot, received more votes than the race for lieutenant governor, the second-highest ranking office in the state. That defied all electoral parameters. It simply made no sense.[159]

As statisticians, political scientists, and computer scientists began scouring the data, no analysis could explain what had happened. Then, "just for kicks, they decided to run a statistical analysis by race." There it was. The greater the number of African Americans in a precinct, the greater the drop-off in votes. Equally important, it wasn't *just* the blacker the district, the more votes that disappeared. There was a strange twist. This phenomenon did not occur with absentee ballots from that area. It didn't happen in districts that leaned just as heavily toward Democrats but were predominately white. It didn't even happen in African American districts with early voting. It only happened when those who lived in predominately African American neighborhoods voted via the machines— the ones that were vulnerable and susceptible to hacking—on election day. Then their votes evaporated. All 127,000 of them. Just gone. Whereas the typical drop-off vote rate from governor to lieutenant governor is 0.8 percent, in these black neighborhoods it was a staggering 13 percent. Then, after that, the tallies on the other contests would go up to regular levels and show none of the statistical anomalies.[160] In the face of this conundrum, the state—Brian Kemp and his elected successor as Georgia's Secretary of State, Brad Raffensperger—saw no need to investigate. Meanwhile, the Democrat, Sarah Riggs Amico, lost her election bid by 123,000 votes.[161]

Lauren Groh-Wargo, Stacey Abrams's campaign manager, tweeted that a poll found that "today, 44% of Georgians believe that people of color and poor Georgians had their votes INTENTIONALLY suppressed in the 2018 election. There is a crisis of faith in the system, because this system is broken, and Georgians know it."[162] But it went beyond Georgia. An analysis by the Associated Press showed that Republicans "won 16 more U.S. House seats" than they should have and held "on to as many as seven" state legislatures "that otherwise could have flipped to Democrats."[163] That was the impact of voter suppression.

The GOP had put in place these suppression techniques, both low-tech and high-tech, to stop the tide of voters—"all these liberal folks"—who knew democracy was on the line in the November midterms and weren't going to sit idly by and let it disappear. There were, in fact, more than 150 citizen-led ballot initiatives in 2018.[164] There was automatic felony re-enfranchisement in Florida that would give 1.4 million returning citizens their voting rights.[165] Nonpartisan redistricting commissions were created in Michigan, Utah, and Missouri to do away with extreme partisan gerrymandering and the stranglehold that had choked "one person, one vote" out of existence in those states.[166] And automatic voter registration in Michigan and Nevada was initiated to lower the barriers to the ballot box for hardworking Americans.[167] All of these were designed to bring some semblance of democracy back to the system.

To breathe life back into a democracy that was gasping for air, however, required that voters, regardless of the barriers, show up. And they did, backed by a phalanx of civil rights organizations that sued, sued, and sued again to breach the wall of voter suppression so that all American citizens could finally cast their ballots. In Georgia, for example, the fight was unending. Civil rights organizations sued the state and local election officials for scrapping more than 10 percent of absentee ballots because of rejected signature matches, for not putting enough machines in predominately black precincts until five P.M. but still trying to close the polls at seven P.M., and for refusing to count tens of thousands of provisional ballots that, because of machine malfunctions, many African Americans and

Asian Americans had to resort to.[168] In addition to the battles in the courts, there was the incredible spirit in the communities. Generous and committed volunteers brought pizza, refreshments, and chairs to those waiting in lines for hours. They drove voters to the polls after hundreds had been shut down. They organized and registered voters. They jumped through all of the obstacles to secure the types of ID necessary so that eligible Americans could vote. They also served as poll watchers and helmed phone lines to provide accurate information to voters when precincts didn't.[169]

Americans mobilized and fought so hard for this democracy in 2018 that they saw the highest voter turnout rate for the midterm elections since 1914.[170] That tsunami of voters had an impact that hit the blue states, as well. The New York state legislature finally had a majority that passed landmark voting rights legislation.[171] When a cabal of New Jersey Democrats tried to sneak through legislation for extreme partisan gerrymandering, other Democrats and progressive activists beat it down. They were clear: Democracy and extreme partisan gerrymandering are incompatible.[172] There were wake-up calls in the red states, too. Major vote suppressors like Kris Kobach in Kansas and Scott Walker in Wisconsin went down in defeat.[173] Lucy McBath, an African American woman whose son had been senselessly shot to death several years earlier, won what was once Newt Gingrich's district by defeating a Republican incumbent who had helped implement Georgia's racially discriminatory voter ID law.[174] Ruth Buffalo not only became the first Native American woman state legislator in North Dakota, but also as a Democrat in a Republican district she defeated the man who sponsored the voter ID law targeted at indigenous peoples.[175] Democrats flipped forty seats in the U.S. House of Representatives and brought the most diverse group of congresspeople ever to D.C. One of the first actions of this new House was H.R. 1—an omnibus bill designed to restore the Voting Rights Act, weaken *Citizens United*, and bring transparency and accountability to American democracy.[176]

The Empire, of course, struck back. Lame duck legislative sessions in Michigan, Ohio, North Carolina, and Wisconsin worked to undermine or undo election results.[177] Florida's legislature recommended a virtual poll tax—payment of court fines and fees—before returning citizens could get their voting rights restored.[178] And, what happened in Texas is but an indication that the struggle for democracy continues.

Texas, which is undergoing a dramatic demographic transformation, sought to silence its growing Hispanic electorate. According to Census data, the Hispanic population increased by nearly 1.5 million since 2010. "Meanwhile," according to the *Texas Tribune*, "the white population has only increased by about 458,000 people." Texas's population is projected to be majority Hispanic in 2022.[179]

That was the backdrop when, shortly after the midterm, Texas's interim secretary of state, David Whitley, called a press conference that would send tremors of joy all the way to the White House. Like Senator Joseph McCarthy in 1950 declaring that he held in his hand the names of hundreds of Communists working in the State Department, Whitley also had an equally dramatic announcement.[180] But this time it wasn't a Red Scare; it was a Brown Scare.

As the *Houston Chronicle* reported, Whitley declared that his office had just "launched a purge of 95,000 people from the voter rolls, saying they do not appear to be U.S. citizens." He added that, working with the Department of Public Safety (DPS), his office found that fifty-eight thousand of those non-citizens had already voted in Texas's elections.[181] Could this be the smoking gun that Trump's Electoral Integrity Commission could not find—lurking all along, deep in the heart of Texas?

"We knew it was happening and now we have proof," crowed James Dickey, the chairman of the Texas Republican Party.[182] Governor Greg Abbott, who had led so much of the voter suppression effort when he was secretary of state, supported Whitley "100 percent."[183] Attorney General Ken Paxton issued a press release vowing to prosecute the miscreants to the full extent of the law. "Every single instance of illegal voting threatens democracy in our state and deprives individual Texans of their voice," Paxton averred. "We're honored to have partnered with the Texas Secretary of State's office in the past on voter initiatives and we will spare no effort in assisting with these troubling cases."[184] Donald Trump was ecstatic. Whitley's announcement was "confirmation of the voter fraud he's long insisted is a national problem."[185] "These numbers are just the tip of the iceberg," Trump tweeted out. "All over the country, especially in California, voter fraud is rampant. Must be stopped." His solution was the old tried-and-untrue: "Strong voter ID!"[186]

That moment of GOP I-told-you-so fervor, however, quickly descended into ignominy.[187] While Whitley had given a "breathless statement to the press," his instructions to the county boards of election were decidedly more measured as he mentioned that the ninety-five thousand matches between the voter rolls and the DPS database were "WEAK."[188] But it was worse than that. He failed to alert the county boards or the media that his office knew well before the press conference that there was a "significant possibility" that thousands of naturalized American citizens were actually on the list.[189] The DPS database doesn't track if, after applying for a driver's license, someone becomes a U.S. citizen, which more than one million had over the twenty-year span of Whitley's list. Indeed, the DPS is "notoriously not up-to-date on peoples' citizenship status."[190] Nonetheless, despite the weak matches, despite the inherent flaws in the DPS database, Whitley didn't give the county officials a chance to double-check the names before he turned over the list of ninety-five thousand people to the state's attorney general.[191]

When election officials in Harris County, where Houston is located, began going through Whitley's list, the full magnitude of the horrific publicity stunt became apparent. They found in just their "initial review that about 60 percent of the names flagged were of naturalized citizens."[192] Harris County officials, stunned by how flawed the list was, decided to slow the purge process down drastically. "We are going to make sure," they said, "we don't improperly disenfranchise anyone."[193] Guadalupe County, after finding that more than half of the names on its list were actually citizens, decided to "not send any letters demanding that the remaining voters in the list prove their citizenship" because those notices "would trigger a 30-day countdown for them to confirm their citizenship status or be tossed from the rolls." Other counties followed suit. The list was too flawed to be of any legitimate use.[194]

What Texas had done, however, was not just to wrongly identify ninety-five thousand people as illegally registered voters but to also label fifty-eight thousand who had actually cast a ballot as criminals. Their names were now on a list circulating in the attorney general's office under the threat of prosecution, a felony conviction, and prison. But, to be clear, it wasn't the act of going to DPS and getting a driver's license that put naturalized citizens on the Brown Scare list. It was registering to vote and then going to the polls. It was the sheer act of exercising their citizenship rights that had put them in the government's crosshairs. One state senator, in the wake of Whitley's debacle, didn't back down. Instead, he went even further and proposed legislation in 2019 that would force county registrars to purge *suspected* (not just verified) noncitizens from the rolls.[195] His bill, if passed, would actually "jail county election officials who balked at carrying out this voting-while-brown law."[196] In short, the Republican leadership in the state of Texas, buoyed by Donald Trump, was more than ready to obliterate American citizens' voter registration simply because they had once been immigrants.

State Senator José Menéndez, chair of the Texas Senate Hispanic Caucus, was incensed: "Voting rights of Latino and naturalized citizens continue to be under attack in Texas," he fumed.[197] José

Rodríguez, a state senator from El Paso, was just as furious. The ramifications of Whitley's "bungled . . . rollout of the controversial citizenship review" were vast. "Many now fear to vote, even though they are eligible." And, equally unacceptable, "Many Texans mistakenly believe evidence of voter fraud has been found." That's "the damage that has been done."[198]

The pushback was, therefore, coming fast and furiously. A phalanx of civil rights organizations—the MOVE Texas Civic Fund, the Jolt Initiative, the League of Women Voters of Texas and the Texas NAACP represented in court by the ACLU of Texas, the national American Civil Liberties Union, the Texas Civil Rights Project, Demos, and the Lawyers' Committee for Civil Rights Under Law—hit Texas hard. In a flurry of lawsuits, they argued that the Fourteenth Amendment had been savaged by the interim secretary of state. U.S.-born citizens weren't on Whitley's list; they didn't get hit with "prove your citizenship or lose your voting rights" notices; and they weren't turned over to the state's attorney general's office for investigation into criminal activity that carried stiff prison sentences. Only those who were naturalized citizens were subjected to that treatment, which was in clear violation of the Fourteenth Amendment's guarantee of "equal protection under the law."[199]

U.S. District Judge Fred Biery agreed. In his decision, which blocked any further purges based on Whitley's infamous Brown Scare list, he issued a scathing rebuke to Texas. The rationale for the state's hunt for rampant voter fraud just did not match up with the facts. As clearly, as plainly, and as precisely as he could, Biery wrote that "there is no widespread voter fraud." And this subsequent mad scramble over ninety-five thousand supposed noncitizens voting "forces officials to figure out 'how to ferret the infinitesimal needles out of the haystack.'" Based on the lie of rampant voter fraud, "perfectly legal naturalized Americans were burdened with what the Court finds to be ham-handed and threatening correspondence from the state which . . . exemplifies the power of government to strike fear and anxiety and to intimidate the least powerful among us."[200]

And there we stand. Without the protections of the Voting Rights Act, American democracy remains imperiled. It is clear that far too many policymakers believe that the right to vote is something to be earned—after, perhaps, paying a modern-day poll tax, or walking miles to the nearest polling station, or standing in line for hours to cast a ballot. It's also clear that, with the gutting of the Voting Rights Act, a major legal and political paradigm shift has taken place. The responsibility for upholding the right to vote has moved off the broad shoulders of the state and been placed squarely on the backs of the individual citizen. States apparently don't have the time to find an accessible polling site, yet Native Americans were given just a few weeks to establish a physical street address if they wanted to vote. Georgia can use a racially discriminatory registration system to put citizens in electoral limbo, but it's the American who must drag a treasure trove of documents to the polling station hoping that one will prove their right to cast a ballot.

In 2018, the people and civil society, therefore, had to "warrior up" and fight an arguably wealthier, entrenched, and more powerful opponent. If they hadn't, if they hadn't exclaimed that "we are the defenders," there wouldn't even be a hope of a United States of America in 2020.

Acknowledgments

How to acknowledge those who bring joy to your life, who ease the load, who light the way, and who provide moral and intellectual sustenance? How to even acknowledge the straight, unflinching "I'm going to tell you what you need to hear, not what you want to hear" friendship? For all that they have brought to me and this work, these mere words of thanks hardly seem adequate. But they're all I have.

First and foremost, to my family. Drew, you are a rock. You amaze me each and every day. I am so proud of you. Aaron, your gentle spirit is like a balm to my soul. Then, there are the brothers. David, I miss you like crazy but I still can feel your love. Earl, oh, Earl. I believe the translation of your name is "the one from whom all greatness flows." (At least, that's what you tell me!) Wendell, stop laughing. I just want you to know, I recognize that you have a sister's back like none other. Smooth as you want to be but will not hesitate to come out of the box when necessary. I love you both. And, my people in Flint. You are strong, more resilient than you should have to be, and simply beautiful—Aunt "Cougar" Lennie, Lisa Anderson, Monica Leverette, and Shirley Sillman. And, to the not quite West Coast side, Uncle Sam and Aunt Barbara, you have always shown how it's done. Grace, intelligence, and class personified. Barry Kountz, always global, always unflinching but always K.C. Thank you.

This book could not have happened without the Dream Team of experts, friends, research assistants, and archivists (and as you know, many of you transcend and occupy several of those categories). Rob

McQuilkin, you are an agent like none other. You heard me, encouraged me, and fought for me. Thank you, Rob. Nancy Miller, we've only just begun and it's already sooooooo good. Really glad we're on this journey together. Speaking of which, Tara Kennedy, to the moon and back (that is my itinerary, right?). You have handled the craziness with skill and aplomb. Dianne Stewart continues to hear me even when I'm not talking. That uncanny ability has made the impossible possible. Thank you. Timothy Rainey II, I don't even know if I have the words to describe how essential your research skills, your professionalism, and your determination have been to this project. You are simply phenomenal. Amir Adem, you stepped in and took that insatiable intellectual curiosity of yours and transformed it into a treasure trove of data and documents. Thank you. Angela Mamaril, you were thrown into the whirlwind and didn't flinch. Thank you. La Shanda Perryman, I remain in awe. The work gets more intricate, the time gets more constrained, the demands become more intense and you just handle it. Handle it with an elegance and precision that is mystifying, magical, and much appreciated. Did I mention "awe"? Thank you. Natasha Trethewey, Brett Gadsden, and Leslie Harris, the love and respect overflows. Even a thousand miles can't stop it. George White Jr., you created the time to take a good hard look at the first draft. Your "Wow, sis!" was golden. Simply golden. I am forever thankful. Susan Whitlock, once again, your discerning eye and brilliance are like guardian angels. Thank you. Finally, to the amazing librarians, curators, and archivists, especially those in the Stuart A. Rose Library at Emory University—Randall Burkett, Pellom McDaniels III, and Sarah Quigley—thank you.

Resources

The following organizations work to preserve voting rights. Some have fearlessly taken on governments that disfranchise American citizens. Others have poured resources into getting people registered to vote and to the polls. They all have done the heavy lifting of democracy.

American Civil Liberties Union (ACLU)
www.aclu.org/

Asian Americans Advancing Justice (AAJC)
www.advancingjustice-aajc.org/

Black Voters Matter Fund
blackvotersmatterfund.org/

Brennan Center for Justice
www.brennancenter.org/

Campaign Legal Center
www.campaignlegalcenter.org/

Common Cause
www.commoncause.org/

Demos
www.demos.org/

Fair Elections Legal Network
fairelectionsnetwork.com/

Fair Fight Action
fairfightaction.com/

FairVote
www.fairvote.org/

Hispanic Federation (HF)
hispanicfederation.org/

Indivisible
www.indivisible.org/

Labor Council for Latin American Advancement (LCLAA)
www.lclaa.org/

Lawyers' Committee for Civil Rights
lawyerscommittee.org/

League of United Latin American Citizens (LULAC)
lulac.org/

League of Women Voters
www.lwv.org/

Let America Vote
www.letamericavote.org/

Moral Mondays
twitter.com/moralmondays

National Association for the Advancement of Colored People
(NAACP)
www.naacp.org/

NAACP Legal Defense and Educational Fund (LDF)
www.naacpldf.org/

Native American Rights Fund/Native American Voting Rights
Coalition
www.narf.org/native-american-voting-rights-coalition/

Poor People's Campaign
www.poorpeoplescampaign.org/

Rock the Vote
www.rockthevote.org/

Transformative Justice Coalition
www.tjcoalition.org/

VoteRiders
www.voteriders.org/

Voto Latino
votolatino.org/

Woke Vote
wokevote.us/

Notes

Chapter One: A History of Disfranchisement

1. Jesse Singal, "Why Black Voters in Milwaukee Weren't Enthused by Hillary Clinton," *New York Magazine*, November 22, 2016, nymag.com/daily/intelligencer/2016/11/why-black-voters-in-milwaukee-werent-enthused-by-clinton.html, accessed March 11, 2017.

2. Tami Luhby, "How Hillary Clinton Lost," CNN, November 9, 2016, www.cnn.com/2016/11/09/politics/clinton-votes-african-americans-latinos-women-white-voters, accessed March 11, 2017.

3. Michael Harthorne, "Hillary Clinton Might Have a Black Voter Problem: African-Americans Aren't Turning Out for Early Voting like They Were in 2012," *Newser*, November 2, 2016, www.newser.com/story/233454/hillary-clinton-might-have-a-black-voter-problem.html, accessed March 11, 2017.

4. Reid Wilson, "Voter Turnout Dipped in 2016, Led by Decline Among Blacks," *The Hill*, May 11, 2017, thehill.com/homenews/campaign/332970-voter-turnout-dipped-in-2016-led-by-decline-among-blacks, accessed June 29, 2017.

5. Ari Berman, "The GOP's Attack on Voting Rights Was the Most Under-Covered Story of 2016," *The Nation*, November 9, 2016, www.thenation.com/article/the-gops-attack-on-voting-rights-was-the-most-under-covered-story-of-2016/, accessed March 11, 2017.

6. "The Parties on the Eve of the 2016 Election: Two Coalitions, Moving Further Apart—the Changing Composition of the Political Parties," Pew Research Center, September 13, 2016, www.people-press.org

/2016/09/13/1-the-changing-composition-of-the-political-parties/, accessed July 25, 2017. For the rightward skewing of the GOP, see Thomas E. Mann and Norman J. Ornstein, *It's Even Worse Than It Looks: How the American Constitutional System Collided with the New Politics of Extremism* (New York: Basic Books, 2012), and E. J. Dionne Jr., *Why the Right Went Wrong: Conservatism—from Goldwater to the Tea Party and Beyond* (New York: Simon & Schuster, 2016).

7. Alexander Keyssar, *The Right to Vote: The Contested History of Democracy in the United States* (New York: Basic Books, 2000), 235; Sam Levine, "Kansas Secretary of State: Only Obstacle Voter ID Causes May Be 'Exerting Calories,'" *Huffington Post*, February 23, 2017, www.huffingtonpost.com/entry/kansas-voter -id_us_58af29b1e4b060480e05ccdb?0tndhnxgbwsysnhfr, accessed July 28, 2017; Carol Anderson, *White Rage: The Unspoken Truth of Our Racial Divide* (New York: Bloomsbury, 2016), 140.

8. Henry Allen Bullock, "The Expansion of Negro Suffrage in Texas," *Journal of Negro Education* 26, no. 3 (Summer 1957): 370.

9. A. A. Taylor, "Democracy Crushed by Caste," *Journal of Negro History* 1, no. 3 (July 1926), 518.

10. Merline Pitre, "A Note on the Historiography of Blacks in the Reconstruction of Texas," *Journal of Negro History* 66, no. 4 (1981): 340–48; John Hope Franklin and Alfred A. Moss Jr., *From Slavery to Freedom: A History of African Americans*, 8th ed. (Boston: McGraw Hill, 2000), 287.

11. Taylor, "Democracy Crushed by Caste," 519.

12. Michael Waldman, *The Fight to Vote* (New York: Simon & Schuster, 2016), 85, 89.

13. Waldman, *The Fight to Vote*, 84.

14. Waldman, *The Fight to Vote*, 94.

15. Bullock, "The Expansion of Negro Suffrage in Texas," 375; "Voter Turnout in Presidential Elections: 1828–2012," American Presidency Project, U.C. Santa Barbara, www.presidency.ucsb.edu/data/turnout .php, accessed July 2, 2017.

16. Waldman, *The Fight to Vote*, 88.

17. Waldman, *The Fight to Vote*, 88.

18. Waldman, *The Fight to Vote*, 85.

19. C. Vann Woodward, *The Strange Career of Jim Crow* (New York: Oxford University Press, 2001), 84.

20. Waldman, *The Fight to Vote*, 142.

21. U.S. Civil Rights Commission, "Voting in Mississippi," 5, www.law .umaryland.edu/marshall/usccr/documents/crl2v94.pdf, accessed July 12, 2017.

22. Jessie Parkhurst Guzman, ed., *Negro Year Book: A Review of Events Affecting Negro Life, 1941–1946* (Tuskegee, AL: Tuskegee Institute, 1947), 70.

23. Anderson, *White Rage*, 70.

24. Anderson, *White Rage*, 89.

25. Guzman, *Negro Year Book*, 70; "Biennial Survey of Education in the United States, 1942–44," (Washington, D.C.: Government Printing Office, 1945), 144.

26. Alabama Voter Literacy Test (c. 1965), www.crmvet.org/info/littest .htm, accessed July 4, 2017.

27. William H. Chafe, Raymond Gavins, and Robert Korstad, *Remembering Jim Crow: African Americans Tell About Life in the Segregated South* (New York: New Press, 2001), 277–80.

28. David C. Colby, "The Voting Rights Act and Black Registration in Mississippi," *Publius* 16, no. 4 (Autumn 1986): 127; *Williams v. Mississippi*, 170 U.S. 213 (1898).

29. Manfred Berg, *The Ticket to Freedom: The NAACP and the Struggle for Black Political Integration* (Gainesville: University of Florida, 2005), 155.

30. "Disenfranchisement by Means of the Poll Tax," *Harvard Law Review* 53, no. 4 (1940): 647, fn15.

31. Women would eventually be incorporated into the requirements after the passage of the Nineteenth Amendment.

32. G. C. Stoney, "Suffrage in the South—Part I: The Poll Tax," Social Welfare History Project, Virginia Commonwealth University,

January 1, 1940, socialwelfare.library.vcu.edu/issues/suffrage-south
-poll-tax/, accessed July 6, 2017.

33. "Disenfranchisement by Means of the Poll Tax," *Harvard Law Review* 53, no. 4 (1940): 648; Dan Nimmo and Clifton McCleskey, "Impact of the Poll Tax on Voter Participation: The Houston Metropolitan Area in 1966," *Journal of Politics* 31, no. 3 (August 1969): 683; G. C. Stoney, "Suffrage in the South—Part I: The Poll Tax."

34. Woodward, *The Strange Career of Jim Crow*, 84.

35. *Screws v. United States*, 325 U.S. 91 (1945); Patrick Phillips, *Blood at the Root: A Racial Cleansing in America* (New York: W. W. Norton, 2016); Gilbert King, *Devil in the Grove: Thurgood Marshall, the Groveland Boys, and the Dawn of a New America* (New York: HarperCollins, 2012).

36. U.S. Civil Rights Commission, "Voting in Mississippi," 19.

37. Stoney, "Suffrage in the South—Part I: The Poll Tax."

38. "Voting Rights: The Poll Tax," Marion Butts Collection, Dallas Public Library, dallaslibrary2.org/mbutts/assets/lessons/L9-voting
+rights/Marion%20Butts%20-%20Voting%20Rights(PPT).pdf, accessed July 6, 2017; Measuring Worth, www.measuringworth.com
/calculators/uscompare/.

39. Berg, *The Ticket to Freedom*, 80.

40. "Voting Rights: The Poll Tax," Marion Butts Collection.

41. "Voting Rights: The Poll Tax," Marion Butts Collection.

42. Stoney, "Suffrage in the South—Part I: The Poll Tax."

43. National Center for Education Statistics, Table 16: Median Family Income by Race, 44, nces.ed.gov/pubs98/yi/yi16.pdf, accessed July 4, 2017.

44. "Voting Rights: The Poll Tax," Marion Butts Collection.

45. Keyssar, *The Right to Vote*, 207.

46. Stoney, "Suffrage in the South—Part I: The Poll Tax."

47. Berg, *The Ticket to Freedom*, 105; David M. Jordan, *FDR, Dewey, and the Election of 1944* (Bloomington: Indiana University Press, 2011), 322.

48. *Newberry v. United States*, 256 U.S. 232 (1921).

49. Leo Alilunas, "The Rise of the 'White Primary' Movement as a Means of Barring the Negro from the Polls," *Journal of Negro History* 25, no. 2 (April 1940): 162.

50. Thurgood Marshall, "The Rise and Collapse of the 'White Democratic Primary,'" *Journal of Negro Education* 26, no. 3 (Summer 1957): 250.

51. Alilunas, "The Rise of the 'White Primary' Movement," 163; Darlene Clark Hine, "Blacks and the Destruction of the Democratic White Primary, 1935–1944," *Journal of Negro History* 62, no. 1 (January 1977): 44.

52. *Williams v. Mississippi*, 170 U.S. 213 (1898).

53. Marshall, "The Rise and Collapse," 251; *Nixon v. Herndon*, 273 U.S. 536 (1927).

54. *United States v. Cruikshank*, 92 U.S. 542 (1875); Hine, "Blacks and the Destruction of the Democratic White Primary, 1935–1944," 43.

55. *Nixon v. Condon*, 286 U.S. 73 (1932); Marshall, "The Rise and Collapse," 251.

56. Marshall, "The Rise and Collapse," 251.

57. Marshall, "The Rise and Collapse," 252; *Grovey v. Townsend*, 294 U.S. 45 (1935).

58. Marshall, "The Rise and Collapse," 252.

59. Hine, "Blacks and the Destruction," 54.

60. *Smith v. Allwright*, 321 U.S. 649 (1944).

61. Hine, "Blacks and the Destruction," 54–55.

62. Marshall, "The Rise and Collapse," 253.

63. Marshall, "The Rise and Collapse," 253.

64. *Terry v. Adams*, 345 U.S. 416 (1953).

65. LeeAnna Keith, *The Colfax Massacre: The Untold Story of Black Power, White Terror, and the Death of Reconstruction* (New York: Oxford University Press, 2008); North Carolina Freedom Monument Project, "The Wilmington Race Riot," www.learnnc.org/lp/editions/nchist-newsouth/4360, accessed July 12, 2017; David S. Cecelski and Timothy B. Tyson, *Democracy Betrayed: The Wilmington Race Riot of 1898 and Its Legacy* (Chapel Hill: University of North Carolina Press, 1998); Paul Ortiz, "Ocoee,

Florida: Remembering 'the Single Bloodiest Day in Modern U.S. Political History,'" *Facing South*, May 14, 2010, www.facingsouth .org/2010/05/ocoee-florida-remembering-the-single-bloodiest-day -in-modern-us-political-history.html/, accessed July 12, 2017.

66. Kevin M. Kruse and Stephen Tuck, *Fog of War: The Second World War and the Civil Rights Movement* (New York: Oxford University Press, 2012).

67. Carol Anderson, *Eyes off the Prize: The United Nations and the African American Struggle for Human Rights, 1944–1955* (New York: Cambridge University Press, 2003), 63–64; Patricia Sullivan, *Lift Every Voice: The NAACP and the Making of the Civil Rights Movement* (New York: New Press, 2009), 318–19; Erica Sterling, "Maceo Snipes: A Man Whose Death Inspired the Teenager Who Led the Movement," Georgia Civil Rights Cold Cases, scholarblogs .emory.edu/emorycoldcases/maceo-snipes/, accessed July 11, 2017.

68. There was a quadruple lynching in Monroe, Georgia, around the same time. See Laura Wexler, *Fire in a Canebrake: The Last Mass Lynching in America* (New York: Scribner, 2003); "Victims of Lynching in Georgia Total 5," *Norfolk Journal and Guide*, August 3, 1946.

69. Christopher S. Parker, *Fighting for Democracy: Black Veterans and the Struggle Against White Supremacy in the Postwar South* (Princeton, NJ: Princeton University Press, 2009); Anderson, *Eyes off the Prize*, 58–59.

70. Sullivan, *Lift Every Voice*, 318–19.

71. Sterling, "Maceo Snipes"; Anderson, *Eyes off the Prize*, 64.

72. Anderson, *Eyes off the Prize*, 64; Sullivan, *Lift Every Voice*, 317–18; U.S. Commission on Civil Rights, "Voting in Mississippi," 7, www .law.umaryland.edu/marshall/usccr/documents/crl2v94.pdf, accessed July 12, 2017.

73. U.S. Commission on Civil Rights, "Voting in Mississippi," 22–26.

74. Colby, "The Voting Rights Act and Black Registration in Mississippi," 126.

75. U.S. Commission on Civil Rights, "Voting in Mississippi," 8.

76. Emilye Crosby, *A Little Taste of Freedom: The Black Freedom Struggle in Claiborne County, Mississippi* (Chapel Hill: University of North Carolina Press, 2005), 69.

77. "Alabama Black Belt Counties Registered Voters: 1960," Black Freedom Struggle in the 20th Century: Federal Government Records, "Black and White Voter Registrations Statistics and Voter Registration Programs" (January 1, 1961 to December 31, 1965 [accession number 001351-019-0492]). Found in Civil Rights during the Kennedy Administration, 1961–1963, Part 2: The Papers of Burke Marshall, Assistant Attorney General for Civil Rights, www.teachingforchange.org/wp-content/uploads/2014/12/1960registeredvoters.pdf, accessed July 3, 2015.

78. Charles S. Bullock and Ronald Keith Gaddie, "Voting Rights Progress in Georgia," *Legislation and Public Policy* 10, no. 1 (Fall 2006): 5.

79. Odd Arne Westad, *The Global Cold War: Third World Interventions and the Making of Our Times* (New York: Cambridge University Press, 2007), 5, 8–72; Jason C. Parker, "Decolonization, the Cold War, and the Post-Columbian Era," *The Cold War in the Third World*, Robert J. McMahon, ed. (New York: Oxford University Press, 2013), 125.

80. Jason C. Parker, *Hearts, Minds, and Voices: US Cold War Public Diplomacy and the Formation of the Third World* (New York: Oxford University Press, 2016); Penny M. Von Eschen, *Satchmo Blows Up the World: Jazz Ambassadors Play the Cold War* (Cambridge, MA: Harvard University Press, 2004); Reinhold Wagnleitner, *Coca-colonization and the Cold War: The Cultural Mission of the United States in Austria After the Second World War* (Chapel Hill: University of North Carolina Press, 1994).

81. Mary L. Dudziak, *Cold War Civil Rights: Race and the Image of American Democracy* (Princeton, NJ: Princeton University Press, 2000).

82. "Who Is Violating the Rights of Man?," *Current Digest of the Russian Press* 8, no. 50 (January 23, 1957): 23.

83. Jason C. Parker, *Hearts, Minds, and Voices*, 7, 109; Memorandum of a Telephone Conversation Between the Secretary of State and the Attorney General (Brownell), Washington, September 24, 1957, 2:15 P.M., *Foreign Relations of the United States, 1955–1957, Foreign Economic Policy; Foreign Information Program*, Volume IX, history.state.gov/historicaldocuments/frus1955-57v09/d208, accessed April 7, 2018.

84. "This Must Be Said!," *Current Digest of the Russian Press* 9, no. 37 (October 23, 1957): 25.

85. Parker, *Hearts, Minds, and Voices*, 109.

86. Dudziak, *Cold War Civil Rights*, 119–20.

87. "This Must Be Said!," *Current Digest of the Russian Press*, 25.

88. "American 'Democracy's' Ways," *Current Digest of the Russian Press* 9, no. 29 (August 28, 1957): 35.

89. Anderson, *Eyes off the Prize*; Brenda Gayle Plummer, *Rising Wind: Black Americans and U.S. Foreign Affairs, 1935–1960* (Chapel Hill: University of North Carolina Press, 1996); Carol Anderson, *Bourgeois Radicals: The NAACP and the Struggle for Colonial Liberation, 1941–1960* (New York: Cambridge University Press, 2013).

90. Emilye Crosby, ed., *Civil Rights from the Ground Up: Local Struggles, a National Movement* (Athens: University of Georgia Press, 2011).

91. Cary Fraser, "Crossing the Color Line in Little Rock: The Eisenhower Administration and the Dilemma of Race for U.S. Foreign Policy," *Diplomatic History* 24, no. 2 (2000): 233–64, DOI: 10.1111/0145 -2096.00211; Michael L. Krenn, "'Unfinished Business': Segregation and U.S. Diplomacy at the 1958 World's Fair," *Diplomatic History* 20, no. 4 (1996): 591–612, DOI: 10.1111/j.1467-7709.1996.tb00288.

92. Keyssar, *The Right to Vote*, 208.

93. Waldman, *The Fight to Vote*, 145.

94. Allan Lichtman, "The Federal Assault Against Voting Discrimination in the Deep South, 1957–1967," *Journal of Negro History* 54, no. 4 (October 1969): 364.

95. Lichtman, "The Federal Assault Against Voting Discrimination," 350.

96. Keyssar, *The Right to Vote*, 208; Gary May, *Bending Toward Justice: The Voting Rights Act and the Transformation of American Democracy* (Durham, NC, and London: Duke University Press, 2015), 97.

97. Lichtman, "The Federal Assault Against Voting Discrimination," 346–67.

98. Waldman, *The Fight to Vote*, 145; Keyssar, *The Right to Vote*, 208.

99. J. Mills Thornton III, *Dividing Lines: Municipal Politics and the Struggle for Civil Rights in Montgomery, Birmingham, and Selma* (Tuscaloosa: University of Alabama Press, 2002), 380–499.

100. Charles S. Bullock III, Ronald Keith Gaddie, and Justin J. Wert, *The Rise and Fall of the Voting Rights Act* (Norman: University of Oklahoma Press, 2016), 18.

101. Quoted in *South Carolina v. Katzenbach*, 383 U.S. 301 (1966).

102. Waldman, *The Fight to Vote*, 159.

103. Denton L. Watson, *Lion in the Lobby: Clarence Mitchell, Jr.'s Struggle for the Passage of Civil Rights Laws* (New York: William Morrow, 1990), 657.

104. Waldman, *The Fight to Vote*, 149.

105. The original jurisdictions met the twin standards to come under the VRA's federal supervision: (a) fewer than half of age-eligible adults voted or were registered to vote in the 1964 election *and* (b) had some type of device, such as a literacy test, as a prerequisite to vote. Based on that, the following were subject to the VRA: Alabama, Georgia, Louisiana, Mississippi, South Carolina, Virginia, and thirty-nine counties in North Carolina. The poll tax was not included in the VRA as a prerequisite device. Texas, therefore, was not one of the original states under the VRA's jurisdiction. That didn't happen until 1972.

106. *South Carolina v. Katzenbach* (1966).

107. Extension of the 1965 Voting Rights Act: Greensboro-Selma Hearings, Box 228, Folder 19, Papers of the Southern Christian Leadership Conference, Stuart Rose Library, Woodruff Library,

Emory University, Atlanta, Georgia (hereafter cited as Papers of the SCLC).

108. *South Carolina v. Katzenbach* (1966).

109. *Allen v. State Bd. of Elections*, 393 U.S. 544 (1969).

110. *Allen v. State Bd. of Elections* (1969); Lorn S. Foster, "Section 5 of the Voting Rights Act: Implementation of an Administrative Remedy," *Publius* 16, no. 4 (Autumn 1986): 17–28; May, *Bending Toward Justice*, 209.

111. *Allen v. State Bd. of Elections* (1969).

112. Berg, *The Ticket to Freedom*, 248; Hank Sanders and Frances M. Beal, "Defending Voting Rights in the Alabama Black Belt," *Black Scholar* 17, no. 3 (May–June 1986): 29.

113. Nicholas Katzenbach quoted in Colby, "The Voting Rights Act and Black Registration in Mississippi," 135.

114. *South Carolina v. Katzenbach* (1966).

115. *South Carolina v. Katzenbach* (1966).

116. John Micklethwait and Adrian Wooldridge, *The Right Nation: Conservative Power in America* (New York: Penguin Books, 2005); Lisa McGirr, *Suburban Warriors: The Origins of the New American Right* (Princeton, NJ: Princeton University Press, 2001); Kevin Kruse, *One Nation Under God: How Corporate America Invented Christian America* (New York: Basic Books, 2015).

117. Keyssar, *The Right to Vote*, 212.

118. Nadine Cohodas, *Strom Thurmond and the Politics of Southern Change* (New York: Simon & Schuster, 1993), 382.

119. May, *Bending Toward Justice*, 217.

120. Berg, *The Ticket to Freedom*, 248.

121. *South Carolina v. Katzenbach* (1966); *Allen v. State Bd. of Elections* (1969).

122. "The Long Goodbye: Is the White Southern Democrat Extinct, Endangered or Just Hibernating?," *Economist*, November 11, 2010, www.economist.com/node/17467202, accessed July 24, 2017.

123. Peter N. Carroll, *It Seemed like Nothing Happened: America in the 1970s* (New Brunswick, NJ: Rutgers University Press, 1990), 38–54, 100–101; Ian Haney López, *Dog Whistle Politics: How Coded Racial Appeals Have Reinvented Racism and Wrecked the Middle Class* (New York: Oxford University Press, 2014), 70–74.

124. Ari Berman, *Give Us the Ballot: The Modern Struggle for Voting Rights in America* (New York: Farrar, Straus and Giroux, 2015), 82, 83.

125. Anderson, *White Rage*, 109; Anderson, *Eyes off the Prize*, 71.

126. Berman, *Give Us the Ballot*, 83.

127. Cohodas, *Strom Thurmond*, 435.

128. Berman, *Give Us the Ballot*, 90.

129. Berg, *The Ticket to Freedom*, 156–57; John Kyle Day, *The Southern Manifesto: Massive Resistance and the Fight to Preserve Segregation* (Jackson: University of Mississippi Press, 2014), 17.

130. Berman, *Give Us the Ballot*, 90–91.

131. Mack H. Jones, *Knowledge, Power, and Black Politics: Collected Essays* (Albany: State University of New York Press, 2014), 157; Allen Tullos, "Crackdown in the Black Belt," *Southern Changes* 7, no. 1 (1985): 5.

132. Raymond Wolters, *Right Turn: William Bradford Reynolds, the Reagan Administration, and Black Civil Rights* (New Brunswick, NJ: Transaction Publishers, 1996); Sean Wilentz, *The Age of Reagan: A History, 1974–2008* (New York: Harper, 2008).

133. Voting Rights Act of 1965 Extension Hearings: Greensboro-Selma, February 13, 1982, Box 228, File 19, Papers of the SCLC.

134. Reginald Stuart, "2 Alabama Rights Workers Are Jailed for Voting Fraud," *New York Times*, January 12, 1982; Art Harris, "Pickens County Flare-Up: The Story of 2 Blacks Found Guilty," *Washington Post*, February 6, 1982.

135. "SCLC Launches Campaign to Free Voting Rights Activists from Unjust Imprisonment," press release, January 22, 1982, Box 228, Folder 19, Papers of the SCLC.

136. Stuart, "2 Alabama Rights Workers Are Jailed for Voting Fraud"; Harris, "Pickens County Flare-Up"; Reverend Joseph Lowery to Mayor Johnny Ford, telegram, January 16, 1982, Box 123, Folder 7, Papers of the SCLC.

137. Stuart, "2 Alabama Rights Workers Are Jailed for Voting Fraud"; Harris, "Pickens County Flare-Up."

138. Emily Bazelon, "The Voter Fraud Case Jeff Sessions Lost and Can't Escape," *New York Times*, January 9, 2017.

139. *Eyes on the Prize*, episode 6, "Bridge to Freedom," directed by Julian Bond and Orlando Bagwell (San Francisco: PBS, 1996).

140. Tullos, "Crackdown in the Black Belt," 3–4.

141. Bazelon, "The Voter Fraud Case Jeff Sessions Lost and Can't Escape."

142. Bazelon, "The Voter Fraud Case Jeff Sessions Lost and Can't Escape."

143. Tullos, "Crackdown in the Black Belt," 2.

144. Ari Berman, "Jeff Sessions, Trump's Pick for Attorney General, Is a Fierce Opponent of Civil Rights," *The Nation*, November 18, 2016, www.thenation.com/article/jeff-sessions-trumps-pick-for-attorney-general-is-a-fierce-opponent-of-civil-rights/, accessed July 21, 2017; Bazelon, "The Voter Fraud Case Jeff Sessions Lost and Can't Escape."

145. "Archive Video: Jeff Sessions 1986 Confirmation Hearing," ABC News, November 18, 2016, www.bing.com/videos/search?q=jeff+sessions+1986+testimony&view=detail&mid=D6E0F114CABED31EDAEBD6E0F114CABED31EDAEB&FORM=VIRE, accessed July 27, 2017.

146. Sanders and Beal, "Defending Voting Rights in the Alabama Black Belt," 33; Berman, "Jeff Sessions, Trump's Pick for Attorney General."

147. Sanders and Beal, "Defending Voting Rights in the Alabama Black Belt," 29; Bazelon, "The Voter Fraud Case Jeff Sessions Lost and Can't Escape."

148. Bazelon, "The Voter Fraud Case Jeff Sessions Lost and Can't Escape."

149. Berman, "Jeff Sessions, Trump's Pick for Attorney General."

150. Sanders and Beal, "Defending Voting Rights in the Alabama Black Belt," 26, 34; Bazelon, "The Voter Fraud Case Jeff Sessions Lost and Can't Escape."

151. Scott Zamost, Drew Griffin, and Curt Devine, "Woman Prosecuted by Jeff Sessions Can't Forgive," CNN, January 9, 2017, www.cnn .com/2017/01/06/politics/marion-three-jeff-sessions/index .html, accessed July 27, 2017.

152. Charles P. Pierce, "You Can Draw a Straight Line from the 2000 Recount to 2016 Voter Suppression: The American Voting System Is Broken—on Purpose," *Esquire*, July 19, 2017, www.esquire .com/news-politics/politics/news/a56423/2000-recount -republican-voter-suppression/, accessed July 22, 2017.

153. Mireya Navarro and Somini Sengupta, "Contesting the Vote: Black Voters; Arriving at Florida Voting Places, Some Blacks Found Frustration," *New York Times*, November 30, 2000, www .nytimes.com/2000/11/30/us/contesting-vote-black-voters-arri ving-florida-voting-places-some-blacks-found.html, accessed July 22, 2017; United States Commission on Civil Rights, "Voting Irregularities in Florida During the 2000 Presidential Election: First-Hand Accounts of Voter Disfranchisement," www.usccr.gov /pubs/vote2000/report/ch2.htm; Richard L. Hasen, *The Voting Wars: From Florida 2000 to the Next Election Meltdown* (New Haven, CT: Yale University Press, 2012), 11–16.

154. David Margolick, "The Path to Florida," *Vanity Fair*, March 19, 2014, www.vanityfair.com/news/2004/10/florida-election-2000, accessed July 22, 2017.

155. Orrin Hatch, "Justice Antonin Scalia: Champion of Liberty," *National Review*, February 25, 2016, www.nationalreview.com /article/431883/justice-antonin-scalia-champion-liberty-judicial -self-restraint, accessed July 23, 2017; "Those 'Activist' Judges: Critiques of Judicial Activism Are, in the End, Rarely Critiques of Judicial Activism," *Economist*, July 8, 2015, www.economist .com/blogs/democracyinamerica/2015/07/judicial-politics-0, accessed July 23, 2017.

156. Jamin B. Raskin, *Overruling Democracy: The Supreme Court vs. the American People* (New York: Routledge, 2003), 22–23.

157. Vincent Bugliosi, *The Betrayal of America: How the Supreme Court Undermined the Constitution and Chose Our President* (New York: Thunder's Mouth Press/Nation Books, 2001), 42.

158. Wendy W. Simmons, "Black Americans Feel 'Cheated' by Election 2000," Gallup News Service, December 20, 2000, www.gallup .com/poll/2188/black-americans-feel-cheated-election-2000 .aspx, accessed July 24, 2017.

159. Roper Center for Public Opinion Research, "How Groups Voted in 2000," Cornell University, ropercenter.cornell.edu/polls/us -elections/how-groups-voted/how-groups-voted-2000, accessed September 24, 2017.

160. Tim Alberta, "Can the GOP Overcome Demographic Change in Red States?," *National Review*, October 31, 2016, www .nationalreview.com/article/441595/voter-demographics -diversifying-republicans-falling-behind, accessed July 24, 2017; "The Changing Composition of the Political Parties: The Parties on the Eve of the 2016 Election—Two Coalitions, Moving Further Apart," Pew Research Center, September 13, 2016, www.people -press.org/2016/09/13/1-the-changing-composition-of-the -political-parties/, accessed July 25, 2017; Keyssar, *The Right to Vote*, 214; Dionne, *Why the Right Went Wrong*, 182; Bullock, Gaddie, and Wert, *The Rise and Fall of the Voting Rights Act*, 96; Leah Wright Rigueur, *The Loneliness of the Black Republican* (Princeton, NJ: Princeton University Press, 2013), 380, fn21.

161. Final Vote Results for Roll Call 374: Fannie Lou Hamer, Rosa Parks, and Coretta Scott King Voting Rights Act Reauthorization and Amendment Act, www.clerk.house.gov/evs/2006/roll374 .xml, accessed June 17, 2017; Charles Babington, "Voting Rights Act Extension Passes in Senate, 98 to 0," *Washington Post*, July 21, 2006, www.washingtonpost.com/wp-dyn/content/article /2006/07/20/AR2006072001217.html, accessed July 23, 2017.

162. Keyssar, *The Right to Vote*, 214.

163. Keyssar, *The Right to Vote*, 215.

164. Anderson, *White Rage*, 143.

165. Ari Berman, "Inside John Roberts' Decades-Long Crusade Against the Voting Rights Act," *Politico*, August 10, 2015, www.politico.com/magazine/story/2015/08/john-roberts-voting-rights-act-121222, accessed July 23, 2017.

166. Berman, "Inside John Roberts' Decades-Long Crusade Against the Voting Rights Act."

167. "U.S. Alleges Discrimination in Mobile Election Case," *New York Times*, May 9, 1981; *City of Mobile v. Bolden*, 446 U.S. 55 (1980); López, *Dog Whistle Politics*.

168. Berman, "Inside John Roberts' Decades-Long Crusade Against the Voting Rights Act."

169. Berman, "Inside John Roberts' Decades-Long Crusade Against the Voting Rights Act."

170. Bullock, Gaddie, and Wert, *The Rise and Fall of the Voting Rights Act*.

171. *Northwest Austin Municipal Utility District Number One v. Holder*, 557 U.S. 193 (2009).

172. "2008 Presidential Election Results in Shelby County Alabama," www.city-data.com/elec08/SHELBY-ALABAMA.html, accessed July 27, 2017.

173. *Gomillion v. Lightfoot*, 364 U.S. 339 (1960).

174. Lorraine C. Minnite, *The Myth of Voter Fraud* (Ithaca, NY, and London: Cornell University Press, 2010).

175. Berman, "The GOP's Attack on Voting Rights Was the Most Under-Covered Story of 2016."

176. Reid Wilson, "Voter Turnout Dipped in 2016, Led by Decline Among Blacks"; Christopher Brennan, "States with New Voting Restrictions Flipped to Trump," *New York Daily News*, November 9, 2016, www.nydailynews.com/news/politics/states-new-voting-restrictions-flip-trump-article-1.2866395, accessed March 12, 2017.

177. Max Rosenthal, "North Carolina GOP Brags About How Few Black People Were Able to Vote Early," *Mother Jones*, November 7, 2016, www.motherjones.com/politics/2016/11/north-carolina -gop-brags-about-how-few-black-people-were-able-vote-early, accessed January 14, 2017.

178. Patrik Jonsson, "What's Behind Fewer African-American Voters at the Polls," *Christian Science Monitor*, June 19, 2017, www .csmonitor.com/USA/Politics/2017/0619/What-s-behind-fewer -African-American-voters-at-the-polls, accessed June 20, 2017.

Chapter Two: Voter ID

1. Omar Villafranca, "Texas' Voter ID Law Is 'Unexplainable on Grounds Other Than Race,' Federal Judge Rules," CBS News, April 13, 2017, www.cbsnews.com/news/army-vet-86-leads-suit -against-texas-voter-id-law/, accessed May 19, 2017.

2. Jeremiah "Jay" Prophet, "An Open Letter from One Disabled Person to Another," *Texas Tribune*, July 21, 2017, www.tribtalk .org/2017/07/21/an-open-letter-from-one-disabled-person-to -another/, accessed July 22, 2017.

3. Sari Horwitz, "Getting a Photo ID So You Can Vote Is Easy. Unless You're Poor, Black, Latino, or Elderly," *Washington Post*, May 23, 2016, www.washingtonpost.com/politics/courts_law /getting-a-photo-id-so-you-can-vote-is-easy-unless-youre-poor -black-latino-or-elderly/2016/05/23/8d5474ec-20f0-11e6-8690 -f14ca9de2972_story.html, accessed September 9, 2017.

4. Christina A. Cassidy, "In Wisconsin, ID Law Proved Insur-mountable for Many Voters," AP News, May 14, 2017, apnews.com /dafac088c90242ef8b282fbebddf5b56, accessed May 14, 2017.

5. Ari Berman, "Iowa's New Voter-ID Law Would Have Disen-franchised My Grandmother: 260,000 Eligible Voters Could Be Blocked from the Polls by the New Law," *The Nation*, April 13, 2017, www.thenation.com/article/iowas-new-voter-id-law-would -have-disenfranchised-my-grandmother/, accessed September 13, 2017; Connor Maxwell and Danielle Root, "Five Truths About Voter

Suppression," Center for American Progress, May 12, 2017, www
.americanprogress.org/issues/race/news/2017/05/12/432339
/five-truths-voter-suppression/, accessed May 13, 2017; Ari Berman,
"Pennsylvania: A Case Study for the Problems with Voter ID Laws,"
Bill Moyers, January 21, 2014, billmoyers.com/2014/01/21
/pennsylvania-a-case-study-for-the-problems-with-voter-id-laws/,
accessed September 13, 2017.

6. Scott Rasmussen, "33 States Have Enacted Voter ID Requirements,"
    Newsmax, July 14, 2017, www.newsmax.com/ScottRasmussen
    /governorship-houses-photo-republicans/2017/07/14/id/801635
    /, accessed July 15, 2017; Zoltan L. Hajnal, Nazita Lajevardi, and
    Lindsay Nielson, "Do Voter Identification Laws Suppress Minority
    Voting? Yes. We Did the Research," *Washington Post*, February 15,
    2017, www.washingtonpost.com/news/monkey-cage/wp/2017/02
    /15/do-voter-identification-laws-suppress-minority-voting-yes-we
    -did-the-research/, accessed February 17, 2017.

7. Helen Colwell Adams, "2000 Election Casts Shadow; Since Florida
    Mess, Moves to Electronic Voting Brings Out Conspiracy Theorists.
    Paper Ballots, Anyone? Don't Laugh," *Sunday (Lancaster, PA)
    News*, March 28, 2004; Richard L. Hasen, *The Voting Wars: From
    Florida 2000 to the Next Election Meltdown* (New Haven, CT:
    Yale University Press, 2012), x.

8. Deborah Barfield and Tom Brune, "Election 2000, the Presidency:
    Distrust Remains for Black Voters," *Newsday*, December 7, 2000.

9. Alexander Keyssar, *The Right to Vote: The Contested History of
    Democracy in the United States* (New York: Basic Books, 2000), 262.

10. Hasen, *The Voting Wars*, ix.

11. David Margolick, "The Path to Florida," *Vanity Fair*, March 19,
    2014, www.vanityfair.com/news/2004/10/florida-election-2000,
    accessed July 22, 2017.

12. Hasen, *The Voting Wars*, 5.

13. Lorraine C. Minnite, *The Myth of Voter Fraud* (Ithaca, NY, and
    London: Cornell University Press, 2010), 99.

14. Hasen, *The Voting Wars*, 46; National Voter Registration Act, (b)(2),
    www.sos.ms.gov/links/elections/home/tab5/NVRAPurging.pdf,

accessed September 23, 2017; *U.S.A. v. Bd of Elec. Commn. for St. Louis City*, 4:2002cv01235 (E.D. Mo.).

15. Minnite, *The Myth of Voter Fraud*, 100.

16. Minnite, *The Myth of Voter Fraud*, 101.

17. Minnite, *The Myth of Voter Fraud*, 100; Brennan Center for Justice, "Missouri, 2000," November 10, 2007, www.brennancenter.org /analysis/Missouri-2000, accessed September 23, 2017.

18. African Americans were 51.8 percent of St. Louis's population in 2000. "St. Louis: Population Profile," www.city-data.com/us -cities/The-Midwest/St-Louis-Population-Profile.html, accessed September 13, 2017.

19. Hasen, *The Voting Wars*, 47.

20. Brennan Center for Justice, "Missouri, 2000."

21. Hasen, *The Voting Wars*, 5.

22. Zachary Roth, *The Great Suppression: Voting Rights, Corporate Cash* (New York: Crown, 2016), 12.

23. Roth, *The Great Suppression*, 10.

24. Leah Wright Rigueur, *The Loneliness of the Black Republican: Pragmatic Politics and the Pursuit of Power* (Princeton, NJ: Princeton University Press, 2015), 306.

25. Roper Center for Public Opinion Research, "How Groups Voted in 2000," Cornell University, ropercenter.cornell.edu/polls/us -elections/how-groups-voted/how-groups-voted-2000/, accessed September 24, 2017.

26. Carol Anderson, *White Rage: The Unspoken Truth of Our Racial Divide* (New York: Bloomsbury, 2016), 139–40.

27. Margolick, "The Path to Florida."

28. Margolick, "The Path to Florida"; "Katherine Harris' 'W' Files," CBS News, August 8, 2001, www.cbsnews.com/news/katherine -harris-w-files/, accessed September 22, 2017; "Contesting the Vote: In One Analysis, Gore Is Clear Winner," *New York Times*, December 4, 2000; Roger Roy, "NAACP Settles Suit Over 2000 Election," *Sun-Sentinel*, September 5, 2002, articles.sun-sentinel .com/2002-09-05/news/0209050114_1_elections-officials-election -day-problems-local-elections, accessed September 22, 2017.

29. Martha Kropf and David C. Kimball, *Helping America Vote: The Limits of Election Reform* (New York: Routledge, 2012), 9.

30. John H. Fund, *Stealing Elections: How Voter Fraud Threatens Our Democracy* (New York: Encounter Books, 2008), 161.

31. Brennan Center for Justice, "Missouri, 2000."

32. "St. Louis Erred in Saying Many Voted Improperly," *Deseret News*, November 5, 2001, www.deseretnews.com/article/872735 /St-Louis-erred-in-saying-many-voted-improperly.html, accessed September 23, 2017.

33. Brennan Center for Justice, "Missouri, 2000."

34. Brennan Center for Justice, "Missouri, 2000."

35. U.S. Election Assistance Commission, "Help America Vote Act," www.eac.gov/about/help-america-vote-act/, accessed September 12, 2017; CASA, "Federal Voter ID Requirements: The Help America Vote Act (HAVA)," civilrights.findlaw.com/other-cons titutional-rights/federal-voter-id-requirements-the-help-america -vote-act-hava.html, accessed September 12, 2017; Evan Woodward, "Carter-Ford Election Report Falls Short," *AlterNet*, August 6, 2001, www.alternet.org/story/11286/carter-ford_election_report _falls_short, accessed September 22, 2017.

36. Hasen, *The Voting Wars*, 47; Kevin Drum, "The Dog That Voted and Other Election Fraud Yarns: The GOP's 10-Year Campaign to Gin Up Voter Fraud Hysteria—and Bring Back Jim Crow at the Ballot Box," *Mother Jones*, July–August 2012, www.motherjones .com/politics/2012/07/voter-suppression-kevin-drum/, accessed September 23, 2017.

37. Quoted in Opinion of Justice Stevens, *Crawford v. Marion County Election Board*, 553 U.S. 181 (2008).

38. Keyssar, *The Right to Vote*, 284.

39. Roth, *The Great Suppression*, 23.

40. Richard L. Hasen, "The Fraudulent Fraud Squad: The Incredible, Disappearing American Center for Voting Rights," *Slate*, May 18, 2007, www.slate.com/articles/news_and_politics/jurisprudence /2007/05/the_fraudulent_fraud_squad.html, accessed September 24, 2017.

41. Hasen, "The Fraudulent Fraud Squad."

42. American Center for Voting Rights, "Vote Fraud, Intimidation and Suppression in the 2004 Presidential Election," July 21, 2005, www .foxnews.com/projects/pdf/Vote_Fraud_Intimidation_Suppression _2004_Pres_Election_v2.pdf, accessed September 30, 2017; U.S. Census Bureau, "The Black Population," August 2001, www.census .gov/prod/2001pubs/c2kbr01-5.pdf, accessed September 30, 2017; East St. Louis, censusreporter.org/profiles/16000US1722255-east -st-louis-il/, accessed September 30, 2017; U.S. Census Bureau, "State and County Facts: Milwaukee, Wisconsin," web.archive.org /web/20140207151149/http://quickfacts.census.gov/qfd/states /55/5553000.html, accessed September 30, 2017; Office of Seattle Mayor Tim Burgess, "Race and Ethnicity Quick Statistics," www .seattle.gov/opcd/population-and-demographics/about-seattle #raceethnicity, accessed September 30, 2017; Census Reporter, Cleveland, Ohio, censusreporter.org/profiles/16000US3916000-cleve land-oh/, accessed September 30, 2017; Thomas E. Mann and Norman J. Ornstein, *It's Even Worse Than It Looks: How the American Constitutional System Collided with the New Politics of Extremism* (New York: Basic Books, 2012), 59–61; Matthew Vadum, "Stranger Than Fiction: Nexis Search Shows the Media's Reported Nexus Between ACORN and Crack Cocaine (Hey, Don't Blame Us: We're Just the Messengers.)," Capital Research Center, October 31, 2008, capitalresearch.org/article/stranger-than-fiction -nexis-search-shows-the-medias-reported-nexus-between-acorn -and-crack-cocaine-hey-dont-blame-us-were-just-the-messengers/, accessed October 1, 2017.

43. Hasen, *The Voting Wars*, 51.

44. Hasen, *The Voting Wars*, 52.

45. Alex Koppelman, "How U.S. Attorneys Were Used to Spread Voter-Fraud Fears," *Salon*, March 21, 2007, www.salon.com/2007/03 /21/us_attorneys_2/, accessed September 24, 2017.

46. Hasen, *The Voting Wars*, 52.

47. Koppelman, "How U.S. Attorneys Were Used to Spread Voter Fraud Fears."

48. Adam Zagorin, "Why Were These U.S. Attorneys Fired?," *Time*, March 7, 2007, content.time.com/time/nation/article/0,8599, 1597085,00.html, accessed September 24, 2017.

49. Eric Lipton and Ian Urbina, "In 5-Year Effort, Scant Evidence of Voter Fraud, *New York Times*, April 12, 2007, www.nytimes.com /2007/04/12/washington/12fraud.html, accessed September 24, 2017.

50. Josh Siegel, "After Voter ID Defeats, Lessons from Indiana's Law That 'Has Stood Test of Time,'" *Daily Signal*, August 7, 2016, dailysignal.com/2016/08/07/after-voter-id-defeats-lessons-from -indianas-law-that-has-stood-test-of-time/, accessed September 25, 2017.

51. Josh Siegel, "After Voter ID Defeats, Lessons From Indiana's Law That 'Has Stood Test of Time' "; Joshua A. Douglas and Eugene D. Mazo, ed., *Election Law Stories* (St. Paul, MN: Foundation Press, 2016), 473.

52. Senate Enrolled Act No. 483, First Regular Session 114th General Assembly (2005), www.in.gov/legislative/bills/2005/SE/SE0483 .1.html, accessed September 30, 2017.

53. ACLU, "Supreme Court Agrees to Review Indiana Voter ID Law: Case Has Broad Implications for Upcoming Elections," September 25, 2007, www.aclu.org/news/supreme-court-agrees-review-indi ana-voter-id-law, accessed September 29, 2017; Opinion of Justice Stevens, *Crawford et al. v. Marion County Election Board*, 553 U.S. 181 (2008); State Defendants' Reply Memorandum in Support of Their Motion for Summary Judgment, *Indiana Democratic Party et al. v. Todd Rokita, Indiana Secretary of State et al.*, 07-25, moritzlaw.osu.edu/electionlaw/litigation/documents/State DefendantsReplyMemoranduminSupportofTheirMotionforSum maryJudgment.pdf, accessed September 30, 2017.

54. *Crawford v. Marion County Election Bd.* (Nos. 07-21 and 07-25), 472 F. 3d 949.

55. *Crawford v. Marion County Election Board et al.*, Reply Brief for Petitioners, No. 07-21, www.americanbar.org/content/dam/aba /publishing/preview/publiced_preview_briefs_pdfs_07_08_07

_21_PetitionerReply.authcheckdam.pdf, accessed September 29, 2017.

56. Siegel, "After Voter ID Defeats."

57. *Crawford v. Marion County Election Board et al.*, Reply Brief for Petitioners, No. 07-21.

58. *Crawford v. Marion County Election Board et al.*, Reply Brief for Petitioners, No. 07-21; Connor Maxwell and Danielle Root, "Five Truths About Voter Suppression," Center for American Progress, May 12, 2017, www.americanprogress.org/issues/race/news/2017 /05/12/432339/five-truths-voter-suppression/, accessed May 13, 2017; Rachel Strange, "Exploring Hoosier Minority Groups: Indiana's Black Population" *InContext*, May–June 2013, www.incontext.ind iana.edu/2013/may-jun/article3.asp, accessed September 30, 2017.

59. Opinion of Justice Stevens, *Crawford v. Marion County Election Board*, 553 U.S. 181 (2008).

60. Opinion of Justice Stevens, *Crawford v. Marion County Election Board*, 553 U.S. 181 (2008); Reply Brief for Petitioners, *Crawford v. Marion County Election Board*, No. 07-21.

61. "Indiana's Income by Race," *InContext*, November 2005, www .incontext.indiana.edu/2005/november/images/race_table1_lg.gif, accessed September 30, 2017; Justice Souter dissent, *Crawford v. Marion County Election Board*, 553 U.S. 181 (2008).

62. Reply Brief for Petitioners, *Crawford v. Marion County Election Board*, No. 07-21.

63. "Black Lawmakers: Burmeister Should Resign Her Position," *Athens Banner-Herald*, November 24, 2005, onlineathens.com /stories/112405/news_20051124053.shtml#.WdBQA7pFw5t, accessed September 30, 2017; Section 5 Recommendation Memorandum: Factual Investigation and Legal Review, August 25, 2005, www.brennancenter.org/sites/default/files/analysis/08-25 -05%20Georgia%20ID%20Preclearance%20Memo%20-%20 DOJ%20Staff.pdf, accessed September 30, 2017.

64. Section 5 Recommendation Memorandum: Factual Investigation and Legal Review, August 25, 2005; Jane Mayer, *Dark Money: The*

Hidden History of the Billionaires Behind the Rise of the Radical Right (New York: Anchor Books, 2017), 403–5.

65. Section 5 Recommendation Memorandum: Factual Investigation and Legal Review, August 25, 2005.

66. John Tanner to Thurbert Baker and Dennis R. Dunn, August 26, 2005, www.brennancenter.org/sites/default/files/analysis/08-26 -05%20Georgia%20ID%20Preclearance%20Letter%20-%20 Tanner.pdf, accessed September 30, 2017; Suevon Lee and Sarah Smith, "Everything You've Ever Wanted to Know About Voter ID Laws," *ProPublica*, March 9, 2016, www.propublica.org/article /everything-youve-ever-wanted-to-know-about-voter-id-laws, accessed March 12, 2017.

67. Anderson, *White Rage*, 138–39.

68. Mann and Ornstein, *It's Even Worse Than It Looks*; "GOP Leader's Top Goal: Make Obama 1-Term President," NBC News, November 4, 2010, www.nbcnews.com/id/40007802/ns/politics-decision_2010 /t/gop-leaders-top-goal-make-obama—term-president/#.WdD -87pFw5s, accessed October 1, 2017.

69. "U.S. Senate: Election 2010," *New York Times*, www.nytimes.com /elections/2010/results/senate.html, accessed October 1, 2017; "U.S. House: Election 2010," *New York Times*, www.nytimes.com /elections/2010/results/house.html, accessed October 1, 2017; "Governor: Election 2010," *New York Times*, www.nytimes.com /elections/2010/results/governor.html, accessed October 1, 2017; Dan Balz, *Washington Post*, "The GOP Takeover in the States," November 13, 2010, www.washingtonpost.com/wp-dyn/content /article/2010/11/13/AR2010111302389.html, accessed October 1, 2017.

70. Nancy MacLean, *Democracy in Chains: The Deep History of the Radical Right's Stealth Plan for America* (New York: Viking, 2017), xvi.

71. Nancy Scola, "Exposing ALEC: How Conservative-Backed State Laws Are All Connected," *Atlantic*, April 14, 2012, www.theatlantic .com/politics/archive/2012/04/exposing-alec-how-conservative

-backed-state-laws-are-all-connected/255869/, accessed August 28, 2017; John Nichols, "ALEC Exposed: Rigging Elections, Looking Toward 2012, ALEC Is Peddling 'Voter ID' Laws to Disenfranchise Voters Least Likely to Support Their Right-wing Candidates," *The Nation*, July 12, 2011, www.thenation.com/article/alec-exposed -rigging-elections/, accessed August 28, 2017.

72. Roth, *The Great Suppression*, 2, 3, 22, 24, 25; Ashantai Hathaway, "Black Homeownership Lower Today Than National Rate During Great Depression," *The Grio*, September 27, 2016, thegrio.com /2016/09/27/black-homeownership-endangered-great-depression/, accessed October 1, 2017.

73. MacLean, *Democracy in Chains*, xiii–xv; Anderson, *White Rage*, 170–71.

74. Justice Ginsburg dissent, *Shelby County v. Holder*.

75. *Citizens United v. Federal Election Commission*, 558 U.S. 310 (2010); Mayer, *Dark Money*, 280–329.

76. Michael Wines, "How Charges of Voter Fraud Became a Political Strategy," *New York Times*, October 21, 2016, www.nytimes.com /2016/10/22/us/how-charges-of-voter-fraud-became-a-political -strategy.html, accessed May 16, 2017.

77. Michael Wines, "Some Republicans Acknowledge Leveraging Voter ID Laws for Political Gain," *New York Times*, September 16, 2016, www.nytimes.com/2016/09/17/us/some-republicans-acknowledge -leveraging-voter-id-laws-for-political-gain.html, accessed May 16, 2017.

78. Charles P. Pierce, "People Have a Right to Vote. Period. More evidence that Voter ID laws are about voter suppression," *Esquire*, September 15, 2016, www.esquire.com/news-politics/politics/news /a48625/wisconsin-voter-suppression-republicans/, accessed April 15, 2018.

79. "Now We Finally Know How Bad Voter Fraud Is in North Carolina," editorial, *Charlotte Observer*, April 24, 2017, www.charlotteobserver .com/opinion/editorials/article146486019.html, accessed April 25, 2017.

80. Justin Levitt, "A Comprehensive Investigation of Voter Impersonation Finds 31 Credible Incidents out of One Billion Ballots Cast," *Washington Post*, August 6, 2014, www.washingtonpost.com/news/wonk/wp/2014/08/06/a-comprehensive-investigation-of-voter-impersonation-finds-31-credible-incidents-out-of-one-billion-ballots-cast/, accessed March 12, 2017.

81. Brynna Quillin, "Why Current Voter ID Laws Are Harmful to American Democracy," *Kennedy School Review*, May 28, 2017, harvardkennedyschoolreview.com/why-current-voter-id-laws-are-harmful-to-american-democracy/, accessed June 11, 2017.

82. Ian Haney López, *Dog Whistle Politics: How Coded Racial Appeals Have Reinvented Racism and Wrecked the Middle Class* (New York: Oxford University Press, 2014).

83. Jennifer L. Eberhardt, Phillip Atiba Goff, Valerie J. Purdie, and Paul G. Davies, "Seeing Black: Race, Crime, and Visual Processing," *Journal of Personality and Social Psychology* 87, no. 6 (December 2004): 876–93; Khalil Gibran Muhammad, *The Condemnation of Blackness: Race, Crime, and the Making of Modern Urban America* (Cambridge, MA: Harvard University Press, 2010).

84. Vadum, "Stranger Than Fiction."

85. Sam Levine, "Kansas Secretary of State: Only Obstacle Voter ID Causes May Be 'Exerting Calories,'" *Huffington Post*, February 23, 2017, huffingtonpost.com/entry/kansas-voter-id_us_58af29b1e4b060480e05ccdb?0tndhnxgbwsysnhfr, accessed July 28, 2017.

86. Sarah Childress, "Why Voter ID Laws Aren't Really About Fraud," *Frontline*, October 20, 2014, www.pbs.org/wgbh/frontline/article/why-voter-id-laws-arent-really-about-fraud/, accessed April 26, 2017.

87. Kim Chandler, "Alabama Photo Voter ID Law to Be Used in 2014, State Officials Say," AL.com, June 25, 2013, blog.al.com/wire/2013/06/alabama_photo_voter_id_law_to.html, accessed October 1, 2017; Sarah Childress, "With Voting Rights Act Out, States Push Voter ID Laws," *Frontline*, June 26, 2013, www.pbs.org/wgbh

/frontline/article/with-voting-rights-act-out-states-push-voter-id
-laws/, accessed October 1, 2017.

88. NAACP-LDF, "Public Housing ID not Valid Voter Photo ID in
Alabama," November 4, 2014, www.naacpldf.org/press-release/pub
lic-housing-id-not-valid-voter-photo-id-alabama, accessed October 1,
2017.

89. Anna Claire Vollers, "Alabama Is 6th Poorest State in Nation:
Poverty Rate at 40 percent in Some Counties," AL.com, July 3,
2017, www.al.com/news/index.ssf/2017/07/alabama_is_6th_poor
est_state_i.html, accessed October 1, 2017.

90. John Sharp, "Rebekah Mason Suggested Closure of DMV Offices
in Majority Black Counties, Report Shows," AL.com, April 8, 2017,
www.al.com/news/mobile/index.ssf/2017/04/rebekah_mason_sug
gested_closur.html, accessed May 20, 2017.

91. Kent Faulk, "NAACP Legal Defense Fund: More Than 100,000
Alabama Registered Voters Can't Cast a Ballot," AL.com,
March 4, 2017, www.al.com/news/birmingham/index.ssf/2017
/03/naacp_legal_defense_fund_more.html, accessed March 5,
2017.

92. Lee and Smith, "Everything You've Ever Wanted to Know About
Voter ID Laws."

93. Faulk, "NAACP Legal Defense Fund."

94. Ian Millhiser, "Breaking: America's Worst Voter Suppression Law
Won't Take Effect for This Election," *ThinkProgress*, August 31,
2016, thinkprogress.org/breaking-americas-worst-voter-suppres
sion-law-won-t-take-effect-for-this-election-773aaa719f20, accessed
July 21, 2017.

95. Quillin, "Why Current Voter ID Laws Are Harmful to American
Democracy."

96. Robert Barnes, "Supreme Court Won't Review Decision That
Found N.C. Voting Law Discriminates Against African Americans,"
Washington Post, May 15, 2016.

97. George Will, "If Texas Goes Blue, Republicans Are Finished,"
National Review, July 20, 2016, www.nationalreview.com/article

/438120/texas-republicans-demographic-change-could-finish
-gop, accessed October 1, 2017.

98. "A Judge Ruled Texas's Second Try at Voter ID Laws Is Illegal.
She's Right," editorial, *Washington Post*, August 26, 2017, www
.washingtonpost.com/opinions/a-judge-ruled-texass-second-try
-at-voter-id-laws-is-illegal-shes-right/2017/08/26/4c565476
-891b-11e7-961d-2f373b3977ee_story.html, accessed August 28,
2017; *Veasey v. Perry*, Civil Action No. 13-CV-00193, October
2014; Lee and Smith, "Everything You've Ever Wanted to Know
About Voter ID Laws."

99. NAACP-LDF, "Texas Court Order Helps Combat Misinformation
Given to Voters," September 19, 2016, www.naacpldf.org/press
-release/texas-court-order-helps-combat-misinformation-given
-voters, accessed October 1, 2017; "A Judge Ruled Texas's Second
Try at Voter ID Laws Is Illegal," editorial, *Washington Post*.

100. Sean Collins Walsh, "Texas House Gives Final Approval to Bill
Aimed at Fixing Voter ID Law," *American Statesman*, May 24,
2017, www.mystatesman.com/news/state—regional-govt—politics
/texas-house-gives-final-approval-bill-aimed-fixing-voter-law
/PqsNH8sW5CH22dER1Zzq2M/, accessed May 24, 2017; Ari
Berman, "Courts Have Blocked Three Discriminatory Texas
Voting Laws in Eight Days," *Mother Jones*, August 24, 2017, www
.motherjones.com/politics/2017/08/courts-have-blocked-three-dis
criminatory-texas-voting-laws-in-eight-days/, accessed August 24,
2017; Manny Fernandez, "Federal Judge Rejects a Revised Voter
ID Law in Texas," *New York Times*, August 23, 2017, www.nytimes
.com/2017/08/23/us/federal-judge-rejects-a-revised-voter-id-law-in
-texas.html, accessed August 24, 2017; Brennan Center for Justice,
"Texas NAACP v. Steen (consolidated with Veascy v. Abbott),"
February 24, 2017, www.brennancenter.org/legal-work/naacp-v
-steen, accessed May 24, 2017; "A Judge Ruled Texas's Second
Try at Voter ID Laws Is Illegal," editorial, *Washington Post*;
NAACP Legal Defense Fund, "NAACP Legal Defense Fund
Statement on Voter ID Bill in Texas," press release, June 2, 2017,

www.naacpldf.org/press-release/naacp-legal-defense-fund
-statement-voter-id-bill-texas, accessed June 2, 2017.

101. Mirren Gidda, "Why It Is So Hard to Vote If You're Black, Poor
or Elderly in America," *Newsweek*, April 11, 2017, www.newsweek
.com/voter-id-laws-texas-minority-voters-strict-states-582405,
accessed May 20, 2017.

102. Ari Berman, "A New Study Shows Just How Many Americans
Were Blocked from Voting in Wisconsin Last Year: Trump Won
the State by 22,748 Votes," *Mother Jones*, September 25, 2017,
www.motherjones.com/politics/2017/09/a-new-study-shows-just
-how-many-americans-were-blocked-from-voting-in-wisconsin
-last-year/, accessed September 25, 2017.

103. Childress, "Why Voter ID Laws Aren't Really About Fraud."

104. Renée Cross, Jim Granato, and Mark P. Jones, "Cross, Granato,
Jones: State Should Focus on Voter Education," *Houston Chronicle*,
April 7, 2017, www.houstonchronicle.com/opinion/outlook/arti
cle/Cross-Granato-Jones-State-should-focus-on-11059285.php?,
accessed May 20, 2017; Michael S. Lynch and Chelsie L. M. Bright,
"How Advertising Campaigns Can Help to Mitigate the Negative
Effects of Voter ID Laws on Turnout," *London School of Economics
Blog*, April 7, 2017, blogs.lse.ac.uk/usappblog/2017/04/07/how
-advertising-campaigns-can-help-to-mitigate-the-negative-effects
-of-voter-id-laws-on-turnout/, accessed May 21, 2017.

105. Todd Richmond, "Judge Rips Wisconsin Officials Over Voter ID
Law Confusion," *Seattle Times*, October 12, 2016, www.seattle
times.com/nation-world/judge-criticizes-wisconsin-for-confusing
-info-on-voting-id/, accessed October 1, 2017; *Frank et al. v. Walker
et al.*, Nos. 16-3003 and 16-3052, and *One Wisconsin Institute,
Inc. et al. v. Thomsen*, Nos. 16-3083 and 16-3091, August 26, 2016.

106. Vann R. Newkirk II, "Voter-Fraud Laws Are All About Race: Courts
Are Recognizing That the Intent of Many New Voter Laws Is Not
to Improve Democracy but to Discriminate," *Atlantic*, August 2,
2016, www.theatlantic.com/politics/archive/016/08/voting-rights
-court-decisions-racism/493937/, accessed April 26, 2017.

107. Villafranca, "Texas' Voter ID Law Is 'Unexplainable on Grounds Other Than Race,' Federal Judge Rules"; Horwitz, "Getting a Photo ID so You Can Vote Is Easy. Unless You're Poor, Black, Latino or Elderly"; Prophet, "An Open Letter from One Disabled Person to Another"; Cassidy and Moreno, "In Wisconsin, ID Law Proved Insurmountable for Many Voters."

Chapter Three: Voter Roll Purge

1. Greg Palast, "The GOP's Stealth War Against Voters," *Rolling Stone*, August 24, 2016, www.rollingstone.com/politics/features /the-gops-stealth-war-against-voters-w435890, accessed May 17, 2017.

2. Connor Maxwell and Danielle Root, "Five Truths About Voter Suppression," Center for American Progress, May 12, 2017, www .americanprogress.org/issues/race/news/2017/05/12/432339 /five-truths-voter-suppression/, accessed May 13, 2017; Mollie Reilly, "Rick Scott Administration Acknowledges Voter Purge Flaws," *Huffington Post*, October 7, 2013, www.huffingtonpost .com/2013/10/07/rick-scottvoter-purge_n_4057074.html, accessed May 17, 2017.

3. Max Greenwood, "Indiana Purges Nearly 500,000 from Voter Rolls," *The Hill*, April 20, 2017, thehill.com/blogs/ballot-box /329659-indiana-purges-nearly-half-a-million-from-voter-rolls, accessed May 16, 2017.

4. Kristina Torres, "Georgia Cancels Registration of More Than 591,500 Voters," *Atlanta Journal-Constitution*, July 31, 2017, www.myajc.com/news/state--regional-govt--politics/georgia -cancels-registration-more-than-591-500-voters/ozSuX227 UpNe18YGQ0hYUJ/, accessed November 26, 2017.

5. Ari Berman, "Trump Administration on the Right to Vote: Use It or Lose It," *Mother Jones*, August 8, 2017, www.motherjones .com/politics/2017/08/trump-administration-on-the-right-to -vote-use-it-or-lose-it/, accessed August 11, 2017.

6. "Pennsylvania Removes Itself from the Interstate Crosscheck System," Medium.com, July 27, 2017, medium.com/@SIIPCam paigns/breaking-news-pennsylvania-removes-itself-from-the-inter state-crosscheck-system-c3a78d126d77, accessed July 27, 2017; Gregory Palast, "Florida's Flawed 'Voter-Cleansing' Program," *Salon*, December 4, 2000, www.salon.com/2000/12/04/voter_file /, accessed September 22, 2017; Leada Gore, "Senate Candidate Mo Brooks Listed as 'Inactive' on Voting Rolls," AL.com, August 15, 2017, www.al.com/news/indes.ssf/2017/08/senate_candidate_mo_ brooks_list.html, accessed August 22, 2017; Pema Levy, "This Republican Candidate Had a Little Trouble Voting on Tuesday," *Mother Jones*, August 17, 2017, www.motherjones.com/politics /2017/08/this-republican-candidate-had-a-little-trouble-voting-on -tuesday/#, accessed November 26, 2017; Vince Grzegorek, "Federal Judge Restores Voting Rights for Thousands in Ohio Purged from the Voter Rolls," Clevescene.com, October 20, 2016, www.clevescene .com/scene-and-heard/archives/2016/09/23/ohios-voter-purge -policy-has-been-ruled-illegal, accessed May 17, 2017.

7. M. L. Schultze, "When Does Not Voting Cost You Your Right to Vote?," WKSU.org, November 20, 2017, wksu.org/post/when-does -not-voting-cost-you-your-right-vote#stream/0, accessed November 22, 2017.

8. Gore, "Senate Candidate Mo Brooks Listed as 'Inactive' on Voting Rolls."

9. Sam Levine, "Listen to Former Felons Who Can Vote Again Explain the Power of the Ballot," *Huffington Post*, November 9, 2017, www .huffingtonpost.com/entry/virginia-restoration-of-voting-rights _us_5a045ea9e4b03deac08b96f9, accessed November 11, 2017; Leigh Chapman, "Ohio: Protect the Voter Rolls from Illegal Purges That Make It Harder for Eligible Citizens to Vote," Let America Vote, August 30, 2017, policy.letamericavote.org/case-study-ohio -voter-purge-161aa76f43dc, accessed October 10, 2017.

10. Richard L. Berke, "Experts Say Low 1988 Turnout May Be Repeated," *New York Times*, November 13, 1988, www.nytimes

.com/1988/11/13/us/experts-say-low-1988-turnout-may-be
-repeated.html, accessed December 5, 2017.

11. J. Mijin Cha, "Registering Millions: The Success and Potential of
the National Voter Registration Act at 20," Demos, www.demos.org
/registering-millions-success-and-potential-national-voter
-registration-act-20, accessed November 27, 2017.

12. American Presidency Project, "Voter Turnout in Presidential
Elections: 1828–2012," www.presidency.ucsb.edu/data/turnout
.php, accessed November 26, 2017; National Voter Registration Act of
1993, Pub. L. 103-31, 107 Stat. 77 (1993). www.gpo.gov/fdsys/pkg
/STATUTE-107/pdf/STATUTE-107-Pg77.pdf, accessed March 28,
2018.

13. National Voter Registration Act of 1993, Pub. L. 103-31, 107 Stat.
77 (1993).

14. National Voter Registration Act of 1993, Pub. L. 103-31, 107 Stat.
77 (1993).

15. Federal Election Commission, "The Impact of the National Voter
Registration Act of 1993 on the Administration of Elections for
Federal Office 1995–1996," www.eac.gov/assets/1/6/The%20
Impact%20of%20the%20National%20Voter%20Registration
%20Act%20on%20Federal%20Elections%201995-1996.pdf,
accessed November 27, 2017.

16. See, for example, Tennessee Secretary of State, "Purging Voter
Registration Information," www.sos.tn.gov/products/elections
/purging-voter-registration-information, accessed May 17, 2017.

17. National Voter Registration Act of 1993, 103rd Congress, 1st sess.

18. Chapman, "Ohio: Protect the Voter Rolls from Illegal Purges That
Make It Harder for Eligible Citizens to Vote."

19. Berman, "Trump Administration on the Right to Vote: Use It or
Lose It."

20. See 52 USC 20507: Requirements with respect to administration
of voter registration, (b)(2).

21. Ari Berman, "The Supreme Court Could Make It Easier for States
to Purge Voters," *The Nation*, May 30, 2017, www.thenation.com

/article/supreme-court-make-easier-states-purge-voters/, accessed May 30, 2017; "Voting Rights Groups to U.S. Supreme Court: Ohio's Method of Purging Voters Is Illegal," Brennan Center for Justice, September 25, 2017, www.brennancenter.org/press-release/voting -rights-groups-us-supreme-court-ohio%E2%80%99s-method -purging-voters-illegal, accessed October 8, 2017; Hannah Yi, Mori Rothman, and Chris Bury, "Why Ohio Has Purged at Least 200,000 from the Voter Rolls," *PBS NewsHour*, July 31, 2016, www.pbs.org /newshour/bb/inside-ohios-fight-voting-rules/, accessed May 17, 2017; Chapman, "Ohio: Protect the Voter Rolls from Illegal Purges That Make It Harder for Eligible Citizens to Vote"; Jane C. Timm, "Trump Administration Stirs Alarm Over Voter Purges," NBC News, August 7, 2017, www.nbcnews.com/politics/supreme-court /trump-administration-stirs-alarm-over-voter-purges-n789706, accessed December 3, 2017; Schultze, "When Does Not Voting Cost You Your Right to Vote?"

22. David A. Graham, "Ohio's Questionable Voter Purge," *Atlantic*, June 3, 2016, www.theatlantic.com/politics/archive/2016/06/ohio -voter-purge/485357/, accessed October 7, 2017.

23. Palast, "The GOP's Stealth War Against Voters."

24. Cleveland, Ohio, www.city-data.com/city/Cleveland-Ohio.html, accessed December 2, 2017.

25. "Cleveland Housing Data," www.towncharts.com/Ohio/Housing /Cleveland-city-OH-Housing-data.html, accessed December 2, 2017.

26. Rich Exner, "Mapping the Ohio Presidential Election Results by County," Cleveland.com, November 10, 2016, www.cleveland.com /datacentral/index.ssf/2016/11/mapping_the_ohio_presidential .html, accessed December 2, 2017.

27. Ari Berman, "As the GOP Convention Begins, Ohio Is Purging Tens of Thousands of Democratic Voters," *The Nation*, July 18, 2016, www.thenation.com/article/as-the-gop-convention-begins -ohio-is-purging-tens-of-thousands-of-democratic-voters/, accessed July 19, 2016; Berman, "Trump Administration on the Right to Vote: Use It or Lose It; Vanita Gupta, "Ohio's Illegal Voter Purges Shouldn't Be Getting Trump Justice Department's Blessing,"

Cleveland.com, October 15, 2017, www.cleveland.com/opinion /index.ssf/2017/10/ohios_illegal_voter_purges_sho.html, accessed October 18, 2017.

28. Yi, Rothman, and Bury, "Why Ohio Has Purged at Least 200,000 from the Voter Rolls."

29. Libby Nelson, "There Are 4,000 People in a Half-Mile Voting Line in Cincinnati Today. This Isn't Okay," *Vox*, November 6, 2016, www .vox.com/presidential-election/2016/11/6/13542680/there-are -4000-people-in-a-half-mile-voting-line-in-cincinnati-today-this -isn-t-okay, accessed January 14, 2017; Kira Lerner, "Meet Trump's Voter Fraud Squad," *ThinkProgress*, July 19, 2017, thinkprogress .org/fraud-squad-8797713d0ef7, accessed July 22, 2017; David Peppers, "Ohio Democrats Expose New Ohio Voting Laws as Modern-Day Literacy Tests, Voter Suppression," *Huffington Post*, April 8, 2016, www.huffingtonpost.com/david-pepper/ohio-dem ocrats-expose-new_b_9643250.html, accessed June 30, 2016.

30. Carol Anderson, *White Rage: The Unspoken Truth of our Racial Divide* (New York: Bloomsbury, 2017, paperback edition), 163; Peppers, "Ohio Democrats Expose New Ohio Voting Laws as Modern-Day Literacy Tests, Voter Suppression."

31. Tony Pugh, "Georgia Secretary of State Fighting Accusations of Disenfranchising Minority Voters," McClatchyDC, October 7, 2016, www.mcclatchydc.com/news/politics-government/article106692837 .html, accessed November 26, 2017.

32. Regina Willis, "More Than 380,000 Georgia Voters Receive 'Purge Notice,'" *Rewire*, July 21, 2017, rewire.news/article/2017/07/21 /more-380000-georgia-voters-received-purge-notice/, accessed July 22, 2017; Nick Knudsen, "The Biggest Story Nobody's Talking About: The Recall of Brian Kemp," *Huffington Post*, November 9, 2017, m.huffpost.com/us/entry/us_5a041b6be4b0c7511e1b3a1c /amp, accessed November 10, 2017.

33. Knudsen, "The Biggest Story Nobody's Talking About."

34. Michael Wines, "Critics See Efforts by Counties and Towns to Purge Minority Voters from Rolls," *New York Times*, July 31, 2016, www.nytimes.com/2016/08/01/us/critics-see-efforts-to-purge

-minorities-from-voter-rolls-in-new-elections-rules.html, accessed May 17, 2017; Rebekah Barber, "Is Georgia's Secretary of State Unjustly Targeting Voting Rights Activists Again?," *Facing South*, October 4, 2017, www.facingsouth.org/2017/10/georgias-secretary -state-unjustly-targeting-voting-rights-activists-again, accessed December 4, 2017.

35. Pugh, "Georgia Secretary of State Fighting Accusations of Disen-franchising Minority Voters"; Torres, "Suit Alleges That Georgia Is Illegally Bumping Voters off Rolls"; Torres, "Georgia Cancels Registration of More than 591,500 Voters."

36. Christopher Ingraham, "7 Papers, 4 Government Inquiries, 2 News Investigations and 1 Court Ruling Proving Voter Fraud Is Mostly a Myth," *Washington Post*, July 9, 2014, www.washingtonpost.com /news/wonk/wp/2014/07/09/7-papers-4-government-inquiries-2 -news-investigations-and-1-court-ruling-proving-voter-fraud-is -mostly-a-myth/, accessed December 7, 2017.

37. Sami Edge and Sean Holstege, "No, Voter Fraud Actually Isn't a Persistent Problem," *Washington Post*, September 1, 2016, www .washingtonpost.com/news/post-nation/wp/2016/09/01/voter -fraud-is-not-a-persistent-problem/, accessed December 4, 2017.

38. Daniel Weeks, "Why Are the Poor and Minorities Less Likely to Vote?," *Atlantic*, January 10, 2014, www.theatlantic.com/politics /archive/2014/01/why-are-the-poor-and-minorities-less-likely-to -vote/282896/, accessed December 7, 2017.

39. Willis, "More Than 380,000 Georgia Voters Receive 'Purge Notice.'"

40. National Voter Registration Act of 1993, 103rd Congress, 1st sess., (3)(e).

41. "Georgia NAACP President Francys Johnson Steps Down," *Atlanta Daily World*, August 3, 2017, atlantadailyworld.com/2017 /08/03/georgia-naacp-president-francys-johnson-steps-down/, accessed December 8, 2017; Sam Levine, "Georgia Is Trying to Block Newly Registered Voters from Taking Part in Fierce Runoff Election," *Huffington Post*, April 21, 2017, www.huffingtonpost .com/entry/georgia-voter-registration-runoff-ossoff_us_58f90 c7ce4b06b9cb91505f8, accessed May 19, 2017.

42. Michael Rey, "Lawsuit: Georgia Illegally Purges Votes," CBS News .com, October 9, 2008, www.cbsnews.com/news/lawsuit-georgia -illegally-purges-votes/, accessed June 5, 2017.

43. Pugh, "Georgia Secretary of State Fighting Accusations of Disenfranchising Minority Voters"; Willis, "More Than 380,000 Georgia Voters Receive 'Purge Notice.'"

44. Ari Berman, "The Man Behind Trump's Voter Fraud Obsession: How Kris Kobach, the Kansas Secretary of State, Plans to Remake America Through Restrictive Voting and Immigration Laws," *New York Times*, June 13, 2017, www.nytimes.com/2017/06/13 /magazine/the-man-behind-trumps-voter-fraud-obsession.html, accessed June 13, 2017; Diamond Naga Siu, "Former Attorney General Holder Calls Kobach a 'Fact-Challenged Zealot,'" *Politico*, July 24, 2017, www.politico.com/story/2017/07/24/holder-kobach -voters-naacp-240902, accessed July 25, 2017; Tomas Lopez and Jennifer L. Clark, "Uncovering Kris Kobach's Anti-Voting History," Brennan Center for Justice, May 11, 2017, www.brennancenter.org /blog/uncovering-kris-kobach%E2%80%99s-anti-voting-history, accessed May 27, 2017.

45. Mark Joseph Stern, "The Presidential Advisory Commission on Election Mendacity: The First Public Meeting of Trump's Voter Fraud Panel Was a Horrifying Parade of Outright Lies," *Slate*, July 19, 2017, www.slate.com/articles/news_and_politics /jurisprudence/2017/07/the_first_public_meeting_of_trump_s _voter_fraud_panel_was_a_parade_of_lies.html, accessed July 19, 2017.

46. Roxana Hegeman, "Uncounted Ballots Fuel Fears About Kobach's Proposals," KIRO 7 News, August 23, 2017, www.kiro7.com/news /uncounted-kansas-ballots-fuel-fears-about-kobachs-proposals /596788663, accessed August 23, 2017.

47. Chelsie Bright, "Kris Kobach and Kansas' SAFE Act," *The Conversation*, July 26, 2017, theconversation.com/kris-kobach-and -kansas-safe-act-81314, accessed December 8, 2017.

48. Stern, "The Presidential Advisory Commission on Election Mendacity."

49. Vann R. Newkirk II, "What's the Real Goal of Trump's Voter-Fraud Commission?" *Atlantic*, July 26, 2017, www.theatlantic.com /politics/archive/2017/07/trump-vote-fraud-commission/534843/, accessed July 26, 2017.

50. Ben Strauss, "'Kris Kobach Came After Me for an Honest Mistake,'" *Politico*, May 21, 2017, www.politico.com/magazine/story /2017/05/21/kris-kobach-voter-fraud-investigation-prosecution -215164, accessed May 22, 2017; Samuel P. Huntington, "The Clash of Civilizations?," *Foreign Affairs* (Summer 1993), www.foreignaf fairs.com/articles/united-states/1993-06-01/clash-civilizations, accessed December 11, 2017.

51. Ben Strauss, "'Kris Kobach Came After Me for an Honest Mistake,'" *Politico*, May 21, 2017, www.politico.com/magazine/story/2017 /05/21/kris-kobach-voter-fraud-investigation-prosecution-215164, accessed May 22, 2017.

52. Jim McLean, "Report: Kansas Election Law Suppressing Turnout," KCUR, March 14, 2017, kcur.org/post/report-kansas-election-law -suppressing-turnout#stream/0, accessed May 21, 2017; Sherrilyn Ifill, "President Trump's Election Integrity Commission Is Illegal and Unconstitutional—That's Why We Filed a Lawsuit," *Salon*, July 27, 2017, www.salon.com/2017/07/27/president-trumps-elec tion-integrity-commission-is-illegal-and-unconstitutional-that-is-why -we-filed-a-lawsuit/, accessed July 27, 2017.

53. Bright, "Kris Kobach and Kansas' SAFE Act."

54. Amrit Cheng, "If You Care About the Right to Vote, Here Are Six Things You Need to Know About Kris Kobach," ACLU, May 17, 2017, www.aclu.org/blog/voting-rights/fighting-voter-suppression /if-you-care-about-right-vote-here-are-six-things-you, accessed May 19, 2017.

55. Cheng, "If You Care About the Right to Vote."

56. Stern, "The Presidential Advisory Commission on Election Mendacity."

57. Pennsylvania Department of State, "The Interstate Crosscheck Program: Things You Should Know."

58. National Association of State Election Directors, "Interstate Voter Registration Crosscheck Program," January 26, 2013.

59. Strauss, "Kris Kobach Came After Me for an Honest Mistake."

60. Palast, "The GOP's Stealth War Against Voters"; Corrie MacLaggan, "Texas Voter Purge Lawsuit Ends with Clarification Memo on Process for Clearing Rolls," *Huffington Post*, October 3, 2012, www .huffingtonpost.com/2012/10/03/texas-voter-purge-lawsuit_n _1937564.html, accessed May 17, 2017.

61. David Catanese, "The 10 Closest States in the 2016 Election: Michigan and New Hampshire replace 2012's nail-biters in Florida and Ohio," *U.S. News & World Report*, November 14, 2016, www .usnews.com/news/the-run-2016/articles/2016-11-14/the-10 -closest-states-in-the-2016-election, accessed March 28, 2018.

62. "Voting Is for White People: The Origins of Crosscheck," Medium .com, April 29, 2017, medium.com/@SIIPCampaigns/voting-is-for -white-people-the-origins-of-crosscheck-c91d5d4532cc, accessed July 19, 2017; Rebecca L. Sanders, "Were up to 58,000 Citizens in Maricopa County Denied Right to Vote?," azcentral.com, May 1, 2017, www.azcentral.com/story/news/politics/elections/2017/05 /02/maricopa-county-voter-registration-citizenship-adrian-fontes /308435001/, accessed May 19, 2017.

63. Strauss, "Kris Kobach Came After Me for an Honest Mistake"; "Greg Palast in Ohio on GOP Effort to Remove African Americans from Voter Rolls in Battleground State," Democracy Now, November 8, 2016, www.democracynow.org/2016/11/8/greg_palast _in_ohio_on_gop, accessed May 17, 2017; Ari Berman, "Trump Election Commissioner's Voter Database Is a Ripe Target for Hackers," *Mother Jones*, October 23, 2017, www.motherjones.com/politics /2017/10/trump-election-commissioners-voter-database-is-a -ripe-target-for-hackers/, accessed October 24, 2017.

64. Palast, "The GOP's Stealth War Against Voters."

65. Sue Sturgis, "How Trump's New 'Election Integrity' Appointee Has Unleashed Chaos on Elections in the South," *Facing South*, May 17, 2017, www.facingsouth.org/2017/05/how-trumps-new-election

-integrity-appointee-has-unleashed-chaos-elections-south, accessed May 19, 2017.

66. Palast, "The GOP's Stealth War Against Voters."

67. Sturgis, "How Trump's New 'Election Integrity' Appointee Has Unleashed Chaos on Elections in the South"; "What Is the Most Common Last Name in the United States," names.mongabay.com /data/1000.html, accessed December 9, 2017.

68. "Chart of Crosscheck's Disparate Impact," projects.aljazeera .com/2014/double-voters/images/infographic2-02.svg, accessed March 28, 2017.

69. Charles D. Ellison, "The GOP Keeps Quietly Purging Black Voters—and Democrats Aren't Doing Anything About It," *The Root*, May 24, 2017, www.theroot.com/the-gop-keeps-quietly-purg ing-black-voters-and-democrat-1795474628, accessed April 13, 2018.

70. Charles P. Pierce, "Kris Kobach's Voter Fraud Commission Is Definitely a Fraud," *Esquire*, October 10, 2017, www.esquire.com /news-politics/politics/a12819768/trump-kobach-voter-fraud -commission/, accessed October 10, 2017.

71. "Greg Palast in Ohio on GOP Effort to Remove African Americans from Voter Rolls in Battleground State," Democracy Now.

72. Sam Levine, "Kris Kobach Proposed Weakening Key Federal Voting Protections in Trump Meeting," *Huffington Post*, October 5, 2017, www.huffingtonpost.com/entry/kris-kobach-nvra_us_598 dcd4le4b08a247273eb29?uh, accessed October 6, 2017; Roxana Hegeman, "Kobach Transcript: Changes to US Election Law Discussed," *Washington Post*, October 26, 2017, www.washing tonpost.com/national/kobach-transcript-changes-to-us-election -law-discussed/2017/10/26/67855e66-ba7d-11e7-9b93 -b97043e57a22_story.html, accessed October 27, 2017; Christopher Ingraham, "Vice Chair of Trump's Voter Fraud Commission Wants to Change Federal Law to Add New Requirements for Voting, Email Shows," *Washington Post*, July 17, 2017, www.washing tonpost.com/news/wonk/wp/2017/07/17/vice-chair-of-trumps -voter-fraud-commission-wants-to-change-federal-law-to-make-it -harder-to-vote-email-shows/, accessed July 18, 2017.

73. Bryan Lowry, "Judge Orders Kris Kobach to Produce Documents He Shared with Donald Trump," Kansascity.com, April 5, 2017, www.kansascity.com/news/politics-government/article142866014 .html, accessed May 21, 2017; Rick Hasen, "Court Fines SOS Kobach $1000 for Misleading Court on NVRA Documents, Allows ACLU to Depose Kobach," *Election Law Blog*, June 23, 2017, elec tionlawblog.org/?p=93347, accessed June 23, 2017; Rick Hasen, "Court Orders Kobach to Produce Voting Document Shared with Trump, Suggests ACLU May Pursue Sanctions Against Kobach," *Election Law Blog*, April 17, 2017, electionlawblog.org/?p=92138, accessed April 17, 2017; Dan Margolies, "Judge Refuses to Reconsider Fine of Kansas Secretary of State Kobach," KCUR, July 6, 2017, kcur.org/post/judge-refuses-reconsider-fine-kansas -secretary-state-kobach#stream/0, accessed July 6, 2017.

74. Abby Phillip and Mike DeBonis, "Without Evidence, Trump Tells Lawmakers 3 Million to 5 Million Illegal Ballots Cost Him the Popular Vote," *Washington Post*, January 23, 2017, www.washing tonpost.com/news/post-politics/wp/2017/01/23/at-white-house -trump-tells-congressional-leaders-3-5-million-illegal-ballots-cost -him-the-popular-vote/, accessed December 10, 2017.

75. Pema Levy, "Pence's Perch atop Trump's Voter Fraud Commission Hints at Suppression Efforts: As Indiana Governor, Pence Cheered a Crackdown on a Major Voter Registration Drive," *Mother Jones*, May 12, 2017, www.motherjones.com/politics/2017/05/how-will -trump-turn-voter-fraud-accusations-voter-suppression/, accessed December 10, 2017; Isaac Chotiner, "Conservative in the Wilderness: Charlie Sykes Was a Conservative Radio Star. Then Trump Won," *Slate*, October 23, 2017, www.slate.com/articles/news_and_politics /interrogation/2017/10/charlie_sykes_was_a_conservative_radio _star_then_trump_won.html, accessed October 26, 2017.

76. "The Bogus Voter-Fraud Commission," editorial, *New York Times*, July 22, 2017, www.nytimes.com/2017/07/22/opinion/sunday/the -bogus-voter-fraud-commission.html, accessed July 23, 2017.

77. Matthew Nussbaum, "Trump Stokes Voter Fraud Fears as Commission Convenes," *Politico*, July 19, 2017, www.politico.com

/story/2017/07/19/trump-pence-voter-fraud-commission-240714, accessed July 19, 2017; "Happy Fourth of July! Show Us Your Papers," *New York Times*, July 3, 2017, www.nytimes.com/2017/07 /03/opinion/voter-fraud-data-kris-kobach.html, accessed July 4, 2017; Jane C. Timm, "States Push New Voter Requirements, Fueled by Trump," NBC News, July 10, 2017, www.nbcnews.com/politics /elections/states-push-new-voter-requirements-fueled-trump -n780611, accessed July 13 2017; "The Bogus Voter-Fraud Commission," editorial, *New York Times*.

78. Alex Horton and Gregory S. Schneider, "Trump's Pick to Investigate Voter Fraud Is Freaking Out Voting Rights Activists," *Washington Post*, June 30, 2017, www.washingtonpost.com/news/post-nation /wp/2017/06/30/trumps-pick-to-investigate-voter-fraud-is-freak ing-out-voting-rights-activists/, accessed December 9, 2017.

79. Kira Lerner, "Meet Trump's Voter Fraud Squad: The Men and Women Tasked with Fighting a Non-existent Demon," *ThinkProgress*, July 19, 2017, thinkprogress.org/fraud-squad-8797713d0ef7, accessed July 22, 2017.

80. Ben Jacobs, "Controversial Rightwing Activist to Join Trump's Election Integrity Commission: J. Christian Adams Has Led Lawsuits Against Jurisdictions with Large Minority Populations in Effort to Purge Voter Rolls," *Guardian*, July 11, 2017, www.theguardian .com/us-news/2017/jul/11/trump-election-integrity-commission -j-christian-adams?CMP=twt_gu, accessed July 11, 2017.

81. Pema Levy, "These Three Lawyers Are Quietly Purging Voter Rolls Across the Country," *Mother Jones*, July 7, 2017, www.motherjones .com/politics/2017/07/these-three-lawyers-are-quietly-purging -voter-rolls-across-the-country/, accessed July 10, 2017; "Civil Rights Groups Launch National Effort to Combat Alarming Voter Purge Attempt," Brennan Center for Justice, November 22, 2017, www.brennancenter.org/press-release/civil-rights-groups-launch -national-effort-combat-alarming-voter-purge-attempt, accessed November 22, 2017; Jane C. Timm, "Vote Fraud Crusader J. Christian Adams Sparks Outrage," NBC News, August 27, 2017, www.nbcnews.com/politics/donald-trump/vote-fraud-crusader-j

-christian-adams-sparks-outrage-n796026, accessed August 27, 2017; Michael Wines, "Culling Voter Rolls: Battling Over Who Even Gets to Go to the Polls," *New York Times*, November 25, 2017, www.nytimes.com/2017/11/25/us/voter-rolls-registration-culling -election.html, accessed November 25, 2017.

82. Ifill, "President Trump's Election Integrity Commission Is Illegal and Unconstitutional—That's Why We Filed a Lawsuit"; Pema Levy, "Trump Election Commissioner Used Dubious Data to Allege an 'Alien Invasion,'" *Mother Jones*, July 18, 2017, www.motherjones .com/politics/2017/07/trump-election-commissioner-used -dubious-data-to-allege-an-alien-invasion/, accessed July 18, 2017.

83. John Wagner, "Trump's Voter Fraud Commission Proves a Magnet for Controversy," *Washington Post*, September 16, 2017, www .washingtonpost.com/politics/trumps-voter-fraud-commission -proves-a-magnet-for-controversy/2017/09/15/1e013fa2-9a30 -11e7-82e4-f1076f6d6152_story.html, accessed September 17, 2017; Kira Lerner, "Democrats on Trump's Voting Commission Iced Out Since First Meeting," *ThinkProgress*, August 22, 2017, thinkprog ress.org/democrats-voting-commission-ceec3ea98a33/, accessed August 23, 2017; Jessica Huseman, "Conflict Mounts Inside Voting Fraud Commission in the Wake of Child Porn Arrest," *ProPublica*, October 17, 2017, www.msn.com/en-us/news/politics/conflict -mounts-inside-voting-fraud-commission-in-the-wake-of-child -porn-arrest/ar-AAtETPp?li-BBmkt5R&ocid-spartanntp, accessed October 18, 2017.

84. Charles Stewart III, "What Is Kris Kobach Up To? A Letter Sent by the President's Election Fraud Commission Reveals a Thin Grasp of How to Answer a Very Real Question," *Politico*, July 3, 2017, www.politico.com/magazine/story/2017/07/03/what-is-kris -kobach-up-to-215332, accessed July 3, 2017.

85. Ari Berman, "Meet the Vote Suppressors and Conspiracy Theorists on Trump's 'Election Integrity' Commission," *The Nation*, July 11, 2017, www.thenation.com/article/meet-the-liars-and-conspiracy -theorists-on-trumps-election-integrity-commission/, accessed July 14, 2017; Asa Royal, "As Trump's Fraud Commission Sought

Data, Some Florida Voters Cancelled Registrations," *Tampa Bay Times*, July 26, 2017, www.tbo.com/blogs/the-buzz-florida-politics /as-trumps-fraud-commission-sought-data-some-florida-voters -cancel-their/2331561, accessed July 27, 2017; Jessica Husseman and Derek Willis, "The Voter Fraud Commission Wants Your Data—But Experts Say They Can't Keep It Safe," *ProPublica*, October 23, 2017, www.propublica.org/article/crosscheck-the -voter-fraud-commission-wants-your-data-keep-it-safe, accessed October 24, 2017; Berman, "Trump Election Commissioner's Voter Database Is a Ripe Target for Hackers"; Amber F. McReynolds, "Trump's voter commission is frightening away Denver voters," *Denver Post*, July 10, 2017, https://www.denverpost.com/2017/07 /10/trumps-voter-commission-is-frightening-away-denver-voters/, accessed May 18, 2019.

86. Soibangla to FN-OVP-Election Integrity Staff, email, June 29, 2017, www.whitehouse.gov/sites/whitehouse.gov/files/docs/comments -received-june-29-through-july-11-2017.pdf, accessed July 14, 2017.

87. Charlie Ticotsky to FN-OVP-Election Integrity Staff, email, June 29, 2017, www.whitehouse.gov/sites/whitehouse.gov/files/docs /comments-received-june-29-through-july-11-2017.pdf, accessed July 14, 2017.

88. Stephen Lehew to FN-OVP-Election Integrity Staff, email, June 29, 2017, www.whitehouse.gov/sites/whitehouse.gov/files/docs/com ments-received-june-29-through-july-11-2017.pdf, accessed July 14, 2017.

89. Mark Joseph Stern, "The Secret Goal of Trump's Voting Commission: It Is Seeking to Gut the Motor Voter Act," *Slate*, July 6, 2017, www.slate .com/articles/news_and_politics/jurisprudence/2017/07/the _secret_goal_of_trump_s_voting_commission_is_to_gut_the_ motor_voter_act.html, accessed July 7, 2017; "Responses to 'Fraud' Commission's Voter File Data Request," Brennan Center for Justice, July 11, 2017, www.brennancenter.org/latest-updates-fraud-commiss ion, accessed July 11, 2017; Stewart, "What Is Kris Kobach Up To?"

90. Stewart, "What Is Kris Kobach Up To?"

91. Celeste Katz, "Kentucky Secretary of State on Voter Data Request: 'Might as Well Let Putin Just Get a Zip Drive,'" *Mic*, July 13, 2017, mic.com/articles/182143/kentucky-secretary-of-state-on-voter-data -request-might-as-well-let-putin-just-get-a-zip-drive#.ppwYo5nYv, accessed December 10, 2017.

92. Jeffrey Toobin, "Trump's Voter-Fraud Commission Heads to New Hampshire," *New Yorker*, September 12, 2017, www.newyorker .com/news/daily-comment/trumps-voter-fraud-commission -heads-to-new-hampshire, accessed September 12, 2017.

93. Phillip Bump, "This Completely Astonishing Interview Totally Undercuts Trump's 'Voter Fraud' Investigation," *Washington Post*, July 19, 2017, www.washingtonpost.com/news/politics/wp/2017/07 /19/this-completely-astonishing-interview-totally-undercuts -trumps-voter-fraud-investigation/, accessed July 29, 2017.

94. Kris W. Kobach, "Exclusive—Kobach: It Appears That Out-of- State Voters Changed the Outcome of the New Hampshire U.S. Senate Race," *Breitbart*, September 7, 2017, www.breitbart.com /big-government/2017/09/07/exclusive-kobach-out-of-state -voters-changed-outcome-new-hampshire-senate-race/, accessed December 10, 2017; Kris Kobach and His 5,313 Fraudulent Voters," editorial, *New York Times*, September 11, 2017, www.nytimes.com /2017/09/11/opinion/kris-kobach-fraudulent-voters.html, accessed September 11, 2017.

95. "Kris Kobach and His 5,313 Fraudulent Voters," editorial, *New York Times*.

96. Pam Fessler, "'Nothing Going On' with Trump Voter Fraud Commission Due to Multiple Lawsuits," NPR, October 26, 2017, www.npr.org/2017/10/26/560089042/nothing-going-on-with -trump-voter-fraud-commission-due-to-multiple-lawsuits, accessed October 26, 2017; Jessica Huseman, "Trump Voter Fraud Commission Is Sued—by One of Its Own Commissioners," *ProPublica*, November 9, 2017, www.propublica.org/article/trump -voter-fraud-commission-dunlap-lawsuit, accessed November 10, 2017; Kurtis Lee, "Democrats on Trump's Voter Fraud Commission

Urge Leaders to Be More Transparent," *Los Angeles Times*, October 25, 2017, www.latimes.com/nation/la-na-pol-trump-voter -fraud-20171024-story.html, accessed October 27, 2017; "GAO to Investigate Presidential Voter Commission," October 26, 2017, www .bennet.senate.gov/?p=release&id=4096, accessed October 27, 2017.

97. Mark Joseph Stern, "Trump Voter Fraud Commission Halts Data Collection amid Torrent of Lawsuits and Complaints," *Slate*, July 10, 2017, www.slate.com/blogs/the_slatest/2017/07/10 /trump_voter_fraud_commission_halts_data_collection_amidst_ lawsuits.html, accessed July 10, 2017.

98. Lauren Rosenblatt, "Trump and Pence Defend Voter Fraud Panel at First Meeting," *Los Angeles Times*, July 19, 2017, www.latimes .com/politics/la-na-pol-trump-voting-commission-20170719-story .html, accessed December 11, 2017; Vann R. Newkirk II, "What's the Real Goal of Trump's Voter-Fraud Commission?," *Atlantic*, July 26, 2017, www.theatlantic.com/politics/archive/2017/07 /trump-vote-fraud-commission/534843/, accessed July 26, 2017.

99. Pema Levy and Ari Berman, "Background Checks for Voting Get Floated at Trump Election Commission Meeting," September 12, 2017, www.motherjones.com/politics/2017/09/background -checks-for-voting-get-floated-at-trump-election-commission -meeting/#, accessed September 12, 2017.

100. Steven Rosenfeld, "The Republican Effort to Rig Elections," *Portside*, September 16, 2017, portside.org/print/2017-09-16 /republican-effort-rig-elections, accessed September 16, 2017.

101. Noah Gordon, "Americans' Deep Racial Divide on Trusting the Police: It Isn't Just Ferguson—Polling Shows That Black Americans Are Wary of Law Enforcement Across the Nation, While Whites Are More Likely to Trust Officers," *Atlantic*, August 20, 2014, www.theatlantic.com/politics/archive/2014/08 /americans-deep-racial-divide-on-trusting-the-police/378848/, accessed December 11, 2017.

102. Sentencing Project, "Felony Disfranchisement," www.sentenc ingproject.org/issues/felony-disenfranchisement/, accessed December 11, 2017.

103. Anderson, *White Rage*, 123–36.

104. Duke Medicine and News Communication, "White and Hispanic Teens More Likely to Abuse Drugs Than African Americans," November 7, 2011, corporate.dukemedicine.org/news_and_pub lications/news_office/news/white-and-hispanic-teens-more-likely -to-abuse-drugs-than-african-americans, accessed November 17, 2015; Maia Szalavitz, "Study: Whites More Likely to Abuse Drugs Than Blacks," *Time*, November 7, 2011, healthland.time .com/2011/11/07/study-whites-more-likely-to-abuse-drugs-than -blacks, accessed August 17, 2015; NAACP, "Criminal Justice Fact Sheet," www.naacp.org/criminal-justice-fact-sheet/, accessed December 11, 2017.

105. Sentencing Project et al., "Democracy Imprisoned: A Review of the Prevalence and Impact of Felony Disenfranchisement Laws in the United States," www.sentencingproject.org/publications /democracy-imprisoned-a-review-of-the-prevalence-and-impact -of-felony-disenfranchisement-laws-in-the-united-states/, accessed December 11, 2017.

106. U.S. Census Bureau, "Quick Facts: Vermont, Maine," www .census.gov/quickfacts/fact/table/VT,ME/PST045216, accessed September 11, 2017.

107. Sentencing Project et al., "Democracy Imprisoned."

108. Florida Center for Investigative Reporting, "How This Floridian Lost His Voting Rights," *ThinkProgress*, November 1, 2016, thinkprogress.org/how-this-floridian-lost-his-voting-rights -a7c69b23776a, accessed May 23, 2017.

109. Conor Friedersdorf, "Will Florida Banish the Ghost of Jim Crow? The State Still Disenfranchises More of Its Eligible Voters Than Any Other—But This Year, It Has the Chance to Change That," *Atlantic*, October 3, 2017, www.theatlantic.com/politics/archive /2017/10/florida-felon-disenfranchisement/541680/, accessed December 11, 2017.

110. Douglas A. Blackmon, *Slavery by Another Name: The Re-Enslavement of Black Americans from the Civil War to World War II* (New York: Anchor Books, 2008, 2009), 7, 112.

111. ACLU, "Felony Disfranchisement Map," www.aclu.org/issues /voting-rights/voter-restoration/felony-disenfranchisement-laws -map, accessed December 11, 2017.

112. "Restoring Ex-felon Voting Rights Could Overhaul the US Political Map, Advocates Say," *Mic*, July 8, 2017, m.mic.com/articles/amp /181632/restoring-ex-felon-voting-rights-could-overhaul-the-us -political-map-advocates-say, accessed July 16, 2017.

113. Florida Center for Investigative Reporting, "How This Floridian Lost His Voting Rights."

114. Vanita Gupta, "The Voter Purges Are Coming," *New York Times*, July 19, 2017, www.nytimes.com/2017/07/19/opinion/donald -trump-voting-rights-purge.html, accessed July 19, 2017. Six states (Idaho, Minnesota, New Hampshire, North Dakota, Wisconsin, and Wyoming) are exempt from the NVRA because, on and after August 1, 1994, they either had no voter-registration requirements or had election-day voter registration at polling places with respect to elections for federal office: www.justice.gov/crt/national-voter -registration-act-1993-nvra.

115. Curt Devine, Drew Griffin, and Scott Bronstein, "The Man Who Helped Purge Thousands from Voter Rolls in North Carolina," CNN, November 5, 2016, www.cnn.com/2016/11/05/politics /north-carolina-voter-rolls/index.html, accessed May 16, 2017.

116. Mark Joseph Stern, "The Purges Are Coming: Jeff Sessions' Justice Department Just Took a Major Stand Against Voting Rights. It's Now Up to the Supreme Court to Protect the Rolls," *Slate*, August 8, 2017, www.slate.com/articles/news_and_politics/juris prudence/2017/08/jeff_sessions_doj_just_gave_states_the _green_light_to_purge_voter_rolls.html, accessed August 10, 2017.

Chapter Four: Rigging the Rules

1. Amicus Curiae Brief of Senators John McCain and Sheldon Whitehouse in Support of Appellees, *Gill v. Whitford*, U.S. Supreme Court, No. 16-1161 (2017); Alexis Farmer, "Redistricting Reform Puts Residents in Charge," Brennan Center for Justice,

December 28, 2017, www.brennancenter.org/blog/redistricting
-reform-puts-residents-charge, accessed December 29, 2017; David
Daley, *Rat F***ed: The True Story Behind the Secret Plan to
Steal America's Democracy* (New York: Liveright Publishing,
2016); Colin Allred, "How the Texas GOP 'Packed and Cracked'
Districts to Dilute Minorities' Voting Rights," *Dallas News*,
July 21, 2017, www.dallasnews.com/opinion/commentary/2017/07
/21/texas-gop-packed-cracked-districts-dilute-minorities-voting
-rights, accessed July 21, 2017.

2. Elizabeth Kolbert, "Drawing the Line: How Redistricting Turned
America from Blue to Red," *New Yorker*, June 27, 2016, www
.newyorker.com/magazine/2016/06/27/ratfcked-the-influence-of
-redistricting?mbid=social_twitter, accessed June 4, 2017.

3. *Baker v. Carr*, 369 U.S. 186 (1962).

4. Andrew Chung, "Fight over Electoral District Boundaries Heads
to Supreme Court," Reuters, September 17, 2017, www.reuters.com
/article/us-usa-court-election/fight-over-electoral-district-bound
aries-heads-to-supremecourtidUSKCN1BS0FR?il=0, accessed
September 21, 2017.

5. "Declining Trust in Government Is Denting Democracy: According
to a New Index, America's Democracy Score Deteriorated in
2016," *Economist*, January 25, 2017, www.economist.com/blogs
/graphicdetail/2017/01/daily-chart-20, accessed January 4, 2018;
Gretel Kauffman, "US No Longer a 'Full Democracy' in 2016
Democracy Index: Where Do We Go from Here?," *Christian Science
Monitor*, January 26, 2017, www.csmonitor.com/USA/2017/0126
/US-no-longer-a-full-democracy-in-2016-Democracy-Index-Where
-do-we-go-from-here, accessed January 4, 2018.

6. Andrew Reynolds, "North Carolina Is No Longer Classified as
a Democracy," *News and Observer*, December 22, 2016, amp
.newsobserver.com/opinion/op-ed/article122593759.html,
accessed December 31, 2017.

7. Robert Draper, "The League of Dangerous Mapmakers," *Atlantic*,
October 2012, www.theatlantic.com/magazine/archive/2012/10
/the-league-of/309084/, accessed July 26, 2017.

8. Cliff Sloan and Michael Waldman, "History Frowns on Partisan Gerrymandering," *Washington Post*, October 1, 2017, www.wash ingtonpost.com/opinions/history-frowns-on-partisan-gerrymander ing/2017/10/01/a6795fca-a491-11e7-ade1-76d061d56efa_story .html, accessed October 6, 2017.

9. Sloan and Waldman, "History Frowns on Partisan Gerrymandering."

10. *Shaw v. Reno*, 509 U.S. 630 (1993).

11. Draper, "The League of Dangerous Mapmakers."

12. William E. Schmidt, "Ending an Era, Wallace Announces He Will Retire," *New York Times*, April 3, 1986, www.nytimes.com/1986 /04/03/us/ending-an-era-wallace-announces-he-will-retire.html, accessed December 29, 2017.

13. Kristin Henze, "Mississippi Mau Mau: Medgar Evers and the Black Freedom Struggle, 1952–1963" (Ph.D. diss., University of Missouri, 2017), 209–10; Jack Bass, "Murder in Mississippi," review of *Blood Justice: The Lynching of Mack Charles Parker* by Howard Smead, *Washington Post*, November 30, 1986, www.washingtonpost.com /archive/entertainment/books/1986/11/30/murder-in-mississippi /f93bbb7a-b2e8-4e14-a85b-deb6bc1c41c3/, accessed January 4, 2018; "Ross Barnett, Segregationist, Dies; Governor of Mississippi in 1960's," *New York Times*, November 7, 1987, www.nytimes.com /1987/11/07/obituaries/ross-barnett-segregationist-dies-governor -of-mississippi-in-1960-s.html, accessed January 4, 2018.

14. Minion K. C. Morrison, *Aaron Henry of Mississippi: Inside Agitator* (Fayetteville: University of Arkansas, 2015), 65; Frank E. Smith, *Congressman from Mississippi* (New York: Pantheon Books, 1964); Dennis J. Mitchell, *Mississippi Liberal: A Biography of Frank E. Smith* (Oxford: University Press of Mississippi, 2001); David Binder, "Jamie Whitten, Who Served 53 Years in House, Dies at 85," *New York Times*, September 10, 1995, www.nytimes .com/1995/09/10/obituaries/jamie-whitten-who-served-53-years -in-house-dies-at-85.html, accessed January 4, 2018.

15. C-Span, "Landmark Cases: *Baker v. Carr*," landmarkcases.c-span .org/Case/10/Baker-V-Carr, accessed January 1, 2018.

16. *Baker v. Carr*, supreme.justia.com/cases/federal/us/369/186/case
.html, accessed January 1, 2018.

17. *Baker v. Carr*; *Wesberry v. Sanders*, 376 U.S. 1 (1964); *Reynolds v. Sims*, 377 U.S. 533 (1964).

18. *Jacobellis v. Ohio*, 378 U.S. 184 (1964).

19. *Davis v. Bandemer*, 478 U.S. 109 (1986).

20. Sarah Koenig, "Congressional Districts Fought in Federal Suit," *Baltimore Sun*, June 19, 2002; Charles S. Bullock III, *Redistricting: The Most Political Activity in America* (Lanham, MD: Rowman Littlefield, 2010), 1–2.

21. Brief of Amici Curiae the American Civil Liberties Union and the Brennan Center for Justice at NYU School of Law in Support of Appellants, *Vieth v. Jubelirer*, 541 U.S. 267 (2004), www.bren nancenter.org/sites/default/files/legal-work/veith.pdf, accessed January 3, 2018; Draper, "The League of Dangerous Mapmakers"; Nicholas R. Seabrook, *Drawing the Lines: Constraints on Partisan Gerrymandering in U.S. Politics* (Ithaca, NY: Cornell University Press, 2017), 1–2.

22. *Vieth v. Jubelirer*, 541 U.S. 267 (2004), supreme.justia.com/cases /federal/us/541/267/opinion.html, accessed January 4, 2018.

23. Anthony J. McGann, Charles Anthony Smith, Michael Latner, and Alex Keena, *Gerrymandering in America: The House of Representatives, the Supreme Court, and the Future of Popular Sovereignty* (New York: Cambridge University Press, 2016), 45.

24. Brief of Amici Curiae the American Civil Liberties Union and the Brennan Center for Justice at NYU School of Law in Support of Appellants, *Vieth v. Jubelirer*, 541 U.S. 267 (2004).

25. Note that the court did not have those qualms about supposedly political issues when it stepped in and stopped the recount of votes in Florida in the 2000 election in *Bush v. Gore*.

26. *Vieth v. Jubelirer*, 541 U.S. 267 (2004).

27. Douglas S. Massey and Nancy A. Denton, *American Apartheid: Segregation and the Making of the Underclass* (Cambridge, MA: Harvard University Press, 1993); Richard Rothstein, *The Color of*

Law: A Forgotten History of How Our Government Segregated America (New York: Liveright Publishing, 2017); Lisa McGirr, *Suburban Warriors: The Origins of the New American Right* (Princeton, NJ: Princeton University Press, 2015); Kevin M. Kruse, *White Flight: Atlanta and the Making of Modern Conservatism* (Princeton, NJ: Princeton University Press, 2005); Nancy Isenberg, *White Trash: The 400-Year Untold History of Class in America* (New York: Penguin, 2016); Nancy MacLean, *Democracy in Chains: The Deep History of the Radical Right's Stealth Plan for America* (New York: Viking, 2017); Thomas E. Mann and Norman A. Ornstein, *It's Even Worse Than It Looks: How the American Constitutional System Collided with the New Politics of Extremism* (New York: Basic Books, 2012); E. J. Dionne Jr., *Why the Right Went Wrong: Conservatism—from Goldwater to the Tea Party and Beyond* (New York: Simon & Schuster, 2016); Jane Mayer, *Dark Money: The Hidden History of the Billionaires Behind the Rise of the Radical Right* (New York: Anchor Books, 2016, 2017); Daley, *Ratf**ked.*

28. McGann et al., *Gerrymandering in America*, 7.
29. Dan Balz, "The GOP Takeover in the States," *Washington Post*, November 13, 2010, www.washingtonpost.com/wp-dyn/content/article/2010/11/13/AR2010111302389.html, accessed January 6, 2018; Daley, *Ratf**ked*; Ari Berman, "The GOP Has Declared War on Democracy: Going Nuclear to Confirm Neil Gorsuch Is the Latest Example of How Republicans Are Thwarting the Will of the People," *The Nation*, April 6, 2017, www.thenation.com/article/the-gop-has-declared-war-on-democracy/, accessed April 6, 2017.
30. Kevin Drum, "Computers Have Revolutionized Gerrymandering. The Supreme Court Should Take Notice," *Mother Jones*, February 26, 2017, motherjones.com/kevin-drum/2017/02/computers-have-revolutionized-gerrymandering-supreme-court-should-take-notice, accessed February 26, 2017.
31. "Electoral Competitiveness in Michigan," Ballotpedia, April 2015, ballotpedia.org/Electoral_competitiveness_in_Michigan, accessed December 29, 2017.

32. Sam Wang and Brian Remlinger, "Can Math Stop Partisan Gerry-mandering?" *Los Angeles Times*, May 5, 2017, www.latimes.com /opinion/op-ed/la-oe-wang-remlinger-gerrymandering-20170505 -story.html, accessed May 21, 2017.

33. McGann et al., *Gerrymandering in America*, 4.

34. Amicus Curiae Brief of Senators John McCain and Sheldon Whitehouse in Support of Appellees, *Gill v. Whitford*, U.S. Supreme Court, No. 16-1161 (2017).

35. Max Greenwood, "Poll Finds Little Support for Deporting DACA Recipients," *The Hill*, October 10, 2017, thehill.com/blogs/blog -briefing-room/news/354702-poll-finds-little-support-for-deport ing-daca-recipients, accessed January 7, 2018; verrit.com/poll -americans-overwhelmingly-support-the-daca-program/, accessed January 7, 2018; David Wright and Tami Luhby, "Polls: Support for Obamacare at All-time High," CNN, February 24, 2017, www .cnn.com/2017/02/24/politics/pew-survey-obamacare-support -record-high/index.html, accessed January 7, 2018; Richard Gonzales, "Only 26 Percent of Americans Support Full Repeal of Obamacare, Poll Finds," NPR, December 2, 2016, www.npr.org /sections/thetwo-way/2016/12/02/504068263/kaiser-poll-only-26 -of-americans-support-full-repeal-of-obamacare, accessed January 7, 2018; Kaiser Tracking Poll Shows CHIP Funding Is Much Higher Priority Than Tax Reform, ccf.georgetown.edu/2017/11/15/kaiser -tracking-poll-shows-chip-funding-is-higher-priority-than-tax-re form/, accessed January 7, 2018.

36. Michael R. Bloomberg, "This Tax Bill Is a Trillion-Dollar Blunder: Congress and President Trump Put Politics Ahead of Smart Reform," *Bloomberg*, December 15, 2017, www.bloomberg.com /view/articles/2017-12-15/this-tax-bill-is-a-trillion-dollar-blunder, accessed January 6, 2018.

37. Bob Bryan, "Republicans Just Received 2 Alarming Reviews of Their Tax Plan," *Business Insider*, December 5, 2017, www.busi nessinsider.com/trump-tax-reform-bill-polls-gallup-quinnipiac -text-gop-2017-12, accessed January 5, 2018.

38. Jonathan Easley, "Poll: Majority Oppose GOP Tax Bill," *The Hill*, December 13, 2017, thehill.com/homenews/administration/364781 -poll-majority-oppose-gop-tax-bill, accessed January 6, 2018; Jennifer Agiesta, "Public Opposition to Tax Bill Grows as Vote Approaches," CNN, December 19, 2017, www.cnn.com/2017/12/19/politics/cnn -poll-tax-bill-opposition-grows/index.html, accessed January 6, 2018; Harry Enten, "The GOP Tax Cuts Are Even More Unpopular Than Past Tax Hikes," *FiveThirtyEight*, November 29, 2017, fivethirtyeight.com/features/the-gop-tax-cuts-are-even-more -unpopular-than-past-tax-hikes/, accessed January 6, 2018.

39. Jack Crowe, "Graham Says GOP Donors Will Jump Ship If Tax Reform Fails," *Daily Caller*, November 9, 2017, dailycaller.com /2017/11/09/graham-says-gop-donors-will-jump-ship-if-tax -reform-fails/, accessed January 6, 2018.

40. Draper, "The League of Dangerous Mapmakers."

41. Michael Li and Thomas Wolf, "5 Things to Know About the Wisconsin Partisan Gerrymandering Case," Brennan Center for Justice, June 9, 2017, www.brennancenter.org/blog/5-things-know-about -wisconsin-partisan-gerrymandering-case, accessed June 17, 2017.

42. Berman, "The GOP Has Declared War on Democracy."

43. Laura Royden and Michael Li, "Extreme Maps," Brennan Center for Justice, www.brennancenter.org/sites/default/files/publications /Extreme%20Maps%205.16.pdf, accessed June 10, 2017; Sam Wang, "Gerrymanders, Part 1: Busting the Both-Sides-Do-It Myth," *Princeton Election Consortium*, September 4, 2017, election .princeton.edu/2012/12/30/gerrymanders-part-1-busting-the-both -sides-do-it-myth/, accessed January 6, 2018; Ari Berman, "North Carolina Is Once Again Found Guilty of Discriminating Against Black Voters," *The Nation*, May 22, 2017, www.thenation.com/article /north-carolina-found-guilty-discriminating-black-voters/, accessed May 22, 2017; Alice Miranda Ollstein, "Alabama Found Guilty of Racial Gerrymandering," *ThinkProgress*, January 20, 2017, think progress.org/alabama-found-guilty-of-racial-gerrymandering -e42f48e19c40, accessed May 4, 2017; Laurel Wamsley, "Federal Court Rules Three Texas Congressional Districts Illegally Drawn,"

NPR, March 11, 2017, www.npr.org/sections/thetwo-way/2017/03
/11/519839892/federal-court-rules-three-texas-congressional-dis
tricts-illegally-drawn, accessed May 4, 2017; Lyle Denniston, "Court
Gives New Guidance on Racial Gerrymandering," *Constitution
Daily* (blog), March 1, 2017, constitutionalcenter.org/blog/court
-gives-new-guidance-on-racial-gerrymandering, accessed May 4,
2017; Elliot Hannon, "Federal Court Rules Texas Republicans
Racially Gerrymandered Districts to Weaken Minority Vote," *Slate*,
March 11, 2017, www.slate.com/blogs/the_slatest/2017/03/11/fed
eral_court_rules_texas_gop_racially_gerrymandered_districts
.html, accessed May 21, 2017; Amber Phillips, "Republican
Redistricting Is Taking a Beating in the Courts (Again)," *Washington
Post*, May 22, 2017, www.washingtonpost.com/news/the-fix/wp
/2017/05/22/republican-redistricting-is-taking-a-beating-in-the
-courts-again/, accessed May 22, 2017.

44. Olga Pierce and Kate Rabinowitz, "'Partisan' Gerrymandering Is
Still About Race," *ProPublica*, October 9, 2017, www.propublica
.org/article/partisan-gerrymandering-is-still-about-race, accessed
October 9, 2017.

45. "The Parties on the Eve of the 2016 Election: Two Coalitions,
Moving Further Apart: The Changing Composition of the Political
Parties," Pew Research Center, September 13, 2016, www.people
-press.org/2016/09/13/1-the-changing-composition-of-the
-political-parties/, accessed January 5, 2018.

46. Mark Joseph Stern, "Georgia Republicans Pass Racial Gerrymander
to Kick Black Voters Out of GOP Districts," *Slate*, March 7, 2017,
www.slate.com/blogs/the_slatest/217/03/07/georgia_republi-
cans_pass_racial_gerrymander.html, accessed May 21, 2017; Aaron
Gould Sheinin, "Democrats Cry Foul as House Republicans Redraw
District Lines," *Atlanta Journal-Constitution*, March 3, 2017, www
.myajc.com/news/state--regional-govt--politics/democrats-cry-foul
-house-republicans-redraw-district-lines/sOOXVi3vMCWJCB7
gpAntTN/, accessed May 4, 2017.

47. Draper, "The League of Dangerous Mapmakers"; Ari Berman,
"Texas's Redistricting Maps and Voter-ID Law Intentionally

Discriminated Against Minority Voters," *The Nation*, March 13, 2017, www.thenation.com/article/texass-redistricting-maps-and-voter-id-law-intentionally-discriminated-against-minority-voters/, accessed May 21, 2017.

48. Berman, "Texas's Redistricting Maps and Voter-ID Law Intentionally Discriminated Against Minority Voters."

49. "Voter Suppression: How the Texas GOP 'Packed and Cracked' Districts to Dilute Minorities' Voting Rights," *Dallas Morning News*, July 21, 2017, www.dallasnews.com/opinion/commentary/2017/07/21/texas-gop-packed-cracked-districts-dilute-minorities-voting-rights, accessed July 21, 2017.

50. Pema Levy, "The National Battle Over Voting Rights Comes Down to Texas: Donald Trump's Justice Department Has Defended the State. Shocker," *Mother Jones*, September 25, 2017, www.motherjones.com/politics/2017/09/the-national-battle-over-voting-rights-comes-down-to-texas/, accessed September 25, 2017; Jim Malewitz and Alexa Ura, "As Court Scoldings Pile Up, Will Texas Face a Voting Rights Reckoning?" *Texas Tribune*, June 16, 2017, www.texastribune.org/2017/06/16/voter-wars-kickoff/, accessed June 16, 2017; Ross Ramsey and Jim Malewitz, "Federal Panel Rules Some of Texas' Congressional Districts Illegal," *Texas Tribune*, March 10, 2017, www.texastribune.org/2017/03/10/federal-panel-rules-texas-congressional-districts-illegal/, accessed May 21, 2017.

51. Dan Schneider, "The Worst Place in America to be Black Is . . . Wisconsin," *Dollars and Sense*, November–December 2015, www.dollarsandsense.org/archives/2015/1115schneider.html, accessed January 7, 2018; Emily Esfahani Smith, "Milwaukee Wisc. Is Most Segregated U.S. City, and Other Quirky Census Facts," *The Blaze*, March 30, 2011, www.theblaze.com/news/2011/03/30/milwaukee-wisc-is-most-segregated-u-s-city-and-other-quirky-census-facts, accessed January 7, 2018.

52. John Nichols, "Democracy Wins One as a Federal Court Strikes a Big Blow Against Gerrymandering," *The Nation*, January 27, 2017, www.thenation.com/article/democracy-wins-one-as-a-federal-court

-strikes-a-big-blow-against-gerrymandering/, accessed May 21, 2017; Michael Wines, "Key Question for Supreme Court: Will It Let Gerrymanders Stand?," *New York Times*, April 21, 2017, www.ny times.com/2017/04/21/us/democrats-gerrymander-supreme-court .html, accessed May 19, 2017; Eric H. Holder Jr., "Gerrymandering Has Broken Our Democracy. The Supreme Court Should Help Fix It," *Washington Post*, October 3, 2017, www.washingtonpost.com /news/posteverything/wp/2017/10/03/eric-holder-redistricting -has-broken-our-democracy-the-supreme-court-should-help-fix-it/, accessed October 3, 2017.

53. Thomas Wolf, "Bringing Whitford into Focus," Brennan Center for Justice, August 8, 2017, www.brennancenter.org/blog/bringing -whitford-focus, accessed August 9, 2017.

54. Wendy R. Weiser and Thomas P. Wolf, "The High Court Must Strike Down Extreme Partisan Gerrymandering," *New York Daily News*, October 4, 2017, www.nydailynews.com/opinion/high-court-strike -extreme-partisan-gerrymandering-article-1.3540650, accessed October 6, 2017.

55. Sloan and Waldman, "History Frowns on Partisan Gerrymandering."

56. David Daley, "Meet the Man Who May End Gerrymandering: A Retired Wisconsin Law Professor's Supreme Court Case Could Save Democracy," *Salon*, March 26, 2017, www.salon.com/2017/03/26 /meet-the-man-who-may-end-gerrymandering-a-retired-wisconsin -law-professors-supreme-court-case-could-save-democracy/, accessed May 20, 2017; *A.M. Joy* on MSNBC, "Supreme Court Gerrymandering Case: Wisconsin and Beyond," transcript, October 8, 2017, www.msnbc.com/am-joy/watch/supreme-court -gerrymandering-case-wisconsin-and-beyond-1065622595526, accessed October 8, 2017.

57. "Politicians Choosing Voters: The Supreme Court Ponders Whether Gerrymandering Has Gone Too Far," *Economist*, October 7, 2017, www.economist.com/news/united-states/21730008-justice-anthony -kennedys-line-questioning-suggests-court-may-decide-it-has, accessed October 6, 2017.

58. Daley, "Meet the Man Who May End Gerrymandering."

59. Andrew Chung, "US Supreme Court to Hear Wisconsin Electoral Redistricting Case," *Christian Science Monitor*, June 19, 2017, www.csmonitor.com/USA/Politics/2017/0619/US-Supreme -Court-to-hear-Wisconsin-electoral-redistricting-case, accessed June 20, 2017.

60. *League of United Latin American Citizens v. Perry*, 548 U.S. 399 (2006).

61. Nicholas Stephanopoulos, "Here's How We Can End Gerrymandering Once and for All," *New Republic*, July 2, 2014, newre public.com/article/118534/gerrymandering-efficiency-gap-better -way-measure-gerrymandering, accessed January 8, 2018.

62. Ian Millhiser, "The Most Exciting Attack on Partisan Gerrymandering in Over a Decade," *ThinkProgress*, April 28, 2016, think progress.org/the-most-exciting-attack-on-partisan-gerry mandering-in-over-a-decade-68ae8b6b2e5e/, accessed June 19, 2017; Wines, "Key Question for Supreme Court: Will It Let Gerrymanders Stand?"

63. "Politicians Choosing Voters: The Supreme Court Ponders Whether Gerrymandering Has Gone Too Far," *Economist*.

64. Nate Cohn and Quoctrung Bui, "How the New Math of Gerrymandering Works," *New York Times*, October 3, 2017, www .nytimes.com/interactive/2017/10/03/upshot/how-the-new -math-of-gerrymandering-works-supreme-court.html, accessed October 7, 2017.

65. Stephen Wolf, "Supreme Court Will Hear Wisconsin Partisan Gerrymandering Case That Could Set a Landmark," *Daily Kos*, June 19, 2017, www.dailykos.com/stories/2017/6/19/1673059/ -Supreme-Court-will-hear-Wisconsin-partisan-gerrymandering -case-that-could-set-a-landmark-precedent, accessed June 19, 2017; Wolf, "Bringing Whitford into Focus"; Linda Greenhouse, "The Supreme Court: Reapportionment; Court Questions Districts Drawn to Aid Minorities," *New York Times*, June 29, 1993, www .nytimes.com/1993/06/29/us/supreme-court-reapportionment -court-questions-districts-drawn-aid-minorities.html, accessed January 1, 2018; Max Boot, "Supreme Court Rules That 'Bizarre'

Districts May Be Gerrymanders," *Christian Science Monitor*, June 30, 1993; *Shaw v. Reno* (1993), 509 U.S. 630.

66. Oral Arguments, *Gill v. Whitford*, No. 16-1161, October 3, 2017, www.supremecourt.gov/oral_arguments/argument_transcripts /2017/16-1611_bpm1.pdf, accessed October 7, 2017, pp. 22–23, 50.

67. Oral Arguments, *Gill v. Whitford*, No. 16-1161, October 3, 2017, 24–25, 60–61.

68. Oral Arguments, *Gill v. Whitford*, No. 16-1161, October 3, 2017, 35–41, 48–49.

69. Oral Arguments, *Gill v. Whitford*, No. 16-1161, October 3, 2017, 11–13.

70. Oral Arguments, *Gill v. Whitford*, No. 16-1161, October 3, 2017, 13–14, 19–20, 27.

71. Oral Arguments, *Gill v. Whitford*, No. 16-1161, October 3, 2017, 14–15.

72. Oral Arguments, *Gill v. Whitford*, No. 16-1161, October 3, 2017, 15–16.

73. Oral Arguments, *Gill v. Whitford*, No. 16-1161, October 3, 2017, 17.

74. Oral Arguments, *Gill v. Whitford*, No. 16-1161, October 3, 2017, 17

75. Oral Arguments, *Gill v. Whitford*, No. 16-1161, October 3, 2017, 28–29.

76. Daley, *Ratf**ked*, xvii.

77. Brennan Center for Justice, "New Report: Extreme Partisan Maps Account for 16–17 Republican Seats in Congress," press release, May 16, 2017, www.brennancenter.org/press-release/new-report -extreme-partisan-maps-account-16-17-republicanseats-congress, accessed May 23, 2017.

78. M. V. Hood and Seth C. McKee, "Trying to Thread the Needle: The Effects of a Redistricting in a Georgia Congressional District," *PS: Political Science and Politics* 42, no. 4 (October 2009), 683.

79. William H. Frey, "Census Shows Pervasive Decline in 2016 Minority Voter Turnout," *Brookings*, May 18, 2017 www.brookings.edu/blog /the-avenue/2017/05/18/census-shows-pervasive-decline-in-2016 -minority-voter-turnout/, accessed January 8, 2017.

80. Sarah McCammon, "Redistricting Reform Advocates Say the Real 'Rigged System' Is Gerrymandering," NPR, March 18, 2017, www

.npr.org/2017/03/18/520551499/redistricting-reform-advocates
-say-the-real-rigged-system-is-gerrymandering.

81. "Arnie Lends Some Muscle to the Campaign Against Gerry-mandering," *Economist*, July 22, 2017, www.economist.com/news
/united-states/21725305-he-compares-politicians-gerrymandered
-districts-overweight-people-who-should-go, accessed July 23, 2017.

82. Dionne, *Why the Right Went Wrong*, 3, 219, 289, 403–4.

83. A. J. Vicens, "The Election in Arizona Was a Mess," *Mother Jones*,
March 24, 2016, www.motherjones.com/politics/2016/03/arizona
-primary-long-lines-voting-restrictions/, accessed June 4, 2017;
Steve Benen, "Controversy Surrounds Long Voting Lines in
Arizona," MSNBC, March 24, 2016, www.msnbc.com/rachel
-maddow-show/controversy-surrounds-long-voting-lines-arizona,
accessed June 4, 2017; Yvonne Wingett Sanchez and Caitlin
McGlade, "Maricopa County Recorder Helen Purcell Takes Blame
for Voter Lines, Says She Won't Resign," azcentral.com, March 23
2016, www.azcentral.com/story/news/politics/electins/2016/03
/23/maricopa-county-recorder-helen-purcell-admits-fault-long-pri
mary-lines/82165730/, accessed June 12, 2017.

84. Randy A. Simes, "Ohio Early Voting Rules Work Against Voters from
Heavily Populated Counties," *UrbanCincy*, November 5, 2012, www
.urbancincy.com/2012/11/ohio-early-voting-rules-work-against-voters
-from-heavily-populated-counties/, accessed December 30, 2017.

85. Christopher Famighetti, Amanda Melillo, and Myrna Pérez,
"Election Day Long Lines: Resource Allocation," Brennan Center
for Justice, www.brennancenter.org/sites/default/files/publications
/ElectionDayLongLines-ResourceAllocation.pdf, accessed June 4,
2017.

86. Charles Stewart III and Stephen Anslabehere, "Waiting to Vote,"
Election Law Journal 14, no. 1 (2015): 47–53; Justin Leavitt,
"'Fixing That': Lines at the Polling Place," *Journal of Law and
Politics* 28, no. 465 (2013): 465–94.

87. Alan S. Gerber, Donald P. Green, and Ron Shachar, "Voting May Be
Habit-Forming: Evidence from a Randomized Field Experiment,"

American Journal of Political Science 47, no. 3 (July 2003): 540–50.

88. Leavitt, " 'Fixing That,' " 465–68; Karen Garloch, Katherine Peralta, and Celeste Smith, "8 Durham County Precincts Got Extended Voting—but Not as Much as the County Wanted," *Charlotte Observer*, November 8, 2016, www.charlotteobserver.com/news/local /article113248708.html, accessed June 4, 2017.

89. Jaeah Lee, "Charts: How Minority Voters Get Blocked at the Ballot Box. It's Not Just Voter ID Laws and Other Restrictions That Stymie Black and Latino Voters," *Mother Jones*, November 3, 2014, www .motherjones.com/politics/2014/11/charts-black-latino-voters -machines-poll-workers/#, accessed December 24, 2017; GAO, "Elections: Observations on Wait Times for Voters on Election Day 2012," September 2014.

90. Famighetti, Melillo, and Pérez, "Election Day Long Lines: Resource Allocation."

91. Victoria McGrane, "Are Voting Rights Being Cut Down?," *Boston Globe*, October 30, 2016, www.bostonglobe.com/news/nation /2016/10/30/continues-struggle-with-universal-voter-access /FylbwdnxoWzFa2Bkil7cKN/story.html, accessed June 4, 2017; Stephanie Mencimer, "Even Without Voter ID Laws, Minority Voters Face More Hurdles to Casting Ballots," *Mother Jones*, November 3, 2014, www.motherjones.com/politics/2014/11/minority-voters -election-long-lines-id/, accessed June 14, 2017; Fatima Hussein, "Republicans Limiting Early Voting in Marion County, Letting It Bloom in Suburbs," *Indianapolis Star*, August 10, 2017, www.indystar .com/story/news/2017/08/10/silencing-vote-data-shows-unequal -barrier-indiana-polls/435450001/, accessed August 10, 2017; Michael C. Herron and Daniel A. Smith, "Race, Party, and the Consequences of Restricting Early Voting in Florida in the 2012 General Election," *Political Research Quarterly* 67, no. 3 (2014): 646–65.

92. Michael Alvarez, Ines Levin, and J. Andrew Sinclair, "Making Voting Easier: Convenience Voting in the 2008 Presidential Election," *Political Research Quarterly* 65, no. 2 (June 2012), 253.

93. Herron and Smith, "Race, Party and the Consequence of Restricting Early Voting in Florida in the 2012 General Election," 649–50.

94. Charlotte Alter, "Detroit Voting Machine Failures Were Widespread on Election Day," *Time*, December 14, 2016, time.com/4599886 /detroit-voting-machine-failures-were-widespread-on-election -day/, accessed January 8, 2018.

95. "Suburban Stats: Current Pickaway County, Ohio Population, Demographics and Stats in 2016, 2017," suburbanstats.org/pop ulation/ohio/how-many-people-live-in-pickaway-county, accessed January 8, 2018.

96. "Suburban Stats: Current Hamilton County, Ohio Population, Demographics and Stats in 2016, 2017," suburbanstats.org /population/ohio/how-many-people-live-in-hamilton-county, accessed January 8, 2018.

97. "Suburban Stats: Current Pickaway County, Ohio Population, Demographics and Stats in 2016, 2017"; "Suburban Stats: Current Franklin County, Ohio Population, Demographics and Stats in 2016, 2017," suburbanstats.org/population/ohio/how-many-people -live-in-franklin-county, accessed January 8, 2018.

98. Ohio Department of Development, "Ohio: African Americans," www.development.ohio.gov/files/research/P7003.pdf, accessed January 8, 2018.

99. Mencimer, "Even Without Voter ID Laws, Minority Voters Face More Hurdles to Casting Ballots."

100. German Lopez, "Southern States Have Closed Down at Least 868 Polling Places for the 2016 Election," *Vox*, November 4, 2016, www.vox.com/policy-and-politics/2016/11/4/13501120/vote -polling-places-election-2016, accessed June 2, 2017.

101. Moshe Haspel and H. Gibbs Knotts, "Location, Location, Location: Precinct Placement and the Costs of Voting," *Journal of Politics* 67, no. 2 (May 2005), 560–61, 565.

102. Zachary Roth, "Study: North Carolina Polling Site Changes Hurt Blacks," MSNBC, November 13, 2015, www.msnbc.com/msnbc /study-north-carolina-polling-site-changes-hurt-blacks, accessed June 2, 2017.

103. "Georgia: Make Elections Fair and Accessible by Keeping Polling Places Open," *Let America Vote*, policy.letamericavote.org/let -america-vote-case-study-polling-place-closures-848db5dafcae, accessed December 4, 2017; Kristina Torres, "Cost-Cutting Moves Spur Fears About Reducing Access to Georgia Voters," *Atlanta Journal-Constitution*, October 11, 2016, politics.myajc.com/news /state--regional-govt--politics/cost-cutting-moves-spur-fears -about-reducing-access-georgia-voters/qu9llnbKd6dSl6yblbB68M /, accessed December 16, 2017.

104. Ari Berman, "Texas's Voter-Registration Laws Are Straight out of the Jim Crow Playbook," *The Nation*, October 6, 2016, www.the nation.com/article/texass-voter-registration-laws-are-straight-out -of-the-jim-crow-playbook/, accessed December 27, 2017; Michael C. Herron and Daniel A. Smith, "The Effects of House Bill 1355 on Voter Registration in Florida," *State Politics and Policy Quarterly* 13, no. 3 (September 2013): 279–305.

105. Alexa Ura, "Texas Voting Law on Language Interpreters Violates Voting Rights Act, Court Says," *Texas Tribune*, August 17, 2017, www.texastribune.org/2017/08/17/texas-voting-law-language -interpreters-ruled-unconstitutional/amp/, accessed August 18, 2017; Joel Anderson, "A Georgia Grandmother Faced Charges After She Helped a Black Voter," *BuzzFeed*, April 4, 2017, www .buzzfeed.com/joelanderson/this-is-what-happened-when-a -georgia-grandmother-went-on, accessed May 20, 2017.

106. Torres, "Cost-Cutting Moves Spur Fears About Reducing Access to Georgia Voters."

Chapter Five: The Resistance

1. Matt Staggs, "Memoir in a Melody: The Outrage in Nina Simone's 'Mississippi Goddam,'" *Signature*, September 27, 2013, www .signature-reads.com/2013/09/memoir-in-a-melody-the-outrage -in-nina-simones-mississippi-goddam/, accessed January 26, 2018.

2. Karlyn Forner, *Why the Vote Wasn't Enough for Selma* (Durham, NC: Duke University Press, 2017), loc. 4356, chapter 7, Kindle.

3. "Best States: About Alabama," *U.S. News and World Report*, www
   .usnews.com/news/best-states/alabama, accessed January 24, 2018.

4. Connor Sheets, "UN Poverty Official Touring Alabama's Black
   Belt: 'I Haven't Seen This' in the First World," AL.com, December 8,
   2017, www.al.com/news/index.ssf/2017/12/un_poverty_official_
   touring_al.html, accessed January 23, 2018.

5. Amy Yurkanin, "Rate of Infant Death in Alabama Increased in
   2016," AL.com, November 16, 2017, www.al.com/news/index.ssf
   /2017/11/rate_of_infant_death_in_alabam.html, accessed January
   23, 2018.

6. "Best States: Alabama," *US News and World Report*.

7. Charles Bethea, "Why Roy Moore's Law-School Professor Nicknamed Him Fruit Salad," *New Yorker*, October 26, 2017, www
   .newyorker.com/news/news-desk/why-roy-moores-law-school
   -professor-nicknamed-him-fruit-salad, accessed December 29, 2017.

8. Stephanie McCrummen, Beth Reinhard, and Alice Crites, "Woman
   Says Roy Moore Initiated Sexual Encounter When She Was 14, He
   Was 32," *Washington Post*, November 9, 2017, www.washington
   post.com/investigations/woman-says-roy-moore-initiated-sexual
   -encounter-when-she-was-14-he-was-32/2017/11/09/1f495878
   -c293-11e7-afe9-4f60b5a6c4a0_story.html, accessed January 1,
   2018; Charles Bethea, "Locals Were Troubled by Roy Moore's
   Interactions with Teen Girls at the Gadsden Mall," *New Yorker*,
   November 13, 2017, www.newyorker.com/news/news-desk/locals
   -were-troubled-by-roy-moores-interactions-with-teen-girls-at-the
   -gadsden-mall, accessed January 26, 2018.

9. Noah Feldman, "Roy Moore Isn't Just Defiant. He's Dangerous,"
   Bloomberg, September 27, 2017, www.bloomberg.com/view/articles
   /2017-09-27/roy-moore-isn-t-just-defiant-he-s-dangerous, accessed
   December 29, 2017; Joshua Green, "Roy and His Rock," *Atlantic*,
   October 2005, www.theatlantic.com/magazine/archive/2005/10
   /roy-and-his-rock/304264/, accessed December 29, 2017.

10. Leada Gore, "Roy Moore Co-authored Course Saying Women
    Shouldn't Run for Office," AL.com, November 29, 2017, www.al

.com/news/index.ssf/2017/11/study_co-authored_by_roy_moore
.html, accessed January 28, 2018.

11. David Corn, "Watch Roy Moore, the Latest GOP Star, Argue for Criminalizing Homosexuality," *Mother Jones*, September 27, 2017, www.motherjones.com/politics/2017/09/watch-roy-moore-the -latest-gop-star-argue-for-criminalizing-homosexuality/, accessed December 29, 2017; Feldman, "Roy Moore Isn't Just Defiant. He's Dangerous"; Tim Murphy, "Roy Moore Is Strangely Nostalgic for Slavery Days," *Mother Jones*, December 7, 2017, www.motherjones .com/politics/2017/12/roy-moore-is-strangely-nostalgic-for-slavery -days/, accessed January 26, 2018; Philip Bump, "Roy Moore: America Was Great in Era of Slavery, Is Now 'Focus of Evil in the World,'" *Washington Post*, December 8, 2017, www.washingtonpost.com/news /politics/wp/2017/12/08/roy-moore-america-was-great-in-era-of -slavery-is-now-focus-of-evil-in-the-world/, accessed January 26, 2018.

12. "After Moore's Alabama Win, Dems See Sliver of Hope in Jones," Access WDUN, September 27, 2017, accesswdun.com/article/2017 /9/587437, accessed January 27, 2018; Bethea, "Why Roy Moore's Law-School Professor Nicknamed Him Fruit Salad."

13. Anna Claire Vollers, "Alabama Is 6th Poorest State in Nation; Poverty Rate at 40 Percent in Some Counties," AL.com, July 3, 2017, www.al.com/news/index.ssf/2017/07/alabama_is_6th_po orest_state_i.html, accessed February 11, 2018.

14. Vollers, "Alabama Is 6th Poorest State in Nation."

15. Sherrilyn A. Ifill to Governor Robert Bentley et al., letter, October 2, 2015, www.naacpldf.org/press-release/alabamas-closures-driver's -license-issuing-offices-impacts-access-photo-voter-id-says, accessed January 11, 2018.

16. Scott Douglas, "The Alabama Senate Race May Have Already Been Decided," *New York Times*, December 11, 2017, www.nytimes.com /2017/12/11/opinion/roy-moore-alabama-senate-voter-suppre ssion.html, accessed January 1, 2018.

17. Douglas, "The Alabama Senate Race May Have Already Been Decided"; Phillip Rawls, "Judge: Bingo Witnesses Aimed to

Suppress Black Voter Turnout," *Tuscaloosa News*, October 21, 2011, www.tuscaloosanews.com/news/20111021/judge-bingo-wit nesses-aimed-to-suppress-black—voter-turnout, accessed February 24, 2018.

18. NAACP Legal Defense Fund, "LDF Files Lawsuit to Challenge Alabama's Racially Discriminatory Photo ID Law," press release, December 2, 2015, www.naacpldf.org/update/ldf-files-lawsuit -challenge-alabama's-racially-discriminatory-photo-id-law, accessed February 24, 2018.

19. Birmingham, AL, DATA USA, datausa.io/profile/geo/birmingham -al/, accessed February 24, 2018; Montgomery, AL, DATA USA, datausa.io/profile/geo/montgomery-al/, accessed February 24, 2018; Center for Budget and Policy Priorities, "Federal Rental Assistance," March 30, 2017, www.cbpp.org/sites/default/files /atoms/files/4-13-11hous-AL.pdf, accessed February 11, 2018; "Alabama: 2016," *Talk Poverty*, talkpoverty.org/state-year-report /alabama-2016-report/, accessed February 24, 2018.

20. NAACP Legal Defense Fund, "LDF Files Lawsuit to Challenge Alabama's Racially Discriminatory Photo ID Law."

21. "Alabama Secretary of State: Voter ID," sos.alabama.gov/alabama -votes/voter/voter-id, accessed February 24, 2018.

22. Sarah Snyder, "NAACP Files Lawsuit Challenging Alabama's Photo ID Law," ABC, December 2, 2015, abc3340.com/news/local /naacp-files-lawsuit-challenging-the-states-photo-id-law, accessed February 24, 2018.

23. Brentin Mock, "Workers, Not Voters, Are Most at Risk Due to Alabama's DMV Closings," CityLab, October 13, 2015, www.citylab .com/equity/2015/10/workers-not-voters-are-most-at-risk-due-to -alabamas-dmv-closings/409957/, accessed January 11, 2018.

24. Mock, "Workers, Not Voters, Are Most at Risk Due to Alabama's DMV Closings."

25. Sam Levine, "There Are Huge Obstacles to Casting a Ballot in Alabama's Special Election," *Huffington Post*, December 14, 2017, www.huffingtonpost.com/entry/alabama-special-election

-voter-id_us_5a2ee40ee4b04617543278f2, accessed January 11, 2018.

26. Federal Communications Commission, "Broadband Availability in America: With Rural Americans Looking for High-Speed Services, Adequate Broadband Speeds Remain out of Reach for Many," January 30, 2015, apps.fcc.gov/edocs_public/attachmatch/DOC -331734A1.pdf, accessed February 11, 2018, p. 5.

27. Ifill to Bentley.

28. Tim Lockette, "Ala. Move to Close Drivers License Facilities 'Discriminatory': ACLU," *Chicago Tribune*, October 2, 2015, www .chicagotribune.com/news/nationworld/ct-alabama-drivers-lice nse-facilities-20151002-story.html, accessed January 14, 2018.

29. Lockette, "Ala. Move to Close Drivers License Facilities 'Discrim-inatory.'" Emphasis added.

30. Ashley Nellis, Ph.D., "The Color of Justice: Racial and Ethnic Disparity in State Prisons," *Sentencing Project*, June 14, 2016, www.sentencingproject.org/publications/color-of-justice-racial -and-ethnic-disparity-in-state-prisons/, accessed February 10, 2018; May Wong, "Bryan Stevenson Highlights Racism, Inequity in Criminal Justice System in Stanford Talk," *Stanford News*, January 15, 2016, news.stanford.edu/2016/01/15/openxchange -stevenson-panel-011516/, accessed February 10, 2018; Bill Quigley, "Fourteen Examples of Racism in Criminal Justice System," *Huffington Post*, July 26, 2010, www.huffingtonpost .com/bill-quigley/fourteen-examples-of-raci_b_658947.html, accessed February 10, 2018; Dan T. Carter, *Scottsboro: A Tragedy of the American South* (New York: Oxford University Press, 1971); Phillip Tutor, "Yellow Mama in All Her Glory," *Anniston (AL) Star*, March 5, 2015, www.annistonstar.com/opinion/phillip -tutor-yellow-mama-in-all-her-glory/article_8545c830-c397-11e4 -b9b8-7b0d334c1203.html, accessed February 27, 2018; Death Penalty Information Center, "Current Death Row Populations by Race," July 1, 2017, deathpenaltyinfo.org/race-death-row-inmates -executed-1976, accessed February 27, 2018; Lindsey Harrison,

"Alabama: Prison Population Demographics vs. Resident Demographics," *Newsmax*, November 5, 2015, www.newsmax.com /fastfeatures/alabama-prison-population-demographics/2015/11 /05/id/700789/, accessed February 27, 2018.

31. Nick Wing, "Alabama's Republican Secretary of State Calls Voting a 'Privilege': Apparently Automatically Giving People Their Constitutional Rights Would Also Be Offensive to Civil Rights Leaders," *Huffington Post*, November 3, 2016, www.huffingtonpost .com/entry/john-merrill-alabama_us_581a4760e4b0c43e6c1d badd, accessed February 10, 2018.

32. German Lopez, "Southern States Have Closed Down at Least 868 Polling Places for the 2016 Election," *Vox*, November 4, 2016, www .vox.com/policy-and-politics/2016/11/4/13501120/vote-polling -places-election-2016, accessed June 2, 2017; Sue Sturgis, "Voting Restrictions Could Affect Alabama's Special U.S. Senate Election," *Facing South*, October 5, 2017, www.facingsouth.org/2017/10 /voting-restrictions-could-affect-alabamas-special-us-senate-elec tion, accessed January 1, 2018.

33. "Groups Asks Alabama to Restore Voters to 'Active' Status: The Southern Poverty Law Center Is Asking Alabama's Secretary of State to Restore Thousands of People to Active Voter Status," *US News and World Report*, August 18, 2017, www.usnews.com/news /best-states/alabama/articles/2017-08-18/groups-asks-alabama -to-restore-voters-to-active-status, accessed February 11, 2018.

34. "Groups Asks Alabama to Restore Voters to 'Active' Status," *US News and World Report*.

35. Alexander Keyssar, *The Right to Vote: The Contested History of Democracy in the United State*, (New York: Basic Books, 2000), 249; *Hunter v. Underwood*, 471 U.S. 222 (1985); Julie Ebenstein, "The Alabama Governor Just Signed a Bill That Will Restore Voting Rights to Thousands of Alabamians," ACLU, May 26, 2017, www.aclu.org/blog/voting-rights/criminal-re-enfranchisment /alabama-governor-just-signed-bill-will-restore-voting, accessed January 14, 2018.

36. Adam Nossiter, "A.C.L.U. Sues Alabama on Ballot Access," *New York Times*, July 22, 2008, www.nytimes.com/2008/07/22/us /22voting.html, accessed January 14, 2018; "Alabama Restores Voting Rights for Thousands of Disenfranchised Citizens," *Democracy Initiative*, May 26, 2017, medium.com/unite4democracy /alabama-restores-voting-rights-for-thousands-of-disenfranchised -citizens-lee6f42905f9, accessed January 11, 2018; Ebenstein, "The Alabama Governor Just Signed a Bill That Will Restore Voting Rights to Thousands of Alabamians."

37. Sturgis, "Voting Restrictions Could Affect Alabama's Special U.S. Senate Election."

38. Mike Cason, "Federal Judges Rule Alabama Must Redraw Legislative Districts," AL.com, January 21, 2017, www.al.com/news /birmingham/index.ssf/2017/01/federal_judges_rule_alabama _mu.html, accessed January 28, 2018.

39. David Leonhardt, "Voter Fraud in Alabama," *New York Times*, December 12, 2017, www.nytimes.com/2017/12/12/opinion /alabama-election-voter-fraud.html, accessed November 11, 2018; ACLU, "Join the Campaign to Let People Vote in Alabama," vote .peoplepower.org/AL, accessed January 14, 2018.

40. Andrew Kaczynski, "Roy Moore in 2011: Getting Rid of Amendments After 10th Would 'Eliminate Many Problems,'" CNN, December 11, 2017, www.cnn.com/2017/12/10/politics/kfile-roy-moore-aroo stook-watchmen/index.html, accessed January 11, 2018.

41. David Smith, "'A Perfect Storm': How Liberal Millennials and African Americans Delivered a Stunning Alabama Result," *Guardian*, December 16, 2017, www.theguardian.com/us-news /2017/dec/16/alabama-senate-election-doug-jones-roy-moore -donald-trump, accessed January 11, 2018.

42. Sturgis, "Voting Restrictions Could Affect Alabama's Special U.S. Senate Election"; John Sharp, "In Alabama Senate Race Between Doug Jones and Roy Moore, Will Black Voters Show Up?," AL.com, November 5, 2017, www.al.com/news/mobile/index.ssf/2017/11 /in_alabama_senate_race_between.html, accessed January 14,

2018; Eugene Scott, "Black Lawmakers Are Stumping for Doug Jones in Alabama. But Is It Too Late?," *Washington Post*, December, 8, 2017, www.washingtonpost.com/news/the-fix/wp /2017/12/08/black-lawmakers-are-stumping-for-doug-jones-in-ala bama-but-is-it-too-late/, accessed January 11, 2018; Sean Sullivan, " 'Doug Jones's Problem': African American Voters Not Energized by Alabama's Senate Race," *Washington Post*, November 24, 2017, www.washingtonpost.com/powerpost/doug-joness-problem-afri can-american-voters-not-energized-by-alabama-senate-race/2017 /11/24/c305a2ec-ce31-11e7-a1a3-0d1e45a6de3d_story.html, accessed January 11, 2018.

43. Bethea, "Why Roy Moore's Law-School Professor Nicknamed Him Fruit Salad."

44. Richard Fausset and Campbell Robertson, "Black Voters in Alabama Pushed Back Against the Past," *New York Times*, December 13, 2017, www.nytimes.com/2017/12/13/us/doug-jones -alabama-black-voters.html, accessed January 11, 2018.

45. Martin Luther King Jr., Letter from a Birmingham Jail, April 16, 1963, okra.stanford.edu/transcription/document_images/unde cided/630416-019.pdf, accessed February 13, 2018.

46. *NAACP v. Patterson*, 357 U.S. 449 (1958); *NAACP v. Alabama ex rel. Flowers*, 377 U.S. 288 (1964).

47. Vann R. Newkirk II, "African American Voters Made Doug Jones a U.S. Senator in Alabama," *Atlantic*, December 12, 2017, www .theatlantic.com/politics/archive/2017/12/despite-the-obstacles -black-voters-make-a-statement-in-alabama/548237/, accessed January 1, 2018; Claire Potter, "Alabama, Goddamn: Join the Progressives Who Rallied the Vote for Doug Jones," *Public Seminar*, December 13, 2017, www.publicseminar.org/2017/12/alabama-god damn/, accessed January 11, 2018; Al Giordano (@AlGiordano), "1. Just spoke with a source in the Mobile (AL) County NAACP . . . ," Twitter, December 12, 2017, 10:58 A.M.

48. Sullivan, " 'Doug Jones's Problem' "; Richard Fausset, "Black Voters Could Sway an Alabama Senate Race Rocked by Scandal," *New York Times*, November 29, 2017, www.nytimes.com/2017/11

/29/us/doug-jones-roy-moore-black-voters.html, accessed March 3, 2018; Scott, "Black Lawmakers Are Stumping for Doug Jones in Alabama. But Is It Too Late?"

49. Vann R. Newkirk II, "How Grassroots Organizers Got Black Voters to the Polls in Alabama," *Atlantic*, December 19, 2017, www .theatlantic.com/politics/archive/2017/12/sparking-an-electoral -revival-in-alabama/548504/, accessed January 11, 2018.

50. Henry Hampton and Steve Fayer, *Voices of Freedom: An Oral History of the Civil Rights Movement from the 1950's Through the 1980's* (New York: Bantam Books, 1990), 213–14; *Eyes on the Prize: Bridge to Freedom*, vol. 6, www.youtube.com/watch?v=nQT7S 8fuzGc, accessed January 18, 2018.

51. Levine, "There Are Huge Obstacles to Casting a Ballot in Alabama's Special Election."

52. Newkirk, "How Grassroots Organizers Got Black Voters to the Polls in Alabama."

53. NAACP Legal Defense Fund, "LDF Launches National 'Reclaim Your Vote' Campaign to Combat Voter Suppression," press release, October 5, 2017, www.naacpldf.org/files/about-us/Reclaim%20Your %20Vote%Campaign%20Press%20Release.pdf, accessed January 11, 2018.

54. Leada Gore, "Alabama's Low Voter Turnout in the Senate Primary: 67 Counties Ranked by Turnout," AL.com, August 23, 2017, www .al.com/news/index.ssf/2017/08/how_low_was_alabamas_voter _tur.html, accessed February 18, 2018; "NAACP Urges College Students and Citizens to Vote," WAAY, www.waaytv.com/content /news/NAACP-urges-college-students-and-citizens-to-vote-this -election-461553813.html, accessed January 14, 2018.

55. Brian Lawson, "Alabama NAACP President Says He Expects Voter Turnout to Be Higher Than 25 Percent," WHNT, December 12, 2017, whnt.com/2017/12/12/__trashed-36/, accessed January 11, 2018.

56. "Vote Out Loud Rally," *Bham Now*, December 9, 2017, bhamnow .com/bhamn-event/vote-out-loud-rally/, accessed January 14, 2018; Amber Grigley, "NAACP Hold Voter Rally Ahead of Senate

Election," ABC, December 11, 2017, abc3340.com/news/local
/naacp-hold-voter-rally-ahead-of-senate-election, accessed January
14, 2018; Alabama State Conference NAACP, "Alabama NAACP
and NPHC Campaign to Recruit Voters," AL NAACP News,
November 17, 2017, www.alnaacp.org/pressreleases/press_release
_20171118_01.pdf, accessed January 14, 2018.

57. NAACP, "NAACP GOTV Helps Mobilize Black Voters in Alabama
Special Election," press release, December 13, 2017, www.naacp.org
/latest/naacp-gotv-helps-mobilize-black-voters-alabama-special
-election/, accessed January 11, 2018.

58. Deborah Barfield Berry, "Rallies, Leafleting and Door Knocking
All Part of Effort to Urge Voters to Cast Ballots in Alabama
Senate Race," *USA Today*, December 10, 2017, www.usatoday.com
/story/news/politics/2017/12/10/rallies-leafleting-and-knocking
-doors-all-part-effortsto-urge-voters-cast-ballots-alabama-senate
-rac/938309001/, accessed January 11, 2018.

59. "President of Alabama NAACP on Democrat Doug Jones' Win,"
All Things Considered, NPR, December 13, 2017, www.npr.org
/2017/12/13/570603424/president-of-alabama-naacp-on
-democrat-doug-jones-win, accessed January 11, 2018.

60. Fausset and Robertson, "Black Voters in Alabama Pushed Back
Against the Past."

61. "President of Alabama NAACP on Democrat Doug Jones' Win,"
All Things Considered.

62. David Detmold, "African Americans Hold the Key to Victory for
Doug Jones in Alabama," *Free Press*, December 11, 2017, freepress
.org/article/african-americans-hold-key-victory-doug-jones-ala
bama, accessed January 11, 2018.

63. Levine, "There Are Huge Obstacles to Casting a Ballot in Alabama's
Special Election."

64. Kira Lerner, "Alabama Elections Chief Wants to Send Citizens to
Prison for 5 Years for Voting: Up to 674 People Who Switched Parties
Between the Primary and Runoff Could Be Charged with a Felony,"
ThinkProgress, October 25, 2017, thinkprogress.org/crossover
-voting-alabama-9b0eda42de54/, accessed October 25, 2017.

65. Connor Sheets, " 'Restoration Clinics' to Help Felons Register to Vote Under New Alabama Law," AL.com, July 11, 2017, www.al .com/news/index.ssf/2017/07/restoration_clinics_to_help-fe .html, accessed January 14, 2018.

66. Author interview with Devon Crawford, telephone, January 16, 2018, notes; "Legal Services Alabama and ACLU of Alabama Provide Training on Alabama's New Voting Rights Restoration Process at Brown Chapel AME," Legal Services Alabama, www .legalservicesalabama.org/gethelp/resources/news_articles/legal -services-alabama-and-aclu-of-alabama-launch-a-new-voting-rights -campaign-at-selmas-brown-chapel-ame.html, accessed January 14, 2018; Rebekah Entralgo and Kira Lerner, "These Alabamians Voting for the First Time Is Pure Joy: 'My Eyes Just Burning. Ain't Nobody Crying,' " *ThinkProgress*, December 12, 2017, think progress.org/the-alabama-senate-race-is-disgusting-these-alaba mans-voting-for-the-first-time-is-pure-joy-1a4b5286c7c0/, accessed January 14, 2018.

67. "Legal Services Alabama and ACLU of Alabama Provide Training on Alabama's New Voting Rights Restoration Process at Brown Chapel AME," Legal Services Alabama.

68. "Legal Services Alabama and ACLU of Alabama Provide Training on Alabama's New Voting Rights Restoration Process at Brown Chapel AME," Legal Services Alabama.

69. Ebenstein, "The Alabama Governor Just Signed a Bill That Will Restore Voting Rights to Thousands of Alabamians."

70. Aaron Klein, "Soros Army in Alabama to Register Convicted Felons to Vote Against Roy Moore," *Breitbart*, December 3, 2017, www .breitbart.com/big-government/2017/12/03/soros-army-alaba ma-reigster-convicted-felons-vote-roy-moore/, accessed January 1, 2018.

71. Ebenstein, "The Alabama Governor Just Signed a Bill That Will Restore Voting Rights to Thousands of Alabamians."

72. Connor Sheets, "Thousands of Alabama Felons Register to Vote in Last-Minute Push," AL.com, November 27, 2017, www.al.com /news/index.ssf/2017/11/advocates_make_last-minute_pus

.html, accessed January 1, 2018; Al Giordano (@AlGiordano), "1. Just spoke with a source."

73. Ari Berman, "Rigged: How Voter Suppression Threw Wisconsin to Trump and Possibly Handed Him the Whole Election," *Mother Jones*, November–December 2017, www.motherjones.com/politics /2017/10/voter-suppression-wisconsin-election-2016/, accessed March 3, 2018; John Bowden, "Ex-CIA Chief: Trump 'Unstable, Inept, Inexperienced, and Also Unethical'," *The Hill*, March 3, 2018, thehill.com/homenews/administration/376547-ex-cia-chief -trump-unstable-inept-inexperienced-and-also-unethical, accessed March 3, 2018.

74. Marwa Eltagouri, "Most Americans Think Trump Is Racist, According to a New Poll," *Washington Post*, March 1, 2018, www .washingtonpost.com/news/politics/wp/2018/03/01/ap-norc-poll -most-americans-say-trump-is-racist/, accessed March 3, 2018.

75. Newkirk, "How Grassroots Organizers Got Black Voters to the Polls in Alabama."

76. Al Giordano (@AlGiordano), "1. Just spoke with a source"; Smith, "'A Perfect Storm': How Liberal Millennials and African Americans Delivered a Stunning Alabama Result."

77. Newkirk, "How Grassroots Organizers Got Black Voters to the Polls in Alabama."

78. "President of Alabama NAACP on Democrat Doug Jones' Win," *All Things Considered.*

79. Berry, "Rallies, Leafleting and Door Knocking All Part of Effort to Urge Voters to Cast Ballots in Alabama Senate Race."

80. Berry, "Rallies, Leafleting and Door Knocking All Part of Effort to Urge Voters to Cast Ballots in Alabama Senate Race."

81. "Alabama Update," Indivisible Ventura, indivisibleventura.org /alabama-update/, accessed January 11, 2018; Indivisible, www .indivisible.org/, accessed February 24, 2018.

82. "Alabama Update," Indivisible Ventura. Emphasis in original.

83. Smith, "'A Perfect Storm': How Liberal Millennials and African Americans Delivered a Stunning Alabama Result"; The Collective PAC, "Doug Jones Isn't Black. Here's Why We Supported Him

Anyway," December 13, 2017, medium.com/@collectivepac/doug
-jones-isnt-black-here-s-why-we-supported-him-anyway-74ce5fb
977c7, accessed January 11, 2018; Charles Bethea, "How the Trump
Resistance Went Pro in Alabama," *New Yorker*, December 15,
2017, www.newyorker.com/news/news-desk/how-the-trump-resis
tance-went-pro-in-alabama, accessed January 11, 2018.

84. Will Drabold, "Black Women Fueled a Grassroots Movement in
Alabama—and May Remake State Politics," *Mic*, December 14,
2017, mic.com/articles/186790/black-women-fueled-a-grassroots
-movement-in-alabama-and-may-remake-state-politics#.900c3k
HfD, accessed January 11, 2018.

85. BlackPAC, www.blackpac.com/, accessed February 25, 2018;
Smith, " 'A Perfect Storm': How Liberal Millennials and African
Americans Delivered a Stunning Alabama Result"; Drabold,
"Black Women Fueled a Grassroots Movement in Alabama—and
May Remake State Politics"; Alabama State Conference
NAACP, "Alabama NAACP and NPHC Campaign to Recruit
Voters."

86. Lauren Zanolli, "To Beat Roy Moore, Black Organizers Need to Get
Out the Youth Vote. Will It Work?," *Guardian*, December 8, 2017,
www.theguardian.com/us-news/2017/dec/08/roy-moore-doug
-jones-alabama-senate-race-black-vote, accessed January 11, 2018;
Al Whitaker, "NAACP: Black Vote Key to Doug Jones' Victory,"
WHNT, December 13, 2017, whnt.com/2017/12/13/naacp-black
-vote-key-to-doug-jones-victory/, accessed January 11, 2018.

87. Newkirk, "How Grassroots Organizers Got Black Voters to the Polls
in Alabama."

88. Drabold, "Black Women Fueled a Grassroots Movement in
Alabama—and May Remake State Politics."

89. Marie Solis, "Black Women 'Saved America' from Roy Moore—Now
Vote Them into Office, Say Political Activists," *Newsweek*,
December 15, 2017, www.newsweek.com/thank-black-women-vote
-office-political-activists-748619, accessed January 11, 2018; Smith,
" 'A Perfect Storm': How Liberal Millennials and African Americans
Delivered a Stunning Alabama Result."

90. Drabold, "Black Women Fueled a Grassroots Movement in Alabama—and May Remake State Politics"; Smith, "'A Perfect Storm': How Liberal Millennials and African Americans Delivered a Stunning Alabama Result."

91. Pew Research Center, "Religious Landscape Study: Blacks," www .pewforum.org/religious-landscape-study/racial-and-ethnic -composition/black/, accessed February 27, 2018.

92. Al Giordano (@AlGiordano), "1. Just spoke with a source."

93. The initial lawsuit forced the state to open some DMVs for one day per week, others for two days per week, and the remaining for two days per month. The judge dismissed the subsequent lawsuit charging the state with implementing a racially discriminatory law. See "Community Pressure and Legal Action Force State of Alabama to Agree to Re-open Drivers Licensing Offices in the Black Belt counties," *Greene County Democrat*, January 5, 2017, greencodem ocrat.com/tag/naacp-legal-defense-and-education-fund-ldf/, accessed January 11, 2018; Anna Beahm, "NAACP Legal Defense Fund 'Disappointed,' Appealing Judge's Dismissal of Alabama Voter ID Lawsuit," AL.com, January 12, 2018, www.al.com/news /birmingham/index.ssf/2018/01/naacp_legal_defense_fund _disap.html, accessed March 3, 2018.

94. Newkirk, "How Grassroots Organizers Got Black Voters to the Polls in Alabama"; VoteRiders, "Alabama's Special Election Is in Your Hands," www.voteriders.org/alabamas-election-in-your-hands/, accessed February 1, 2018; Patt Morrison, "Disenfranchised Because of Voter ID Bureaucracy? VoteRiders and Kathleen Unger Can Help," *Los Angeles Times*, December 6, 2017, www.latimes .com/opinion/op-ed/la-ol-patt-morrison-unger-vote-riders-2017 1206-htmlstory.html, accessed February 25, 2018; VoteRiders, "Voter ID Clinics," www.voteriders.org/get-involved/voter-id-clinics /, accessed February 25, 2018.

95. Rick Hasen (@rickhasen), Twitter, January 4, 2018, 5:50 P.M.

96. "President of Alabama NAACP on Democrat Doug Jones' Win," *All Things Considered*.

97. Al Giordano (@AlGiordano), "1. Just spoke with a source."

98. "Alabama Update," Indivisible Ventura. Emphasis in original.

99. Connor Sheets, "How a Former Sharecropper in an SUV Helped Drive Doug Jones to Victory in Alabama's Black Belt," AL .com, December 13, 2017, www.al.com/news/index.ssf/2017/12 /how_a_former_sharecropper_in_a.html, accessed March 3, 2018.

100. Jessica Weiss, "How Black Women Helped Doug Jones to Victory in Alabama," Univision, December 13, 2017, www.univision.com /univision-news/politics/how-black-women-helped-doug-jones-to -victory-in-alabama, accessed January 11, 2018; Newkirk, "How Grassroots Organizers Got Black Voters to the Polls in Alabama"; "Alabama Update," Indivisible Ventura; Mobile NAACP, "Vote Out Loud Rally."

101. Matt Fernandez, "NAACP Provides Free Rides to Polls," WIAT, December 12, 2017, www.wiat.com/news/naacp-provides-free -rides-to-polls/906167838, accessed January 14, 2018; Olivia Stump, "List of NAACP Locations to Give Voters Ride to Poll Locations," WKRG, December 12, 2017, www.wkrg.com/news /local-news/list-of-naacp-locations-to-give-voters-ride-to-poll -locations/906240728, accessed March 3, 2018.

102. Senate Majority PAC, www.senatemajority.com/about/, accessed March 3, 2018; Senate Majority PAC, "Senate Majority PAC Statement on Alabama Senate Race," press release, December 12, 2017, www.senatemajority.com/frontpage/2017/senate-majority -pac-statement-alabama-senate-race/, accessed January 11, 2018; John Eligon, "Democrats Draw Vivid Lesson from Alabama: Mobilize Black Voters," *New York Times*, December 14, 2017, www.nytimes.com/2017/12/13/us/doug-jones-alabama-black -voters.html, accessed January 11, 2018.

103. Newkirk, "How Grassroots Organizers Got Black Voters to the Polls in Alabama."

104. Drabold, "Black Women Fueled a Grassroots Movement in Alabama—and May Remake State Politics."

105. Newkirk, "How Grassroots Organizers Got Black Voters to the Polls in Alabama."

106. Ryan C. Brooks, "In the Lead-Up to Doug Jones' Win, Groups Actually Spent Million Trying to Mobilize Black Voters," *BuzzFeed*, December 18, 2017, www.buzzfeed.com/ryancbrooks /in-the-lead-up-to-doug-joness-win-groups-actually-spent, accessed January 11, 2018.

107. Eligon, "Democrats Draw Vivid Lesson from Alabama: Mobilize Black Voters."

108. McCrummen, Reinhard, and Crites, "Woman Says Roy Moore Initiated Sexual Encounter When She Was 14, He Was 32."

109. Bethea, "Locals Were Troubled by Roy Moore's Interactions with Teen Girls at the Gadsden Mall."

110. David A. Graham, "The Republican Party Slinks Back to Roy Moore: A Month After the First Allegations of Sexual Misconduct Against the U.S. Senate Hopeful in Alabama, the GOP Steps Down from the Moral High Ground," *Atlantic*, December 5, 2017, www.theatlantic.com/politics/archive/2017/12/roy-moore-re -endorsements/547529/, accessed March 3, 2018; Benjamin Hart, "Poll: 71 Percent of Alabama Republicans Think Roy Moore Allegations Are Made Up," *New York Magazine*, December 3, 2017, nymag.com/daily/intelligencer/2017/12/poll-most-alaba ma-republicans-think-moore-allegations-fake.html, accessed March 5, 2018; "Roy Moore Accuser Admits She Wrote Part of Yearbook Inscription Attributed to Alabama Senate Candidate," *Fox News*, December 8, 2017, www.foxnews.com/politics/2017/12 /08/roy-moore-accuser-admits-forged-part-yearbook-inscription -attributed-to-alabama-senate-candidate.html, accessed March 3, 2018; Sara Boboltz, "Fox News Corrects Story Claiming Roy Moore Accuser 'Forged' Candidate's Signature: A Handwriting Expert Has Verified That the Woman's Yearbook Signature Belongs to Senate Candidate Moore, According to Gloria Allred," *Huffington Post*, December 9, 2017, www.huffingtonpost.com /entry/fox-news-corrects-story-claiming-roy-moore-accuser

-forged-candidates-signature_us_5a2c1d58e4b0a290f051304f, accessed March 3, 2018; Callum Borchers, "Sean Hannity Gave Roy Moore an Ultimatum. Then He Went Soft," *Washington Post*, November 15, 2017, www.washingtonpost.com/news/the-fix/wp /2017/11/15/sean-hannity-gave-roy-moore-an-ultimatum-then -he-went-soft/, accessed March 3, 2018; Tanya Dua, Maxwell Tani, and Kate Taylor, "Here's How Advertisers Have Responded to Hannity's Coverage of the Roy Moore Allegations," *Business Insider*, November 15, 2017, www.businessinsider.com/sean -hannity-roy-moore-advertisers-boycott-keurig-2017-11, accessed March 3, 2018; Greg Evans, "Six Companies Won't Advertise on 'Hannity' After Roy Moore Interview," *Deadline*, November 12, 2017, deadline.com/2017/11/sean-hannity-roy-moore-advertisers -keurig-1202206708/, accessed March 3, 2018; Sara Boboltz, "Even More Advertisers Are Dropping Sean Hannity Over His Roy Moore Coverage: Reddi Whip, Green Mountain Coffee and Dollar Shave Club Are Among the Growing List," *Huffington Post*, November 16, 2017, www.huffingtonpost.com/entry/adverti sers-sean-hannity-roy-moore-coverage_us_5a0b6582e4b00a6 eece4f0aa, accessed March 3, 2018; Mike Cason, "Gov. Kay Ivey to Vote for Roy Moore in U.S. Senate Race," AL.com, November 17, 2017, www.al.com/news/index.ssf/2017/11/gov_kay_ivey_to_vote _for_roy_m.html, accessed March 3, 2018.

111. Bruce Riley Ashford, "Should Conservatives Vote for Roy Moore?," opinion, *Fox News*, December 11, 2017, www.foxnews.com /opinion/2017/12/11/should-conservatives-vote-for-roy-moore .html, accessed March 3, 2018.

112. Rosalind S. Helderman and David Weigel, "As Alabama Prepares to Vote, Republican Sen. Richard Shelby Says State 'Deserves Better' Than Moore," *Washington Post*, December 10, 2017, www.washingtonpost.com/news/post-politics/wp/2017/12/10 /as-alabama-prepares-to-vote-republican-sen-richard-shelby -says-state-deserves-better-than-moore/, accessed February 27, 2018.

113. Louis Nelson, "Shelby: My State of Alabama 'Deserves Better' Than Moore," *Politico*, December 10, 2017, www.politico.com /story/2017/12/10/shelby-alabama-moore-senate-288642, accessed February 27, 2018.

114. Ian Schwartz, "Roy Moore Interviewed by Hannity: 'Generally' Didn't Date Girls in Late Teens, Accusations 'Never Happened,'" *Real Clear Politics*, November 10, 2017, realclearpolitics.com /video/2017/11/10/roy_moore_interviewed_by_hannity_gene rally_didnt_date_girls_in_late_teens_accusations_never_hap pened.html, accessed March 3, 2018.

115. John Sharp, "'Shame on You': Gov. Kay Ivey Faces Criticism on Roy Moore Support. But Will She Benefit Politically?," AL.com, November 21, 2017, www.al.com/news/mobile/index.ssf/2017/11 /shame_on_you_gov_kay_ivey_face.html, accessed March 3, 2018.

116. Helderman and Weigel, "As Alabama Prepares to Vote, Republican Sen. Richard Shelby Says State 'Deserves Better' Than Moore."

117. Michael Graham, "Commentary: Why Roy Moore Is Surging in Alabama," *CBS News*, December 5, 2017, www.cbsnews.com /news/commentary-why-roy-moore-is-surging-in-alabama/, accessed March 3, 2018.

118. Jess Bidgood, "In Race Against Roy Moore, Democratic Candidate Is Mostly on His Own," *New York Times*, November 19, 2017, www.nytimes.com/2017/11/19/us/jones-alabama-democrats .html, accessed April 17, 2018.

119. Weiss, "How Black Women Helped Doug Jones to Victory in Alabama"; Detmold, "African Americans Hold the Key to Victory for Doug Jones in Alabama"; Kira Lerner, "Black Alabamians Discuss Their Decisive Role in Doug Jones' Victory: 'That's the Power of the Sister Vote,'" *ThinkProgress*, December 13, 2017, think progress.org/black-voters-alabama-election-067d73324dcc/, accessed January 11, 2018; Sullivan, "'Doug Jones' Problem': African American Voters Not Energized by Alabama's Senate Race."

120. *Roland Martin News One Now*, transcript, December 21, 2017.

121. Lawson, "Alabama NAACP President Says He Expects Voter Turnout to Be Higher Than 25 Percent"; Joshua Field, Charles Posner, and Anna Chu, "Uncounted Votes: The Racially Discriminatory Effects of Provisional Ballots," Center for American Progress, October 29, 2014, www.americanprogress.org/issues /race/reports/2014/10/29/99886/uncounted-votes/, accessed March 4, 2018.

122. Sherrilyn Ifill, "Black Voters in Alabama Mattered Way Before Doug Jones Beat Roy Moore," *Time*, December 19, 2017, time.com /5071404/alabama-black-voters-doug-jones-roy-moore/, accessed January 11, 2018.

123. *Roland Martin News One Now*, transcript.

124. U.S. Disability Statistics by State, County, City and Age: Alabama, Montgomery County, www.disabled-world.com/disability/stati stics/scc.php, accessed March 4, 2018.

125. *Roland Martin News One Now*, transcript.

126. *Roland Martin News One Now*, transcript.

127. Newkirk, "How Grassroots Organizers Got Black Voters to the Polls in Alabama."

128. Lerner, "Black Alabamians Discuss Their Decisive Role in Doug Jones' Victory"; Lerner, "These Alabamians Voting for the First Time Is Pure Joy."

129. Nate Cohn, "Why Turnout Shifts in Alabama Bode Well for Democrats: Turnout of Black Voters Surged, and Trump's Less Educated Version of the Republican Coalition Has Eroded a Traditional G.O.P. Edge," *New York Times*, December 13, 2017, www.nytimes.com/2017/12/13/upshot/alabama-turnout -republican-problem.html, accessed March 4, 2018; Paul Gattis, "As Donald Trump Wins, How Did Madison County Vote?," AL .com, November 9, 2016, www.al.com/news/huntsville/index.ssf /2016/11/as_donald_trump_wins_how_did_m.html, accessed March 4, 2018; "2017 Alabama U.S. Senate Election Results: U.S. Senate Voting Results by Alabama County," AL.com, December 13, 2017, www.al.com/new/index.ssf/page/2017_alabama_us

_senate_election_results.html, accessed March 4, 2018; Bethea, "How the Trump Resistance Went Pro in Alabama"; Jesse Singal, "Why Black Voters in Milwaukee Weren't Enthused by Hillary Clinton," *New York Magazine*, November 22, 2016, nymag.com /daily/intelligencer/2016/11/why-black-voters-in-milwaukee -werent-enthused-by-clinton.html, accessed March 11, 2017; Michael Harthorne, "Hillary Clinton Might Have a Black Voter Problem: African-Americans Aren't Turning Out for Early Voting like They Were in 2012," *Newser*, November 2, 2016, www.newser .com/story/233454/hillary-clinton-might-have-a-black-voter -problem.html, accessed March 11, 2017; Tami Luhby, "How Hillary Clinton Lost," CNN, November 9, 2016, www.cnn.com /2016/11/09/politics/clinton-votes-african-americans-latinos -women-white-voters/, accessed March 11, 2017.

130. *When We Were Kings*, directed by Leon Gast, Universal Home Entertainment, 2002, DVD.

131. Brooks, "In the Lead-Up to Doug Jones' Win, Groups Actually Spent Millions Trying to Mobilize Black Voters."

132. Errol Louis, "Of Course, Selma Made the Difference for Doug Jones," CNN, December 13, 2017, www.cnn.com/2017/12/13 /opinions/of-course-selma-made-the-difference-for-doug-jones -louis/index.html, accessed January 14, 2018.

133. Sharp, "In Alabama Race between Doug Jones and Roy Moore, Will Black Voters Show Up?"; Newkirk, "How Grassroots Organizers Got Black Voters to the Polls in Alabama"; Newkirk, "African American Voters Made Doug Jones a U.S. Senator in Alabama."

134. "Alabama Secretary of State Explains Why He's Backing Roy Moore," WBUR, December 11, 2017 www.wbur.org/hereandnow /2017/12/11/alabama-secretary-of-state-john-merrill, accessed March 4, 2018.

135. Drabold, "Black Women Fueled a Grassroots Movement in Alabama—and May Remake State Politics."

136. Dante Chinni, "Buried Inside the Alabama Election, a Lesson for the GOP in 2018," NBC News, December 17, 2017, www.nbcnews

.com/politics/first-read/buried-inside-alabama-election-lesson
-gop-2018-n830476, accessed March 4, 2018; "2017 Alabama U.S.
Senate Election Results: U.S. Senate Voting Results by Alabama
County," AL.com; Matthew Bloch, Nate Cohn, Josh Katz, and
Jasmine Lee, "Alabama Election Results: Doug Jones Defeats Roy
Moore in U.S. Senate Race," *New York Times*, December 12, 2017,
www.nytimes.com/elections/results/alabama-senate-special
-election-roy-moore-doug-jones, accessed April 14, 2018.

137. "Exit Poll Results: How Different Groups Voted in Alabama,"
Washington Post, December 13, 2017, www.washingtonpost.com
/graphics/2017/politics/alabama-exit-polls/, accessed March 4,
2018; Weiss, "How Black Women Helped Doug Jones to Victory
in Alabama."

138. Gabrielle Gurley, "Black Alabamians Voted for Themselves,"
Prospect, December 15, 2017, prospect.org/article/black-alaba
mians-voted-themselves, accessed January 14, 2018; Drabold,
"Black Women Fueled a Grassroots Movement in Alabama—and
May Remake State Politics"; Cohn, "Why Turnout Shifts in
Alabama Bode Well for Democrats"; Lerner, "Black Alabamians
Discuss Their Decisive Role in Doug Jones' Victory"; Bethea,
"How the Trump Resistance Went Pro in Alabama."

139. Alexander C. Kaufman, "Roy Moore Supporters Start Crying
Voter Fraud Immediately After Doug Jones Wins: 'They Cheated,
Soros Interfered,'" *Huffington Post*, December 13, 2017, www
.huffingtonpost.co.za/2017/12/13/roy-moore-supporters-start
-crying-voter-fraud-immediately-after-doug-jones-wins_a
_23305645/, accessed January 1, 2018; Alan Pyke, "Clinging to
the Spotlight, Roy Moore Demands New Vote Because Black Voter
Surge Must Have Been Fraud," *ThinkProgress*, December 28,
2017, thinkprogress.org/roy-moore-sues-for-new-election-fdd088
938157/, accessed December 28, 2017.

140. Weiss, "How Black Women Helped Doug Jones to Victory in
Alabama."

Conclusion: At the Crossroads of Half Slave, Half Free

1. "Only 24% of Americans Think Their Country Is Heading in the Right Direction: Poll," *CNBC*, October 7, 2017, www.cnbc.com /2017/10/07/only-24-percent-of-americans-think-their-country-is -heading-in-the-right-direction-poll.html, accessed March 17, 2018; Ryan Sit, "Donald Trump Is an Embarrassment to Most Americans, Who Don't Want Him as a Role Model to Their Children: Poll," *Newsweek*, January 25, 2018, www.newsweek.com/donald-trump -quinnipiac-poll-role-model-embarrassment-moral-leader-approval -791028, accessed March 17, 2018.

2. Luis Sanchez, "Poll: Americans Trust Mueller More Than Trump on Russia," *The Hill*, February 26, 2018, thehill.com/policy/national -security/375734-poll-americans-trust-mueller-more-than-trump -on-russia, accessed March 17, 2018.

3. Charles Pierce, "Mueller Has the Goods Now, and Trump Knows It," *Esquire*, February 16, 2018, www.esquire.com/news-politics -politics/a18212230/what-mueller-indictments-mean/, accessed February 16, 2018; Scott Shane, "The Fake Americans Russia Created to Influence the Election," *New York Times*, September 7, 2017, www.nytimes.com/2017/09/07/us/politics/russia-facebook -twitter-election.html, accessed March 17, 2018; David Voreacos and Steven T. Dennis, "Mueller Accuses Russians of Pro-Trump/ Anti-Clinton Meddling," *Bloomberg*, February 16, 2018, www.bloom berg.com/news/articles/2018-02-16/u-s-charges-13-russians-3 -companies-for-hacking-election, accessed March 17, 2018.

4. Pierce, "Mueller Has the Goods Now, and Trump Knows It"; Jerry Zremski, "Russian Trolls Pushed Rally in Buffalo—Then Urged Blacks Not to Vote," *Buffalo News*, March 10, 2018, buffalonews .com/2018/03/10/russian-trolls-pushed-rally-in-buffalo-and-urged -blacks-not-to-vote/, accessed March 11, 2018.

5. Pierce, "Mueller Has the Goods Now, and Trump Knows It"; Cristiano Lima and Elizabeth Castillo, "A Caged Clinton and Fake 'Woke Blacks': 9 Striking Findings from the Mueller Indictment,"

Politico, February 16, 2018, www.politico.com/story/2018/02/16 /mueller-indictment-hillary-clinton-key-findings-415692, accessed March 17, 2018. Emphasis in original.

6. Zremski, "Russian Trolls Pushed Rally in Buffalo—Then Urged Blacks Not to Vote"; Lima and Castillo, "A Caged Clinton and Fake 'Woke Blacks'"; Scott Shane, "These Are the Ads Russia Bought on Facebook in 2016," *New York Times*, November 1, 2017, www.ny times.com/2017/11/01/us/politics/russia-2016-election-facebook .html, accessed March 17, 2018; Eric Frazier, "My Feminist Daughter's Problem with Hillary Clinton," *Charlotte Observer*, November 6, 2016, www.charlotteobserver.com/opinion/opn-columns-blogs /eric-frazier/article112633448.html, accessed March 17, 2018.

7. Thomas Frank, "Did Russia's Social Media Campaign to Discourage Black Voters Cost Clinton the Election?," *BuzzFeed*, February 20, 2018, www.buzzfeed.com/thomasfrank/did-russias-social-media -campaign-to-discourage-black, accessed March 17, 2018.

8. Zremski, "Russian Trolls Pushed Rally in Buffalo—Then Urged Blacks not to Vote"; Pierce, "Mueller Has the Goods Now, and Trump Knows It."

9. Pierce, "Mueller Has the Goods Now, and Trump Knows It."

10. Ari Berman, "American Democracy Is Now Under Siege by Both Cyber-Espionage and GOP Voter Suppression," *The Nation*, July 12, 2017, www.thenation.com/article/american-democracy-is-now -under-siege-by-both-cyber-espionage-and-gop-voter-suppression/, accessed March 11, 2018.

11. Carol Anderson, *White Rage: The Unspoken Truth of Our Racial Divide* (New York: Bloomsbury, 2016, 2017), 138–54.

12. Berman, "American Democracy Is Now Under Siege by Both Cyber-Espionage and GOP Voter Suppression"; Lawrence Norden, "Clear and Present Danger to U.S. Vote," Brennan Center for Justice, March 5, 2018, www.brennancenter.org/analysis/clear-and-present -danger-us-vote, accessed March 10, 2018.

13. "Population Estimates for Indiana Counties, 2010–2015," www .stats.indiana.edu/population/popTotals/2015-county-estimates

.asp, accessed March 17, 2018; Rachel Strange, "Exploring Hoosier Minority Groups: Indiana's Black Population," *InContext* 14, no. 3 (May–June 2013), www.incontext.indiana.edu/2013/may-jun /article3.asp, accessed March 17, 2018.

14. Garet Williams, "Report: The GOP in Indiana Is Making It Harder for Democrats to Vote," *Vox*, August 11, 2017, www.vox.com/policy -and-politics/2017/8/11/16131498/report-indiana-gop-early -voting-indianapolis, accessed March 5, 2018; Mark Joseph Stern, "After Obama's 2008 Win, Indiana GOP Added Early Voting in White Suburbs, Cut It in Indianapolis," *Slate*, August 10, 2017, www.slate.com/blogs/the_slatest/2017/08/10/the_indiana_gop _cut_early_voting_in_area_with_black_democrats_after_2008 .html, accessed March 5, 2018; Sam Levine, "Indiana Republicans Keep Blocking Early Voting in a Major Democratic County," *Huffington Post*, August 10, 2017, www.huffingtonpost.com/entry /indiana-republicans-early-voting_us_598cacdfe4b09096 4295b5ca, accessed March 12, 2018; Ed Kilgore, "How the Indiana GOP Used Uneven Early Voting Rules to Tamp Down Democratic Votes," *New York Magazine*, August 10, 2017, nymag.com/daily /intelligencer/2017/08/how-the-indiana-gop-skewed-early-voting -opportunities.html, accessed March 12, 2018.

15. Rebekah Barber, "Is Georgia's Secretary of State Unjustly Targeting Voting Rights Activists Again?," *Facing South*, October 4, 2017, www.facingsouth.org/2017/10/georgias-secretary-state-unjustly -targeting-voting-rights-activist-again, accessed March 5, 2018; Spencer Woodman, "Register Minority Voters in Georgia, Go to Jail," *New Republic*, May 5, 2015, newrepublic.com/article/121715 /georgia-secretary-state-hammers-minority-voter-registration -efforts, accessed March 15, 2018.

16. Barber, "Is Georgia's Secretary of State Unjustly Targeting Voting Rights Activists Again?"; Woodman, "Register Minority Voters in Georgia, Go to Jail."

17. Berman, "American Democracy Is Now Under Siege by Both Cyber-Espionage and GOP Voter Suppression."

18. Michael Wines, "Some Republicans Acknowledge Leveraging Voter ID Laws for Political Gain," *New York Times*, September 16, 2016, www.nytimes.com/2016/09/17/us/some-republicans-acknow ledge-leveraging-voter-id-laws-for-political-gain.html, accessed May 16, 2017.

19. Zachary Roth, "Black Turnout Down in North Carolina After Cuts to Early Voting," *NBC News*, November 7, 2016, www.nbcnews .com/storyline/2016-election-day/black-turnout-down-north -carolina-after-cuts-early-voting-n679051, accessed March 18, 2018.

20. Mark Joseph Stern, "New Hampshire Republicans Are Close to Passing Their Trump-Inspired Poll Tax," *Slate*, January 3, 2018, slate.com/news-and-politics/2018/01/new-hampshire-senate-passes -poll-tax-to-suppress-student-voting.html, accessed March 18, 2018.

21. Hedrick Smith, "The Oregon Idea—Make Voting Easy," *Bill Moyers*, October 19, 2016, billmoyers.com/story/oregon-idea-make -voting-easy/, accessed March 6, 2018.

22. Smith, "The Oregon Idea—Make Voting Easy"; Jonathan Brater, "Update: Oregon Keeps Adding New Voters at Torrid Pace," Brennan Center for Justice, August 19, 2016, www.brennancenter .org/analysis/update-oregon-keeps-adding-new-voters-torrid-pace, accessed March 15, 2018; Sean McElwee, Brian Schaffner, and Jesse Rhodes, "How Oregon Increased Voter Turnout More Than Any Other State," *The Nation*, July 27, 2017, www.thenation.com/article /how-oregon-increased-voter-turnout-more-than-any-other-state/, accessed March 6, 2018.

23. Smith, "The Oregon Idea—Make Voting Easy."

24. Lonnie Wong, "California Looks at Colorado Voter Reform Model," Fox 40, May 27, 2015, fox40.com/2015/05/27/california -looks-at-colorado-voter-reform-model/, accessed March 4, 2018; "Legislative Oversight Hearing on Colorado Model of Elections: Report from California Observers," May 21, 2015, www.govbuddy .com/directory/press/CA/legislative-oversight-hearing-on-colorado -model-of-elections-report-from-california-observers/37391/, accessed March 4, 2018.

25. "New California Law to Expand Youth Voter Participation," *LA Sentinel*, March 2, 2018, lasentinel.net/new-california-law-to-expand-youth-voter-participation.html, accessed March 2, 2018.

26. Nicole Flatow, "Colorado Legislature Passes Major Voting Rights Expansion Bill," *ThinkProgress*, May 2, 2013, thinkprogress.org/colorado-legislature-passes-major-voting-rights-expansion-bill-9de254d63e15/, accessed March 2, 2018; Mary Plummer, "More Changes Ahead for California Voters in 2017," KPCC, December 26, 2016, www.scpr.org/news/201612/26/67391/more-changes-ahead-for-california-voters-in-2017, accessed March 3, 2018.

27. Smith, "The Oregon Idea—Make Voting Easy"; Brennan Center for Justice, "Automatic Voter Registration," February 10, 2018, www.brennancenter.org/analysis/automatic-voter-registration, accessed March 2, 2018.

28. Jonathan Brater, "Automatic Voter Registration in Illinois Is a Landmark Advance," Brennan Center for Justice, August 28, 2017, www.brennancenter.org/blog/automatic-voter-registration-illinois-landmark-advance, accessed March 6, 2018; Aaron Barksdale, "Millions of New Voters in Illinois Could Change American Politics: The Fight to Expand Voting Rights Through Automatic Voter Registration Is Happening Right Now, State by State," *Vice Impact*, September 27, 2017, impact.vice.com/en_us/article/9k3dx7/millions-of-new-voters-in-illinois-could-change-american-politics, accessed March 2, 2018.

29. Smith, "The Oregon Idea—Make Voting Easy"; Brennan Center for Justice, "Automatic Voter Registration."

30. McElwee, Schaffner, and Rhodes, "How Oregon Increased Voter Turnout More Than Any Other State"; Smith, "The Oregon Idea—Make Voting Easy"; "The Largest US Cities: Cities Ranked 1 to 100," City Mayor Statistics, www.citymayors.com/gratis/uscities_100.html, accessed March 18, 2018.

31. "Tracking Congress in the Age of Trump: An Updating Tally of How Often Every Member of the House and the Senate Votes with or Against the President," *FiveThirtyEight*, March 14, 2018, projects

.fivethirtyeight.com/congress-trump-score/, accessed March 18, 2018.

32. Will Drabold, "How Cities Are Bypassing States to Explore Registering Hundreds of Thousands to Vote," *Mic*, January 5, 2018, mic.com/articles/187178/how-cities-are-bypassing-states-to-exp lore-registering-hundreds-of-thousands-to-vote#.n3SpuKTkz, accessed March 2, 2018; Dylan Matthews, "Polls Show Americans Are Closer to Democrats Than Donald Trump on Immigration: Americans Want to Help DREAMers, Don't Want a Wall, and Don't Want to Cut Immigration Levels," www.vox.com/policy-and -politics/2018/2/3/16959458/immigration-trump-compromise -public-opinion-poll-dreamers-wall, accessed March 19, 2018; "Latino Working Families Cannot Afford the GOP Tax Plan," *Unidos US*, www.unidosus.org/issues/economy/federal-budget, accessed March 19, 2018.

33. "How Groups Voted: US Elections 2016," *Roper Center*, ropercenter .cornell.edu/polls/us-elections/how-groups-voted/groups-voted -2016/, accessed March 18, 2018; "Exit Poll Results: How Different Groups Voted in Alabama," *Washington Post*, December 13, 2017, www.washingtonpost.com/graphics/2017/politics/alabama-exit -polls/, accessed March 19, 2018; Rev. Dr. William Barber, "The Unbearable Hypocrisy of Roy Moore's Christian Rhetoric: This Isn't Christianity, It's an Extreme Form of Republican Religionism," *NBC News*, November 18, 2017, www.nbcnews.com/think/opinion /unbearable-hypocrisy-roy-moore-s-christian-rhetoric-ncna821921, accessed December 30, 2017.

34. Joshua A. Douglas, "Expanding Voting Rights Through Local Law," *American Constitution Society for Law and Policy*, October 2017, www.acslaw.org/sites/default/files/Expanding_Voting_Rights _Through_Local_Law_-_ACS_Issue_Brief.pdf, accessed March 6, 2018.

35. David Anderson, "Delaware Absentee Voting Is Easier," DelawarePolitics.net, July 29, 2017, www.delawarepolitics.net /delaware-absentee-voting-is-easier, accessed March 4, 2018.

36. New Mexico Senate Democrats, "New Mexico Senate Passes Legislation to Greatly Expand Voter Registration Time Period," KRWG, March 1, 2017, krwg.org/post/new-mexico-senate-passes -legislation-greatly-expand-voter-registration-time-period, accessed March 9, 2018; New Mexico Legislature, "2018 Regular Session—SB 224," www.nmlegis.gov/Legislation/Legislation?chamber=S&leg type=B&legno=224&year=18&AspxAutoDetectCookieSupport=1, accessed March 18, 2018.

37. "CT Passes Election Day and Online Voter Registration," *Demos*, May 9, 2012, www.demos.org/press-release/ct-passes-election-day -and-online-voter-registration, accessed March 4, 2018.

38. Keith Brekhus, "Democratic Led Minnesota Senate Approves Expanding Early Voting and Voting Rights," *Politicus*, May 12, 2015, www.politicususa.com/2015/05/12/democratic-led-minne sota-senate-approves-expanding-early-voting-voting-rights.html, accessed March 6, 2018.

39. Mary Spicuzza, "Milwaukee to More Than Double Early Voting Sites for 2018 Elections," *Milwaukee Sentinel Journal*, November 15, 2017, www.jsonline.com/story/news/local/milwaukee/2017 /11/15/milwaukee-more-than-double-early-voting-sites-2018 -elections/867191001/, accessed March 4, 2018.

40. "Expanding Voting Rights," Policy Brief, Local Progress: The National Municipal Policy Network, September 2013, localprogress .org/wp-content/uploads/2013/09/expanding_voting_rights.pdf, accessed March 6, 2018; Drabold, "How Cities Are Bypassing States to Explore Registering Hundreds of Thousands to Vote"; Jeff Daly, "Hours Expand for Early Voting in Macon County," *Now Decatur*, March 5, 2018, www.nowdecatur.com/2018/03/05/hours-expand -for-early-voting-in-macon-county/, accessed March 6, 2018.

41. Ezra Kaplan, "Georgia Democratic Lawmakers Hope to Expand Voters' Rights," WMC Action News 5, January 28, 2017, www.wm cactionnews5.com/story/34371675/georgia-democratic-law makers-hope-to-expand-voters-rights, accessed March 6, 2018.

42. Emily Guskin and Scott Clement, "Poll: Nearly Half of Americans Say Voter Fraud Occurs Often," *Washington Post*, September 15, 2016, www.washingtonpost.com/news/the-fix/wp/2016/09/15/poll -nearly-half-of-americans-say-voter-fraud-occurs-often/, accessed March 18, 2018.

43. Bryan Lowry, "His Own Witness Doesn't Back Kobach Claims That Illegal Votes Cost Trump Popular Vote," *Kansas City Star*, March 13, 2018, www.kansascity.com/news/politics-government /article204976839.html, accessed March 14, 2018; Sam Levine, "Top ACLU Voting Rights Lawyer Rips into Trump Expert's Evidence of Kansas Voter Fraud," *Huffington Post*, March 9, 2018, www.huffingtonpost.com/entry/aclu-hans-von-spakovsky_us_5aa 33fe0e4b01b9b0a3b7c9b, accessed March 10, 2018; Sherman Smith, "ACLU: Report to Kris Kobach Shows 5 Illegal Voters out of 1.3 Million Ballots," *Topeka Capital Journal*, March 9, 2018, www .cjonline.com/news/20180308/aclu-report-to-kris-kobach-shows -5-illegal-voters-out-of-13-million-ballots, accessed March 11, 2018.

44. Barksdale, "Millions of New Voters in Illinois Could Change American Politics."

45. "AP Analysis Shows How Gerrymandering Benefited GOP in 2016," June 27, 2017, www.mlive.com/news/index.ssf/2017/06/ap _analysis_shows_how_gerryman.html, accessed March 19, 2018.

46. Anderson, *White Rage*, 163–68; Berman, "How Voter Suppression Threw Wisconsin to Donald Trump and Possibly Handed Him the Whole Election."

47. Carlos Ballesteros, "Trump Is Nominating Unqualified Judges at an Unprecedented Rate," *Newsweek*, November 17, 2017, www .newsweek.com/trump-nominating-unqualified-judges-left-and -right-710263, accessed March 19, 2018; "The Senate Is Rushing Through Trump's Judicial Nominees. These Embarrassments Prove It," *Washington Post*, December 17, 2017, www.washing tonpost.com/opinions/the-senate-is-rushing-through-trumps -judicial-nominees-these-embarrassments-prove-it/2017/12/17

/9123f6a4-e1da-11e7-8679-a9728984779c_story.html,   accessed March 19, 2018.

48. Joanne B. Freeman, *The Field of Blood: Violence in Congress and the Road to Civil War* (New York: Farrar, Straus and Giroux, 2018).

49. Kari A. Frederickson, *The Dixiecrat Revolt and the End of the Solid South, 1932–1968* (Chapel Hill: University of North Carolina Press, 2001); Manfred Berg, *"The Ticket to Freedom": The NAACP and the Struggle for Black Political Integration* (Gainesville: University Press of Florida, 2005); Mary L. Dudziak, *Cold War Civil Rights: Race and the Image of American Democracy* (Princeton, NJ: Princeton University Press, 2000).

50. David Remnick, "Donald Trump and the Stress Test of Liberal Democracy," *New Yorker*, March 19, 2018, www.newyorker.com /magazine/2018/03/19/donald-trump-and-the-stress-test-of -liberal-democracy, accessed March 11, 2018; Steven Levitsky and Daniel Ziblatt, *How Democracies Die* (New York: Crown, 2018); David Frum, *Trumpocracy: The Corruption of the American Republic* (New York, NY: Harper, 2018).

51. Abraham Lincoln, "House Divided Speech," June 16, 1858, www .abrahamlincolnonline.org/lincoln/speeches/house.htm, accessed March 18, 2018.

Afterword: "We Are Going to Warrior Up"

1. Michael Brice-Saddler, "GOP Senator: It's a 'great idea' to make it harder for 'liberal folks' to vote," *Washington Post*, November 16, 2018, https://www.washingtonpost.com/politics/2018/11/16/cindy -hyde-smith-its-great-idea-make-it-harder-liberal-folks-vote/?utm _term=.ea4fa9c86360, accessed March 20, 2019.

2. Michael Brice-Saddler and Deanna Paul, "A senator refuses to apologize for joking about 'public hanging' in a state known for lynch-ings," *Washington Post*, November 12, 2018, https://www.washing tonpost.com/politics/2018/11/11/senator-mississippi-joked

-about-public-hanging-her-black-opponent-called-it-reprehensible
/?utm_term=.2f3f95c5e4f3, accessed March 20, 2019.

3. *ABC News Turning Point*, "Murder in Mississippi: The Price of
    Freedom," Anthony Ross Potter (producer), (New York: ABC News,
    1994), VHS.

4. Adam Serwer, "The Cruelty Is the Point: President Trump and his
    supporters find community by rejoicing in the suffering of those
    they hate and fear," *The Atlantic*, October 3, 2018, https://www
    .theatlantic.com/ideas/archive/2018/10/the-cruelty-is-the-point
    /572104/, accessed March 24, 2019; Nicole Narea, "A Year in
    Trump Corruption: Here's every time Trump has profited off the
    presidency," *Washington Monthly*, January/February/March/2018,
    https://washingtonmonthly.com/magazine/january-february
    -march-2018/a-year-in-trump-corruption/, accessed March 24, 2019;
    Holmes Lybrand, "Fact-checking Trump's Notion that White
    Nationalism is not a Rising Threat," CNN.com, March 16, 2019,
    https://www.cnn.com/2019/03/16/politics/fact-checking-trump
    -on-threat-of-white-nationalism/index.html, accessed March 24,
    2019; "Trump Sides with Russia against FBI at Helsinki Summit,"
    BBC.com, July 16, 2018, https://www.bbc.com/news/world-europe
    -44852812, accessed March 24, 2019; Greg Miller, *The Apprentice:
    Trump, Russia and the Subversion of American Democracy* (New
    York: HarperCollins, 2018); Kate Lyons, " 'I believe Putin': Trump
    Dismissed US Advice on North Korea Threat, says McCabe," *The
    Guardian*, February 17, 2019, https://www.theguardian.com/us
    -news/2019/feb/18/i-believe-putin-trump-dismissed-us-advice
    -on-north-korea-threat-says-mccabe, accessed March 24, 2019;
    S. Erdem Aytaç and Susan Stokes, "Americans just set a turnout
    record for the midterms, voting at the highest rate since 1914. This
    explains why," *Washington Post*, November 20, 2018, https://www
    .washingtonpost.com/news/monkey-cage/wp/2018/11/20
    /americans-just-set-a-turnout-record-for-the-midterms-voting-at
    -the-highest-rate-since-1914-this-explains-why, accessed March 19,

2019; Zack Beauchamp, "The midterm elections revealed that America is in a cold civil war," *Vox*, November 7, 2018, https://www .vox.com/midterm-elections/2018/11/7/18068486/midterm -election-2018-results-race-surburb, accessed April 5, 2019.

5. Paul Weyrich—"I don't want everybody to vote" (Goo Goo), https://www.youtube.com/watch?v=8GBAsFwPglw, accessed March 28, 2019; Jennifer Rubin, "GOP Autopsy Report Goes Bold," *Washington Post*, March 18, 2013, https://www.washingtonpost .com/blogs/right-turn/wp/2013/03/18/gop-autopsy-report-goes -bold/?utm_term=.27c861de7f22, October 31, 2018.

6. Jenni Monet, "North Dakota's Voter ID Law Seen as Retaliatory and Privileged," *Medium*, November 4, 2018, https://medium .com/@missmonet/north-dakotas-voter-id-law-seen-as-retaliatory -and-privileged-51a02e2cc798, accessed April 6, 2019.

7. German Lopez "North Dakota's New Voting Restrictions Seemed Aimed at Native Americans who Vote Democrat," *Vox*, October 31, 2018, https://www.vox.com/policy-and-politics/2018/10/31/180 47922/north-dakota-voter-id-suppression-heitkamp, accessed April 6, 2019; Rebecca Hersher, "Key Moments in the Dakota Access Pipeline Fight," *NPR*, February 22, 2017, https://www.npr.org /sections/thetwo-way/2017/02/22/514988040/key-moments-in -the-dakota-access-pipeline-fight, accessed April 16, 2019; Jenni Monet, "North Dakota's Voter ID Law Seen as Retaliatory and Privileged," *Medium*, November 4, 2018, https://medium.com /@missmonet/north-dakotas-voter-id-law-seen-as-retaliatory-and -privileged-51a02e2cc798, accessed April 6, 2019.

8. Jamie Azure, "North Dakota's Voter ID Law Aimed to Silence Native American Voters, Instead it Rallied My Tribe," *Washington Post*, November 1, 2018, https://www.washingtonpost.com/outlook /2018/11/01/north-dakotas-voter-id-law-aimed-silence-native -american-voters-instead-it-rallied-my-tribe/?utm_term=.9094 e34a92fa, accessed April 6, 2019.

9. Maggie Astor, "A Look at Where North Dakota's Voter ID Controversy Stands," *New York Times*, October 19, 2018 https://

www.nytimes.com/2018/10/19/us/politics/north-dakota-voter
-identification-registration.html, accessed April 6, 2019.

10. North Dakota Indian Affairs Commission, "Tribal Nations," http://
indianaffairs.nd.gov/tribal-nations/, accessed April 6, 2019; Jenni
Monet, "North Dakota's Voter ID Law Seen as Retaliatory and
Privileged," *Medium*, November 4, 2018, https://medium.com/@
missmonet/north-dakotas-voter-id-law-seen-as-retaliatory-and-privi
leged-51a02e2cc798, accessed April 6, 2019.

11. Dan McGull, "Has North Dakota's Voter ID Law Made it Harder
for Native Americans to Vote?" *Snopes*, October 15, 2018, https://
www.snopes.com/fact-check/north-dakota-native-american-voters/,
accessed April 6, 2019.

12. NARF, *Brakebill, et al v. Jaeger*, https://www.narf.org/cases/nd
-voter-id/, accessed April 6, 2019.

13. Ruben Kimmelman, "Judge Rules Native Americans in North
Dakota Must Comply with Voter ID Law," NPR, November 2, 2018,
https://www.npr.org/2018/11/02/663417341/judge-rules-native
-americans-in-north-dakota-must-comply-with-voter-id-law,
accessed April 6, 2019.

14. Jenni Monet, "North Dakota's Voter ID Law Seen as Retaliatory
and Privileged," *Medium*, November 4, 2018, https://medium
.com/@missmonet/north-dakotas-voter-id-law-seen-as-retaliatory
-and-privileged-51a02e2cc798, accessed April 6, 2019.

15. Katie Reilly, "North Dakota's Voter ID Law Disproportionately
Affects Native Americans. Here's How They're Mobilizing to Fight
It," *Time*, November 2, 2018, http://time.com/5442434/north
-dakota-voting-law-native-american-activism/, accessed April 6, 2019.

16. Jay Michaelson, "North Dakota's Racist Voter ID Law Is Already
Backfiring," *The Daily Beast*, November 1, 2018, https://www
.thedailybeast.com/north-dakotas-racist-voter-id-law-is-already
-backfiring, accessed April 6, 2019.

17. Katie Reilly, "North Dakota's Voter ID Law Disproportionately
Affects Native Americans. Here's How They're Mobilizing to Fight
It," *Time*, November 2, 2018, http://time.com/5442434/north

-dakota-voting-law-native-american-activism/, accessed April 6, 2019.

18. Jay Michaelson, "North Dakota's Racist Voter ID Law Is Already Backfiring," *The Daily Beast*, November 1, 2018, https://www.thedailybeast.com/north-dakotas-racist-voter-id-law-is-already-backfiring, accessed April 6, 2019.

19. Matt Vasilogambros, "Polling Places in Black Communities Continue to Close Ahead of November Elections," *Governing*, September 5, 2018, https://www.governing.com/topics/politics/sl-polling-place-close-ahead-of-november-elections-black-voters.html, accessed March 23, 2019.

20. Charles Bethea, "A Win in the Battle to Vote in Georgia," *New Yorker*, August 24, 2018, https://www.newyorker.com/news/news-desk/a-win-in-the-battle-to-vote-in-georgia, accessed March 23, 2019.

21. U.S. Census, "Randolph County, GA," https://www.census.gov/quickfacts/fact/table/randolphcountygeorgia/PST045217, accessed March 23, 2019; Jada Haynes, "Randolph County board proposes closing multiple polls: 'No indication' of poll closure proposal before Wednesday," *Albany Herald*, August 16, 2018, https://www.albanyherald.com/news/local/randolph-county-board-proposes-closing-multiple-polls/article_08500c00-76b5-584f-9526-3e6198bffc3a.html, accessed March 23, 2019.

22. Charles Bethea, "A Win in the Battle to Vote in Georgia," *New Yorker*, August 24, 2018, https://www.newyorker.com/news/news-desk/a-win-in-the-battle-to-vote-in-georgia, accessed March 23, 2019.

23. Doug Richards, "Consultant behind plan to close Randolph Co. polling places did it before, but not on this scale," WXIA—11 Alive, August 20, 2018, https://www.11alive.com/article/news/local/consultant-behind-plan-to-close-randolph-co-polling-places-did-it-before-but-not-on-this-scale/85-585898906, accessed March 24, 2019.

24. Charles Bethea, "A Win in the Battle to Vote in Georgia," *New Yorker*, August 24, 2018, https://www.newyorker.com/news/news

-desk/a-win-in-the-battle-to-vote-in-georgia, accessed March 23, 2019; "Martin Luther Coon . . . er King," https://www.youtube .com/watch?v=thJXKW43pnM, accessed March 31, 2019.

25. "Backlash grows over poll closures in predominantly black Georgia county," CBS News, August 22, 2018, https://www.cbsnews.com /news/backlash-grows-over-poll-closures-in-predominantly-black -georgia-county/, accessed March 23, 2019.

26. Khushbu Shah, " 'Textbook voter suppression': Georgia's bitter election a battle years in the making," *The Guardian*, November 10, 2018, https://www.theguardian.com/us-news/2018/nov/10/georgia -election-recount-stacey-abrams-brian-kemp, accessed December 25, 2018.

27. Carol Anderson, "Brian Kemp's Lead in Georgia Needs an Asterisk," *The Atlantic*, November 7, 2018, https://www.theatlantic.com /ideas/archive/2018/11/georgia-governor-kemp-abrams/575095 /, accessed March 24, 2019.

28. Charles Bethea, "A Win in the Battle to Vote in Georgia," *New Yorker*, August 24, 2018, https://www.newyorker.com/news/news -desk/a-win-in-the-battle-to-vote-in-georgia, accessed March 23, 2019.

29. Vanessa Williams, "Georgia Groups Call on GOP Gubernatorial Nominee Brian Kemp to Step Down as the State's Elections Chief," *Washington Post*, August 8, 2018, https://www.washingtonpost .com/news/powerpost/wp/2018/08/08/georgia-groups-call-on -gop-gubernatorial-nominee-brian-kemp-to-step-down-as-the -states-elections-chief/?utm_term=.2982ebdd8ac1, accessed March 24, 2019; Felicia Sonmez, "Jimmy Carter Calls on Brian Kemp to Resign as Georgia Secretary of State," *Washington Post*, October 29, 2018, https://www.washingtonpost.com/politics/jimmy-carter-calls -on-brian-kemp-to-resign-as-georgia-secretary-of-state/2018/10 /29/074df8e2-db96-11e8-b732-3c72cbf131f2_story.html?utm_ term=.1f03ce10c6b4, accessed March 25, 2019.

30. Carrie Dan, "Poll: Abrams and Kemp Virtually Tied in Georgia Gubernatorial Race," NBC News, October 24, 2018, https://www

.nbcnews.com/politics/first-read/poll-abrams-kemp-virtually-tied -georgia-gubernatorial-race-n924061, accessed March 24, 2019.

31. Mark Joseph Stern, "Brian Kemp's Bid for Governor Depends on Erasing the Black Vote in Georgia: It's working," *Vox*, August 17, 2018, https://slate.com/news-and-politics/2018/08/georgia-voter -suppression-brian-kemps-bid-for-governor-depends-on-erasing -the-black-vote-its-working.html, accessed April 5, 2019.

32. Bob Moser, "The GOP's Sneakiest Voter Suppression Tactic," *The New Republic*, October 31, 2018, https://newrepublic.com/article /151966/gops-sneakiest-voter-suppression-tactic, accessed March 23, 2019.

33. Igor Derysh, "Voter-suppression shuffle: Officials close only polling site in majority-Latino Kansas town," *Salon*, October 24, 2018, https://www.salon.com/2018/1/24/officials-close-only-polling-site -in-majority-latino-kansas-town/, accessed December 15, 2018.

34. Jamil Smith, "Jamil Smith: How Can African Americans Escape the 'Plantation' If We Can't Vote?" *Rolling Stone*, August 20, 2018, https://www.rollingstone.com/politics/politics-features/republ ican-voter-suppression-713557/, accessed August 20, 2018.

35. "Backlash grows over poll closures in predominantly black Georgia county," CBS News, August 22, 2018, https://www.cbsnews.com /news/backlash-grows-over-poll-closures-in-predominantly-black -georgia-county/, accessed March 23, 2019.

36. Mark Joseph Stern, "Brian Kemp's Bid for Governor Depends on Erasing the Black Vote in Georgia: It's working," *Vox*, August 17, 2018, https://slate.com/news-and-politics/2018/08/georgia-voter -suppression-brian-kemps-bid-for-governor-depends-on-erasing -the-black-vote-its-working.html, accessed April 5, 2019.

37. Jada Haynes, "Randolph County board proposes closing multiple polls: 'No indication' of poll closure proposal before Wednesday," *Albany Herald*, August 16, 2018, https://www.albanyherald.com /news/local/randolph-county-board-proposes-closing-multiple -polls/article_08500c00-76b5-584f-9526-3e6198bffc3a.html, accessed March 23, 2019; U.S. Census, Randolph County, GA,

https://www.census.gov/quickfacts/fact/table/randolphcounty
georgia/PST045217, accessed March 23, 2019.

38. Jamil Smith, "Jamil Smith: How Can African Americans Escape
the 'Plantation' If We Can't Vote?" *Rolling Stone*, August 20, 2018,
https://www.rollingstone.com/politics/politics-features/republi
can-voter-suppression-713557/, accessed August 20, 2018.

39. "ACLU of Georgia Demands Randolph County Board of Elections
and Registration Reject Proposal to Close More Than 75% of
Polling Places in Majority African-American Communities,"
August 14, 2018, https://www.acluga.org/en/press-releases/aclu
-georgia-demands-randolph-county-board-elections-and-registra
tion-reject-0, accessed March 28, 2019; Victor Blackwell, Devon M.
Sayers and Pamela Kirkland, "Election board takes less than a
minute to reject proposal to close 7 of 9 polling places in majority-
black county," CNN.com, August 24, 2018, https://www.cnn.com
/2018/08/24/us/randolph-county-polling-closures-vote/index
.htm, accessed March 23, 2019.

40. Bob Moser, "The GOP's Sneakiest Voter Suppression Tactic," *The
New Republic*, October 31, 2018, https://newrepublic.com/article
/151966/gops-sneakiest-voter-suppression-tactic, accessed March 23,
2019.

41. Igor Derysh, "Voter-suppression shuffle: Officials close only
polling site in majority-Latino Kansas town," *Salon*, October 24,
2018, https://www.salon.com/2018/1/24/officials-close-only-polling
-site-in-majority-latino-kansas-town/, accessed December 15, 2018.

42. David Remnick, "The Midterm Elections Are a Referendum on
Donald Trump," *The New Yorker*, November 5, 2018, https://www
.newyorker.com/magazine/2018/11/05/the-midterm-elections
-are-a-referendum-on-donald-trump, accessed March 28, 2019;
Steve Benen, "Paul Ryan Warns that if Dems win, they'll hold
Trump Accountable," MSNBC, May 3, 2018, http://www.msnbc
.com/rachel-maddow-show/paul-ryan-warns-if-dems-win-theyll
-hold-trump-accountable, accessed March 28, 2019; Karl Evers-
Hillstrom, "Midterms: Gun control groups outspend NRA and

other gun rights rivals," OpenSecrets.org, October 26, 2018, https://www.opensecrets.org/news/2018/10/2018-gun-control -outspends-nra-rights/, accessed March 28, 2019; Kristina Monllos, "2-page Ad in the New York Times Calls out NRA-backed Members of Congress," *Ad Week*, February 21, 2018, https://www.adweek .com/brand-marketing/2-page-ad-in-the-new-york-times-calls-out -nra-backed-members-of-congress/, accessed March 28, 2019; Jason Mark, "The Climate-Wrecking Industry . . . and How to Beat It," *The Nation*, August 30, 2018, https://www.thenation.com /article/the-climate-wrecking-industry-and-how-to-beat-it/, accessed April 2, 2019; Alexander Tucciarone, press release, "New Report: Corruption Fuels the Student Loan Debt Crisis," Roosevelt Institute, June 26, 2018 http://rooseveltinstitute.org/corruption-fuels-student -loan-debt-crisis/, accessed April 2, 2019.

43. Jonathan Shorman, "Judge troubled by clerk's 'LOL' remark, but won't order another Dodge City polling site," *The Wichita Eagle*, November 1, 2018, https://www.kansas.com/news/politics-govern ment/article220998870.html, accessed March 28, 2019.

44. Roxana Hegeman, "New Voters Get Notices Listing Wrong Dodge City Polling Site," *AP News*, October 26, 2018, https://www.hppr .org/post/new-voters-get-notices-listing-wrong-dodge-city-polling -site, accessed December 15, 2018.

45. Matt Pearce, "Buses, carpools stay idle in Dodge City as vote-suppression fears fail to materialize," *Los Angeles Times*, November 6, 2018, https://www.latimes.com/politics/la-na-pol -midterm-election-day-updates-get-out-the-vote-buses-carpools -stay-1541535299-htmlstory.html, accessed December 15, 2018; Katie Moore, "Ford County sees slight uptick in voter turnout," *Dodge City Daily Globe*, November 15, 2018, https://dodgeglobe .com/news/20181115/ford-county-sees-slight-uptick-in-voter -turnout, accessed December 15, 2018; "Kris Kobach is the G.O.P. at Its Worst," *New York Times*, August 8, 2018, https://www.nyti mes.com/2018/08/08/opinion/editorials/kris-kobach-kansas -gop-primary.html, accessed March 28, 2019.

46. Matt Pearce, "Buses, carpools stay idle in Dodge City as vote-suppression fears fail to materialize," *Los Angeles Times*, November 6, 2018, https://www.latimes.com/politics/la-na-pol -midterm-election-day-updates-get-out-the-vote-buses-carpools -stay-1541535299-htmlstory.html, accessed December 15, 2018; "Volunteers Flock to Dodge City to Give Election Day Rides," *US News and World Report*, November 6, 2018, https://www.usnews .com/news/best-states/kansas/articles/2018-11-06/volunteers -flock-to-dodge-city-to-give-election-day-rides, accessed December 15, 2018.

47. Roxana Hegeman, "ACLU sues Dodge City over voting access for Hispanics," *AP News*, October 26, 2018, https://www.apnews.com /a30208bd208a45fba85f3c89771ac216, accessed March 28, 2019.

48. Roxana Hegeman, "ACLU sues Dodge City over voting access for Hispanics," *AP News*, October 26, 2018, https://www.apnews .com/a30208bd208a45fba85f3c89771ac216, accessed March 28, 2019; Daniel Mortiz-Rabson, "Kansas Election Official Writes 'LOL' After ACLU Seeks to Publicize Information About Voter Help Line," *Newsweek*, November 2, 2018, https://www.newsweek .com/kansas-election-official-lol-aclu-voting-help-line-1199849, accessed March 28, 2019.

49. Roxana Hegeman, "ACLU sues Dodge City over voting access for Hispanics," *AP News*, October 26, 2018, https://www.apnews .com/a30208bd208a45fba85f3c89771ac216, accessed March 28, 2019; Roxana Hegeman, "Dodge City clerk turns to hired legal gun in election fight," *AP News*, November 23, 2018, https://www.apnews .com/77cc6cd0f1254d2eb0ef0bbed751c247, accessed December 15, 2018; Matt Pearce, "Buses, carpools stay idle in Dodge City as vote-suppression fears fail to materialize," *Los Angeles Times*, November 6, 2018, https://www.latimes.com/politics/la-na-pol -midterm-election-day-updates-get-out-the-vote-buses-carpools -stay-1541535299-htmlstory.html, accessed December 15, 2018.

50. Shirley Christian, "Hispanic Workers Revitalize a Town," *New York Times*, January 29, 1998, https://www.nytimes.com/1998

/01/29/us/hispanic-workers-revitalize-a-town.html, accessed March 28, 2019; James Fallows, "The Story of Ernestor," *The Atlantic*, July 2016, https://www.theatlantic.com/national/archive/2016 /07/ernestor-de-la-rosa/489977/, accessed March 28, 2019; Jonathan Shorman, "Concern raised about double voting in Dodge City polling place lawsuit," *Wichita Eagle*, November 1, 2018, https://www.kansas.com/news/politics-government/article22094 2645.html, accessed April 4, 2019; Roxana Hegeman, "Iconic Dodge City moves its only polling place outside town," *AP News*, October 18, 2018, https://www.apnews.com/70e4a2665b0644bf8 84c60c25405c076, accessed April 7, 2019; Nomin Ujiyediin, "Judge: It's Too Late to Open a Second Polling place in Dodge City," KCUR, November 1, 2018, https://www.kcur.org/post /judge-its-too-late-open-second-polling-place-dodge-city#stream/0, accessed December 15, 2018. For color-blind racism see, Eduardo Bonilla-Silva, "The Structure of Racism in Color-Blind, 'Post-Racial' America," *American Behavioral Scientist*, 59, no. 11 (2015), https://doi.org/10.1177/0002764215586826.

51. Jonathan Shorman, "Concern raised about double voting in Dodge City polling place lawsuit," *Wichita Eagle*, November 1, 2018, https://www.kansas.com/news/politics-government/article2209 42645.html, accessed April 4, 2019.

52. *Veasey, et al v. Perry, et al*, No. 14-41127 (October 14, 2014); Richard Fausset, "North Carolina's Gerrymandered Map Won't Be Redrawn for the Midterms," *New York Times*, September 4, 2018, https://www.nytimes.com/2018/09/04/us/court-north-carolina -gerrymandering.html, accessed April 16, 2019.

53. Vann Newkirk II and Adam Harris, "Fighting for the Right to Vote in a Tiny Texas County," *The Atlantic*, November 1, 2018, https://www.theatlantic.com/politics/archive/2018/11/prairie-view -m-students-file-suit-over-voting-hours/574600, accessed December 19, 2018; Michael Barajas, "In the Midterms, Texans Face a 'Panoply of Voter Suppression," *Texas Observer*, November 5, 2018,

https://www.texasobserver.org/in-the-midterms-texans-face-a
-panoply-of-voter-suppression/, accessed December 19, 2018.

54. Vann Newkirk II and Adam Harris, "Fighting for the Right to
Vote in a Tiny Texas County," *The Atlantic*, November 1, 2018,
https://www.theatlantic.com/politics/archive/2018/11/prairie
-view-m-students-file-suit-over-voting-hours/574600, accessed
December 19, 2018; Michael Barajas, "On Election Day, Students
Rally for Voting Rights at Texas' Oldest HBCU," *Texas Observer*,
November 6, 2018, https://www.texasobserver.org/on-election-day
-students-rally-for-voting-rights-at-texas-oldest-hbcu/, accessed
December 19, 2018; *Symm v. U.S*, 439 U.S. 1105 (1979).

55. Michael Barajas, "On Election Day, Students Rally for Voting
Rights at Texas' Oldest HBCU," *Texas Observer*, November 6, 2018,
https://www.texasobserver.org/on-election-day-students-rally-for
-voting-rights-at-texas-oldest-hbcu/, accessed December 19, 2018.

56. Vann Newkirk II and Adam Harris, "Fighting for the Right to Vote
in a Tiny Texas County," *The Atlantic*, November 1, 2018, https://
www.theatlantic.com/politics/archive/2018/11/prairie-view-m
-students-file-suit-over-voting-hours/574600, accessed December 19,
2018.

57. Also see Alabama A&M and Oakwood University, Sherrilyn Ifill to
Linda Hairston, letter, November 2, 2018, https://www.scribd.com
/document/392226502/NAACP-Letter, accessed April 4, 2019.

58. Kia Morgan-Smith, "Prairie View students demand to be counted,
file federal lawsuit to prevent voter suppression," *The Grio*,
October 25, 2018, https://thegrio.com/2018/10/25/prairie-view
-voter-suppression-lawsuit/, accessed December 19, 2018; Amber
Phillips, "Ted Cruz built a brand on being the most hated man in
Washington. Now what? *Washington Post*, May 10, 2016, https://
www.washingtonpost.com/news/the-fix/wp/2016/05/10/ted-cruzs
-dilemma-should-he-stay-the-guy-washington-loves-to-hate/?utm
_term=.291fa83ed667, accessed April 4, 2019; Jake Richardson,
"Election 2018: How Much Money Did Texas Senate Candidate

Beto O'Rourke Raise In Campaign Contributions?" *International Business Times*, November 9, 2018, https://www.ibtimes.com /election-2018-how-much-money-did-texas-senate-candidate-beto -orourke-raise-campaign-2730967, accessed April 4, 2019; Matt Zdun, "Ted Cruz's lead over Beto O'Rourke narrows to 3.6, UT-Tyler poll says," *Texas Tribune*, October 31, 2018, https://www .texastribune.org/2018/10/31/ted-cruz-beto-orourke-poll-uttyler -texas/, accessed April 4, 2019.

59. Alex Ura, "Prairie View A&M students sue Waller County over early voting sites," *Texas Tribune*, October 22, 2018, https://www .texastribune.org/2018/10/22/prairie-view-m-students-sue-waller -county-over-early-voting-sites/, accessed December 19, 2018.

60. Michael Barajas, "On Election Day, Students Rally for Voting Rights at Texas' Oldest HBCU," *Texas Observer*, November 6, 2018, https://www.texasobserver.org/on-election-day-students-rally-for -voting-rights-at-texas-oldest-hbcu/, accessed December 19, 2018; "Prairie View A&M students sue Texas county, allege voter suppression of black citizens," NBC News, October 24, 2018, https://www .nbcnews.com/news/nbcblk/prairie-view-m-students-sue-texa -county-allege-voter-suppression-n924141, accessed December 19, 2018.

61. Brianna Stone, "Election is Over, but Prairie View A&M students' voter-suppression suit goes on," *Dallas News*, November 9, 2018, https://www.dallasnews.com/news/2018-elections/2018/11/09 /prairie-view-am-voter-suppression-lawsuit-still-pending-after -election-day/, accessed December 19, 2018.

62. Alex Ura, "Prairie View A&M students sue Waller County over early voting sites," *Texas Tribune*, October 22, 2018, https://www .texastribune.org/2018/10/22/prairie-view-m-students-sue-waller -county-over-early-voting-sites/, accessed December 19, 2018.

63. Alex Ura, "Prairie View A&M students sue Waller County over early voting sites," *Texas Tribune*, October 22, 2018, https://www .texastribune.org/2018/10/22/prairie-view-m-students-sue-waller -county-over-early-voting-sites/, accessed December 19, 2018.

64. Brianna Stone, "Election is over but Prairie View A&M students' voter suppression suit goes on," *Dallas News*, November 9, 2018, https://www.dallasnews.com/news/2018-elections/2018/11/09/prairie-view-am-voter-suppression-lawsuit-still-pending-after-election-day/, accessed December 19, 2018.

65. Kira Lerner, "States purged 16 million voters from the rolls before the 2016 election: Voter purges disproportionately affect low-income and minority voters," *Think Progress*, July 20, 2018, https://thinkprogress.org/states-purged-16-million-voters-from-the-rolls-before-the-2016-election-1c5688dcaad7/, accessed April 5, 2019.

66. Greg Bluestein, "AJC poll shows a deeply divided Georgia and tough numbers for Kemp," *Atlanta Journal-Constitution*, January 18, 2019, https://www.ajc.com/news/state—regional-govt—politics/ajc-poll-shows-deeply-divided-georgia-and-tough-numbers-for-kemp/8dqIoXplj5o0kujop427PN/, accessed April 5, 2019.

67. Rebekah Barber, "Is Georgia's Secretary of State Unjustly Targeting Voting Rights Activists Again?" *Facing South*, October 4, 2017, www.facingsouth.org/2017/10/georgias-secretary-state-unjustly-targeting-voting-rights-activist-again, accessed March 5, 2018; Spencer Woodman, "Register Minority Voters in Georgia, Go to Jail," *New Republic*, May 5, 2015, newrepublic.com/article/121715/Georgia-secretary-state-hammers-minority-voter-registration-efforts, accessed March 15, 2018.

68. Khushbu Shah, "'Textbook voter suppression': Georgia's bitter election a battle years in the making," *The Guardian*, November 10, 2018, https://www.theguardian.com/us-news/2018/nov/10/georgia-election-recount-stacey-abrams-brian-kemp, accessed December 25, 2018.

69. *Finding Justice: Voter Suppression*, documentary, executive producers Dwayne Johnson, Dany Garcia, and dream hampton, BET, aired March 29, 2019.

70. Vann Newkirk II, "In the Georgia Governor's Race, the Game Is Black Votes," *The Atlantic*, October 12, 2018, https://www.theatlantic.com/politics/archive/2018/10/georgia-race-mired

-minority-vote-suppression-charges/572854/, accessed April 5, 2019.

71. Jonathan Brater and Rebecca Ayala, "What's the Matter with Georgia?" Brennan Center, October 12, 2018, https://www.brennancenter.org/blog/whats-matter-georgia, accessed November 4, 2018.

72. Khushbu Shah, "'Textbook voter suppression': Georgia's bitter election a battle years in the making," *The Guardian*, November 10, 2018, https://www.theguardian.com/us-news/2018/nov/10/georgia-election-recount-stacey-abrams-brian-kemp, accessed December 25, 2018.

73. *Finding Justice: Voter Suppression*, documentary, executive producers Dwayne Johnson, Dany Garcia, and dream hampton, BET, aired March 29, 2019.

74. Anne Gearan and Felicia Sonmez, "Trump says Democrat Abrams would turn Georgia into a 'sanctuary city'," *Washington Post*, November 4, 2019, https://www.washingtonpost.com/politics/trump-says-democrat-abrams-would-turn-georgia-into-a-sanctuary-city/2018/11/04/719dd164-deb0-11e8-85df-7a6b4d25cfbb_story.html?utm_term=.053b85af5d3e, accessed April 5, 2019; Amy Gardner, "GOP claims of voter fraud threat fuel worries about ballot access in November," *Washington Post*, October 13, 2018, https://www.washingtonpost.com/politics/crackdowns-on-potential-voter-fraud-fuel-worries-about-ballot-access-in-november/2018/10/13/764db388-c0cd-11e8-be77-516336a26305_story.html?utm_term=.214b46f1f474, accessed April 5, 2019; Ben Nadler, "AP FACT CHECK: Kemp wrong on Abrams comments," *AP News*, October 25, 2018, https://www.apnews.com/dedaa5c71f654f9e86d78d31fc3ce1d8, accessed April 9, 2019. Madeleine Aggeler, "The Undeniable Awfulness of Stacey Abrams' Opponent Brian Kemp," *The Cut*, October 23, 2018, https://www.thecut.com/2018/10/brian-kemp-georgia-governor-race-voter-suppression.html, accessed April 6, 2019; *Finding Justice: Voter Suppression*, documentary, executive producers Dwayne Johnson, Dany Garcia, and dream hampton, BET, aired March 29, 2019.

75. Madeleine Aggeler, "The Undeniable Awfulness of Stacey Abrams' Opponent Brian Kemp," *The Cut*, October 23, 2018, https://www.thecut.com/2018/10/brian-kemp-georgia-governor-race-voter-suppression.html, accessed April 6, 2019; Curt Devine and Drew Griffin, "6 million Georgia voters' records exposed: 'Could have easily been compromised'," CNN.com, August 14, 2018, https://www.cnn.com/2018/08/14/politics/georgia-brian-kemp-voter-data/index.html, accessed April 5, 2019; Richard Elliot, "Investment company sues Brian Kemp over $500K loan," *Atlanta Journal-Constitution*, June 12, 2018, https://www.ajc.com/news/local/investment-company-sues-brian-kemp-over-500k-loan/ynD1uG eLpQ2m3NViHpXVjI/, accessed April 5, 2019.

76. Ben Nadler, "Voting Rights Become a Flashpoint in Georgia Governor's Race," *AP News*, October 9, 2018, https://www.apnews.com/fb011f39af3b40518b572c8cce6e906c, accessed April 5, 2019.

77. "Voting in Mississippi," https://ballotpedia.org/Voting_in_ Mississippi, accessed April 7, 2019; Vann Newkirk II, "What's Missing From Reports on Alabama's Black Turnout," *The Atlantic*, December 7, 2017, https://www.theatlantic.com/politics/archive/2017/12/can-doug-jones-get-enough-black-voters-to-win/547574/, accessed April 7, 2019, "New York Allow for No-Excuse Absentee Voting Amendment (2021)," https://ballotpedia.org/New_York _Allow_for_No-Excuse_Absentee_Voting_Amendment_(2021), accessed April 7, 2019.

78. Bill Barrow, "In Georgia, claims of vote suppression and publicity stunts," *AP News*, October 14, 2018, https://apnews.com/56239d 657f1445dd8bf958b9acfa75bd, accessed April 6, 2019; Ben Nadler, "Georgia Republican candidate for governor puts 53,000 voter registrations on hold," *USA Today*, October 11, 2018, https://www.usatoday.com/story/news/politics/elections/2018/10/11/georgia-republican-candidate-brian-kemp-puts-53-000 -voter-registrations-hold/1608507002/, accessed April 6, 2019.

79. Brentin Mock, "Where Voter Suppression Hits Hardest in Georgia," *City Lab*, October 18, 2018, https://www.citylab.com

/equity/2018/10/where-voters-color-are-suppressed-hardest
-georgia/573367/, accessed December 28, 2018.

80. Bill Barrow, "In Georgia, claims of vote suppression and publicity
stunts," *AP News*, October 14, 2018, https://apnews.com/56239d
657f1445dd8bf958b9acfa75bd, accessed April 6, 2019.

81. Ciara Cummings, "County says misunderstanding, Black Voters
Matter says suppression," October 17, 2018, WRDW, https://www
.wrdw.com/content/news/Black-seniors-headed-to-vote-kicked
-off-Black-Voters-Matter-bus-497738561.html, accessed April 8,
2019.

82. For the impact of face-to-face get out the vote strategies, see, Todd
Rogers, Craig R. Fox, and Alan S. Gerber, "Why People Vote:
Voting as Dynamic Social Expression" for *The Behavioral
Foundations of Policy*, edited by Eldar Shafir, https://www.inn
ovations.harvard.edu/sites/default/files/rethinking.pdf, accessed
April 9, 2019.

83. *Finding Justice: Voter Suppression*, documentary, executive
producers Dwayne Johnson, Dany Garcia, and dream hampton,
BET, aired March 29, 2019.

84. Mark Niesse, "Black senior citizens ordered off Georgia bus taking
them to vote," *Atlanta Journal-Constitution*, October 16, 2018,
https://www.ajc.com/news/state-regional-govt-politics/black
-senior-citizens-ordered-off-georgia-bus-take-them-vote/42lZxI
GOFluFo637TEc9jp, accessed April 8, 2019.

85. Ciara Cummings, "County says misunderstanding, Black Voters
Matter says suppression," October 17, 2018, WRDW, https://www
.wrdw.com/content/news/Black-seniors-headed-to-vote-kicked
-off-Black-Voters-Matter-bus-497738561.html, accessed April 8,
2019.

86. Dan MacGuill, "Did Officials in Georgia Stop a Bus Filled with
Black Seniors Going to Vote?" *Snopes*, October 22, 2018, https://
www.snopes.com/fact-check/georgia-black-voters-bus/, accessed
April 9, 2019.

87. *Finding Justice: Voter Suppression*, documentary, executive producers Dwayne Johnson, Dany Garcia, and dream hampton, BET, aired March 29, 2019.

88. Dan MacGuill, "Did Officials in Georgia Stop a Bus Filled with Black Seniors Going to Vote?" *Snopes*, October 22, 2018, https://www.snopes.com/fact-check/georgia-black-voters-bus/, accessed April 9, 2019.

89. *Finding Justice: Voter Suppression*, documentary, executive producers Dwayne Johnson, Dany Garcia, and dream hampton, BET, aired March 29, 2019.

90. Ciara Cummings, "County says misunderstanding, Black Voters Matter says suppression," October 17, 2018, WRDW, https://www.wrdw.com/content/news/Black-seniors-headed-to-vote-kicked-off-Black-Voters-Matter-bus-497738561.html, accessed April 8, 2019.

91. Ciara Cummings, "County says misunderstanding, Black Voters Matter says suppression," October 17, 2018, WRDW, https://www.wrdw.com/content/news/Black-seniors-headed-to-vote-kicked-off-Black-Voters-Matter-bus-497738561.html, accessed April 8, 2019.

92. Dan MacGuill, "Did Officials in Georgia Stop a Bus Filled with Black Seniors Going to Vote?" *Snopes*, October 22, 2018, https://www.snopes.com/fact-check/georgia-black-voters-bus/, accessed April 9, 2019.

93. P.R. Lockhart, "'This is voter suppression': black seniors in Georgia ordered off of bus taking them to vote" *Vox*, October 17, 2018, https://www.vox.com/identities/2018/10/17/17990110/georgia-senior-ciizens-bus-removal-balck-voters-matter-suppression, accessed April 8, 2019

94. Rebecca Tippett, "The North Carolina Electorate: Asian & Hispanic Voters," Carolina Population Center, University of North Carolina-Chapel Hill, November 1, 2016, https://demography.cpc.unc.edu/2016/11/01/the-north-carolina-electorate-asian-hispanic-voters/, accessed April 9, 2019.

95. Louis Jacobson, "Donald Trump's Pants on Fire claim that millions of illegal votes cost him popular vote victory," *Politifact*, November 28, 2016, https://www.politifact.com/truth-o-meter /statements/2016/nov/28/donald-trump/donald-trumps-pants -fire-claim-millions-illegal-vo/, accessed April 10, 2019.

96. Carol Anderson, "Trump consistently lied to Americans in the State of the Union address," *The Guardian*, February 6, 2019, https://www.theguardian.com/commentisfree/2019/feb/06 /trump-consistently-lied-to-americans-in-the-state-of-the-union -address, accessed April 10, 2019; Chris McGreal, "Defiant Trump warns of 'caravans and crime' in last minute push for votes," *The Guardian*, November 6, 2018, https://www.theguardian.com/us -news/2018/nov/06/defiant-donald-trump-warns-of-caravans-and -in-last-minute-push-for-midterm-votes, accessed April 12, 2019.

97. Suzanne Gamboa, "Nearly 500 children are still separated from their migrant parents," NBC News, August 31, 2018, https://www .nbcnews.com/storyline/immigration-border-crisis/nearly-500 -children-are-still-separated-their-migrant-parents-n905461, accessed April 11, 2019.

98. Amanda Holpuch, " 'I live in fear': under Trump, life for America's immigrants can change in a flash," *The Guardian*, October 18, 2018, https://www.theguardian.com/us-news/2018/oct/18/immig ration-ice-deportation-undocumented-trump, accessed April 11, 2019; Samantha Schmidt, "ICE detains a Polish doctor and green-card holder who has lived in the U.S. for nearly 40 years," *Washington Post*, January 22, 2018, https://www.washingtonpost .com/news/morning-mix/wp/2018/01/22/ice-detains-a-polish -doctor-and-green-card-holder-who-has-lived-in-the-u-s-for-nearly -40-years/?utm_term=.f2a66a71dd8c, accessed April 10, 2019.

99. Erin Teachman, "ICE: A Bureaucracy of Terror," *Medium*, May 29, 2018, https://medium.com/@newmethos/ice-a-bureaucr acy-of-terror-52b089f99fc4, accessed April 10, 2019; McKay Coppins, "The Outrage Over Family Separation Is Exactly What Stephen Miller Wants," *The Atlantic*, June 19, 2018, https://www

.theatlantic.com/politics/archive/2018/06/stephen-miller-family -separation/563132/, accessed April 10, 2019.

100. Travis Fain, "Federal subpoenas demand 'tsunami' of NC voter records," WRAL, September 5, 2018, https://www.wral.com /federal-subpoenas-demand-tsunami-of-nc-voter-records /17821061/, accessed April 8, 2019; Alek Kemeny, "ICE's voter registration subpoena could stifle turnout, cause racial profiling, professor says," *Duke Chronicle*, October 3, 2018, https://www .dukechronicle.com/article/2018/10/ices-voter-registration -subpoena-could-stifle-turnout-cause-racial-profiling-professor -says, accessed April 8, 2019; Laura Leslie, "State elections board to challenge federal voter records subpoenas, WRAL, September 7, 2018, https://www.wral.com/state-elections-board -to-challenge-federal-voter-records-subpoena/17826204/, accessed April 8, 2019.

101. Sam Levine and Ryan J. Reilly, "Trump DOJ Official Overseeing Voter Fraud Hunt Subpoenas Millions of Voting Records," *Huffington Post*, September 5, 2019, https://www.huffpost.com /entry/north-carolina-voting-subpoenas_n_5b902f1434b0cf7b0 03c0806, accessed April 8, 2019.

102. Richard Fausset, Alan Blinder, and Michael Wines, "Justice Dept. Demand for North Carolina Voting Records Extended to D.M.V.," *New York Times*, September 7, 2018, https://www .nytimes.com/2018/09/07/us/north-carolina-voting.html, accessed April 8, 2019; Sam Levine and Ryan J. Reilly, "Trump DOJ Official Overseeing Voter Fraud Hunt Subpoenas Millions of Voting Records," *Huffington Post*, September 5, 2019, https://www.huffpost.com/entry/north-carolina-voting-subpoen as_n_5b902f1434b0cf7b003c0806, accessed April 8, 2019.

103. Sam Levine and Ryan J. Reilly, "Trump DOJ Official Overseeing Voter Fraud Hunt Subpoenas Millions of Voting Records," *Huffington Post*, September 5, 2019, https://www.huffpost.com /entry/north-carolina-voting-subpoenas_n_5b902f1434b0cf7b0 03c0806, accessed April 8, 2019.

104. Richard Fausset, Alan Blinder, and Michael Wines, "Justice Dept. Demand for North Carolina Voting Records Extended to D.M.V.," *New York Times*, September 7, 2018, https://www.nytimes.com /2018/09/07/us/north-carolina-voting.html, accessed April 8, 2019

105. Laura Leslie, "State elections board to challenge federal voter records subpoenas," WRAL, September 7, 2018, https://www .wral.com/state-elections-board-to-challenge-federal-voter -records-subpoena/17826204/, accessed April 8, 2019.

106. Molly McKitterick, "ICE's Demand for Millions of NC Voting Records Explained," *Voice of America*, September 10, 2018, https://www.voanews.com/a/ice-s-demand-for-millions-of-nc -voting-records-explained/4565786.html, accessed April 7, 2019; Alek Kemeny, "ICE's voter registration subpoena could stifle turnout, cause racial profiling, professor says," *Duke Chronicle*, October 3, 2018, https://www.dukechronicle.com/article/2018 /10/ices-voter-registration-subpoena-could-stifle-turnout-cause -racial-profiling-professor-says, accessed April 8, 2019; Kevin Miller, "Maine's member of voter fraud panel says it had 'pre- ordained' goal of backing up Trump's claims," *Press Herald*, August 3, 2018, https://www.pressherald.com/2018/08/03 /dunlap-accuses-white-house-of-falsely-implying-widespread -voter-fraud/, accessed April 11, 2019.

107. Jonathan Blitzer, "Jeff Sessions Is Out, But His Dark Vision for Immigration Policy Lives On," New Yorker, November 8, 2018, https://www.newyorker.com/news/news-desk/jeff-sessions-is -out-but-his-dark-vision-for-immigration-policy-lives-on, accessed April 11, 2019.

108. Travis Fain, "Federal subpoenas demand 'tsunami' of NC voter records," WRAL, September 5, 2018, https://www.wral.com /federal-subpoenas-demand-tsunami-of-nc-voter-records/17821061 /, accessed April 8, 2019.

109. Alek Kemeny, "ICE's voter registration subpoena could stifle turnout, cause racial profiling, professor says," *Duke Chronicle*,

October 3, 2018, https://www.dukechronicle.com/article/2018
/10/ices-voter-registration-subpoena-could-stifle-turnout-cause
-racial-profiling-professor-says, accessed April 8, 2019.

110. Paige St. John and Joel Rubin, "ICE held an American man in
custody for 1,273 days. He's not the only one who had to prove his
citizenship," *Los Angeles Times*, September 17, 2018, https://
www.latimes.com/local/lanow/la-me-citizens-ice-20180427
-htmlstory.html, accessed April 11, 2019; Christine Hauser,
"U.S. Citizen Detained by ICE Is Awarded $55,000 Settlement,"
New York Times, October 29, 2018, https://www.nytimes.com
/2018/10/29/us/ice-detains-woman-california.html, accessed
April 11, 2019; David Bier, "U.S. Citizens Targeted by ICE: U.S.
Citizens Targeted by Immigration and Customs Enforcement in
Texas," Cato Institute, August 29, 2018, https://www.cato.org
/publications/immigration-research-policy-brief/us-citizens
-targeted-ice-us-citizens-targeted, accessed April 11, 2019.

111. Alek Kemeny, "ICE's voter registration subpoena could stifle
turnout, cause racial profiling, professor says," *Duke Chronicle*,
October 3, 2018, https://www.dukechronicle.com/article/2018
/10/ices-voter-registration-subpoena-could-stifle-turnout-cause
-racial-profiling-professor-says, accessed April 8, 2019.

112. Laura Leslie, "State elections board to challenge federal voter
records subpoenas," WRAL, September 7, 2018, https://www
.wral.com/state-elections-board-to-challenge-federal-voter
-records-subpoena/17826204/, accessed April 8, 2019.

113. Laura Leslie, "State elections board to challenge federal voter
records subpoenas," WRAL, September 7, 2018, https://www
.wral.com/state-elections-board-to-challenge-federal-voter
-records-subpoena/17826204/, accessed April 8, 2019.

114. Alek Kemeny, "ICE's voter registration subpoena could stifle
turnout, cause racial profiling, professor says," *Duke Chronicle*,
October 3, 2018, https://www.dukechronicle.com/article/2018
/10/ices-voter-registration-subpoena-could-stifle-turnout-cause
-racial-profiling-professor-says, accessed April 8, 2019; Charles

Duncan, "Hurricane Florence was among the costliest disasters on record. Here's NOAA's tally," *Charlotte News Observer*, February 8, 2019, https://www.newsobserver.com/news/state /north-carolina/article225974185.html, accessed April 12, 2019.

115. Richard Fausset, Alan Blinder, Sydney Ember, Timothy Williams, and Serge F. Kovaleski, "North Carolina's 'Guru of Elections': Can-Do Operator Who May Have Done Too Much," *New York Times*, December 8, 2018, https://www.nytimes.com/2018/12 /08/us/politics/north-carolina-election-frau-dowless.amp.html, accessed December 15, 2018.

116. Doug Bock Clark, "The Tearful Drama of North Carolina's Election-Fraud Hearings: How Mark Harris, a prominent Republican pastor in Charlotte, lost his way in the Ninth Congressional District," *New Yorker*, February 24, 2019, https:// www.newyorker.com/news/dispatch/the-tearful-drama-of-north -carolinas-election-fraud-hearings, accessed March 7, 2019; Nathaniel Rakich, "What Comes Next in that Contested Election in North Carolina," *FiveThirtyEight*, December 13, 2018, https:// fivethirtyeight.com/features/the-fight-over-election-fraud-in -north-carolina-could-drag-on-for-months/, accessed December 22, 2018; Chris Cillizza, "There's something VERY fishing going on in North Carolina," CNN.com, December 4, 2018, https://www .cnn.com/2018/12/04/politics/north-carolina-9-absentee-voting -fraud-investigation/index.html, accessed January 2, 2019.

117. Drew Griffin, "NC-9 scandal: More than a thousand absentee ballots possibly destroyed," WTHI-TV, December 6, 2018, https://www.wthitv.com/content/national/502035622.html, accessed January 2, 2019.

118. Doug Bock Clark, "The Tearful Drama of North Carolina's Election-Fraud Hearings: How Mark Harris, a prominent Republican pastor in Charlotte, lost his way in the Ninth Congressional District," *New Yorker*, February 24, 2019, https://

www.newyorker.com/news/dispatch/the-tearful-drama-of-north
-carolinas-election-fraud-hearings, accessed March 7, 2019.

119. Chris Kromm, "N.C. GOP blamed black group for absentee ballot
scheme led by GOP operative," *Facing South*, December 21, 2018,
https://www.facingsouth.org/2018/12/nc-gop-blamed-black-group
-absentee-ballot-scheme-led-gop-operative, accessed January 2,
2019.

120. Chris Kromm, "N.C. GOP blamed black group for absentee
ballot scheme led by GOP operative," *Facing South*, December 21,
2018, https://www.facingsouth.org/2018/12/nc-gop-blamed
-black-group-absentee-ballot-scheme-led-gop-operative, accessed
January 2, 2019.

121. Chris Kromm, "N.C. GOP blamed black group for absentee
ballot scheme led by GOP operative," *Facing South*, December 21,
2018, https://www.facingsouth.org/2018/12/nc-gop-blamed
-black-group-absentee-ballot-scheme-led-gop-operative, accessed
January 2, 2019.

122. Michael Biesecker and Gary D. Robertson, "North Carolina official had asked feds to act in voting case," *AP News*, December 21,
2018, https://apnews.com/73c059acc31e4047a89cc0d1a8ce8710,
accessed December 21, 2018.

123. Amy Gardner and Beth Reinhard, "N.C. election board's warnings to local and federal prosecutors about alleged election fraud
drew little action," *Washington Post*, December 21, 2018, https://
www.washingtonpost.com/politics/nc-election-officials-sounded
-alarm-about-alleged-election-fraud-to-federal-prosecutors-in-janu
ary-2017/2018/12/21/240e09a0-0539-11e9-b5df-5d3874f1ac36
_story.html?utm_term=.8d671le15bee, accessed December 21,
2018.

124. Richard Fausset, Alan Blinder, Sydney Ember, Timothy
Williams, and Serge F. Kovaleski, "North Carolina's 'Guru of
Elections': Can-Do Operator Who May Have Done Too Much,"
New York Times, December 8, 2018, https://www.nytimes.com

/2018/12/08/us/politics/north-carolina-election-frau-dowless
.amp.html, accessed December 15, 2018.

125. Sam Levine, "North Carolina Election Board Finds Evidence of
Significant Fraud to Help GOP Candidate," *Huffington Post*,
February 18, 2019, https://www.huffpost.com/entry/north-carol
ina-election-fraud-evidence_n_5c6ae122e4b01757c36e79ae,
accessed February 18, 2019; Amanda Lamb, "Woman who collected
absentee ballots in 9th Congressional District race says she feels
duped," WRAL, December 4, 2018, https://www.wral.com
/woman-who-collected-absentee-ballots-in-9th-congressional
-district-says-she-feels-duped/18040395/, accessed January 2,
2019; Kevin Morris and Myrna Pérez, "North Carolina's Election
Fiasco is About Voter Suppression, Not Voter Fraud," Brennan
Center, December 6, 2018, https://www.brennancenter.org/blog
/north-carolinas-election-fiasco-about-voter-suppression-not
-voter-fraud, accessed December 16, 2018; Dylan Scott, "What
we know about the alleged election fraud plot in North Carolina,"
Vox, December 8, 2018, https://www.vox.com/policy-and-politics
/2018/12/7/18128973/north-caorlina-9th-district-voter-election
-fraud-mccrae-dowless, accessed January 2, 2019; Erin Durkin,
"North Carolina election still undecided amid absentee ballot
fraud inquiry," *The Guardian*, December 5, 2018, https://www
.theguardian.com/us-news/2018/dec/05/north-carolina-election
-still-undecided-amid-absentee-ballot-inquiry, accessed January 2,
2019.

126. "North Carolina man implicated in voting fraud scheme turns in
hundreds of absentee ballots," ABC News, December 5, 2018,
https://www.abcactionnews.com/news/national/north-carolina
-man-implicated-in-voting-fraud-scheme-turns-in-hundreds-of
-absentee-ballots, accessed January 2, 2019; Chris Cillizza,
"There's something VERY fishy going on in North Carolina,"
CNN.com, December 4, 2018, https://www.cnn.com/2018/12
/04/politics/north-carolina-9-absentee-voting-fraud-investi
gation/index.html, accessed January 2, 2019.

127. Erin Durkin, "North Carolina election still undecided amid absentee ballot fraud inquiry," *The Guardian*, December 5, 2018, https://www.theguardian.com/us-news/2018/dec/05/north-caro lina-election-still-undecided-amid-absentee-ballot-inquiry, accessed January 2, 2019.

128. Paul Specht, "NC GOP misleads about NC election fraud investigation," *Politifact*, December 4, 2018, https://www.politifact.com /north-carolina/statements/2018/dec/04/north-carolina-repub lican-party/nc-gop-misleads-about-nc-election-fraud-investigat/, accessed January 2, 2019.

129. Sasha Ingber, "Amid Fraud Allegations, North Carolina Election Board Won't Certify House Race," *NPR*, December 1, 2018, https://www.npr.org/2018/12/01/672531061/amid-fraud-allega tions-state-election-board-wont-certify-north-carolina-house-ra, accessed January 2, 2019.

130. "Documents detail how absentee ballots gathered in NC vote," *AP News*, December 23, 2018, https://www.apnews.com/ab20c 7bd12464a4383abfdc2bd88ca92, accessed December 23, 2018.

131. Drew Griffin, "NC-9 scandal: More than a thousand absentee ballots possibly destroyed," WTHI-TV, December 6, 2018, https://www.wthitv.com/content/national/502035622.html, accessed January 2, 2019.

132. "The North Carolina midterm debacle shows us where the real threat to elections lies," *Washington Post*, December 3, 2018, https://www.washingtonpost.com/opinions/an-honest-vote-in -north-carolinas-9th-congressional-district-were-not-so-sure/2018 /12/03/ff211a9a-f734-11e8-863c-9e2f864d47e7_story.html?utm _term=.87e9e01e2b7f, accessed January 2, 2019.

133. Pema Levy, "Republicans Finally Have an Election Fraud Scandal. And None of Them Want to Talk About It," *Mother Jones*, December 4, 2018, https://www.motherjones.com/politics/2018 /12/republicans-finally-have-a-voter-fraud-scandal-and-none-of -them-want-to-talk-about-it/, accessed January 2, 2019; Carol Anderson, "Our Democracy is Being Stolen. Guess Who the

Thieves Are," *New York Times*, March 14, 2019, https://www
.nytimes.com/2019/03/14/opinion/voting-fraud-north-carolina
.html, accessed March 14, 2019.

134. Paul Specht, "NC GOP misleads about NC election fraud investigation," *Politifact*, December 4, 2018, https://www.politifact.com
/north-carolina/statements/2018/dec/04/north-carolina-republi
can-party/nc-gop-misleads-about-nc-election-fraud-investigat/,
accessed January 2, 2019.

135. Eli Rosenberg, "The shoe-leather reporting boosting North
Carolina's explosive election fraud investigation," *Washington Post*,
December 5, 2018, https://www.washingtonpost.com/politics
/2018/12/05/shoe-leather-reporting-boosting-north-carolinas
-explosive-election-fraud-investigation/?utm_term=.635fc353
abd8, accessed January 2, 2019.

136. Erin Durkin, "North Carolina election still undecided amid
absentee ballot fraud inquiry," *The Guardian*, December 5, 2018,
https://www.theguardian.com/us-news/2018/dec/05/north
-carolina-election-still-undecided-amid-absentee-ballot-inquiry,
accessed January 2, 2019.

137. Matthew Burns, "Filled with bombshell revelations, 9th District
hearing ends with new election," WRAL, February 21, 2019,
https://www.wral.com/filled-with-bombshell-revelations-9th
-district-hearing-ends-with-new-election/18200098/, accessed
April 14, 2019; Laura Barrón-López, "N.C. elections board orders
new race in disputed House district," *Politico*, February 21, 2019,
https://www.politico.com/story/2019/02/21/north-carolina
-election-mark-harris-documents-1197404, accessed February 21,
2019; Amy Gardner, "Candidate's son warned father of N.C.
political operative's alleged tactics," *Washington Post*, February 20,
2019, https://www.washingtonpost.com/politics/candidates-son
-warned-father-of-nc-political-operatives-tactics/2019/02/20/a1fb
fecc-3521-11e9-a400-e481bf264fdc_story.html?utm_term=.
1693de5e6e37, accessed April 14, 2019.

138. Laura Barrón-López, "Mark Harris says he won't run in North Carolina election do-over," *Politico*, February 26, 2019, https://www.politico.com/story/2019/02/26/mark-harris-says-he-wont-run-in-north-carolina-election-do-over-1188036, accessed April 14, 2019; Amy Gardner and John Wagner, "N.C. political operative indicted, and prosecutor signals that more charges are likely," *Washington Post*, February 23, 2019, https://www.washington post.com/politics/north-carolina-political-operative-indicted-in-election-fraud-case-that-upended-congressional-race/2019/02/27/b0d5f004-3aaf-11e9-aaae-69364b2ed137_story.html?utm_term=.44fa50f7003d, accessed March 13, 2019.

139. Tamar Hallerman and Mark Niesse, "Feds to give Georgia $10 million to upgrade outdated voting machines," *Atlanta Journal-Constitution*, March 29, 2018, https://www.ajc.com/news/state—regional-govt—politics/feds-give-georgia-million-upgrade-outdated-voting-machines/B8IbGwxNJxtPFloEXn4aIL/, accessed February 2, 2019; J. Peter Bruzzese, "Microsoft to end support for Windows 2000, XP SP2 July 13: Windows XP users can extend support at no cost by upgrading to SP3, but Windows 2000 users have no such option," *InfoWorld*, May 10, 2010, https://www.infoworld.com/article/2626857/microsoft-to-end-support-for-windows-2000—xp-sp2-july-13.html, accessed February 2, 2019.

140. Carol Anderson, "Brian Kemp, Enemy of Democracy," *New York Times*, August 11, 2018, https://www.nytimes.com/2018/08/11/opinion/sunday/brian-kemp-enemy-of-democracy.html, accessed April 14, 2019.

141. Portions of this section reprinted from Anderson, "Brian Kemp, Enemy of Democracy."

142. Richard DeMillo, "Georgia's Election System Can't Be Trusted: Under attack from outside, and undermined from within," *Bloomberg*, December 18, 2017, https://www.bloomberg.com/opinion/articles/2017-12-18/georgia-s-election-system-can-t-be-trusted, accessed August 10, 2018.

143. Jeremy Stahl, "Incompetence or a Cover-Up? Georgia destroyed election data right after a lawsuit alleged its voting system might have been hacked," *Slate*, October 27, 2017, https://slate.com /technology/2017/10/georgia-destroyed-election-data-right -after-a-lawsuit-alleged-the-system-was-vulnerable.html, accessed August 10, 2018

144. Phil Bolton, "KSU's 'Year of Russia' Has Guarded View of Improved U.S.-Russian Relations," *Global Atlanta*, March 18, 2017, https://www.globalatlanta.com/ksus-year-russia-guarded -view-improved-u-s-russian-relations/, accessed August 10, 2018.

145. James Salzer, "Kemp's office concludes election data not lost in server wipe," *Atlanta Journal-Constitution*, October 31, 2017, https://www.ajc.com/news/state—regional-govt—politics/kemp -office-concludes-election-data-not-lost-server-wipe/KRXneAW bc5ck43B7aSKYnN/?icmp=np_inform_variation-control, accessed August 10, 2018.

146. Arielle Kass, "Thousands of provisional ballots remain uncounted in Fulton County," *Atlanta Journal-Constitution*, November 7, 2018, https://www.ajc.com/news/local-govt—politics/thousands -provisional-ballots-remain-uncounted-fulton-county/XJHEhx b3AZNdqh45Slh4SN/, accessed December 25, 2018.

147. William Brent Ney to Cheryl Ringer, letter, December 21, 2017 (letter in author's possession).

148. Arielle Kass, "Thousands of provisional ballots remain uncounted in Fulton County," *Atlanta Journal-Constitution*, November 7, 2018, https://www.ajc.com/news/local-govt—politics /thousands-provisional-ballots-remain-uncounted-fulton-county /XJHEhxb3AZNdqh45Slh4SN/, accessed December 25, 2018.

149. Charles P. Pierce, "Brian Kemp's Election Ratf*cking 101: Lock Up the Voting Machines!" *Esquire*, November 8, 2018, https:// www.esquire.com/news-politics/politics/a24847675/geroge -election-voting-machines/, accessed February 2, 2019.

150. Cyrus Farivar, "Judge to Georgia voting officials: You're terrible at digital security," *ARS Technica*, September 18, 2018,

https://arstechnica.com/tech-policy/2018/09/georgias -electronic-voting-system-will-remain-for-now-judge-rules/, accessed April 14, 2019.

151. Johnny Kauffman, "Georgia Set to Vote Using 'Vulnerable' Machines Despite Federal Cash Boost," WABE, April 6, 2018, https://www.wabe.org/georgia-set-vote-using-vulnerable-machi nes-despite-federal-cash-boost/, accessed February 2, 2019.

152. Pema Levy, "Equipment Malfunctions and Voting Machine Shortages Bring Long Lines in Georgia," *Mother Jones*, November 6, 2018, https://www.motherjones.com/politics/2018 /11/equipment-malfunctions-and-voting-machine-shortages -bring-long-lines-in-georgia/, accessed December 19, 2018.

153. P.R. Lockhart, "Voting hours in parts of Georgia extended after technical errors create long lines," *Vox*, November 6, 2018, https://www.vox.com/policy-and-politics/2018/11/6/18068492 /georgia-voting-gwinnett-fulton-county-machine-problems-mid term-election-extension, accessed December 25, 2018.

154. David Gilmour, "Long delays and broken machines plague voters in Georgia: Many people left without casting a ballot after waiting hours," *The Daily Dot*, November 6, 2018, https://www.dailydot .com/layer8/georgia-election-2018-midterms-technical -problems/, accessed December 19, 2018.

155. P.R. Lockhart, "Voting hours in parts of Georgia extended after technical errors create long lines," *Vox*, November 6, 2018, https://www.vox.com/policy-and-politics/2018/11/6/18068492 /georgia-voting-gwinnett-fulton-county-machine-problems -midterm-election-extension, accessed December 25, 2018.

156. Audrey Washington and Tom Regan, "Long lines, voting issues reported at several polling places in metro Atlanta," WSB-TV, November 7, 2018, https://www.wsbtv.com/news/local/long-lines -voting-issues-reported-at-polling-places-across-metro-atlanta /867629575, accessed December 25, 2018.

157. Arielle Kass, "Thousands of provisional ballots remain uncounted in Fulton County," *Atlanta Journal-Constitution*, November 7,

2018, https://www.ajc.com/news/local-govt—politics/thousands-prov
isional-ballots-remain-uncounted-fulton-county/XJHEhxb
3AZNdqh45Slh4SN/, accessed December 25, 2018; Alan Judd,
"Did voting problems influence outcome in Georgia election?"
Atlanta Journal-Constitution, November 9, 2018, https://www
.ajc.com/news/scattered-problems-emerge-georgia-voting
/oQxJq2DOKu8o32pd0mvAxN/, accessed December 25, 2018;
AJC staff, "Live Voting Updates: Polls are closed—at least most
of them," *Atlanta Journal-Constitution*, November 6, 2018,
https://www.ajc.com/news/state—regional-govt—politics/live
-updates-georgians-head-the-polls/DtYWWHcxngbl4SdVaD
AyDL/, accessed December 19, 2018.

158. Ontaria Woods, "We waited almost 5 hours to vote in my
Georgia precinct. How convenient for Kemp," *Washington Post*,
November 7, 2018, https://www.washingtonpost.com/outlook
/2018/11/07/we-waited-almost-hours-vote-my-georgia-precinct
-how-convenient-kemp/?utm_term=.689eec5bfd80, accessed
December 19, 2018.

159. Michael Harriot, "Exclusive: Thousands of Black Votes in
Georgia Disappeared and No One Can Explain It," *The Root*,
February 9, 2019, https://www.theroot.com/exclusive-thousands-of
-black-votes-in-georgia-disappea-1832472558, accessed February 9,
2019.

160. Coalition for Good Governance, "Georgia's 127,000 Missing
Votes Disproportionate Vote Loss in African Neighborhoods,"
February 8, 2019.

161. Michael Harriot, "Exclusive: Thousands of Black Votes in
Georgia Disappeared and No One Can Explain It," *The Root*,
February 9, 2019, https://www.theroot.com/exclusive-thousands
-of-black-votes-in-georgia-disappea-1832472558,   accessed
February 9, 2019.

162. @fairfightaction, February 20, 2019; @gwlauren, February 18, 2019.

163. David A. Lieb, "AP: GOP won more seats in 2018 than suggested
by vote share," *AP News*, March 21, 2019, https://www.apnews

.com/9fd72a4c1c5742aead977ee27815d776, accessed March 31, 2019.

164. Dana Goldstein and Kirk Johnson, "Voters Weigh In on Key Issues Through More Than 150 Ballot Initiatives," *New York Times*, November 6, 2018, https://www.nytimes.com/2018/11 /06/us/politics/ballot-initiatives-referendum.html, accessed December 28, 2018.

165. Florida Amendment 4, Voting Rights Restoration for Felons Initiative (2018), Ballotpedia, https://ballotpedia.org/Florida_ Amendment_4,_Voting_Rights_Restoration_for_Felons_ Initiative_(2018), accessed January 2, 2019; Jaden Urbi and Jordan Malter, "This midterm ballot initiative could unlock 1.5 million Florida votes in 2020," CNBC, October 25, 2018, https://www.cnbc.com/2018/10/25/amendment-4-voting-rights -restoration-florida-former-felons.html, accessed January 2, 2019; Tim Mak, "Over 1 Million Florida Felons Win Right to Vote with Amendment 4," NPR, November 7, 2018, https://www.npr.org /2018/11/07/665031366/over-a-million-florida-cx-felons-win -right-to-vote-with-amendment-4, accessed January 2, 2019.

166. Dana Goldstein and Kirk Johnson, "Voters Weigh In on Key Issues Through More Than 150 Ballot Initiatives," *New York Times*, November 6, 2018, https://www.nytimes.com/2018/11 /06/us/politics/ballot-initiatives-referendum.html, accessed December 28, 2018; Erick Trickey, "A Grassroots Call to Ban Gerrymandering," *The Atlantic*, September 23, 2018, https:// www.theatlantic.com/politics/archive/2018/09/a-grassroots -movement-in-michigan-has-gerrymandering-in-the-crosshairs /570949/, accessed December 28, 2019; Michael Krafcik, "Proposal 2, Proposal 3 pass, changing election laws and districts in Michigan," WWMT, November 6, 2018, https://wwmt.com /news/election/proposal-2-proposal-3-could-change-elections -and-districts-in-michigan, accessed December 28, 2018; "Michigan Proposal 2, Independent Redistricting Commission Initiative (2018), Ballotpedia, https://ballotpedia.org/Michigan_Proposal_2,

_Independent_Redistricting_Commission_Initiative_(2018), accessed December 28, 2018; Jay Riestenberg, "Who is Behind the Legal Challenge to Nonpartisan Redistricting in Michigan?" Common Cause, May 7, 2018, https://www.commoncause.org /democracy-wire/who-is-behind-michigan-redistricting-initiative -challenge/, accessed December 28, 2018; Tom McCarthy, "Billionaires join final push over Michigan's 'rigged' voting map," *The Guardian*, October 30, 2018, https://www.theguardian.com /us-news/2018/oct/30/michigan-gerrymandering-redistricting -voters-not-politicans, accessed December 28, 2018; Jonathan Oosting, "Conservative groups spending $1.2M to defeat Proposal 2 redistricting commission," *Detroit News*, October 23, 2018, https://www.detroitnews.com/story/news/local/michigan/2018 /10/23/devos-proposal-2-redistricting-opposition/1743725002/, accessed December 28, 2018.

167. Dana Goldstein and Kirk Johnson, "Voters Weigh In on Key Issues Through More Than 150 Ballot Initiatives," *New York Times*, November 6, 2018, https://www.nytimes.com/2018 /11/06/us/politics/ballot-initiatives-referendum.html, accessed December 28, 2018; "Michigan Proposal 3, Voting Policies in State Constitution Initiative (2018)," Ballotpedia, https://ballot pedia.org/Michigan_Proposal_3_Voting_Policies-in_State_ Constitution_Initiative_(2018), accessed December 28, 2018.

168. Chris Joyner and Jennifer Peebles, "AJC Analysis: Absentee voting pitfalls tripped thousands of Ga. Voters," *Atlanta Journal-Constitution*, December 20, 2018, https://www.ajc.com /news/state—regional-govt—politics/ajc-analysis-absentee -voting-pitfalls-tripped-thousands-voters/5Qu6ynxydaKrT 4leledtPL/, accessed January 4, 2019; Curt Devine and Drew Griffin, "Georgia county tosses out hundreds of minority absentee ballots," CNN.com, October 21, 2018, https://www.cnn.com /2018/10/20/politics/gwinnett-county-absentee-ballots/index .html, accessed December 25, 2018; Mark Niesse and Tyler Estep, "High rate of absentee ballots thrown out in Gwinnett,"

Atlanta Journal-Constitution, October 15, 2018, https://www
.ajc.com/news/state—regional-govt—politics/high-rate-absen
tee-ballots-thrown-out-gwinnett/azdOsCxX2X6mT8PTrgZlJI/,
accessed December 25, 2018; Mark Niesse, "Georgia election
board votes on counting absentee ballots in governor's race,"
Atlanta Journal-Constitution, November 11, 2018, https://www
.ajc.com/news/state—regional-govt—politics/georgia-election
-board-votes-counting-absentee-ballots-governor-race/J6jf5RklT
e4DhFXICFdtBI/, accessed December 25, 2018; Tyler Estep,
"Federal judge to order Ga. Counties to stop absentee ballot rejec-
tions," *Atlanta Journal-Constitution*, October 24, 2018, https://
www.ajc.com/news/local-govt—politics/breaking-judge-proposes
-injunction-absentee-ballot-rejections/drBFCpDG2KmnlkJ
wQxItMJ/, accessed December 25, 2018; Becca J. G. Godwin and
Arielle Kass, "Voting hours extended at three Fulton County
locations in Atlanta," *Atlanta Journal-Constitution*, November 6,
2018, https://www.ajc.com/news/local-govt—politics/voting
-hours-extended-three-fulton-county-locations-atlanta/tExhQ
6zdkAcLMPfrR0fMSN/, accessed December 25, 2018; P.R.
Lockhart, "Voting hours in parts of Georgia extended after
technical errors create long lines," *Vox*, November 6, 2018,
https://www.vox.com/policy-and-politics/2018/11/6/18068492
/georgia-voting-gwinnett-fulton-county-machine-problems
-midterm-election-extension, accessed December 25, 2018;
Anjali Enjeti, "Reckoning With Georgia's Increasing Suppression
of Asian American Voters," *Longreads*, December 2018, https://
longreads.com/2018/12/19/reckoning-with-georgias-increasing
-suppression-of-asian-american-voters/, accessed April 15, 2019;
Mark Niesse, "Judge orders review of provisional ballots in
Georgia election," *Atlanta Journal-Constitution*, November 13,
2018, https://www.ajc.com/news/state—regional-govt—politics
/judge-orders-review-provisional-ballots-georgia-election
/ZM2yd0QGkyZ8ZilIyVpF3H/, accessed December 25, 2018;
Jeremy Bauer-Wolf, "At Spelman, Taking Voting Rights Seriously,"

Inside Higher Ed, November 12, 2018, https://www.insidehigh ered.com/news/2018/11/12/spelman-president-tells-students -confirm-their-votes-counted, accessed December 25, 2018.

169. Ontaria Woods, "We waited almost 5 hours to vote in my Georgia precinct. How convenient for Kemp," *Washington Post*, November 7, 2018, https://www.washingtonpost.com/outlook /2018/11/07/we-waited-almost-hours-vote-my-georgia-prec inct-how-convenient-kemp/?utm_term=.689eec5bfd80, accessed December 19, 2018; Vote Riders, "2018 Impact Report," https:// www.voteriders.org/wp-content/uploads/2019/02/VoteRiders -2018-Impact-Report-v3.pdf; Anjali Enjeti, "Reckoning With Georgia's Increasing Suppression of Asian American Voters," *Longreads*, December 2018, https://longreads.com/2018/12/19 /reckoning-with-georgias-increasing-suppression-of-asian-amer ican-voters/, accessed April 15, 2019; Sue Halpern, "The National Hotline for Voter Complaints Has Received More than Twenty Thousand Calls on Election Day," *New Yorker*, November 6, 2018, https://www.newyorker.com/news/dispatch/the-national-hotline -for-voter-complaints-has-received-more-than-twenty-thousand -calls-on-election-day, accessed April 15, 2019; AJC staff, "Live Voting Updates: Polls are closed—at least most of them," *Atlanta Journal-Constitution*, November 6, 2018, https://www.ajc .com/news/state—regional-govt—politics/live-updates-georg ians-head-the-polls/DtYWWHcxngbl4SdVaDAyDL/, accessed December 19, 2018.

170. S. Erdem Aytaç and Susan Stokes, "Americans just set a turnout record for the midterms, voting at the highest rate since 1914. This explains why," *Washington Post*, November 20, 2018, https://www.washingtonpost.com/news/monkey-cage/wp/2018 /11/20/americans-just-set-a-turnout-record-for-the-midterms -voting-at-the-highest-rate-since-1914-this-explains-why, accessed March 19, 2019

171. Ari Berman, "The Law That Just Passed In New York Is A Huge Win For Voting Rights," *Mother Jones*, January 14, 2019,

https://www.motherjones.com/politics/2019/01/new-york
-passes-huge-voting-rights-expansion/, accessed April 15, 2019;
Jesse McKinley, "Early Voting and Other Changes to Election
Laws Are Coming to New York," *New York Times*, January 10,
2019, https://www.nytimes.com/2019/01/10/nyregion/voting
-reform-election-ny.html, accessed April 15, 2019.

172. Mark Joseph Stern, "How Progressive Activists Killed New
Jersey Democrats' Gerrymandering Scheme," *Slate*, December 17,
2018, https://slate.com/news-and-politics/2018/12/new-jersey
-democratic-partisan-gerrymandering-amendment-is-dead-prog
ressive-activists-killed-it.html, accessed April 15, 2019; Brent
Johnson, "Obama's former attorney general speaks out against
redistricting plan that could give N.J. Democrats more power,"
NJ.com, December 16, 2018, https://www.nj.com/news/2018
/12/obamas-former-attorney-general-speaks-out-against
-redistricting-plan-that-could-give-nj-democrats-more-power
.html, accessed April 15, 2019.

173. Sam Levine, "Kris Kobach Loses Kansas Governor's Race to
Democrat Laura Kelly: Her victory over a key ally of the presi-
dent comes two years after the state overwhelmingly voted for
Donald Trump," *Huffington Post*, November 6, 2019, https://
www.huffpost.com/entry/laura-kelly-kansas-governor_n_5bdcb-
4b6e4b09d43e31ee97a, accessed April 15, 2019; Dan Merica,
"Scott Walker loses bid for third term in Wisconsin," CNN.com,
November 7, 2018, https://www.cnn.com/2018/11/07/politics
/wisconsin-governor-scott-walker-tony-evers/index.html, accessed
April 15, 2019.

174. Jelani Cobb, "The Crucial Significance of Lucy McBath's Win in
Georgia's Sixth Congressional District," *New Yorker*, November 17,
2019, https://www.newyorker.com/news/daily-comment/the
-crucial-significance-of-lucy-mcbaths-win-in-georgias-sixth
-congressional-district, accessed April 15, 2019.

175. Maggie Astor, "Meet the Native American Woman Who Beat
the Sponsor of North Dakota's ID Law," *New York Times*,

November 13, 2019, https://www.nytimes.com/2018/11/13/us /politics/north-dakota-ruth-buffalo.html, accessed April 15, 2019.

176. Ari Berman, "Democrats' First Order of Business: Making It Easier to Vote and Harder to Buy Elections," *Mother Jones*, January 4, 2019, https://www.motherjones.com/politics/2019 /01/democrats-first-order-of-business-making-it-easier-to-vote -and-harder-to-buy-elections/, accessed March 12, 2019; Amy Sherman, "House Democrats and HR 1: Voting rights expansion or federal power grab?" *Politifact*, February 8, 2019, https://www .politifact.com/truth-o-meter/article/2019/feb/08/democrats -seek-expand-voting-access-2020-election-/, accessed March 12, 2019; Testimony of Sherrilyn Ifill, President and Director-Counsel, NAACP Legal Defense and Educational Fund, Inc., Hearing on H.R. 1, the "For the People Act of 2019," January 29, 2019, https://www.naacpldf.org/wp-content/uploads/Sherrilyn -Ifill-HR1-Testimony-1-29-18-FINAL.pdf, accessed January 29, 2019.

177. Vann R. Newkirk II, "How the Minority Wins," *The Atlantic*, December 12, 2018, https://www.theatlantic.com/politics/archive /2018/12/gop-maneuvers-rule-minority-party/577948/, accessed April 15, 2019; Ari Berman, "Republicans Brazenly Gut Voting Rights in Lame Duck Before They Lose Power," *Mother Jones*, December 3, 2018, https://www.motherjones.com/politics/2018 /12/republicans-brazenly-gut-voting-rights-in-lame-duck -before-they-lose-power/, accessed December 28, 2018; Emily Badger, "Are Rural Voters the 'Real' Voters? Wisconsin Republicans Seem to Think So," *New York Times*, December 6, 2018, https:// www.nytimes.com/2018/12/06/upshot/wisconsin-republicans -rurual-urban-voters.html, accessed December 17, 2018; Stephen Wolf, "Voting Rights Roundup: Michigan GOP passes lame-duck power grabs for GOP Governor to sign," *Daily Kos*, December 21, 2018, https://www.dailykos.com/stories/2018/12/21/1820572 /-Voting-Rights-Roundup-Michigan-GOP-passes-lame-duck -power-grabs-for-GOP-governor-to-sign, accessed December 21,

2018; David Eggert, "Michigan GOP advances bill to make ballot drives harder," *Daily Herald*, December 13, 2018, https://www.dailyherald.com/article/20181213/news/312139996, accessed December 28, 2018.

178. Sam Levine, "Florida Lawmakers Move To Block People With Court Debts From Voting," *Huffington Post*, March 18, 2019, https://www.huffpost.com/entry/florida-felony-disenfranchisement-bill_n_5c901a9de4b04ed2c1ad8366, accessed March 20, 2019.

179. Alex Ura and Naema Achmed, "Hispanic Texans on pace to become largest population group in state by 2022," *Texas Tribune*, June 21, 2018, https://www.texastribune.org/2018/06/21/hispanic-texans-pace-become-biggest-population-group-state-2022/, accessed April 12, 2019.

180. Joseph McCarthy, "Enemies from Within" Speech Delivered in Wheeling, West Virginia (1950), https://liberalarts.utexas.edu/coretexts/_files/resources/texts/1950%20McCarthy%20Enemies.pdf, accessed April 12, 2019; "'Communists in Government Service,' McCarthy Says," February 9, 1950, https://www.senate.gov/artandhistory/history/minute/Communists_In_Government_Service.htm, accessed April 12, 2019.

181. Jeremy Wallace, "Texas moves to purge 95,000 voters suspected to be non-citizens," *The Houston Chronicle*, January 26, 2019, https://www.chron.com/news/politics/texas/article/Texas-is-purging-95-000-voters-suspected-to-be-13562186.php, accessed April 12, 2019.

182. Chuck Lindell, "Specter of illegal Texas voters draws skepticism," *Austin Statesmen*, January 30, 2019, https://www.statesman.com/news/20190128/specter-of-illegal-texas-voters-draws-skepticism, accessed February 21, 2019.

183. Alex Ura and Emma Platoff, "Opposition to Texas Secretary of State David Whitley's nomination mounts, imperiling his future in the job," *Texas Tribune*, February 21, 2019, https://www.texastribune.org/2019/02/21/texas-senate-democrat-secretary

-of-state-david-whitley-jose-rodriguez/, accessed February 21, 2019.

184 "AG Paxton: Texas Secretary of State's Office Discovers Nearly 95,000 People Identified by DPS as Non-U.S. Citizens are Registered to Vote in Texas," press release, January 25, 2019, https://www.texasattorneygeneral.gov/news/releases/ag-paxton-texas-secretary-states-office-discovers-nearly-95000-people-ident ified-dps-non-us-citizens, accessed February 21, 2019.

185. Jeremy Wallace, "Texas moves to purge 95,000 voters suspected to be non-citizens," *The Houston Chronicle*, January 26, 2019, https://www.chron.com/news/politics/texas/article/Texas-is-purging-95-000-voters-suspected-to-be-13562186.php, accessed April 12, 2019.

186. Sam Levine, "Trump Amplifies Misleading Allegations of Voter Fraud in Texas: Texas officials said 95,000 non-citizens may be on voter rolls, but that number is suspect," *Huffington Post*, January 30, 2019, https://www.huffpost.com/entry/trump-texas-voter-fraud_n_5c4dceb4e4b06ba6d3be02e8, accessed March 13, 2019.

187. Jeremy Wallace, "Harris County pushes back against state's call for voter purge," *Houston Chronicle*, January 28, 2019, https://www.houstonchronicle.com/news/politics/texas/article/Harris-County-pushes-bakc-against-state-s-call-13567454.php, accessed January 29, 2019.

188. Sean Morales-Doyle and Rebecca Ayala, "There's Good Reason to Question Texas' Voter Fraud Claims," Brennan Center, January 29, 2019, https://www.brennancenter.org/blog/theres-good-reason-question-texas-voter-fraud-claims, accessed January 29, 2019.

189. Alex Ura, " 'This relationship is in tatters': How Texas' voter citizenship review frayed its relationship with local officials," *Texas Tribune*, February 23, 2019, https://www.texastribune.org/2019/02/23/how-texas-voter-rolls-review-frayed-its-relationship-counties/, accessed March 13, 2019.

190. Jeremy Wallace, "Harris County pushes back against state's call for voter purge," *Houston Chronicle*, January 28, 2019, https://www.houstonchronicle.com/news/politics/texas/article/Harris-County-pushes-bakc-against-state-s-call-13567454.php, accessed January 29, 2019; Carol Anderson, "Our Democracy Is Being Stolen. Guess Who the Thieves Are," *New York Times*, March 14, 2019, https://www.nytimes.com/2019/03/14/opinion/voting-fraud-north-carolina.html, accessed March 14, 2019.

191. Alex Ura, " 'This relationship is in tatters': How Texas' voter citizenship review frayed its relationship with local officials," *Texas Tribune*, February 23, 2019, https://www.texastribune.org/2019/02/23/how-texas-voter-rolls-review-frayed-its-relationship-counties/, accessed March 13, 2019.

192. Carol Anderson, "Our Democracy Is Being Stolen. Guess Who the Thieves Are," *New York Times*, March 14, 2019, https://www.nytimes.com/2019/03/14/opinion/voting-fraud-north-carolina.html, accessed March 14, 2019.

193. Jeremy Wallace, "Harris County pushes back against state's call for voter purge," *Houston Chronicle*, January 28, 2019, https://www.houstonchronicle.com/news/politics/texas/article/Harris-County-pushes-bakc-against-state-s-call-13567454.php, accessed January 29, 2019.

194. Alex Ura, "The AG's office told lawmakers it isn't investigating voters on Texas' citizenship review list. It told a local official the opposite," *Texas Tribune*, February 11, 2019, https://www.texastribune.org/2019/02/11/texas-ags-office-said-it-was-investigating-voters-citizenship-review-l/, accessed February 11, 2019.

195. Ashley Lopez, "GOP Bills Would Force Registrars to Remove People Flagged as Potential Noncitizens from Voter Rolls," KUT, February 25, 2019, https://www.kut.org/post/gop-bills-would-force-registrars-remove-people-flagged-potential-noncitizens-voter-rolls, accessed March 12, 2019.

196. Carol Anderson, "Our Democracy Is Being Stolen. Guess Who the Thieves Are," *New York Times*, March 14, 2019, https://www

.nytimes.com/2019/03/14/opinion/voting-fraud-north-carolina .html, accessed March 14, 2019.

197. Jeremy Wallace, "Harris County pushes back against state's call for voter purge," *Houston Chronicle*, January 28, 2019, https:// www.houstonchronicle.com/news/politics/texas/article/Harris -County-pushes-bakc-against-state-s-call-13567454.php, accessed January 29, 2019.

198. Alex Ura and Emma Platoff, "Opposition to Texas Secretary of State David Whitley's nomination mounts, imperiling his future in the job," *Texas Tribune*, February 21, 2019, https://www.texas tribune.org/2019/02/21/texas-senate-democrat-secretary-of -state-david-whitley-jose-rodriguez/, accessed February 21, 2019.

199. Alex Ura, "Another group of civil rights organizations sues Texas over voter citizenship review," *Texas Tribune*, February 4, 2019, https://www.texastribune.org/2019/02/04/civil-rights-groups -sue-texas-over-voter-citizenship-review/, accessed April 13, 2019.

200. Emma Platoff, "Federal judge temporarily blocks Texas from purging voters in citizenship review," *Texas Tribune*, February 27, 2019, https://www.texastribune.org/2019/02/27/federal-blocks -texas-purging-voters-citizenship-review/, accessed March 12, 2019.

Index

A Note on the Author

Carol Anderson is the Charles Howard Candler Professor and Chair of African American Studies at Emory University. She is the author of *White Rage*, which won the National Book Critics Circle Award, *Bourgeois Radicals*, and *Eyes off the Prize*. She lives in Atlanta, Georgia.